THE ETHICS OF WAR

THE ETHICS
OF WAR

Barrie Paskins
&
Michael Dockrill

University of Minnesota Press
Minneapolis

First published in the United States of America
by the University of Minnesota Press, 1979

© 1979 by Barrie Paskins and
Michael Dockrill

Library of Congress Cataloging in Publication Data

Paskins, Barrie.
   The ethics of war.

   Bibliography: p.
   Includes index.
   1. War and morals. 2. Military ethics.
I. Dockrill, M.L., joint author. II. Title.
U22.P37   172'.4   79-10798
ISBN 0-8166-0885-7

Photoset in Great Britain by
Specialised Offset Services Ltd., Liverpool
and printed by
Unwin Brothers Limited, Old Woking

Contents

FOR OUR PARENTS

'God has specially appointed me to this city, as though it were a large thorough-bred horse which because of its great size is inclined to be lazy and needs the stimulation of some stinging fly ... All day long I never cease to settle here, there, and everywhere, rousing, persuading, reproving every one of you. You will not easily find another like me, gentlemen, and if you take my advice you will spare my life.'

Socrates (Plato *Apology* 30e)

Preface

This book is addressed to the common reader, and to students and colleagues whose work impinges on the study of war.

It is an experiment in practical philosophy by a philosopher and a historian. We originally intended to contribute separate sections to it but as the work progressed it became increasingly clear that the final text would need to be the integrated product of one hand – it is the responsibility of Barrie Paskins. Of the material from which it is made, Michael Dockrill contributed the historical parts, Barrie Paskins the theoretical and philosophical. Our book attempts to synthesise a wide variety of ideas. We have not hesitated to trespass on other people's expertise but have not tried to construct an introduction to strategy, for example, or to ethics. If the reader finds some of our summary outlines of subjects bordering our own somewhat breathless, and feels impelled to pursue the issues into fuller studies, then we will count ourselves amply rewarded.

The book was written in the Department of War Studies, King's College, London and owes much to students and colleagues there. In particular, Wolf Mendl read the manuscript and made many helpful suggestions; our understanding of nuclear deterrence has been greatly enhanced by Laurence Martin. Sydney Bailey, Paul Ramsey and other friends in the Council on Christian Approaches to Defence and Disarmament provided invaluable stimulus. What philosophical steel there is in the argument derives largely from the example and work of Bernard Williams. Our theoretical view of war and international relations has been hammered out in the International Political Theory Group organised by Michael Donelan. Our thoughts on riot control developed in a working party of the Council for Science and Society gently guided by Jerome Ravetz. The work could never have been done without the generous establishment by the Ministry of Defence of a Lectureship in the Ethical Aspects of War which is currently held by Barrie Paskins. As always the ideas took shape in innumerable conversations with Susie Paskins, who also read the manuscript and contributed many improvements of detail and structure.

Our mistakes, of course, are our own.

B.P.

M.D.

Introduction

This book is an introduction to the ethical aspects of war. Faced with the idea of there being an ethics of war many people are tempted to react in one of two ways: by adopting whatever manner comes naturally when a pious sermon on a tedious subject threatens; or in blank disbelief ('Surely you mean the unethics of war?') Our purpose is not to preach, though we do try to show what ethics of war is like. What we have written is an experiment in practical philosophy. Ethics is that branch of philosophy which flourishes (or withers) when the philosopher directs his attention to the moral life. No one will doubt that a good deal of moralising about war has taken place at one time or another. We have tried to make philosophical sense of this moralising and the anti-moralistic polemics which it has called forth.

We are trying, among other things, to offer a restatement of some parts of the so-called just war tradition. We attempt to be guided by inherited ideas but we also make certain innovations and jettison some long-cherished, much-travelled luggage. There are several excellent, erudite expositions of the received tradition, but they tend to sheer away from the many doubts that spring to mind when one reflects critically upon the enterprise of moralising about war. The result is a vacuum. Anyone who approaches the tradition as part of a study of politics, international relations, law, or history of ideas comes away with a good deal of detailed knowledge but no sense of perspective. He is told how many conditions must be satisfied if a war is to meet Thomas Aquinas' notion of justice and what view Vitoria and Suarez took of the dispute over whether a war can be just on both sides. But he is left to shift for himself if he desires to relate this body of ideas to Hobbes and the theorists of power politics; or to Grotius, the League of Nations and current international law; or to Tolstoy, Gandhi and contemporary proponents of nonviolence. The student of theology gets equipped to reiterate an ancient tradition and to point out that something has been done to demonstrate its bearing on nuclear weapons policy, but hardly to engage the non-religious in informed dialogue. The philosopher, if he looks at our subject at all, usually does so from a great distance. It is but one example of some extremely abstract issue; other exemplars will serve as well, and there is no need to enquire too closely about what is peculiar to war. For good or ill, we propose to let a little air (if not light) into this vacuum: our main aim is to confront head-on the sceptic about ethics of war.

We have not tried to be comprehensive. The question 'What sense does it make to think of applying moral ideas to war?' is very abstract. To make it more concrete, we have chosen to examine three issues from recent history and contemporary politics in some detail: the planting of bombs by 'terrorists' and 'freedom fighters'; the bombing by one state of the villages, towns and cities of another state; and nuclear deterrence. These three things all fall under the rubric 'the bombing of cities'. One of their common features is that each of them extends the killing beyond the battlefield. In one way or another, more than just the army is threatened by the bombing of cities. The extension beyond (or of) the battlefield is nothing new. In the Old Testament numerous populations are exterminated. In the *Iliad* the Trojan heroes lament the fact that if their city falls then their wives will be carried off into slavery. Carthage was destroyed utterly and the siege is an immemorial weapon that kills indiscriminately. For all its antiquity, indiscriminate warfare remains a relatively compact, familiar and urgent problem.

I

Area Bombing

We begin with the bombing by one state of the cities, towns and villages of another state. The bombing campaigns of World War II culminated in the dropping of the two atom bombs on Hiroshima and Nagasaki and thus ushered in the post-war world in which nuclear deterrence influences all levels of warfare and the guerrilla and counter-insurgent clash under the nuclear umbrella. The area bombing of 1939-45 is the immediate precursor of our current predicament and through it our present murkier problems can be seen more clearly.

We aim to consider what bearing a version of the just war idea has upon area bombing. It is necessary first of all to try to see those distant campaigns through the eyes of some of the people involved. For one very important problem concerns the relation between what people actually do in history and moral concepts such as that of just war. A rough outline of the perceptions of a few of the many, very different people caught up in the planning and execution of the bombing will serve our purpose.

The participants we want to discuss saw themselves as having a job to do. Their task was to find a way of waging war which would avoid the disasters of World War I. To the surprise of almost everyone it had been a long not a short war and its outcome had hung in the balance for years on end. The losses in blood and treasure had been enormous. Some of the proponents of air power doubtless hoped that there would not be another war but hoping was not part of their job: their duty was to be ready if war should come. From 1919 to 1938 resources were scarce in two respects: total military budgets were very limited, and those who favoured area bombing were competing with claimants who were lobbying on behalf of other strategies and other services. In both peace and war they were under pressure to plead the best case they could so one should not be surprised if cool analytic appraisals of the prospects were lacking. This is not to say that moral issues were ignored. As we shall see, some at least of those involved thought that they could answer 'the' moral questions.

1. World War I

Military aviation had begun in earnest shortly before World War I. In 1911 and 1912 the Italians used aircraft, balloons and airships in the Tripoli war and by 1914 the British, French, German, Italian and Russian armed forces were more or less organised for military flying. In each of these countries a small band of the faithful saw a prodigious future for war in or from the air[1], but at the outbreak of war military leaders had accepted aircraft in only one role: reconnaissance.[2] Yet the primitive machines designed for information-gathering proved to be serviceable as fighters and bombers. War-time evolution of new types was rapid. Purpose-built bombers were soon appearing. Bomb-sights and direction-finding wireless telegraphy were introduced and hand grenades lobbed from the cockpit gave way to finned artillery shells, and then to bombs tailored for the new bomb racks.[3] The first bombs weighed as little as ten pounds, but by the armistice 250 lbs was standard and development was looking to 2000 pounders.

In World War I airpower was used mainly in support of land forces.[4] The pilot had four principal tasks: to locate enemy troop concentrations and movements; to spot for artillery; to prevent enemy planes from doing the same; and, as the war progressed, to bomb rail and supply facilities behind enemy lines. Precision bombing of German factories and raw material plants remained technically impossible, but it became relatively easy to bomb cities, using the argument that the morale of enemy workers was a legitimate target. Throughout the war long-range bombing was sporadic and on a small scale, though from 1916 onwards the French bombed German cities in retaliation for German attacks on Paris and other French towns. In 1914-15 British planes of the Royal Naval Air Service (RNAS) raided German Zeppelin factories and other military targets, while from 1915 to 1918 Germany hit London and other English towns. Her first attacks were by rigid airships designed by Graf Ferdinand von Zeppelin. Defence against these became very effective before the end of 1916. Bombing by Gotha aeroplanes began in May 1917, to be called off almost a year later after several raids on London. Forty-three Gotha and Giant aircraft set out on the night of 19-20 May 1918 and thirteen found their targets. They caused considerable damage, but anti-aircraft batteries and British fighters shot down six. As in the

[1] For details see Neville Jones *The Origins of Strategic Bombing* 25-47.

[2] Some commanders (e.g. Haig) were reluctant to concede even the reconnaissance role, *ibid.* 48-9.

[3] *ibid.* 20-1.

[4] *ibid.* 20-1, 69-76, 98-102, 165-70.

earlier case of the rigid airships, the advantage was swinging back from attack to defence.[5]

The Gotha raids provoked a public outcry for retaliation but suitable aircraft were lacking and for the British High Command in France the western front was the only priority; they opposed the use of aircraft outside the battle zone. Some attacks on German towns were, however, made from the end of 1916, and in April 1918 Britain established an independent bombing force.[6]

In numerical terms the bombing of cities in World War I was not impressive. Against England, for example, there were 208 airship and 435 aeroplane sorties. Fewer than 300 tons of bombs were dropped. About 1300 people were killed and about 3000 injured. Yet a widespread fear of city bombing had taken hold and in June 1918 the Chief of the Air Staff suggested to the British War Cabinet that the next war would open with a massive air strike against a capital city. This idea, like so many canvassed by the proponents of air power, was to remain untested and untestable until World War II. Winston Churchill (as Minister of Munitions) had asserted in a memorandum of October 1917 that, to judge from British experience, air strikes against Germany would serve only to strengthen German resolve.

2. *Inter-war developments*

The inter-war history of bombing[7] had three largely unrelated elements: experience, preparation for major war, and theory.

Experience was very limited. General Jan Christian Smuts, charged to reconsider the problem of air power in the light of German raids on English towns in the summer of 1917, had recommended the establishment of an independent air service.[8] This came into being as the Royal Air Force on 1 April 1918, but the army and navy firmly expected that their parts of the force would be restored at the end of the war. The new organisation was therefore soon fighting for its life. Early in 1919 General Hugh Trenchard[9] as Chief of the Air Staff did

---

[5] *ibid.* Chs 2-6.

[6] *ibid.* 16-21 for the pre-history of the independent bombing force.

[7] For some details see Robin Higham *Air Power: A Concise History*. Jones 14 suggests that the main problems with strategic bombing had been identified before 1915, but that by 1939 'the fact that these problems even existed had been forgotten'.

[8] Churchill's memorandum was a riposte to the two Smuts reports of July and August 1917. See Charles Webster and Noble Frankland *The Strategic Air Offensive Against Germany 1939-45* I 47.

[9] Sir Hugh Montague Trenchard (1873-1956) served as an army officer in South Africa, 1899-1902, and succeeded Sir David Henderson as Commander of the Royal Flying Corps in-the-Field, 1915. Chief of the Air Staff, 1918 and 1919-29; Commissioner of Metropolitan Police, 1931-35.

much to secure the future of the RAF when he succeeded in showing that it could police Iraq at a third of the cost of an army presence. His cheap colonial airforce subsequently served in Aden, on India's north-west frontier, and in other restless parts of the Empire. Such experience had very little bearing on the bombing war fought between 1939 and 1945, though not everyone anticipated this in the inter-war period.

The Italian effort against Ethiopia, basically a colonial action against a divided and relatively defenceless enemy, was similarly irrelevant. Somewhat more salient, perhaps, was the Japanese onslaught against China in the 'thirties. In 1931 first-class Japanese pilots and aircraft were pitted against a Chinese force consisting of few fighters and virtually no bombers, flown largely by incompetent mercenaries. Air opposition was speedily disposed of and the Japanese settled down to strategic bombing. In the next round of hostilities in 1937, the Chinese moved their bases out of range of Japanese fighters. Japan riposted with advanced refuelling fields but at one point Japanese bombers were withdrawn from attacking Chinese airfields because of high losses. It taught the Japanese the need for fighter cover even against scanty Chinese resistance. In the Spanish Civil War Italy, Russia and Germany got some practice. The Luftwaffe came out of the war better placed to cooperate in blitzkrieg. There was some terror bombing (most notoriously of Guernica) which frightened many British and French politicians, but it was not of the type later experienced. With some exceptions in the fight against China, bombing raids on cities between the wars had one vital common feature: none of them faced significant resistance. Theorists had not noticed the swing of advantage from attack to defence during the raids on Britain of 1915-18 and experience before 1939 provided little additional evidence that the victims of aerial bombardment might try with considerable effect to protect themselves.

Preparation for major war was very patchy. In Germany a disguised airforce was developed under Hitler. In supreme command was Goering, a World War I fighter pilot who saw it in a tactical role. The one prominent German advocate of strategic bombing, General Walter Wever, was killed in an air crash in 1936. It has been suggested that Hitler's strategy of blitzkrieg allowed no room for a strategy of area bombing, though of course tactical bombing raids might destroy cities.[10] On the Soviet Union the evidence is confused, but it is clear that the purges of 1936-38 eliminated any possiblity that readers of the theorists of air power would have any influence. By 1939

[10] Cajus Bekker *The Luftwaffe War Diaries* 59, 182. The Luftwaffe was not equipped for area bombing: it lacked a heavy four-engined bomber.

Soviet heavy bombers were obsolete. The United States possessed an independent naval airforce throughout the inter-war period. In command of it in the twenties was Rear Admiral William A. Moffatt, head of the Bureau of Aeronautics 1921-33. Moffatt opposed the extravagant ideas of the principal American proponent of strategic bombing, General William Mitchell. By 1925 Moffatt had developed a capability for aircraft carrier operations. In that year Mitchell was court-martialled. In the isolationist US the idea of area bombing was unlikely to gain much support. But Mitchell's friends kept his ideas alive and evolved a doctrine of offensive strategic bombing. By 1941 bomber advocates were firmly entrenched in the leadership of the US Army Air Corps. Unlike Mitchell, they did not at first realise the importance of fighter protection. In the United Kingdom the RAF had three roles: colonial policing, air defence, and resistance against invasion. Trenchard did not believe that there was a defence against bombers – the civilian population would have to grin and bear it until enemy morale was smashed from the air. There was therefore little work on all-round city defence. A counter-strike deterrent force of bombers was initiated in 1923 but the RAF soon stopped ordering long-range heavy bombers, opting instead for cheaper medium bombers incapable of striking beyond Paris but useful as fighter bombers in colonial operations. In no country before 1939 did preparations remotely approach what was demanded by the theorists of air power.

3. Inter-war theorists

Theory was well advanced in the UK before the end of World War I. Among the early advocates of strategic bombing were F.W. Lanchester, P.R.C. Groves and Sir Frederick Sykes. One representative British view of bombing is found in *Paris or the Future of War* written in 1925 by Basil Liddell Hart before he began to believe that a future major war would be decisively different *on land* from that of 1914-18. *Paris* makes the explicit assumption that 'any future wars' fought in the manner of World War I 'must mean the breakdown of Western civilisation'. So the question for the strategist is 'Is there an alternative?'[11] 'The aim of a nation in war is to subdue the enemy's will to resist, with the least possible human and economic loss to itself.'[12] It may be unnecessary to destroy the enemy's armed forces, the costly aim of war on the western front. 'Of what use is decisive victory in battle if we bleed to death as a result of it?'[13] The task is to find the weakest link in a highly organised state:

[11] *Paris* 10.   [12] *ibid.* 25.   [13] *ibid.* 26.

if we can demoralise one section of the nation, the collapse of its will to
resist compels the surrender of the whole – as the last months of 1918
demonstrated.[14]

The next question, therefore, is

how the moral attack takes effect, and how the will of an enemy people is
reduced to a degree that they will sue for peace rather than face a
continuation of the struggle. Put in a nutshell, the result is obtained by
dislocating their normal life to a degree that they will prefer the lesser evil
of surrendering their policy, and by convincing them that any return to
'normalcy' – to use President Harding's term – is hopeless unless they do
surrender.[15]

Liddell Hart supports his view that every man has his breaking-point
with two observations, one speculative and one concerned with the
slender evidence available in 1925. He speculates that

History, even Anglo-Saxon history, shows that nations bow to the
inevitable, and abandon their policy rather than continue a struggle once
hope has vanished. No war between civilized people has been ... anywhere
nearly carried to the point of extermination. The living ... retain the
power to admit defeat, and since wars, therefore, are ended by surrender
and not by extermination, it becomes apparent that defeat is the result not
of loss of life, save, at the most, indirectly and partially, but by [sic] loss of
morale.[16]

In addition he considers that World War I experience supports his
argument in favour of area bombing. He points out that between May
1915 and May 1918, despite strong air and ground defences, German
air raids on London caused 244 fires, the complete destruction of 174
buildings and serious damage of 619, at an estimated total cost of over
£2 million – all this by means of a mere 13 Zeppelins, 128 aeroplanes
and 300 tons of bombs. He finds impressive the effect of bombing on
Cleveland (output of pig iron cut by one-sixth) and Hull ('Women,
children, babies in arms, spending night after night huddled in
sodden fields, shivering under a bitter wintry sky').[17]

Liddell Hart does not fail to examine 'the ethical objection' to
bombing cities. He thinks it

is based on the seeming brutality of an attack on the civilian population,
and the harmful results to the aggressor of any outrage of the human
feelings of the neutral peoples. The events of the last war have, however,

[14] *ibid.* 27.
[15] *ibid.* 35. It should be noted that writers of this period consistently refer to morale
as 'moral'.
[16] *ibid.* 37.
[17] *ibid.* 46.

acclimatized the world to the idea that in a war between nations the damage cannot be restricted merely to paid gladiators. When, moreover, the truth is realized that a swift and sudden blow of this nature inflicts a total of injury far less than when spread over a number of years, the common sense of mankind will show that the ethical objection to this form of war is at least not greater than to the cannon-fodder wars of the past.[18]

Liddell Hart subsequently lost interest in area bombing as a key to the next war, since a consideration of the tank led him to believe that land war would in future be very different from the stalemate of the trenches. But some others in British defence thinking, and particularly some more closely bound up than was Liddell Hart with the fortunes of the RAF, continued to think that the bombing of cities would be central to future major war. (We will examine a prominent RAF dissenter from this view below.)

The most careful theorist of airpower between the wars, the Italian General Giulio Douhet (1868-1930), exerted no influence in the UK. The horrors of aerial bombardment had been vividly imagined by H.G. Wells before World War I[19] and Douhet was among those who wrote studies of the military possibilities as early as 1909. He had entered the Italian army many years before the first aeroplanes, had promoted other mechanical novelties before aviation caught his attention, and in 1916 was imprisoned for sending memoranda highly critical of Italian military policy to a member of the Italian cabinet. He was exonerated after the Italians suffered military catastrophe at Caporetto in 1917 and the decision of his court-martial was formally repudiated and expunged in 1920. The following year he attained the rank of general and published the first edition of his major work, later to be known in English as *Command of the Air*. His influence increased with the rise of Mussolini, who was impressed by his doctrines. By 1927 political pressures had so eased that Douhet felt able to publish a second edition in which he repudiated various qualifications which prudence had dictated in the pre-Mussolini period. The book was translated only after his death: into French in 1932, from French for the US army air corps in 1933, into German in 1935. *The RAF Quarterly* carried an abstract in April 1936 and a complete translation of his main military writings became available in England and the United States at the end of 1942, in time to be used as one of the theoretical justifications for the bombing of Germany. His influence outside his own country is debatable; he was dead before China forced Japan to adopt extensive fighter protection.

---

[18] *ibid.* 50.
[19] *War in the Air* (1908).

Douhet makes two large assumptions: (a) Airpower adds a new dimension to war, shifting the advantage decisively to the attack, since no effective defence against bombers can be foreseen. (b) Bombardment of civilian centres will shatter civilian morale.

These two views are obviously interconnected. If one's opponent has no defence and one's own resources are unlimited then (b) is certainly correct: if need be one can bomb and kill every enemy citizen. Their will to resist will probably break at some point before one does this. But if they can defend themselves against one's attacks, or if the devastation one can wreak is limited, then there are two key variables: the degree to which one can penetrate the enemy's defences, and the point at which the enemy's morale breaks. (One's own ability and willingness to undergo losses might also be an important factor.) The 'twenties yielded little clue to either of the key variables but Douhet makes much of the World War I German offensive against England:

> every time an aerial offensive was carried out resolutely it accomplished its purpose.[20]

Douhet fully appreciated that Italy possessed limited resources and would face some defences. He tried to solve the problem of the two key variables with his notion of the command of the air:

> To have command of the air means to be in a position to prevent the enemy from flying while retaining the ability to fly oneself.[21]
>
> To prevent the enemy from flying does not, of course, mean to prevent even his flies[22] from flying. In the absolute sense, it will certainly hardly be possible to destroy *all* the enemy's means of flying. The command of the air will be gained when the enemy's planes are reduced to a negligible number incapable of developing any aerial action of real importance in the war as a whole. ... Command of the air ... means *to have the ability to fly against an enemy so as to injure him, while he has been deprived of the power to do likewise.*[23]

To this general concept of the command of the air, Douhet adds some specific observations. In all bombing operations '*the objective must be destroyed completely in one attack, making further attack on the same target*

---

[20] *The Command of the Air* 20. An interesting discussion of Douhet and related thinkers, nearly contemporary with Douhet's full publication in English, is Edward Warner 'Douhet, Mitchell, Seversky: Theories of Air Warfare' in *Makers of Modern Strategy* (ed.) Edward Mead Earle 485-503.

[21] Douhet 26.

[22] Thus the translation. Douhet has in mind the more modest objective of stopping the enemy's fliers.

[23] *ibid.* 83.

unnecessary'.[24] 'With the air arm it is easy to strike but not to parry' so it is necessary to resign oneself *'to submit to enemy attacks in order to use all possible means for launching the greatest offensives against the enemy'.*[25] This doctrine is perhaps made more tolerable in Douhet's eyes by the insistence that aerial warfare is to be conducted from the outbreak of war 'with the greatest possible intensity':[26] he is confident that it will be a short war. Also, he is concerned only with fighter defences. He is silent about air-raid shelters and anti-aircraft guns; had the demand for these competed with the allocation of resources for breaking enemy defences and bombing enemy cities he would doubtless have dismissed them: 'No local defence can be very effective when confronted by an aerial offensive of this magnitude; therefore, the expenditure of men and resources for such a purpose goes against the principles of sound war economy'.[27]

Douhet expressed views with a bearing on ethical issues. He claims that with the coming of air war

> No longer can areas exist in which life can be lived in safety and tranquillity, nor can the battlefield be limited to actual combatants. On the contrary, the battlefield will be limited only by the boundaries of the nations at war, and all of their citizens will become combatants since all of them will be exposed to the aerial offensives of the enemy. There will be no distinction any longer between soldiers and civilians.[28]

If war is fought as Douhet counsels, this obliteration of distinctions will be carried further: 'bombing objectives should always be large.'[29] He recognises that aerial bombardment is frightful but

> Mercifully, the decision will be quick in this kind of war, since the decisive blows will be directed at civilians, that element of the countries at war least able to sustain them. These future wars may yet prove to be more humane than wars in the past in spite of all, because they may in the long run shed less blood. But there is no doubt that nations who find themselves unprepared to sustain them will be lost.[30]

Part of Douhet's argument is concerned with the use of poison gas. The technical aspects of this are not important for our theme, but in passing Douhet comments on the significance of international law, which forbade the use of poison gas.[31] He says

> It is useless to delude ourselves. All the restrictions, all the international agreements made during peacetime are fated to be swept away like dried leaves on the winds of war. A man who is fighting a life-and-death fight –

[24] *ibid.* 22.   [28] *ibid.* 14.
[25] *ibid.* 93.   [29] *ibid.* 22.
[26] *ibid.* 92.   [30] *ibid.* 54-5.
[27] *ibid.* 50.   [31] 1925 Gas Protocol.

as all wars are nowadays – has the right to use any means to keep his life. War means cannot be classified as human and inhuman. War will always be inhuman, and the means which are used in it cannot be classified as acceptable or not acceptable except according to their efficacy, potentiality, or harmfulness to the enemy. The purpose of war is to harm the enemy as much as possible; and all means which contribute to this end will be employed, no matter what they are. He is a fool if not a patricide who would acquiesce in his country's defeat rather than go against those formal agreements which do not limit the right to kill and destroy, but simply the ways of killing and destroying. The limitations applied to the so-called inhuman and atrocious means of war are nothing but international demagogic hypocrisies. As a matter of fact, poison gases are being experimented with everywhere – and certainly not for purely scientific purposes. Just because of its terrible efficacy, poison gas will be largely used in the war of the future. This is the brutal fact; and it is better to look it squarely in the face without false delicacy and sentimentalism.[32]

On most matters the views of the American General William Mitchell coincided with those of Douhet. A fiery propagandist in the cause of airpower, Mitchell did not develop a clear and systematic statement of his position and is perhaps most interesting for his undoubted influence in the US and the close knowledge of technological problems and constraints which he possessed and which Douhet lacked. One other difference lies in their attitude to the relation between bombers and bomber protection. Douhet, as we have seen, was dismissive of city defence. He claimed that enemy airforces should be dealt with not by combat in the air but by the destruction of ground installations and factories. In the second edition of his book he went further, insisting that specialised aircraft should be sacrificed to economy. Insistent on the primacy of the bomber strike, he argued that the basic type of airforce equipment should be the 'battleplane', performing the roles of both fighter and bomber. In a footnote to the 1942 English translation, Douhet's editor suggested that the Flying Fortress met this specification. Now if, unlike Douhet, one anticipates heavy enemy resistance or very resilient enemy morale then one will want the best possible fighters for air combat and the best purpose-built bombers. It is here that Mitchell diverges from Douhet. In 1925 he was writing:

> It was proved in the European war that the only effective defense against aerial attack is to whip the enemy's air forces in air battles.[33]

Mitchell never ceased to stress the importance of good fighter-protection.

---

[32] Douhet 147.
[33] William Mitchell *Winged Defense* 199.

An interesting if muted pre-war critic of area bombing theory is J.C. Slessor.[34] His *Air Power and Armies* was based on lectures given at the Joint Staff College, Camberley, in 1931-34 and appeared in 1936. It begins with a reconsideration of armies and approaches the question of air-power slowly, with many bets hedged. The object of a land campaign, Slessor thinks, is always to defeat the enemy's army and is therefore always directed against the enemy's land forces, their communications and system of supply.[35] The main importance of aircraft in World War I was army cooperation. Up to 1918 the primary object of all air operations, with one exception, was to secure air superiority and enable reconnaissance and artillery aircraft to carry on their work of close cooperation. The one exception was 'the group of units known as the Independent Force RAF' and Slessor holds that implicit in the establishment of this force was the view that

> the primary object, the service of first importance that air forces could perform for the land forces, was the purely ancillary service of reconnaissance and observation.[36]

The purpose of *Air Power and Armies*, however, is not to labour these important ancillary services but to draw attention to

> the positive influence which can be exerted by an air striking force in direct attacks upon objectives on the ground.[37]

This can be crucial and Slessor thinks that the RAF underrates it.

Slessor makes no mention of the idea that the next war will begin with an air strike against a capital city, the suggestion, it will be recalled, of the Chief of the Air Staff in June 1918. He sees city bombing as occupying a different place in the next war: 'A stage may occur ... in which the ultimate aim of the enemy is the reduction of this country by air measures.'[38] If so, the enemy will first have to face a ground struggle for possession of air bases in the Low Countries from which the air invasion of England can be mounted. Until the enemy army has been driven back behind its own frontiers, the primary

[34] Sir John Charlesworth Slessor (1897-   ) served with the Royal Flying Corps, 1915-18, and was Director of Plans at the Air Ministry, 1937-41. Air Representative at Anglo-French Conversations, 1939, and Anglo-American Conversations, Washington 1941. Commander Fifth Group Bomber Command 1941-42; Assistant Chief of the Air Staff (Policy), 1942-43; Commander-in-Chief Coastal Command, 1943-44; Commander-in-Chief RAF Mediterranean and Middle East, 1944-45; Air Member for Personnel, 1945-47; Commandant, Imperial Defence College, 1948-49; Chief of the Air Staff, 1950-52.

[35] Slessor 2-3.
[36] *ibid.* 2.
[37] *ibid.*
[38] *ibid.*

object of British forces in the field must be to defeat enemy ground strength. Once the enemy has been driven back, the ultimate reduction of the enemy nation from the air 'may (and very likely will)' take place.[39] Slessor does not make explicit his reason for expecting war to develop in this way. Perhaps he was partly influenced by the bases a likely enemy would probably need: a land campaign would have to precede aerial bombardment if the initiative was with Germany. And, as pointed out above, the RAF had opted for medium-bombers that could not strike beyond Paris if operating from airfields in England. Also present in Slessor's reasoning may have been his telling criticism of the idea of command of the air. He points out that we do not now talk of command of the sea but of control of the sea, and the same should hold when we think about the air:

> The reason is to be found in the same quality, the capacity for *evasion*, at sea of the submarine, in the air of the aeroplane. Once warfare gets into the third dimension, whether above or below the surface, the cubic area of the battle-field is so immense that absolute command is hardly ever practicable.[40]

It would be desirable to destroy the enemy's air forces if this were possible but

> the unlimited opportunities for evasion have the result that the most we can hope for in a war against a first-class enemy is to throw air forces on the defensive, to neutralize them, to enable our own aircraft to work with the minimum of interference, and to reduce enemy air action against our own forces to the minimum. And even this limited result can only be secured by hard and continuous fighting.[41]

Douhet had conceded that it would 'hardly be possible to destroy *all* the enemy's means of flying', but Slessor argues that the prospects are much bleaker: the enemy's air defences are unlikely to be destroyed even by hard and continuous fighting. If that is correct then an attacker who hopes ultimately to defeat the UK by means of city bombing is going to need those bases in the Low Countries to give his bombers and their fighter cover the best chance against our defences.

Analysis of the methods used to obtain air superiority during World War I in Palestine and on the Somme led Slessor to propound two main principles.

(a) 'Even assuming approximately equal resources on both sides in personnel, training, and equipment, air superiority can be gained and

---

[39] *ibid.* 3. Slessor does not comment on the possibility of using French airfields if France should be an ally.
[40] *ibid.* 5.
[41] *ibid.*

must be maintained firstly by the adoption of a resolute bombing offensive against the vital centres of the enemy.'[42] This will throw the enemy onto the defensive in two ways: First, he will be forced to use up his strength in defence, devoting aircraft to the protection of his vital centres instead of to their primary task, which alone can be decisive in his favour, of striking at our vital centres. Secondly, by judicious selection of objectives, we may be able to force the enemy to allocate even these defensive aircraft to places which for military or political reasons he cannot afford to leave unguarded, instead of to those centres which are decisively important for the ongoing battle.

(b) The offensive against the enemy's vital centres must be supplemented by direct action against his airforces. Such measures will be directed against his airforces both on the ground and in the air.

Slessor supports this part of his argument with a careful definition of 'vital centres' – an 'over worked and loosely used' phrase:

> Strictly speaking a vital centre is an organ or centre in a man, an army or a nation, the destruction or even interruption of which will be fatal to continued vitality.[43]

Material destruction of a vital centre may not be necessary: e.g. if a set of railway junctions is vital, it may be sufficient to prevent trains running through them long enough to inflict logistical damage on an army in the field. It may be possible to do this without destroying the junctions. Slessor is alive to the strategic importance of other targets than vital centres. War is a human activity and human nature being what it is, decisions in war are influenced by factors other than those of cold military expediency. There are therefore quite likely to be centres not in the strict sense vital but nevertheless so important that no government can afford to leave them unprotected. He finds it hard to be definite about such imponderables but instances London during World War I. Despite the importance of Woolwich arsenal and other munitions in the London area, there is no doubt that from a strictly military viewpoint the UK tied up far too many aircraft in the defence of London against the very weak and sporadic raids launched against it. These attacks could not possibly have led to the defeat of our forces in the field or our fleets at sea. But the government could not afford to leave unprotected the capital city and greatest centre of population, commerce and finance in view of the possible social and political consequences of serious attack, however unlikely. Slessor has such examples in mind when he suggests the diversionary tactics mentioned above.

---

[42] *ibid.* 15.
[43] *ibid.* 16.

Slessor is anxious to avoid giving the impression that he 'underrates the possibly terrible effects of air bombardment on the morale of a civilian population'.[44] The first serious air operations against German industrial areas were, he thinks, initiated in October 1917 as a reprisal rather than to reduce the German output of munitions. But 'it is worth while asking ourselves – though we can never know the answer' what contribution bombing made to the breaking of German civilian will to resist which, he considers, was so important in the defeat of their armies in the field.

> In air operations against the means of production the weight of attack will inevitably fall hardest upon a vitally important, and not by nature very amenable, section of the community – the industrial workers, whose morale and sticking power cannot be expected to equal that of the disciplined soldier.[45]

Slessor mentions the point in order not to discuss it further.

He recalls that the debate about airpower has been polarised. On the one hand, Sir Douglas Haig and other devotees of the western front had opposed independent air operations in any form. Slessor plainly does not agree with them and permits himself a moment of fun – he wonders how much harm has been done by the constant use of the misleading word 'independent'. On the other hand is his true target:

> The claim ... submitted in the past, for instance, by Sir Frederick Sykes and today by Brig. Gen. Groves ... to the effect that 'the necessary uses of aircraft with the Army and Navy being ensured, any available margin of air power should be employed on an independent basis for definite strategic purposes'.[46]

Slessor points out that 'for some obscure reason' Sykes and Groves reserve the word 'strategic' for operations against enemy towns and industrial areas. Neither of them, he thinks, has made it clear how, when or by whom it is to be decided that the 'necessary uses of aircraft' for the other services have been adequately ensured so that a surplus is now available for other purposes. He is not surprised to learn that it was found 'difficult ... to arrive at any agreement as to the minimum tactical and grand tactical requirements of the Army and Navy'. 'No final agreement', according to Slessor, 'ever was arrived at, or ever can be.'[47]

Before 1939, theory far outran experience and technology in the

---

[44] *ibid.* 65.
[45] *ibid.*
[46] *ibid.* 69.
[47] *ibid.* 69-70.

claims it made for the area bombing of the villages, towns and cities of enemy states. The theory, by no means universally held, was that the disastrous land war of World War I could be avoided if states would engage instead in the quicker and ultimately perhaps less brutal war in the air. There was no hope of preventing all enemy flying, but the implications of this were far from clear: theorists differed among themselves, for example, about the importance of fighter protection. Would theory have been less self-confident and shrill if there had not been the intense competition for resources and in some countries the struggle for an independent air service? The question is as unanswerable as it is important.

4. Germany on the offensive, 1939-40

World War II began with Germany on the offensive. The air component in the onslaught was principally shaped by Hitler, Goering and Erhard Milch. Milch, as an artilleryman, had served on the western front as an aircraft observer from July 1915. In 1920 he wrote a paper on airpower for the Defence Ministry and it appears that at that time he saw fighterplanes as the key to air supremacy, bombers as having secondary importance. In the 'twenties he worked as technical director for civil airlines and when Goering was elected to the Reichstag as a Nazi deputy the two men became friends. During the slump of 1929-33 Milch thoroughly reformed the German state airline Lufthansa, describing himself as ruthless. In April 1932 Hitler spoke to him at length about the works of Douhet,[48] and said that in future a powerful airforce would occupy a position of equality with the army. The following year he persuaded Milch to accept the post of state secretary in the new air ministry. Goering became Reich Plenipotentiary for Aviation with Milch as his deputy secretary of state and they set to work to expand the secret airforce. Goering's preoccupation with other tasks left Milch in effective control and (unlike proponents of air power in other countries) he enjoyed virtually unlimited funds. His first Chief of Air Staff, the army Lieut.-General Walther Wever, persuaded Milch of the need for heavy bombers capable of attacking the UK, but this was not the first priority. Heinkel had on the drawing board only a medium-range bomber suitable for strikes against France, Poland and Czechoslovakia. Dornier and Junkers developed a four-engine bomber for use against shipping lanes. In the war scare of October 1933 Milch was determined that the airforce would defend Berlin and the Ruhr

[48] David Irving *The Rise and Fall of the Luftwaffe* 27.

industrial belt. In July 1934 his plan was to build 4021 aircraft by 1935; Hitler and Goering wanted more. Milch urged that the need was for airfields and more trained men but Goering, wanting a propaganda airforce, overruled him. The Luftwaffe was officially founded on 1 March 1935 with Goering, as commander-in-chief, constantly pressing for an increase in aircraft numbers. In May 1936 Wever issued the first Luftwaffe training manual:

> Air power carries the war right into the heart of enemy country from the moment war breaks out. It strikes at the very root of the enemy's fighting power and of the people's will to resist.[49]

The Luftwaffe's duty was first to fight for air supremacy. When this was achieved it was to provide, where necessary, support in the land and sea battles or to attack the enemy's resources – industrial potential, food supplies, vital import routes, transport and government centres. Terror bombing of the civilian population was expressly forbidden. The following month Wever died in an air crash.

In that same June 1936, Goering removed the head of the Luftwaffe's technical department and replaced him by Ernst Udet, a World War I fighter pilot and friend of Milch. Hitler mistakenly regarded Udet as technically competent. He was lazy and easy-going. In 1939 he was appointed director-general of the vast Office of Air Force Equipment and presided over the development of the Junker 88 high-speed bomber. Among thirty-two technical criticisms of this plane was its tendency to self-ignite in the air. Before Udet's suicide in 1941 made room for Milch to assume control of production and direct the Luftwaffe's re-birth, Udet had denounced his old friend as a Jew.[50] But this is to anticipate.

In 1937 Milch wrote a memorandum to Goering insisting that the Luftwaffe would never be big enough to meet every strategic demand and suggesting that they plan to cross frontiers and destroy enemy airforces and air bases without a declaration of war. This, Milch thought, would provide the command of the air on which Douhet laid such stress. Goering by now saw Milch as a potential rival for his job and probably ignored the memorandum. He reorganised the Luftwaffe, promoting two other men to equal rank with Milch, who was no longer to be his deputy but did retain control over administration. In 1937-38 Milch encouraged collaboration with the RAF. Senior British and French officers were shown German installations and programmes. In return, Milch saw British shadow factories, met Churchill and embarrassed his hosts at a formal dinner

---

[49] *ibid*. 47.
[50] *ibid*. 135-7, 327.

by asking how radar detection was progressing. Increasing Anglo-German tension in 1938 prompted a Luftwaffe enquiry into the prospects of air war against Britain. This suggested that the airforce should support ground operations in the west; engage in reprisal raids (!) on Paris and London; bomb English docks, armament factories, Channel ports, and airfields; and attack British shipping.

By September 1939 the Luftwaffe was the largest air force in the world: 4,093 front-line aircraft including 1,176 bombers, 408 twin-engined fighters, 771 single-engine fighters. A strength before mobilisation of 370,000 men with 107,000 in flak, 58,000 in signals, 20,000 aircrew, and 1,500 paratroopers.[51] Its main weaknesses in Milch's view were that it was more organised for home defence than for attack, and insufficiently integrated with the other armed services. Its airfields were too small for the new generation of aircraft and no long-range strategic bombers were ready until November. There were no night bombers, no bombs larger than 100 lbs, no air torpedoes, no modern mines, no modern armaments, no bombsights, few air-to-air communication facilities. Despite its size, it had a weak substructure in both manufacture and servicing.

The first decisive air struggle of the war was the Battle of Britain. In Poland the Luftwaffe had served mainly in army cooperation, except for one saturation bombardment of Warsaw. In the conquest of France and the Low Countries, having destroyed French airfields and planes, it again provided close support for the army, bombing Rotterdam by mistake after the city had surrendered. After Dunkirk, the land battle which Slessor had expected to precede any serious aerial bombardment was over. Milch urged Goering to invade Britain with the Luftwaffe at once, but Goering did not think it could be done. Hitler was hoping that England would make peace and did not order an air attack during June 1940. He permitted no more than scattered night raids 'designed to intimidate the population and to give crews operational training'.[52]

The Luftwaffe planned to attack the RAF in two stages: first to annihilate the fighter defences; then in daylight operations to roll northwards gaining complete air ascendancy while at the same time making complementary attacks on the air industry. The invasion would take place four weeks from the start: to pave the way for it, British trade would be disrupted by attacks on Channel ports and shipping, and the English Channel closed by night-and-day

[51] *ibid.* 81.
[52] Derek Wood and Derek Dempster *The Narrow Margin: the Battle of Britain and the Rise of Air Power 1930-40* 23.

bombing.[53] On 17 July the Luftwaffe attacked supply lines and on the 21st Hitler demanded that invasion be made possible by 15 September. But the navy insisted that air supremacy be obtained first. Goering called for more determined attacks on British shipping. The whole country would be 'unsettled' by bombing, though south coast ports would be spared because the army would need unloading facilities. The prime targets would be the RAF and the British aero-engine industry. Nuisance raids would begin at once to prevent the concentration of British defences. RAF fighters would be forced to fly defensively against German bombers only to be destroyed by escorting German fighters.

But it was not so simple. Goering believed that air attack would force Britain to surrender, while Hitler thought that the invasion would be a mere police operation.[54] Despite pressure from his Chief of Staff, Hans Jeschonnek, Goering refused to permit terror raids on London. His assumptions about the time needed to destroy the RAF were far too optimistic. Of the two available types of escort fighter, the twin-engine Me 110 was useless against superior British Spitfires and Hurricanes and the single-engine Me 109 could barely reach London. The Luftwaffe was unable to destroy the British radar installations.[55] German efforts to draw the RAF into battle by the despatch of fighter squadrons were ignored by British commanders. Bomber formations with heavy fighter escort could not be ignored, but RAF losses were insufficient to permit the Luftwaffe to progress to phase two – the roll-back northwards. The British air industry was producing new aircraft twice as quickly as the German.

On 6 August Goering ordered heavily escorted bombers to attack within the vicinity of London by day in order to overwhelm British fighter defences. London was to be left alone and the experiment would be abandoned if German losses were too high. Bad weather delayed the assault, which began on 13 August. It did not defeat the RAF, German losses being consistently higher. After the 19th, day attacks except to provoke fighter battles were abandoned. Day and night attacks on airfields, dock targets and factories (especially aircraft factories) were tried in early September, to try and force RAF fighters to come up and be destroyed. But fighter escorts were directed to remain with the bombers at all times and were therefore more vulnerable to the RAF. British fighter cover had been withdrawn to

[53] In an order of 30 June, Goering insisted that the prime requirement was to smash 'the enemy air force' but that 'every effort should be made to avoid unnecessary loss of life amongst the civil population'. Cf. also Führer directive No. 17, 1 August 1940. Wood and Dempster 220-1 and 227; Bekker 150.
[54] Wood and Dempster 221-2; Bekker 148-50.
[55] Bekker 145-6.

bases round London where the single-engined Me 109 was at the limit of its fuel endurance. What the Luftwaffe required if it was to obtain control (if not command) of the air was a series of daylight attacks on London to provoke the RAF into a massed confrontation. On the night of 24 August, as a result of bad navigation, a flight of German aircraft strayed over central London and killed nine civilians. The RAF retaliated by bombing Berlin on the 25th and four more attacks on Berlin followed. Milch's subordinates demanded mass daylight raids on London, claiming that morale was more fragile there than in Berlin; Goering dismissed this as nonsense. On 2 September Hitler authorised the start of reprisal raids against London. On the 7th, Goering took personal command of the operation and for the last time in daylight over 300 bombers and 600 Me 109 and Me 110 fighters attacked docks and oil installations in London; losses Luftwaffe 41, RAF 28. The biggest (night) raid was on the 15th: 60 German losses, 26 RAF. Before the 15th, Goering and his advisers had believed that the RAF was at its last gasp, but they were mistaken. There was indeed an acute shortage, but of trained pilots, not aircraft. On the 16th, Goering ordered the continuation of night attacks against London (where night defences were thin) and a renewed fighter campaign to deplete RAF Fighter Command wherever they could be found and to enable German bombers to range at will. The background to his action was shifting: on 14 September Hitler told his commanders-in-chief that the poor weather was to blame for the Luftwaffe's lack of air supremacy and he put off the invasion until the 17th in the hope that control could be secured by then. On the 17th he ordered indefinite postponement of the invasion and on the 19th directed that the invasion fleet should not be augmented. The Battle of Britain ended on 31 October.

The Luftwaffe had borne the brunt of the fighting since July and got the blame for failing to win the Battle of Britain. But it has been argued that the failure was Hitler's for not ordering saturation bombing of London in fine weather against weak defences. Perhaps that would have made possible German air supremacy, but it should be remembered that Hitler was attempting to fight a limited war against Britain. He hoped that the UK would come to terms without the need to defeat her armed forces. Until early September he was still refusing to attack residential areas in London saying that this was to be kept in reserve as a 'final reprisal'. He may have thought that bombing London would bring about the final collapse of British resistance: he said 'if eight million people go mad, it might very well turn into a catastrophe'.[56] And he was half-heartedly preparing for

[56] Irving 97, 98, 105.

invasion. But the concept of limited war – of doing less than one is militarily capable of doing for political reasons – imposed constraints upon the German offensive. Had the onslaught against airfields and radar in southern England been sustained instead of being abandoned later in favour of the attack on London; or had the attack on London come earlier; or had the German navy and army contented themselves with something less than they in fact demanded by way of air supremacy then the battle might have been won. Instead Germany had now to concentrate on her own air defences against the mounting attacks by Bomber Command.

What does the experience of the Battle of Britain imply for the theory of air power sketched above? The broad question is best considered in two parts. (a) What was Germany trying to do? Despite Goering's pretensions, it seems clear enough that the German offensive was a combined operation, much more the sort of thing envisaged by Slessor than the bypassing of armies suggested by Liddell Hart and Douhet. (b) Would Germany have done better to engage in the other sort of strategy? In 1939 she was incapable of a major bomber offensive. It might be suggested that she should have acquired this capability earlier but this is open to at least two doubts: it is entirely possible that a four-engined bomber force could have been built up, given Germany's industrial limitations, only at the expense of the other air facilities that had served so well in the blitzkrieg campaigns;[57] and it is far from clear that a mere plethora of bombers, without strong fighter protection, would have done any better against the RAF than the fighters which failed to win the Battle of Britain.[58] But given influential proponents of Douhet's ideas and a freedom from such incompetents as Udet, perhaps a bomber victory would have been possible. Even so, a problem remains. Hitler hoped to draw Britain into a separate peace and later became obsessed with his plan to invade Russia. None of the theorists of air power had ever suggested that one could use the bombing of cities in limited war to persuade a power still in a position to fight to surrender instead. The theory was that by breaking the cities' morale one would destroy the opponent's ability to fight.

The Battle of Britain had settled one question beyond, one would have thought, all reasonable doubt. It showed that in some circumstances at least, seizing control (still more, command) of the air was a lengthy and difficult business. The advantage in this conflict had clearly been with the defence: his fighters operating fresh from nearby bases; his pilots, if forced to bale out, not thereby lost as

---

[57] Bekker 228.
[58] Higham 128; Bekker 134-6.

prisoners-of-war; his efforts at coordination controlled by radar – with these, the defender could put up a very creditable fight. If he was to be defeated at all then one would require specialised fighters to match his fighter-planes, whether or not one *in addition* needed fighter protection for bombers or could leave them to fend for themselves. On this question, Mitchell was proved right and Douhet wrong, though ironically the US took a long time to see the point. Of course, each new situation is different and one could argue that the lesson of the last experience did not apply; but a prima facie case had been made out that control of the air was exceedingly difficult. Slessor was vindicated as against Douhet, though in a campaign of the kind envisaged not by Douhet but by Slessor.

5. *Britain and the US on the offensive, 1940-44*

Having managed not to be defeated in the Battle of Britain, the RAF went on to the offensive. The air attack on Germany became, from 1942, an allied effort involving both British Bomber Command and the US Eighth Army Air Force. (The latter was amalgamated with the Fifteenth (Italy) in 1944 to form the US Strategic Air Forces in Europe.) The two bomber forces had different equipment and theory. As is well known, the US favoured 'pinpoint' bombing while Bomber Command was wedded to the notion of area bombing. The distinction between selective and indiscriminate killing is so important in ethics that it is vital from the outset to be clear about the relation between American and British theory and practice.

An example from 1943 may serve to clarify the issue. The Casablanca Conference (21 January) issued a directive on the allied bombing offensive which was so vague as to leave the decisive choices on what to do to the American and British bomber commanders – General Ira C. Eaker (Eighth Air Force) and Sir Arthur Harris (Bomber Command). According to the Eaker plan,

> it is better to cause a high degree of destruction in a few really essential industries than to cause a small degree of destruction in many industries.[59]

Later, on 14 May, the Combined Chiefs of Staff approved a joint RAF/USAAF bomber offensive – 'Pointblank'. Although the first paragraph of the campaign plan emphasises the offensive against morale, 76 precision targets are picked out, falling into six groups – submarine bases, submarine construction yards, the aircraft industry, the ball-bearings industry, oil production, synthetic rubber plants, and

[59] Webster and Frankland II, 15.

military transport vehicles. There would be precision bombing of these selected targets by day and night 'where tactical considerations permit' together with area bombing of cities associated with the selected targets. Harris opposed the plan bitterly. He held to the view expounded above that the war would be won, and could only be won, by the area bombing of cities causing the collapse of popular morale: any attempt to single out other targets was a wasteful diversion of resources from the essential task.[60] The issues between Eaker and Harris were tactical and strategic. (Among the tactical questions: what was it possible to hit and with what degree of accuracy? Central to the strategic questions: what sort of bombing would do most towards winning the war?)

The British official historians of the RAF offensive remark trenchantly that

> the moral issue was not really an operative factor. The choice between precision and area bombing was not conditioned by abstract theories of right and wrong, nor by interpretations of international law. It was ruled by operational possibilities and strategic intentions.[61]

The Eighth Air Force carried out 'a number of area attacks in Germany' and 'the American bomber forces in the Far East' adopted 'wholeheartedly the policy of area bombing against Japan which found an ultimate expression in the discharge of the atomic bomb'.[62] The disagreement between Eaker and Harris was not moral but, like the earlier divergence of view between on the one hand Douhet and Liddell Hart's *Paris* and on the other Slessor, was a disagreement about tactics and strategy. (Though this is not to suggest that Eaker and Harris would have rejected moral considerations any more than Liddell Hart or Slessor.) Slessor writes of the controversy: 'I regarded it all as a matter not of legality but of expediency.'[63]

February 1942 was a crucial month. The first deliberate air attack on German civilians had occurred on 16 December 1940, when Mannheim was bombed in reprisal for the German devastation of Coventry. (The night bombing of civilians in the Berlin industrial belt on 25 April 1940 was described as 'unintentional', industry having been the objective.) At the end of 1940 Bomber Command was still attempting to operate plans for precision bombing of selected industrial targets very like those proposed later in the Eaker Plan. But existing bombers could neither find nor hit such targets and January-

---

[60] *ibid.* 18-19.
[61] *ibid.* 22.
[62] *ibid.* 21-2.
[63] *The Central Blue* 214.

March 1941 saw a search for larger objectives, to be bombed until new navigational aids should become available. Accordingly, the industrial centres of large towns were increasingly selected (e.g. Berlin, Düsseldorf, Bremen, Cologne, Hamburg). Bomber Command did not possess control (still less command) of the air at this time. The Luftwaffe fighter force, operating now over home territory, aided by ground flak and unhampered by problems of range, took a heavy toll. The Allies did not possess an adequate long-range fighter and the slow, lightly-armed bombers were an easy target. A single example of the losses must suffice. On 7 November 1941, 400 RAF bombers attacked Berlin, Mannheim, the Ruhr, Cologne and Boulogne: 37 did not return.

Target	No. sent	No. lost	Percentage lost
Berlin	169	21	12.5%
Mannheim	55	7	13%
Ruhr	43	9	21%

There was no one person who could reasonably be blamed for such casualties: they were inevitable given the resilience of German defences, the vulnerable state of the attackers, and the Allied determination to strike at targets which were understandably well-protected. But blame was nevertheless attached to Sir Charles Peirse, commander-in-chief of Bomber Command, and on 22 February 1942 he was replaced by Sir Arthur Harris.

The Official History captures this bleak time so well that it is worth quoting at length:

> the force was in dire need of inspired leadership. Its operations up to 1942 had revealed themselves as gravely disappointing. ... Confidence in the future of Bomber Command had seriously diminished in high, as also sometimes in public, places ... The force, which represented the original and fundamental idea behind the creation of the Royal Air Force as a separate service, was in danger of eclipse before it had received many of its basic requirements such as more effective aircraft, better bombs, and radar guidance, and also at a time when the American air generals were striving for acceptance of related ideas in the preparations of their own strategic air forces. Nor was it only from above that Bomber Command was threatened. Its effectiveness ultimately depended on the behaviour of the crews who manned it, and, though the morale of the force was by no means broken, there were signs that it was delicately poised. Severe casualties had been sustained and little compensating success had been achieved. The public showed little appreciation either of the hazards or the hardships which confronted those who night after night embarked upon what was often a fruitless search in the dark.

Moreover, Sir Arthur Harris, unlike some more fortunate commanders, did not inherit a force, which, while still appearing to be in the doldrums, had, in fact, surmounted its growing pains. In some respects, it is true, Bomber Command was, in February 1942, upon the verge of significant advances. The Lancasters[64] were about to come into operational service and the introduction of *Gee*[65] was imminent. To this extent things were getting better, but in other ways, apart from the fact that for so long so few Lancasters were available and that, in some ways, *Gee* was a disappointment, things were getting worse. The German night fighter force, for example, was growing incomparably more effective, and Bomber Command casualties were more likely to rise than to decline. The great material reinforcements which had once been expected from the United States had also been gravely curtailed.[66]

A week before Harris' promotion, the plans for 1942 were issued (14 February). These gave formal expression to the policy of aerial bombardment: the objectives were to destroy German capacity and will to make war and to help Russia; the new bombers and navigational aids would be deployed as they became available in attacks on the centres of west and north-west Germany. The *primary* objective of the bombing was, for the first time, officially stated to be the morale of industrial workers: men and not their factories were to be the direct object of city bombing. It was not for the authors of the 1942 plans to adjudicate the claim that airpower alone could win the war, and could win it alone. So the plans do not mention Douhet's doctrine of the decisiveness of air power. But at the tactical level, and the level of air force strategy, the idea of bombing to destroy morale was adopted unequivocally for the first time in the history of human warfare. It would not be until two years later that the Allies had to make up their minds about the relation between this airforce strategy (not, as we have seen, shared by the US Eighth) and grand strategy which governs land, sea and air forces. Meanwhile, Harris and his staff were at liberty to evolve, within the framework of official policy, the technique of starting a conflagration in the centre of a town selected for bombing with the hope that the conflagration would consume the whole town.[67]

[64] The Lancaster was a heavy four-engined bomber introduced in March 1942. Harris described it as 'incomparably the most efficient' British bomber, surpassing all the others 'in range, bombload, ease of handling, freedom from accident and in casualty rate'. Webster and Frankland II 92.

[65] Gee was a radar aid to navigation and target identification. For details see Webster and Frankland I 316.

[66] *ibid.* III 78.

[67] Note that Harris preferred high explosive as being more effective than incendiaries; see Denis Richards and Hilary St John Saunders *Royal Air Force 1939-45* II 132.

In a memorandum dated 14 February, A.V. Alexander, First Lord of the Admiralty, stated that he had no objection to area bombing but that aircraft would also be needed for the Battle of the Atlantic and in the Indian Ocean. He requested six-and-a-half Wellington squadrons for Coastal Command, and two bomber squadrons for Ceylon. He was later to demand more planes for long-range reconnaissance which could be provided only at the expense of Bomber Command. On 25 February, three days after Harris's appointment, Sir Stafford Cripps, Lord Privy Seal, expressed doubts in the House of Commons about the effectiveness of devastation bombing and suggested a change in policy. On 4 March Sir Archibald Sinclair, the Secretary of State for Air, spoke to the House about the introduction of new bomber-types and the intention to resume the area offensive at the earliest possible moment. His speech reflects the anxiety that Bomber Command would lose its squadrons to other functions (e.g. reconnaissance) which the Air Staff believed they could not perform. It also indicates disquiet about the Anglo-American alliance. Given the need to encourage USAAF staffs to concentrate on the European rather than the Pacific theatre, the Air Ministry could hardly speak openly against an American strategy which it viewed with dismay; furthermore, any criticism of the RAF bombing offensive would weaken those American lobbyists who favoured a Europe-first allocation of bombers.

On 30 March 1942 the celebrated controversy between Churchill's scientific adviser Lord Cherwell and Sir Henry Tizard began to find expression in cabinet papers.[68] Cherwell wrote to Churchill saying he was absolutely convinced that devastation bombing would destroy German morale:

> Investigation seems to show that having one's house demolished is most damaging to morale. People seem to mind it more than having their friends or even relatives killed.

Large numbers of heavy bombers must be produced. These must each survive fourteen sorties. Better navigational and aiming accuracy is required, and no diversion from devastation bombing. 50 per cent of bombs must find their targets.

Tizard's rejoinder appears on 20 April. Cherwell has overestimated the rate of production and the amount of bombs that can be dropped. Bombers would be destroyed at too great a rate. It is doubtful whether the 58 towns with over 100,000 inhabitants can easily be located and hit. Only 25 per cent of bombs will find their targets. Success in the war really depends on progress by the Red

[68] Webster and Frankland I 332-6.

Army. The result of devastation bombing would be damaging but not decisive. The policy would not have an important effect until 1943 and is altogether too risky. Such a strategy could be effective only if a truly huge bomber fleet could be deployed: British efforts should be directed to attacks on German shipping.

A month later (20 May) the Singleton report on the effects of air attacks on Germany[69] could come to no firm conclusions. It could be quoted to justify any argument. Harris wrote to Churchill on 17 June: the need was to adopt a proper policy of mass bombing of Germany. Bomber Command alone could win the war, but all bombers would have to be returned to it. Victory could be obtained by air power but not by indecisive and bloody land campaigns. The day before, Admiral Sir Dudley Pound, the First Sea Lord, had called for greater concentration on the war at sea. On 17 September Churchill told Sinclair that Bomber Command must be expanded and concentrated on Germany, but some squadrons would have to be transferred to other commands. Churchill, acutely aware of Britain's economic weakness and ever sceptical about cut-and-dried methods for winning the war, never gave Bomber Command the strength that Harris and Tizard considered essential, though Tizard's influence with him was greater than Cherwell's and Harris was able to boast frequent meetings and a unique intimacy with the Prime Minister.

Just over a week before Harris' appointment, Albert Speer was given control of the German armaments industry (13 February). Milch was already in effective command of air production, having on Udet's suicide in June 1941 inherited 'a veritable clinic of ailing projects, ill-planned industry and corrupt organisation'.[70] Milch had set to work at once on expanding production of both fighters and bombers. With the failure to win the Battle of Britain and the growing Allied bomber offensive against Germany, he was persuaded of the need to give priority to fighter-planes: with good defences, perhaps the Allies could be made to fail as Germany had in the Battle of Britain; and a new weapon – the flying bomb – might terrorise the British into abandoning the struggle. Milch was far from sanguine. He had been on leave during the preliminary stages of Hitler's planning for the attack on Russia and was dismayed by it. The war on two fronts and later the Allied drive up from the south of Europe resulted in a great many conflicting demands on the Luftwaffe, so that its efficiency was impaired. But as late as July 1943, though increasingly pessimistic about the war's outcome, Milch still harboured hopes which were not entirely unreasonable: a maximum effort might halt the Allied

[69] *ibid.* 337.
[70] Irving 141.

bomber offensive, while German fighters would protect the missile launching pads on the Channel coast. A flying bomb could be launched every twelve minutes – London would be unable to endure such a pounding. After a few days, morale in the capital would collapse. The new weapon was thus enshrined in the old strategy of morale bombing made possible by control of the air.

Relations between Milch and Speer were sometimes strained.[71] Speer made efforts to annex Milch's empire; in October 1943, Milch tried unsuccessfully to prod Goering into persuading Hitler to stop Speer raiding aircraft factories for skilled workers. The following month, Speer warned Milch that his production programme, based partly on Milch's own fighter priorities and partly on an increase in bombers insisted upon by Goering, was too ambitious: the supplies would not be forthcoming. But in the main it was a fruitful collaboration and fighter output expanded at a level very damaging to the Allies.[72]

The quarrel which destroyed Milch's power concerned the Messerschmitt 262 jet aeroplane. It first flew in July 1942 but did not enter service until autumn 1944. Despite his post-war denials, the aircraft designer and maker Wilhelm Messerschmitt was responsible for the delay and for pushing Hitler to demand that a bomber version of the plane be given top priority. With the Allied air offensive increasingly punishing and the resulting desire for a counter-strike force, Hitler readily agreed that the jet would make a desirable fast bomber. Messerschmitt was also poisoning his mind against Milch. By October 1943 a good deal of thought was being given to the prevention of Allied landings in France. Hitler told Goering on 27 October that this was more important than city defence.[73] Milch warned his superiors that the defence of aeroplane factories was also a top priority since the factories were the basis of German military strength. Goering ignored Milch's advice. The Me 262 was at this time vital if Germany was to regain air superiority. General Adolf Galland, the Inspector of the German Fighter Forces, wanted to use it as a fighter whereas Hitler demanded a fighter-bomber. In January 1944 the pattern repeated itself: on 4 January, Hitler, obsessed with a possible Allied invasion, once more ordered the production of a jet fighter-bomber. Milch could do little to correct Hitler's belief that the Me 262 was fully equipped for bombing. (In fact, the necessary equipment was being fitted only slowly.) On 22 January, a 1,000

[71] Our account follows Irving 146-7, 169, 148-9. Ever diplomatic, Speer claims that the relationship was cordial: *Inside the Third Reich* 282, 287.
[72] Speer 489.
[73] *ibid.*

plane reprisal attack on London without the jet was disastrous – only 30 tons of bombs fell within the LCC area, and bomber losses were heavy. On 23 May Milch confessed to Hitler that none of the Me 262s so far produced could carry bombs. The two men quarrelled and Milch was slowly dropped from office. The Führer congratulated him on the success of the flying bomb campaign, but Milch's transfer to the post of deputy Armament Minister and assistant to Speer left him without power for most of the year before, on 4 May 1945, he was arrested by British troops. After his fall, the Luftwaffe drifted into confusion.

Despite the conflicting direction of Milch, Goering, Speer and Hitler the Luftwaffe was at times a formidable defensive force. Between June 1941 and July 1943 Milch increased aircraft production by 270 per cent. By June 1944 fighter production was at fifteen times the rate of summer 1941. Milch encouraged the flying bomb project, though mercifully no one in the Reich seized the opportunity presented by Heisenberg's work on atomic fission. In the three-and-a-quarter years between February 1942 and the end of the war in Europe there were times when the Luftwaffe had one of the two Allied bomber forces beaten. For example, the US Eighth Air Force was compelled to break off its daylight offensive after October 1943; and Bomber Command suffered 'in the operational sense ... more than a failure ... a defeat'[74] in the Battle of Berlin (November 1943-March 1944). But the revival of the USAAF dates from December 1943-February 1944 and at no time did Germany enjoy a complete respite from Allied bombing.

1942 saw the first 1,000 bomber raids. Harris proposed the scheme on 18 May and Portal[75] and Churchill agreed the next day. On 30 May 1,046 bombers set out for Cologne. 1,455 tons of bombs were dropped and 600 acres of the built-up area destroyed, no considerable part of the city escaping damage. Only 40 bombers, 3.8 per cent of the force, were destroyed; 116 were damaged, 12 beyond repair. This degree of losses was far from crippling but the German defences had not been swamped: anti-aircraft guns were bringing down bombers at the rate of one every eight minutes. Essen was attacked by 956 aircraft on 1 June: the bombs fell over a wide area with little damage to the city of the Krupp works. 3.2 per cent of the force was destroyed, 10.3 per cent damaged. Of 1,006 bombers sent against Bremen on 25 June,

---

[74] Webster and Frankland II 193.

[75] Marshal of the Royal Air Force Sir Charles Frederick Algernon Portal (1893-1971). Served in Europe 1914-18; Air Member for Personnel 1939-40; Air Officer Commander-in-Chief, Bomber Command 1940; Chief of the Air Staff 1940-45; Controller, Atomic Energy, Ministry of Supply, 1946-51.

49 – 4.9 per cent – were lost. Harris then discontinued the 1,000 bomber raids for the rest of 1942, urging Churchill to help him build up the force. In 1942, such massive raids could be mounted only if Training Units were added to the force – regular combat use of these would have severely disrupted training.[76]

The daily average number of RAF bombers available for Bomber Command operations did not increase much between November 1941 (506 planes) and January 1943 (515), though introduction of the Lancaster brought a decided improvement in quality. By August 1943 the daily average had jumped dramatically to 787. Bomber Command fought three mighty battles in 1943, known as the battles of the Ruhr (March-July), of Hamburg (July-August), and of Berlin (November-March 1944). Between August and November, many operations were part of 'the campaign on the road to Berlin'. The authors of the British Official History remark that

> the striking power of Bomber Command developed during the Battle of the Ruhr was enormously greater than anything which had previously been brought to bear by any air force. Britain, in spite of her military defeats, her persistent maritime perils and her consequently generally defensive strategy, had, with the vigorous support of her sister Dominions, nevertheless created an offensive air weapon which, though less mighty than once planned, was vastly more formidable than the German air power which in the last years of peace had helped to intimidate the Anglo-French alliance into abdication and which, in the first year of war, had extended British air defences to their utmost. Such a force as was now disposed in Bomber Command would, in the days of crystal gazing before the war, undoubtedly have given rise to optimistic expectations of an immediate and complete 'knock-out blow'.[77]

Not only was there no 'knock-out blow', 'the evidence of the Battle of the Ruhr' made it 'difficult to judge whether, in a long-drawn campaign of that sort, Bomber Command would become the victim or the victor'.[78]

The battle began well, employing new targetting techniques. High-speed Mosquito aircraft using the navigational aid 'Oboe' dropped flares to guide the bomb-aimers. In the first attack (5-6 March) 160 acres of Essen were laid waste, and over another 450 acres at least three-quarters of the buildings were demolished or damaged by fire. The Krupp steel works were 'deliberately and repeatedly hit'[79] in this and subsequent raids. The Mosquito 'Pathfinder' force was not infallible: 'It was always easy to make the kind of mistake which once led the Pathfinders to mistake Dobrany for Pilsen and a lunatic

---

[76] Richards and Saunders II 132-8.   [78] *ibid.* 138-9.
[77] Webster and Frankland II 138.   [79] *ibid* 135.

asylum for the Skoda works.'[80] But, in operations which were within the Mosquitoes' range, accuracy was greatly improved: in that first attack on Essen, for example, 153 of the 345 bombers delivered their bombs to within three miles of the aiming point(!). Not that Oboe made possible pinpoint attacks: it generally produced

> aiming errors which varied between six hundred yards and a mile or more, and in addition to these errors, those of the main force aiming at the markers also have to be taken into account.[81]

The Official History sums up the experience in this battle within the area where Oboe was operative thus:

> the revolutionary advances in the technique of bombing which it demonstrated had made Bomber Command into an effective bludgeon but ... they had not yet enabled it to develop the potential of a rapier.[82]

A related aspect of the campaign which has a bearing on the ethical aspects of the Allied offensive is well brought out by Webster and Frankland:

> Now it happened, of course, that in the great towns and cities of Germany, these centres were generally congested areas of residential property and seldom, though Essen is an obvious exception, contained major industrial installations ... It is not intended at this point to enter into a discussion as to whether it would have been more or less desirable to aim at factories rather than areas of housing, but it should be clear from what has been said that it would undoubtedly have been much less economical to do so and that to cause destruction of buildings, let alone machinery, in the suburbs comparable to that which could be achieved against houses at the centres would have required a much greater force, either than Bomber Command possessed, or, indeed, was ever to possess.[83]

This was despite the immensity of the RAF bombing force at the time, which is rightly stressed by Webster and Frankland in the passage quoted above. With housing the technically inescapable main target, the destruction of factories 'could be regarded', as Sir Arthur Harris put it, 'as a bonus'.[84]

While Bomber Command was grimly enjoying the successes of the battles of the Ruhr and of Hamburg, the US Eighth Air Force was suffering unsustainable losses. Their strategy was one of deep penetration in daylight by self-defending Flying Fortresses (B17s) without fighter protection. They were hitting at vitally important targets, e.g. Schweinfurt, a centre of the German ball-bearings industry. A sortie on 17 August 1943 experienced a 19 per cent loss

---

[80] *ibid.* 134-5. Slessor, writing after the war, considered the Pathfinder force undesirable: *Central Blue* 373.
[81] Webster and Frankland II 135.   [82] *ibid.* 136.   [83] *ibid.* 122:   [84] *ibid.*

rate, 60 out of 376; on 14 October, out of 291 aircraft sent against Schweinfurt, 148 were destroyed.[85] The British Official History comments that

> the theory of the self-defending bomber formation had, in the face of a properly organised and resolute fighter force, been shown to be a myth.[86]

The Luftwaffe seemed to have won a decisive victory for control of the air over Germany, at any rate in daylight. The Battle of Berlin opened in November and was conducted almost entirely by Bomber Command while the Eighth Air Force recovered from its mauling over Schweinfurt. On 7 December Sir Arthur Harris made a remarkable boast. He had as usual been exuding confidence while lobbying for increased resources and now wrote an official letter to the Air Ministry claiming that on certain carefully stated assumptions

> the Lancaster force alone should be sufficient but only just sufficient to produce in Germany by April 1st 1944, a state of devastation in which surrender is inevitable.[87]

It is not certain that Harris' argument is to be taken at face value. He was in the middle of a massive battle and confronted with the prospect that resources earmarked for Bomber Command might instead be diverted to the very different objectives of those engaged in pre-invasion planning. But his assertion is interesting if only because it is clear and categorical, and because his declared hopes were disappointed for reasons which are still subject to debate. Harris claimed that if certain quantifiable conditions could be brought about (e.g. destruction of 40 per cent of German built-up areas) then 'surrender is inevitable'. He made no reference to the morale factor or to the problems of an orderly transfer of power. And he ignored the fact that his force was in no position to damage severely the widely-scattered German aircraft industry. To put the point in terms of the two variables mentioned earlier, Harris discounted the variable of morale in a situation where he was unable to control the variable of the enemy's capacity for self-protection.

Within this framework of unexamined assumptions, Harris was circumspect:

> It cannot be too strongly emphasised that even a minor change in any of the following factors would entirely alter the picture:
> (i) failure of Lancaster production to come up to schedule;
> (ii) increase in the ratio of our losses to sorties;
> (iii) failure in development or delivery of the navigational aids on which the rate of efficiency of our attacks largely depends.[88]

---

[85] Higham 134.
[86] Webster and Frankland II 40.
[87] *ibid.* 56. The whole letter is reprinted 55-7.
[88] *ibid.*

His letter did not refer to another matter which must have been in his mind: the Allies were planning to begin Operation Overlord in May 1944, and it was to be a combined operation involving all Allied forces in Europe including Bomber Command. Harris, understandably, given his attachment to the idea of victory by bombing alone, was planning an air offensive that would make Overlord unnecessary.

Harris said that 15,052 Lancaster sorties would be required to achieve the outcome he envisaged, with the loss of 752 aircraft. In the event 14,652 sorties were flown for the loss of 681 aircraft. Geography, the German defences and the weather were all against Harris' plan. Berlin was a very distant target, so that protection and targetting were more difficult than in the earlier battles of the Ruhr and Hamburg. A casualty rate near to the maximum Harris had provided for was accompanied by a marked decline in efficiency to be accounted for not, as Harris had supposed, by failures in development or delivery, but by operational problems. For years, Harris had blocked the objections of his critics on the ground that they were ignorant of operational factors; in the Battle of Berlin he seemed to have misunderstood the operational powers of the bombing system at his disposal. On the day before 1 April, in an operation forming part of the offensive whose main target was Berlin, Bomber Command suffered the worst disaster in its history: of 832 aircraft sent against Nuremberg, 95 failed to return and 71 were damaged. Harris understood the problem very well: the previous year, the US Eighth Air Force had been beaten for lack of long-range protection; now, at last, Harris demanded for Bomber Command 'night fighter support on a substantial scale'.[89]

The US possessed the necessary aeroplane. The P51 Mustang, most successful long-range fighter of the war, could fly at 375 mph at 5,000 feet, 400 mph at 10,000 feet, 440 mph at 35,000 feet. Still more important than this considerable speed, the Mustang could, with droppable fuel tanks, accompany bombers 660 miles from base. It began to appear in December 1943 and enabled the Allies to secure air superiority over Germany.

The use to be made of the massive Allied system of bombers and long-range fighters was the subject of vigorous in-fighting in the first half of 1944. In August 1943 the Allied conference at Quebec had approved the appointment of Sir Trafford Leigh-Mallory as Commander-in-Chief of the Allied Expeditionary Air Force, but the relation between this organisation and the strategic bomber forces remained undecided at the end of 1943. In January 1944 the US Eighth and Fifteenth Air Forces were placed under the overall

[89] *ibid.* 193. See also Martin Middlebrook *The Nuremberg Raid* 30-1.

command of the charismatic General Carl Spaatz.[90] Spaatz and Harris exhibited a marked tendency to ignore suggestions from Leigh-Mallory, whose position was rendered increasingly anomalous. Eisenhower demanded complete operational control of Bomber Command and Spaatz's force. Churchill toyed with the idea of appointing a commander for the whole of Britain's air forces in the person of Air Chief Marshal Sir Arthur Tedder.[91] But the Chiefs of Staff, intent on preserving the independence of their several services, were against the scheme and Churchill backed down. In March 1944 Portal and Eisenhower agreed that the *strategic* plan Overlord would be framed by Tedder in consultation with Spaatz and Harris; Leigh-Mallory would prepare the tactical air plan under Tedder's 'supervision'. (The American General Arnold later forced the substitution of 'direction' for 'supervision'.) Tedder would be Deputy Supreme Commander under Eisenhower and also – as Churchill had wanted – supreme air commander.

Leigh-Mallory had prepared an ambitious plan for the disruption of French railways. For now that it was widely agreed that the war would probably end only with hard land fighting, the Allies faced a problem which pre-war air strategists had not foreseen: the military need to bomb a potentially friendly nation and former ally. Planning for the possibility that Germany might suddenly collapse under the weight of strategic bombing continued in the form of Operation Rankin.[92] But a land victory presented very different problems. Germany enjoyed excellent interior communications. She was defending a circle from the centre and able to bring up her reserves by land; whereas the Allies had to attack the circle from outside and to bring their very large land forces by sea. The German railway system was the best in the world and there were therefore very pressing military reasons for striking against German railways and roads. By

---

[90] General Carl Spaatz, Commanding General of the US (Army) Eighth Air Force based in England. From February 1943 he commanded the North-West African Air Force in the Tunisian, Sicilian and Italian campaigns. Appointed Commander-in-Chief of the US Strategic Air Forces in Europe, January 1944. From July 1945, Commander of the US Strategic Air Forces in the Pacific.

[91] Marshal of the Royal Air Force Sir Arthur William Tedder (1890-1967). Served in Europe 1914-18; Air Officer Commanding RAF Far East 1936-38; Director-General of Research and Development, Air Ministry 1938-40; Air Officer Commander-in-Chief Middle East 1941-43; Air Commander-in-Chief Mediterranean Air Command 1943; Deputy Supreme Commander Allied Forces 1943-45; Chief of the Air Staff 1946-50.

[92] Operation Rankin, planned by the Combined Chiefs of Staff during 1943, for rapid occupation of the Continent in the event of a German collapse. Webster and Frankland III 12.

the same token, there was a military imperative for hitting French railways.

Leigh-Mallory's plan required cooperation from the strategic bombing forces. Spaatz and Harris continued to be difficult. Spaatz refused to take orders from Leigh-Mallory; Harris insisted that Bomber Command could only launch 'mass fire raising on very large targets'[93] (and of course the area bombing of France was harder to stomach than the selective bombing of transport installations that happened to be in France). Spaatz and Harris both argued that the German economy would recover while Allied bombers were engaged over France. The favoured strategy of Spaatz and Arnold was different from that of Harris, the Americans believing that selective strikes against oil-producing installations would force the Luftwaffe to concentrate in defence of oil. It would then be possible to use the Mustang to destroy the German air force in the air. Thus, according to Spaatz and Arnold, selective bombing of oil would directly damage a crucial element in the enemy war potential and indirectly secure command of the air. Spaatz, like Harris, was still committed to the idea of a decisive independent strategic air offensive, but unlike him wanted it to be against selective targets and preferably under American control.

Although Harris' arguments against Leigh-Mallory's plan were difficult to challenge on technical grounds, the Air Staff was not convinced by them. On 27 February 1944 Portal directed Air Marshal Sir Norman Bottomley to conduct experimental precision bombing of targets in France. Six marshalling yards were chosen and during March all were bombed successfully. This tended to refute Harris and the issue now lay between Leigh-Mallory and Spaatz. Initially, Leigh-Mallory gained his point. Tedder intervened on 24 March, rejecting for the immediate future the plan for an attack on oil and telling Spaatz to concentrate on communications. The Ministry of Economic Warfare had weakened the oil argument by pointing out that Germany possessed large secure reserve stocks. Spaatz continued his offensive against oil but agreed to bomb French railways. Portal estimated that French casualties would be about 10,000. This dismayed Churchill and the War Cabinet, but Eisenhower declared that political arguments could not override military necessities. Churchill was worried by the odium that would accrue to Britain in France from the presence of Bomber Command in the joint campaign. He appealed to Roosevelt, who backed Eisenhower. By June, Bomber Command was devoting the bulk of its efforts to targets in France and other occupied territories. This gave a breathing space to German

[93] Webster and Frankland III 21.

towns, as Harris and Spaatz had predicted; but the Allied air forces benefitted, too, at a time when fighter defence over Germany was at the height of its powers. By 6 September the campaign over France had done its work and Eisenhower all but called it off. The occupation of France, as it proceeded apace, altered the military balance radically, progressively depriving the Luftwaffe of its early warning areas. Leigh-Mallory's plan for the attainment of air superiority in 1944* and disruption of German communications in France and western Germany was accompanied, at Spaatz's insistence, by an informal oil offensive. Eisenhower gave Spaatz informal permission for this on 19 April and it was initiated on 12 May by 935 bombers of the US Strategic Air Forces in Europe. Spaatz and independent economic experts exerted mounting pressure for an expansion of the effort, which, it was argued, could force Germany to surrender by the end of 1944. The British staff were soon chafing at their inability to control operations which, it seemed, were increasingly being decided at Supreme Headquarters Allied Expeditionary Forces (SHAEF).

6. *The Portal memorandum*

On 1 August Portal drafted an astonishing memorandum. He stated that the object of any renewed air offensive 'was not primarily, as had been the case in previous attacks on targets of this nature, to reduce war production, nor was it designed to throw Germany into utter chaos': the aim would be to preserve some form of German government. The dangerous alternative to organised surrender was that there might be a guerrilla campaign in Germany which would force the Allies to occupy the whole country and assume full responsibility for its administration. The need was to influence high military and political authorities in Germany to surrender, or to secure a regime which would surrender. It would be necessary to undermine the morale first of these authorities, then secondly of the armed forces, and finally of the civilian population. German civilian morale was hard to break and the High Command's morale would not be much affected by bombing unless its authority had already been severely reduced by other factors. Victory when virtually gained by other means might be consolidated, hastened and controlled by a blow from the air of 'catastrophic force'. Berlin would be the most useful target, since 5 per cent of the population lived there and it was the centre of government. 20,000 tons of bombs would need to be dropped on the city in four days and three nights. This would knock the city out. It could soon be repaired, but in the short run such a blow would have an effect on the morale of the Berlin population which might influence the German High Command at a decisive moment. Similar blows against Hamburg, Cologne, Frankfurt and Munich were also considered in the memorandum since they would involve smaller Allied losses. 'Immense devastation could be produced if the entire attack was concentrated on a single big town other than Berlin and the effect would be especially great if the town was one hitherto relatively undamaged.'[94]

This memorandum has an importance in the intellectual history of warfare which appears to have escaped notice. Major writers in the just war tradition and Clausewitz are agreed that war is to be thought about in relation to the conditions which one hopes to produce by means of war. The just war theorists make the point by insisting that war be conducted only for the sake of peace; Clausewitz, perhaps assuming that real peace is never to be found in the world of international relations, puts the point in his celebrated maxim, that war is 'a continuation of political activity by other means'.[95] Portal's memorandum seems to be the first item in the copious theoretical literature on aerial bombing which makes any serious effort to consider the political significance of bombing, its implications for 'peace' or the post-war world. The representative authors discussed above all take the population's morale to be a unitary thing. At most, they draw a distinction between the morale of trained soldiers and that of untrained civilians. What Portal saw was that there is no magic or automatic connection between popular morale and political will. He was able to draw the vital distinction between these two things because he was shrewd enough to realise that an orderly transfer of power was not the only possibility. Clausewitz says that in war

> Force ... is thus the *means* of war; to impose our will on the enemy is its object. To secure that object we must render the enemy powerless; and that, in theory, is the true aim of warfare. That aim takes the place of the object, discarding it as something not actually part of war itself.[96]

The theorists of air power, both opponents and proponents of a decisive strategic air offensive, had discarded the ultimate object. But Clausewitz discarded it knowing what he was doing; he disregarded the political dimension only in those conditions where it was possible and desirable to pursue one's ultimate object as though it were enough to seek merely to disarm one's opponent. The air power theorists proceeded less reflectively and never raised the question of whether there might be conditions in which the political objective

[94] *ibid.* III 53-5.
[95] *On War* I.1.24, tr. Howard and Paret.
[96] *ibid.* I.1.2.

would need to be re-examined, to see how it impinges on military conduct. From 1916 to 1944, it seems, they never once thought of it.

The view of strategic bombing taken in the Portal memorandum was very different from that of Sir Arthur Harris. The memorandum amounted to a severe indictment of general area attack because it suggested that the long-drawn-out war of attrition waged by the RAF since 1940 was unlikely to have any significant effect on German morale. The Air Staff were now envisaging three tasks for Harris's bombers: an all-out offensive against oil; attacks on German communications; and 'Thunderclap', as the final and catastrophic blow against German morale was known. The distinctions between selective and indiscriminate bombing had never in practice been thoroughly clear-cut, and the line separating various types of tactical and support bombing from the strategies of Harris and Spaatz became increasingly blurred as the Allied armies' advance made some at least of Spaatz's and Harris' targets salient to the other components in the invasion of Germany. The bomber forces were so large by this time that the pressure for choice between competing plans was not great. As we have seen, Portal, Tedder, Spaatz and Harris had incompatible ideas about what use to make of the bombers. But none was able to impose his view upon the others, and to the end of the war Allied bombing was a muddled compromise.

7. *Final offensive against Germany, 1944-45*

On 1 November 1944 Harris, who was continuing the indiscriminate bombing of German towns despite instructions to the contrary, made his reply to a memorandum by Tedder dated 25 October, which had been sent to him by Portal and which was critical of Bomber Command. Harris inveighed against any sort of detailed pattern to the bombing offensive other than that required for the general offensive against German towns. Those 'outside the immediate Command' he dismissed as ignorant of the decisive effects of weather and tactical factors. The offensive had to be spread and divided in order to spread, divide and deceive the German defences. Bomber Command's relatively low casualty rate was 'mainly due to foxing the enemy by such methods' – Harris ignored the declining effectiveness of German defences. His immediate intention was to destroy Magdeburg and Halle.

In Bomber Command we have always worked on the principle that bombing anything in Germany is better than bombing nothing.[97]

[97] Webster and Frankland III 82.

In the last eighteen months, Bomber Command had virtually destroyed forty-five of the sixty leading German cities, two-and-a-half cities a month. The task was nearing completion: all that was now required was the destruction of Magdeburg, Halle, Leipzig, Dresden, Chemnitz, Breslau, Nuremberg, Munich, Coblenz, Karlsruhe together with the further destruction of Berlin and Hanover. This accomplishment would 'do more towards accelerating the defeat of Germany than the armies have yet done – or will do'.[98]

A lengthy correspondence ensued. Notice Portal's tone in a letter of 12 November:

> You refer to a plan for the destruction of the 60 leading German cities, and to your efforts to keep up with, and even to exceed, your average of 2½ such cities devastated each month; I know that you have long felt such a plan to be the most effective way of bringing about the collapse of GERMANY.[99] Knowing this, I have, I must confess, at times wondered whether the magnetism of the remaining German cities has not in the past tended as much to deflect our bombers from their primary objectives as the tactical and weather difficulties which you described so fully in your letter of 1st November ... If I knew you to be as wholehearted in the attack of oil as in the past you have been in the matter of attacking cities I would have little to worry about.[100]

Harris' growing irritation at the criticisms of his strategy by Portal and other air leaders led him to ask, on 18 January 1945, whether Portal should consider 'whether it is best for the prosecution of the war and the success of our arms, which alone matters, that I should remain in this situation'.[101] The authors of the Official History explain Portal's failure to accept Harris' resignation in terms of Harris' achievements and 'greater prestige than any other (commander-in-chief) in the Royal Air Force'.[102]

Webster and Frankland are surely right when they say that Bomber Command operations between October 1944 and May 1945, if the most spectacular of the war, were also 'perhaps, the least interesting'.[103] But there is one exception to which they properly devote considerable attention: the destruction of Dresden. On 28 March 1945 Churchill sent to Ismay and Portal a memorandum, parts of which he was subsequently to amend. It was, according to Webster and Frankland, 'among the least felicitous of the Prime Minister's long series of war-time minutes'.[104] Churchill wrote:

[98] *ibid.* 81-2.
[99] Capitals in original.
[100] *ibid.* 84.
[101] *ibid.* 93.
[102] *ibid.*
[103] *ibid.* 183.
[104] *ibid.* 112.

It seems to me that the moment has come when the question of the bombing of German cities simply for the sake of increasing the terror, should be reviewed. Otherwise we shall come into control of an utterly ruined land. We shall not, for instance, be able to get housing materials out of Germany for our own needs because some temporary provision would have to be made for the Germans themselves. The destruction of Dresden remains a serious query against the conduct of Allied bombing. I am of the opinion that military objectives must henceforward be more strictly studied in our interests rather than that of the enemy.

The Foreign Secretary has spoken to me on this subject, and I feel the need for more precise concentration upon military objectives, such as oil and communications behind the immediate battle zone rather than on mere acts of terror and wanton destruction, however impressive.[105]

The argument that it was necessary to think about post-war conditions continued, of course, the line of thought noted above in the Portal memorandum of 1 November 1944, and the amended memorandum preserved this. What Churchill was persuaded to delete was the reference to Dresden and terror.[106]

To assess Churchill's 'infelicity' it is necessary to go back to the beginning of 1945. On 25 January a Joint Intelligence Report was issued on the further bombing of Berlin. Such devastation would not, it was thought, lead to breakdown of the German will to war but, by creating confusion and unleashing floods of refugees, would help the Soviet Union on the eastern front. 25,000 tons of Anglo-American bombs (a good round figure) in four days and three nights would materially assist Russia and show her that her allies wanted to help her. On the same day Harris suggested to Bottomley that the main attack on Berlin should be supplemented by actions against Chemnitz, Leipzig and Dresden, which were also refugee and communication centres. On the same day, too, Churchill asked Sinclair what plans the RAF had for 'basting the Germans in their retreat from Breslau'.[107] Portal considered that the oil campaign should still be the first priority together with jet factories and submarine yards; but on that understanding

we should use available effort in one big attack on Berlin and attacks on Dresden, Leipzig, Chemnitz, or any other cities where a severe blitz will not only cause confusion in the evacuation but will also hamper the movement of troops from the East.[108]

[105] *ibid.*
[106] The deletions appear in a memorandum from Churchill to Ismay and Portal, 1 April 1944: *ibid.* 117.
[107] *ibid.* 101.
[108] 26 January 1945; *ibid.* 101.

Sinclair replied to Churchill on 26 January:

> You asked me last night whether we had any plan for harrying the German retreat from Breslau.
> The target which the enemy may offer in a large scale retreat Westward to Dresden and Berlin is best suited to Tactical Air Forces. This is particularly so now when cloud often makes it impossible to bomb from high level ... It would be extremely difficult for our heavy bombers to interfere with enemy movements by direct attack on their lines of retreat ... I feel strongly that the best use of our heavy bombers at the present time lies in maintaining the attack upon German oil plants whenever the weather permits. The benefits of these attacks are felt equally by the Russians and by ourselves and nothing should be allowed to interfere with them. There may, however, be occasions when the weather is unsuitable for attacks on the comparatively small targets presented by the oil plants but yet would permit area attacks on Eastern Germany. These opportunities might be used to exploit the present situation by the bombing of Berlin and other large cities in Eastern Germany, such as Leipzig, Dresden and Chemnitz ...
> To achieve results of real value, a series of heavy attacks would probably be required, and weather conditions at this time of year would certainly prevent these being delivered in quick succession. The possibility of these attacks being delivered on the scale necessary to have a critical effect on the situation in Eastern Germany is now under examination.[109]

Churchill replied irritably on the same day:

> I did not ask you about plans for harrying the German retreat from Breslau. On the contrary, I asked whether Berlin, and no doubt other large cities in East Germany, should not now be considered especially attractive targets. I am glad that this is 'under examination'. Pray report to me tomorrow what is going to be done.[110]

It should not be supposed that Sinclair was labouring under some moral scruple in this exchange with the Prime Minister: on 21 May Sinclair received a letter from a Member of Parliament declaring himself

> all for the bombing of working-class areas in German cities. I am Cromwellian – I believe in 'slaying in the name of the Lord', because I do not believe you will ever bring home to the civil population of Germany the horrors of war until they have become tasted in this way.[111]

Sinclair replied that he was 'delighted to find that you and I are in complete agreement about ... bombing policy generally'.[112]

The day after the exchange between Churchill and Sinclair,

[109] *ibid*. 102.　　[111] *ibid*. 115.
[110] *ibid*. 103.　　[112] *ibid*.

Bottomley directed Harris to conduct a 'severe blitz' on Dresden, Leipzig, Chemnitz and any other likely cities 'with the particular object of exploiting the confused conditions which are likely to exist in the above-mentioned cities during the successful Russian advance'.[113] Churchill initialled without comment an assurance that the attacks would be carried out as soon as weather conditions permitted. Thus, Harris received formal instructions known to the Prime Minister to carry out the policy which he, Harris, had suggested informally and which two months later Churchill was to describe as 'mere acts of terror and wanton destruction'.

At the Yalta conference, a Red Army memorandum asked the Western Allies to paralyse Nazi communications by striking at the centres of Berlin and Leipzig (4 February). This was almost all the interest shown by the Soviet Union in the strategic air offensive. Indeed, insofar as eastern Germany was the target, Russia seemed anxious to restrict her allies to the west of a bombing line between Berlin and Dresden. But the British plan, whose formulation had included numerous references to Soviet interests, proceeded. (The Russian memorandum refers only to Berlin and Leipzig, not to Chemnitz: 'No evidence has come to light that the Russians asked specifically for the bombing of Dresden.')[114]

On 13-14 February 800 Lancasters of Bomber Command attacked Dresden by night in what Webster and Frankland call 'one of the most devastating attacks of the war in Europe'.[115] 400 daylight bombers of the US Strategic Air Forces in Europe followed up on the 14th, 200 on the 15th, and 400 on 2 March. German sources put the casualties from the Lancaster attack alone at over 32,000.

On 17 February the Associated Press war correspondent at SHAEF issued a despatch to the effect that 'Allied Air Chiefs' had made the 'long-awaited decision to adopt deliberate terror bombing of German population centres as a ruthless expedient to hastening Hitler's doom'.[116] The despatch occasioned great embarrassment in the US and UK. Webster and Frankland consider that it 'undoubtedly contributed to the widespread misunderstanding of the conduct of the British Air Staff and of the Commander-in-Chief, Bomber Command, which has prevailed ever since'.[117] It suggested that a radically new kind of bombing policy had been adopted, and adopted by military commanders no longer under proper political control. Sinclair, whose

[113] *ibid.* 103.
[114] *ibid.* 105.
[115] *ibid.* 109. See also David Irving *The Destruction of Dresden.*
[116] Webster and Frankland III 13.
[117] *ibid.*

task it was to defend the bombing policy against critics who included such formidably respectable people as the Marquess of Salisbury and George Bell, Bishop of Chichester,[118] had not conceded in any of his private or public pronouncements that one of the objects of area bombing was the reduction of civilian and especially industrial morale by the bombing of housing and public utilities. He 'usually and, on public occasions, invariably suggested that Bomber Command was aiming at military or industrial installations, as, of course, it sometimes was'.[119] He did not deny that severe and sometimes vast damage was done to residential areas, but he implied or sometimes stated that this was incidental and regrettable. On 28 October 1943 he had explained to Portal that only in this way could he satisfy the enquiries of the Archbishop of Canterbury, the Moderator of the Church of Scotland and other religious leaders since moral condemnation of the bomber offensive by them might disturb the morale of the bomber crews.[120] Sir Arthur Harris took a different view of the morale question, wondering whether the official line might not give his men the impression that they were being asked to do things which the Air Ministry was ashamed to admit. And whatever Sinclair's attitude to confidentiality, Harris frequently made plain the objects of the bombing offensive. As Lord Salisbury put it to Sinclair on 26 November 1943, Harris' declared resolve that the Battle of Berlin should continue until ' "the heart of Nazi Germany ceases to beat" ' seemed to bring us up short against the repeated Government declarations that we are bombing only military or industrial targets'.[121] Government discretion and Harris' candour gave the impression, confirmed by the Associated Press story, of a divergence of policy between military commanders and political authority. As we have seen, although there were hard-fought differences of policy within the administration, this simple-minded analysis did not fit the confidential facts:

> Neither the Air Staff nor Sir Arthur Harris can justly be accused of waging war in a different moral sense from that approved by the Government.[122]

8. Was the Allied offensive a success?

Whatever one's view of the ethics of war, an ineluctably important

[118] Fourth Marquess of Salisbury (1861-1947): Lord Privy Seal 1924-29; Leader of the House of Lords 1925-29. Rt Rev. George Kennedy Alan Bell (1883-1958): Dean of Canterbury 1924-29; Bishop of Chichester 1929-58.
[119] Webster and Frankland III 116.
[120] *ibid.*   [121] *ibid.*   [122] *ibid.* 117.

question concerning the Allied bomber offensive against Germany is: Was it a success? Let us look at this question under four headings: Did the offensive hurt the enemy? Did it tie down and destroy the German air force and air defences? Did it weaken the German industrial base? Did it destroy Germany's will to fight?

Hurting the enemy. There were times during World War II when Britain was powerless to do anything more in her fight against Germany than to hurt the enemy. The morality of bombing the enemy population under such conditions will be examined later but it is surely undeniable that there was on the Allied side the will to hurt the enemy and that the bombing offensive enabled Britain to do 'him' grave harm. This was inflicted at the cost of the lives of many brave airmen, who may or may not have had a personal desire to punish the aggressor. The damage they did was enormous, and this amounted to some kind of success. The value of this success has to be assessed both in terms of whatever intrinsic value is to be found in punishment and also by reference to the instrumental value of reassuring the British people that they were not totally powerless and of giving some (albeit unappreciated) indication to Stalin that Britain was still fighting.

Tying down and destroying the German air forces and air defence. The bombing of German cities enforced a diversion of some planes from the eastern front. It threw Germany on to a defensive posture in the air and eventually the Allied system of bombers and fighters managed to destroy the Luftwaffe in air combat, and to swamp German anti-aircraft batteries. There was a limited success, made possible by something close to command of the air, in the precision bombing of V1 and V2 bases. Here too, therefore, one has to recognise success. One cannot weigh the merits of the compromise offensive actually mounted against the pure Harris plan, the pure Spaatz strategy, etc. without entering into niceties of speculation beyond the scope of this book. But one thing seems indisputable: the defeat of the Luftwaffe needed the Mustang. Pre-war theorising of the Douhet type, and war-time insistence on bombers at the expense of fighters, retarded this development and cost a large number of Allied lives in the indefensible, allegedly self-defending Flying Fortresses and in the disastrous Battle of Berlin. It will be recalled that Mitchell was stressing the need for good fighter protection as early as 1925.

Weakening the German industrial base. At no stage during the war were the Allied bomber forces in a position to destroy Germany's industrial base in a short, catastrophic offensive. The most that could be hoped for, therefore, was to weaken and if possible destroy it over a long period – the kind of time-scale that permitted adaptation of the German economy to new conditions. The damage could be done through the impact of bombing on labour, on the material factors in production, or on both.

German air-raid shelters were on the whole good and the percentage of the work force killed or diverted into caring for casualties was remarkably small. Fred Iklé, in a book comparing World War II experience with that which might be expected in a nuclear war, describes the German losses as negligible.[123] Bombing did bring an increase in absenteeism, loss of efficiency through fatigue and nervous tension, but this was over-estimated in even the most cautious British estimates and the German work force soon adapted to all but the severest of air-raids (the British population had done the same). An effect more of the war as a whole than of the bombing campaign was the diversion of skilled labour into the armed forces; of some importance was the diversion of skilled workers into making the precision instruments and sophisticated communication systems demanded for defence against the Allied bombers. An ironic fact observed by J.K. Galbraith and his team in Hamburg after the war was that the destruction of hotels and other luxury industries increased the percentage of the population available for war-work.[124] Richard Titmuss suggests that in Britain an average of six working days was lost to the search for accommodation when a person's home was destroyed. In Germany it was probably much less, since it was much easier to enforce labour and in many cases there was not much accommodation left to search for.[125] In sum, bombing had an effect on German (and occupied countries') labour, but it was by no means decisive.

British estimates consistently overrated the bombers' destruction of the material factors in German industry through failure to appreciate a simple difference: a much smaller force is needed to render a house unliveable in than to make work in a factory impossible. Estimates of the destruction of homes were fairly accurate because destruction observed from the air showed pretty plainly which houses were uninhabitable. But irreparable damage to heavy machinery generally required a direct hit by a high-explosive bomb of at least 500 lbs, or an uncontrollable fire. Many factories seen to have lost their roofs were able to resume almost at once; much machinery was removed with surprising speed from factories in a worse state to other cover near by. In 1944 Germany built some oil refineries underground but such measures were exceedingly costly in men and

---

[123] *The Social Impact of Bomb Destruction* 214-21.
[124] J.K. Galbraith *The Affluent Society* 138-40. For a fuller account there is the United States Strategic Bombing Survey (316 vols.).
[125] Iklé 16, 40.

materials: Britain managed to put only seven aircraft factories underground during the war. Perhaps more important was the German success in the devolution of certain key industries (e.g. aircraft, machine tools). The Allies never succeeded in locating, still less destroying from the air, these scattered vitals. The Krupp works whose damaging occasioned such pride (and which shook Albert Speer) was less important than was assumed: it was devoted to design rather than volume production and the effort was readily taken up elsewhere. The pre-war theorists of air power had not asked themselves whether it would be possible to destroy or severely damage industry. In the event it proved not to be possible.

Breaking the will to fight. As we have seen, pre-war theory laid great stress on 'the moral factor' and to the last Sir Arthur Harris believed that the undermining of German morale was the way to win the war. The high importance attached to Operation Rankin showed that few were prepared to gainsay the idea. The expectation that bombing would produce panic was, as pointed out above, strong in some minds: all the evidence suggests that the expectation was mistaken.[126] On morale more generally, Iklé summarises as follows the findings of the US Strategic Bombing Survey:

> Before the end of World War II it was thought that bombing destruction would lower civilian morale and that low morale would lead to lessened war production or even to a revolt against the government, forcing it to surrender. The fallacy of this premise lies in the fact that two quite different types of 'morale' are involved ... The German language has a different word for each kind of 'morale': consequently the German intelligence reports in World War II concerning the civilian home front always clearly distinguished between the two. These reports correctly showed that bombing destruction lowered *Stimmung*, the 'passive morale' or the way people felt. But the low Stimmung did not destroy *Haltung*, the 'active morale' or the way people actually behaved under stress. Habits, discipline, the fear of punishment, and the lack of alternative courses of action left the behaviour (*Haltung*) of the civilian population unaffected by the low feelings and depressed mood (*Stimmung*).[127]

Those who expected to break German morale never pondered what would have been involved in mounting a revolt against the Nazi administration, another failure of political imagination closely connected with that pointed out above in connection with the Portal memorandum. This non-political imagination is perhaps understandable in the military men who were the theorists of air power. They were right in thinking that massive aerial bombardment

[126] *ibid.* 15.
[127] *ibid.* 198.

would make the survivors feel low but overlooked the difficulties these wretches would have in translating their feelings into action.

It is tempting to try and draw together these four factors – hurting the enemy, destroying his air defences, weakening the German industrial base, destroying Germany's will to fight – and to find a general answer to the general question 'Was the bombing on the whole effective?' But the temptation has to be resisted, since the general question cannot be given any meaning. There is no one overriding objective against which the bombing can be weighed. Once one has considered it under several headings, one has given to the subject all the unity that it is capable of possessing.

This might seem an unduly sceptical claim. It might be suggested that the general question, the one that really matters, is the question of what contribution the bombing made to victory. But in fact this question is both over-ambitious and seriously misleading. Only a god could answer it because it is quite beyond human capacity to review and assess all of the implications, positive and negative, of the bombing. For example, if one really wants to come to a balanced judgment on the overall merits, one requires to know what the costs of the bombing were to coastal defences and the protection of convoys in the Atlantic; what losses in Asia were occasioned by the ear-marking of resources for Bomber Command; what alternative uses could have been made of the skills and scarce materials that went into the bombers; and so on. An interesting question, no doubt, but too ambitious. Even more important for our theme, the question is seriously misleading, for it discounts one of the four factors just reviewed: the importance of hurting the enemy is not adequately accounted for if one merely considers the imponderable effect of such hurt on the eventual German defeat and the morale of the eventually victorious Allies. It was a long war and, especially since issues were at stake which seemed momentous to many of those involved, the hurting of the enemy had a day-to-day and month-by-month significance that is quite lost if one sees the thing as wholly a self-effacing pursuit of a distant, eventually attained goal. Of course, victory was always the eventual hope. But the meaning of the word 'hope' changed as the war progressed. In 1940 it was a tenacious refusal to give in, and a millennial dream of a time when the UK would hit back with glorious effectiveness; by 1945 it was a confident expectation. The notion of goal-directed activity, in which everything is done for the sake of the supreme objective, made far better sense in 1945 than in 1940. In the early part of the war, the UK hit back by bombing largely because it was the only thing she could do of a warlike kind. To ask what contribution such hitting made to victory is to ask a thoroughly misleading question. For no one was in a position to envisage victory as a practical objective. To insist on 'objective' analysis, disregarding the perspective of the participants, is to lose all touch with any sort of history that càn hope to illuminate ethical judgment.

Closely connected with this point is what might have struck the reader as a curious feature of our argument: in a chapter devoted to area bombing we have made no attempt to define 'area bombing'. This is not because definitions are impossible.[128] Rather, it seems to us that what is impressive about the bombing debates is that definitions of 'area' and 'strategic bombing' played no part in them. The various controversialists each had their ideas about what to do but there was no common vocabulary for the discussion of different kinds of bombing and, given the course of the debate, no use for such a uniform vocabulary. It would have been a very different campaign if Harris, Spaatz, Portal, etc. had been people with occasion to see the need for a set of uniform definitions distinguishing strategic from tactical bombing. Each knew what he wanted only too well. But each knew perfectly well also what the others wanted, and why he was against it. They had no use for a definition and we, attempting to render the story in terms not wholly alien to the participants, have therefore avoided a definition.

When invited to reflect on the ethics of war, people often bring forward two incompatible ideas, both false. One is that everything which happens in war is done in the heat of battle, on the spur of the moment. (This is often thought to mean that no one can ever be to blame for anything that happens in war.) The other view is that everything that happens in war is done in a spirit of the coldest expediency, clearly separable ends being seen as justifying any means that might appear conducive to their attainment. What the Allied bombing campaign suggests is something altogether more complicated. Each of the controversialists had his own ideas about means (ways of using the bombers) and about ends (what various uses of the bombers would achieve, and how the achievement would fit into the overall pursuit of victory). Each of the participants lived through years of war in which the prospects of victory changed beyond all recognition. In the case of at least some of the participants (e.g. Harris) it is sometimes very hard to determine whether they are firmly convinced of the merits of certain means and seeking for ends to fit, or whether they are attached to certain ends and seeking the most promising means. Each is an individual with a stake in the acceptance

---

[128] See e.g. Webster and Frankland I 6ff.

of a view he has already propounded, and a representative of an interest group that stands to lose if his propounded view is rejected. The best one can do for the idea that war is a matter of the ruthless pursuit of victory is to say that it was perhaps an ideal of some of these persons, that they would have liked to think their problem through in terms of means to victory, and subordinate means to the means to victory, and so on. But it by no means follows that the campaign was merely a product of the heat of battle. We have traced a little of the immense quantity of thought that went into it, dating at least from Wells' imaginings in 1908 and Douhet's earliest writings on the subject in 1909. Impassioned thought, side-tracked by individual and group interest, devoted at times to the modest task of hurting the enemy because victory has not yet risen over the horizon, devoted at all times to the day-to-day business of lobbying for a cherished project in which means and ends are jumbled together – this is the reality with which the student of ethics of war finds himself confronted. Part of the same reality is, perhaps, the ideal of a thoroughly ruthless policy of employing whatever means seem likeliest to produce victory.

9. The atom-bombing of Japan

Two bomber sorties which were not part of the war in Europe require some discussion – the missions against Hiroshima (6 August 1945) and Nagasaki (9 August). Most of the facts about the two atom bomb raids are so well known that it is possible to be fairly brief.

The availability of nuclear weapons in World War II is attributable entirely to pre-war developments in Europe and to activity during the war in Europe and the US; it is a mere accident of history that the bomb was first used outside the European theatre. The triumph of Nazism in Germany had three major consequences for nuclear physics and physicists. Numerous distinguished scientists, being subjected to persecution or the threat of persecution or finding themselves revolted by the tyranny, fled from Germany to the US and UK. In some cases of appointments to important physics jobs under the Reich, Nazi zeal received more weight than scientific excellence. And the Hitlerite attitude to modern physics, together with the personal opposition of some of the remaining nuclear physicists to the regime, occasioned a lack of urgency about a military nuclear programme and arguably some active efforts to delay and prevent Nazi attainment of the atom bomb.

By September 1939 there were (native or refugee) scientists in Britain, France, US, Germany, and Japan who knew of the theoretical possibility that there might be a way of producing a nuclear explosion.

The precise character of such an explosion was unknown; it was even uncertain whether the thing was scientifically and technically feasible.[129] What was clear was that to find out whether nuclear explosions were possible would require a great deal of time, money and scarce expertise. Japan did not possess the resources for such an effort but Germany and the Western Allies did.

In Germany, Hitler at first inclined to rely upon the relatively new, but by September 1939 well-tried, tactics of blitzkrieg to win the series of short wars he was expecting to have to fight. He was subsequently to give his blessing to such innovations as the V1 and V2. Hitler had a healthier respect for modern ballistics than for modern ('Jewish') physics, but it is conceivable that had the will existed among those nuclear scientists who remained in the Reich he could have been persuaded to sanction a nuclear weapons programme. One major source for the understanding of the absence of any such will is an article contributed to *Nature* by the great physicist Werner Heisenberg, the principal authority on nuclear energy remaining in Germany during the war.[130] According to Heisenberg:

> Almost simultaneously with the outbreak of the war, news reached Germany that funds were being allocated by the American Military authorities for research on atomic energy. In view of the possibility that England and the United States might undertake the development of atomic weapons, the Heereswaffenamt created a special research group ... whose task it .was to examine the possibilities of the technical exploitation of atomic energy.[131]

This research group was a long time reporting. Perhaps the delay is partly attributable to opposition to the regime; but certainly Reich scientists never understood fully the nature of an atomic bomb explosion. A report was finally sent to Speer in June 1942 and he decided, on the strength of it, to give high priority to work on the construction of a uranium pile to provide nuclear power; development of an atom bomb in time for use during the war was seen as an outside chance unworthy of the allocation of scarce resources. Heisenberg explains that the bomb project 'could not have succeeded under German war conditions ... In 1942, German industry was already stretched to the limit'.[132] This is not very convincing. Had Speer been persuaded that there was an appreciable risk of an Allied atom bomb,

---

[129] In 1939 Tizard and Lindemann doubted that 'any practical form of bomb could be made with uranium' for several years: Margaret Gowing, *Britain and Atomic Energy 1939-45* 37-87. Only Chadwick dissented from this view (*ibid.* 42).

[130] 'Research in Germany on the Technical Application of Atomic Energy.'

[131] Quoted Batchelder 32-3.

[132] *ibid.* 30.

it seems extremely unlikely that his fertile and ruthless mind would have failed to squeeze out the resources needed for a German research project. Heisenberg's formidable colleague C.F. von Weizsäcker seems more plausible when he writes:

> We had such a precise knowledge of the difficulties inherent in the production of an atom bomb and considered them so formidable that it had never occurred to us that America would be in a position to produce atom bombs during the war.[133]

German intelligence was wrong about the date when US funds began to be spent on the atom bomb; German scientists were of course also wrong if they truly did believe that no Allied bomb would be ready during the war (but not the war against Germany!). Work began in earnest in Britain in April 1940,[134] but the US official commitment began only on the day before Pearl Harbor. Without a vigorous campaign by the research scientists it might never have begun at all, and British resources alone could not have completed the work in time.[135]

Enrico Fermi, the first man to split the atom (in 1934), arrived in the US early in 1939 and on 16 March (the day after Germany marched into Prague) he tried without success to interest the US Navy in the possibilities of nuclear explosions. On 11 October, having previously been thwarted by President Roosevelt's preoccupation with the newly-started war in Europe, the scientists were able to present the President with a letter bearing the signature of Einstein, who had the great merit of possessing a public reputation in America. On 1 November Roosevelt responded by establishing a committee which for several months did nothing. A second letter with Einstein's signature in March 1940 emphasised the potential of nuclear power and pointed out that nuclear research was being expanded and intensified at the Kaiser Wilhelm Institute in Berlin. The first US funds ($6,000 for graphite and uranium) were allocated about this time but as late as September 1941 it was possible for the head of the section then responsible for the nuclear research committee to argue that this area of research should be stopped until after the war: for the research work was at that moment at an impasse, and there were projects with less remote chances of success competing for limited funds. Then came breakthroughs in Britain and California, and in November 1941 a high-powered committee reported in favour of large US commitment, estimating that bombs could be made 'within three or four years'.[136]

[133] *ibid.* 31.
[134] Gowing 37-44.

[135] *ibid.* 66, 72-3.
[136] *ibid.* 122; Batchelder 22-4.

The scientists who had urged that the possibility of atomic bombs be explored were concerned that Hitler might get the bomb first. They gave little thought to what should be done if the Allies acquired the first bomb, or to what should be done after the war. They saw themselves as confronting an unprecedented emergency and acted accordingly. Intelligence reports suggested that German research was advancing and the truth was discovered only in November 1944. One of the physicists working on the Allied project then said to a military colleague, 'Isn't it wonderful that the Germans have no atom bomb? Now we won't have to use ours'. The officer replied, 'Of course you understand, Sam, if we have such a weapon, we are going to use it.'[137]

The pre-war airpower theorists had not envisaged anything like the atom bomb. Their intricate calculations were all concerned with ordinary high explosives. But, as Portal's memorandum of 1 November 1944 demonstrated, there was at least one strategic idea in existence by late 1944 which would provide a use for the atom bomb: if one of the roles of strategic air power was to end a war through a catastrophic air strike which would persuade a defeated government to surrender then the atom bomb would be an ideal weapon. Portal had had to reckon on an enormous fleet of bombers and to calculate anxiously the relation between the speed with which they could devastate a town and the rate at which the town could recover. The damage could be done so much more quickly with a single atom bomb as to radically alter the variable of enemy adaptiveness to aerial bombardment.

The first atom bomb was exploded in the New Mexico desert on 16 July 1945. The Allies were by this time confronting a Japan which was, as people often express it, already defeated but not yet willing to surrender. The meaning of this somewhat paradoxical expression is that Japan could no longer reasonably hope to obtain military victory or stave off military defeat or annihilation so long as her enemies continued to prosecute the war vigorously; yet Japanese leaders were unwilling to surrender – some of them favouring a fight to the death of every Japanese under arms. It was a situation very like that envisaged in Portal's memorandum.

A great deal of argument has focussed on the range of options open to the Allies. One point is clear: it is far too simple to claim that the choice was a straightforward one between bombing Hiroshima and Nagasaki or fighting one's way, island by island, to Tokyo with enormous loss of life. The US Army argued that victory could be obtained only by destroying the Japanese land forces, and it was

[137] Batchelder 37.

estimated that this might involve a million Allied casualties. The US
Navy and Air Force claimed that the war could be won with far less
Allied casualties by means of the naval blockade and/or a strategic air
offensive which had already inflicted massive damage on Japan. The
Navy and Air Force arguments had considerable force for, despite the
worryingly high morale of Japanese kamikaze pilots and the spirited
defence put up by the remnants of the Japanese air defences, the Allies
possessed command of the sea and air. But such a strategy would take
time. Could the US afford to wait? The Soviet Union was on the point
of declaring war on Japan. The longer she participated in the Pacific
war before it was won, the greater claims she would have in an area of
the world in which the US had staked out a very great interest through
pre-war investment and four years of extremely bloody fighting.
Raymond Aron puts the point with characteristic vigour: 'Soviet
participation ... would deprive the United States of some of the spoils
of a victory which it had in fact won by its own efforts alone.'[138]

Another complication is what the US knew of the state of Japanese
political will. Japan was known to have been putting out official peace
feelers in May and June 1945 and on 12 July (four days before the first
atom bomb test) the US intercepted a message from the Japanese
Foreign Minister to the Japanese ambassador in Moscow. It said in
part:

> See [Foreign Commisar] Molotov before his departure for Potsdam ...
> Convey His Majesty's strong desire to secure a termination of the war ...
> Unconditional surrender is the only obstacle to peace.[139]

Subsequent telegrams, also intercepted, made it 'clear as crystal'[140]
that at the very least there was a powerful and authoritative part of the
Japanese government prepared to surrender if only the Allies would
permit the retention of the Japanese emperor. It is now widely known
that the Japanese government was deeply split into a war party and a
peace party; that the emperor had been opposed to war in 1941 and
powerless to avert it; that the Allies decided belatedly that the
emperor should keep his throne. But these things were not clear in
July 1945: the US had reason before the Potsdam conference to think
that she could secure Japanese surrender possibly before the Soviet
Union entered the Pacific War. But she did not act on this knowledge.
Some suggest that it would have been politically impossible for the US
administration to take advantage of its (partial) knowledge because it
was a prisoner of public opinion which would accept nothing less than

138 *The Imperial Republic* 22.
139 Batchelder 83.
140 *ibid.* 85.

unconditional surrender. This is a remarkably unconvincing argument: the US did settle for something less (carefully concealed, of course, in a diplomatic formula) and the popularity of the administration's glorious victory was not noticeably diminished.

At Potsdam, the question of Japan was discussed by the politicians only marginally; the only serious consultations on the subject were between military chiefs-of-staff. This seems to be more remarkable than it is usually taken to be. One of the more interesting unanswerable questions of World War II is what the Japanese response would have been if, at Potsdam, the Russians had been asked to enter the war against Japan and such a formal invitation had been embodied in the Potsdam declaration. We now know that Japanese of all persuasions were exceedingly worried about the Soviet threat. Molotov had suggested on 29 July that the US and UK address a formal request to the Soviet government that it should declare war on Japan. The possibility of using such a request *instead of* a 'Thunderclap' bombing raid to persuade the Japanese government to surrender appears not to have been even considered. Russia entered the war after Hiroshima, thus standing to gain at any future peace settlement but contributing at best marginally to the securing of Japan's surrender.

Some of the nuclear scientists, unaware of the diplomatic and political opportunities just pointed out, tried to suggest an alternative to the use of the atom bomb against Japan. At a lunch on 31 May, Arthur Compton suggested to Secretary of War Stimson that a non-military demonstration of the bomb might persuade the Japanese to surrender. Present at the lunch were all members of the committee set up to advise on nuclear projects. Stimson put forward Compton's suggestion for discussion round the table. It was rejected: the Japanese would suspect trickery; they would make every effort to shoot down the demonstration plane if the time and place were announced in advance, as it presumably would have to be; the bomb might fail to work; Japanese weather conditions were so changeable that one could not announce a time and place in advance and be confident of being able to drop the bomb there and then; if a demonstration failed to produce surrender, the advantage of surprise would have been lost irretrievably.[141] (What does 'surprise' mean here? Certainly not the military initiative.) The idea of a non-military demonstration was pressed subsequently but always encountered similar obstacles.

Roosevelt had died on 12 April 1945 bequeathing Truman, so far as

[141] *ibid.* 90.

is known, no opinion on how the bomb should be used. Truman learned of the bomb's existence only after he had been sworn in as President. He consulted with his advisers (Roosevelt's team whom Truman had asked to stay in office) and spoke with Churchill before deciding what to do. The advisory committee, having pondered suggestions including those of a demonstration explosion, recommended unanimously that the bomb be used against Japan as soon as possible. Truman is quoted as saying

> I then agreed to the use of the atomic bomb if Japan did not yield.
> I had reached a decision after long and careful thought. It was not an easy decision to make. I did not like the weapon. But I had no qualms if in the long run millions of lives could be saved.[142]

Truman told Stimson that the bomb should be dropped on a 'military target'. Stimson was supplied with the names of five cities 'of great importance to the Japanese production effort ... because of their size and manufacturing or industrial significance'. These were Hiroshima, Niigata, Nagasaki, Kikura, and Kyoto. Kyoto was struck from the list because it was the ancient capital of Japan and a centre of Japanese art and culture: it was spared as the old cultural centre named Dresden had not been. On 25 July orders to bomb one of the four remaining targets were sent to the commanding general of the Strategic Air Forces in the Pacific, a person familiar from an earlier part of this narrative – Spaatz.

Some commentators have raised the question of why the bomb was dropped on a city rather than on a more purely military target, and have argued that the reason was that by 1945 the distinction between civilian and military objectives had for all practical purposes been eroded. There is some truth in this view, in that the utility of bombing cities had been the subject of eloquent advocacy since 1916. But it was not the case, as the debates discussed above make plain, that by July 1945 no one could any longer recognise the distinction between city bombing and the bombing of other objectives. Spaatz for one had been heavily involved in disputes in Europe which presupposed the possibility of making the relevant distinctions and was hardly the man to accept orders without counter-argument if so minded. Why, then, were cities chosen? After all, the principal opponents in the Japanese cabinet to accession to the Allied terms of surrender on other issues than that of the emperor were mainly military men. Robert Batchelder suggests that

> Had the target been a supply dump of equipment essential to the defense

---

[142] Gowing 373.

of the Kyushu invasion beaches, the impact upon General Anami and his friends might have been greater than was that of the destruction of Hiroshima.[143]

Anami's war faction attempted to conceal and minimise the damage to Hiroshima – they were certainly not persuaded by it to accept surrender.

Plans had been laid that if the first attack did not secure surrender than it would be followed in a few days by a second. It was intended when the first bomb was dropped on 6 August that the second would be used, should occasion arise, on 11 August. Weather conditions worsened and it became clear that bombing on 11 August would be impossible. The mission that destroyed Nagasaki was *not* delayed but brought forward to 9 August. Why? There appears to be only one explanation (unless one assumes that the move was merely an inexplicable bungle). The bombing of Hiroshima was followed by another event outside US control: Russia entered the war against Japan on 8 August. If the Japanese had failed to surrender after Hiroshima but had then surrendered after the Soviet declaration of war and before the second atom bomb then the Russian claim to a share of the spoils of victory would have been strengthened. If one accepts Aron's view quoted above that the US wanted and was entitled to enjoy the victory it had won alone then the haste in bombing Nagasaki is understandable.

The raid on Hiroshima had been preceded by a warning contained in the Potsdam declaration:

2. The prodigious land, sea and air forces of the United States, the British Empire, and China, many times reinforced by their armies and air fleets from the West, are poised to strike the final blows upon Japan ...

3. The result of the futile and senseless German resistance to the might of the aroused free peoples of the world stands forth in awful clarity as an example to the people of Japan. The might that now converges on Japan is immeasurably greater than that which, when applied to the resisting Nazis, necessarily laid waste the lands, the industry, and the method of life of the whole German people. The full application of our military power, backed by our resolve, will mean the inevitable and complete destruction of the Japanese homeland ...

13. We call upon the Government of Japan to proclaim now the unconditional surrender of all the Japanese armed forces, and to provide proper and adequate assurances of their good faith in such action. The

---

[143] Batchelder 157. General Korechika Anami, War Minister and former military adviser to the Emperor, was a leader of those who favoured a last-ditch fight against the US. He committed suicide on 15 August 1945.

alternative for Japan is complete and utter destruction.[144]

Batchelder comments on this address to a proud and intelligent people:

> The *threat* of 'utter destruction' did not hint at the existence of a new and overwhelmingly powerful weapon; neither did the *hope* extended to Japan include any mention of the retention of the Emperor.[145]

It was known in the US that there were in Japan physicists capable of understanding the message 'We possess nuclear weapons' and indeed this message was rather quaintly taped to three instrument boxes which were to be dropped by parachute from a second plane at the same time as the atom bomb was dropped by the first pláne over Nagasaki. The message was found, turned over to Japanese naval intelligence and finally transmitted to the addressee long after the surrender. The Western Allies did not try to find out what leverage the peace party in the Japanese government could exert before Hiroshima using as a crowbar the knowledge Japanese scientists possessed of the potential for nuclear explosions. Had the case been argued out in the US and then in Tokyo *before* Hiroshima, would the war party have been forced to give in before the Russian declaration of war and before Nagasaki? The Allies did not make the experiment so we do not know.

A very thorough historian sums up the part played by Hiroshima and Nagasaki in Japan's decision to surrender thus:

> The atomic bombing of Hiroshima and Nagasaki *and the Soviet Union's declaration of war* did not produce Japan's decision to surrender, for that decision – in embryo – had long been taking shape. What these events did was to create that unusual atmosphere in which the heretofore static factor of the Emperor could be made active in such an extraordinary way as to work what was *virtually a political miracle*.[146]

We have already stressed the importance of Russia's intervention and it remains to consider the 'political miracle'. Political decisions in Japan were taken by the military. The Emperor was little more than a figurehead in whose name decisions were taken. By the 1940s it had become all but inconceivable that he should intervene. Yet he did intervene, twice. After Nagasaki, the Cabinet was hopelessly split and rehearsed its arguments in front of the Emperor. He declared for

---

[144] *ibid.* 92. Casualties at Hiroshima 64,000 killed, 72,000 injured; at Nagasaki 39,000 killed, 25,000 injured (Gowing 380). Scarcely 'complete and utter destruction'.

[145] Batchelder 91.

[146] Robert J.C. Butow *Japan's Decision to Surrender* 231.

peace. The Cabinet endorsed his influential, but not authoritative, decision and sued for peace, accepting the Potsdam declaration 'with the understanding that the said declaration does not comprise any demand which prejudices the prerogatives of His Majesty as a Sovereign Ruler'.[147] The Allies replied in terms preserving in the letter the demand for unconditional surrender while in fact conceding the Japanese condition. This again split the Japanese Cabinet, but again the Emperor spoke for peace, thus ending World War II. As one writer has put it

> We demanded unconditional surrender, then dropped the bomb [twice!] and accepted conditional surrender.[148]

General J.F.C. Fuller writes that by June 1945 only the demand for unconditional surrender stood between the Western Allies and a 'highly advantageous' peace with Japan.[149] The Emperor, retained in office, played an important part in the orderly post-war government of occupied and then independent Japan.

What, then, is one to make of the bombing of Hiroshima and Nagasaki? Neither was the most lethal raid of the war. Taken together, and together with the Russian intervention in the Pacific, they can be fitted into the theory contained in the Portal memorandum that air power can have a use in putting an end to a war already all but won. But in this role their success was a very near-run thing: the Emperor's decisive intervention was not a certainty, nor even a predictable possibility, but a miracle. The two raids could easily have provoked a war party coup, the total eclipse of the peace party, and a further prolongation and intensification of the war.[150] Finally, they were not the only option apart from the Army's proposed bloodier strategy. A variety of less lethal political, diplomatic and military alternatives were not tried. Some but not all of these would have enhanced Soviet power in the Pacific.

[147] Batchelder 139.
[148] Hanson W. Baldwin *Great Mistakes of the War* 92.
[149] J.F.C. Fuller *The Second World War: a Strategical and Tactical History*, 391-4.
[150] Butow 199.

II

Deterrence and Terrorism

Since 1945 the military situation has changed so much and so irreversibly that many of the questions which were important to the pre-war theorists and to those conducting the Allied bombing offensive have lost their currency. We look later into the problem of whether the same ethical traditions have a bearing both on World War II and on the contemporary world. But before that can be done it is necessary to venture an outline account of the present military situation. To do this in the historical manner essayed in Chapter One would be impossibly cumbrous and besides would convey the misleading impression that it is possible in the dark late-seventies to get a decent historical perspective on the post-war world – the necessary detachment, information and perspective are not yet available. We therefore resort to an intuitive, fragmentary presentation aimed to locate in their proper context the twin themes of nuclear deterrence and terrorism.

1. War and international relations

Before World War II, ideas about air-power did not underlie any great part of systematic thinking about international relations. If there was a dominant theory about the interstate system then its organising concept in the minds of idealists was the League of Nations. The states of the inter-war period were widely seen as constituting a family. The League's arrangements were the best hope for keeping the peace in this somewhat unruly family. If the League broke down, the traditional mechanisms of power-political diplomacy might avert war but there was no other systematic guarantee apart from the League against the outbreak of another ruinous world war. States pursued their own perceived self-interest, so the theory went, except insofar as a respect for the League restructured their priorities and activity. Perceived self-interest had not prevented World War I and could not be relied on to avert a new catastrophe. The task of military strategic thinking was to determine what measures would be required if war occurred. No military idea was seen as having any implications for the structure of international relations. On the contrary: the military facts being what they were, it was even more imperative that the League should work and bloody war be averted. The idea of air power even at its most grandiose was the idea of a military means, not of a principle of order within the interstate system.[1]

There now exists a widely shared theory about nuclear deterrence which goes far beyond the consideration of mere military means: nuclear weapons are thought to structure both peace and war. Military preparations are no longer made only against the day when the system breaks down and fails to keep the peace; military measures are thought to be constitutive of what is meant by peace, and are important guarantors, if not the sole guarantors, of the system of international relations. The pre-1945 theorists of air power thought their job well done if they could tell us how to win a war most economically should peace break down; contemporary nuclear strategy is seen as bearing, among other things, the heavier burden of enabling the participants in the international system to live together in (relative) peace. Before 1939 it was possible to think about international relations without having to do much thinking about bombing, and to theorise about bombing without the need for any profound study of the international system. Today, the two are seen as inextricably bound up and it would be mere ignorant folly to attempt a consideration of one without reference to the other. The naiveté about politics which we have repeatedly encountered in the story of airpower to 1945 was understandable and arguably excusable; one may think that contemporary theorists are also naive about politics, but they cannot be silent about the political implications of nuclear deterrence – at most, the quarrel will be about the substance of the politics, not about whether politics is at all relevant.

Nuclear theory has such gothic complexity that it is necessary for our purposes to oversimplify enormously, though not, we think, unfairly.[2]

Between 1949, when the USSR detonated its first nuclear device, and 1962, four changes occurred within the constant, if fluctuating, context of East-West confrontation. Nuclear weapons became

[1] Political realists increasingly challenged reliance on the League (see in particular E.H. Carr *The Twenty Years' Crisis*). But realism did not suggest that military measures had any role beyond the traditional one of being the final resort when international order broke down.

[2] For a short introduction see Laurence Martin *Arms and Strategy*, Ch.1. Philip Green *Deadly Logic* provides a fair but biting critique of some fundamental deterrence theories, and has a useful bibliography. For more recent material see publications by the International Institute of Strategic Studies.

plentiful. Delivery systems altered beyond recognition. The number of nuclear powers increased, and theory burgeoned. We consider these points in turn.

Nuclear weapons became plentiful. Atom bombs which had been few throughout the forties and whose scarcity appears to have played an important part in the decision to bomb Nagasaki were now stockpiled in very large numbers, and the still more destructive hydrogen bomb also proliferated.

The systems for getting nuclear weapons to their target also altered beyond recognition. In place of vulnerable bombers, the US possessed by 1962 three separate ways of getting nuclear explosives to the desired place: the bomber system, the land-based missile system, and the submarine system. As we have seen, the debate about Hiroshima made crucial reference to the ability of the Japanese air force to interfere with a demonstration test. The bombing offensive against Germany was largely a story of the interplay between a vulnerable offensive and a formidable defence of fighters and anti-aircraft guns. We have argued that, given the level of armaments available during World War II, the two key variables were the enemy's morale and his ability to fend off and recover from one's bombing (to which might be added one's own will and ability to sustain losses). Except for Hiroshima and Nagasaki, all major raids in World War II permitted recovery or at least adaptation on the part of the enemy state. Even in the case of the two atom bombings, Allied calculations had to pay careful attention to the possibility of adaptation.

The abundance of nuclear weapons and delivery systems has changed all this drastically. It would be an exaggeration to claim that there is no possibility of adaptation to nuclear bombardment.[3] But even those who argue that it would be possible to fight, survive and win a nuclear war, freely concede that the possibility is highly problematic. Immensely more damage would be done with a speed which represents a difference in kind and not merely of degree: a city would be wrecked in minutes rather than days. With so many bombs and rockets, a far greater loss rate could be sustained by the power launching the nuclear strike and yet the state under attack still suffer arguably irreparable damage. The abundance of radioactive fallout is a new and largely unpredictable variable.

2. Nuclear devastation and political theory

Modern technology threatens to destroy any state that undergoes

---

[3] See, e.g. Fred Iklé *The Social Impact of Bomb Destruction*.

nuclear bombardment. Modern ideas about what constitutes a state are various and confused, but the problem in political theory can be sketched without much difficulty. At present, most people tend to identify a state, and to distinguish it from other states, by reference to the territory it effectively controls and/or by reference to 'the things it stands for'. If a group of people is moved from one part of the world to another they may constitute the same nation or the same people (e.g. the Jewish people) as before, but they will not constitute the same state as they did before the move. Thus physical movement destroys states.

Now suppose that the same group of people living in the same territory change their political system fundamentally, whether of their own free will or because forced to do so from outside. Then there is doubt about whether they constitute the same state as before. For example, the Nazi state disappeared in 1945 and it would be incorrect to say that the Nazi state was split into two states – East and West Germany – with a few years of occupation interrupting its sovereignty. Radical internal change, like physical movement, can therefore destroy a state.

It seems entirely possible that the extent of devastation caused by a major nuclear bombardment would destroy all the *states* subject to it. Not only would the loss of life be very great and material civilisation be largely destroyed; those things which make a thing the same state with a continuous history would be destroyed. For territorial integrity and political institutions would be most unlikely to survive. This is more important for our thinking about nuclear deterrence than is usually realised. Some would be disposed to dismiss it as mere pedantry, of no importance and perhaps obscene when the real question is the prospect of ruinous major nuclear war. We are unable to agree. A good deal of strategic and military thinking is going on about the possibility of surviving a major nuclear war and it seems merely irresponsible for those of us whose expertise is in political theory rather than in the quantification of material destruction to shun the discussion. The result would only be that, like pre-1945 thinking about air power, the new debates are conducted in a political vacuum where the crassest blunders of political thinking find no resistance.

We wish, therefore, to draw attention to the failure of those considering the prospects of after-holocaust life to ponder the deep uprooting of our thought (which is also their thought) that would result from the destruction of contemporary states. All Western thinking about nuclear deterrence is conducted in a political tradition that derives in various complex ways from the political revolution, perhaps best symbolised in the treaty of Westphalia (1648),[4] which replaced a medieval cosmos understood in religious terms with a system of sovereign states whose relations are thought about in secular terms. It is in the language that has resulted from this revolution that nuclear deterrence is necessarily both propounded and criticised. No other thought-world is available. The idea of fighting and surviving a nuclear war is therefore vastly more complex than is usually understood. For it involves deep problems of identity. It may well be that many individual human beings would survive even a massive nuclear war. But in addition to the obvious questions about the emotional state these wretches would be in, there is a political question. Does it make sense to say that the survivors would be Russians, Americans, Chinese, etc? Given current ideas about the state (and what else can one go by?), the answer is probably No. The survivors are likely to be without political identity.

This is a considerable difficulty for those who argue that in some sense a nuclear war can be fought and won. Their argument focusses on the extent of material damage and deaths, adaptation in cities, etc. They develop their thinking within orthodox political theory, taking as their guide perceived state self-interest. Their maxim is: 'Do what is conducive to, or necessary in, the interest of the state of which you are a subject.' This is all very well before a nuclear war, but if the war destroys that state which one was trying to serve then what is one to do? The political rationale for seeking to survive a nuclear war is deeply obscure.

A third change in East-West relations in the period 1949-62 is that the weapons spread to states which did not possess them in 1945. Most crucially, of course, the USSR acquired a set of nuclear weapons and delivery systems commensurate with that of the US. The West came to face, in addition to the morally appalling prospect of inflicting nuclear devastation on the Soviet Russia, the perhaps more widely felt distressing possibility of suffering nuclear bombardment at the hands of the USSR. On Christmas Day 1954, having been galvanised into action by the Bikini tests of the hydrogen bomb, Bertrand Russell read over the BBC radio a message entitled 'Man's Peril' which he had persuaded Albert Einstein to sign. He said

> There lies before us, if we choose, continued progress in happiness, knowledge and wisdom. Shall we instead choose death because we can not forget our quarrels? I appeal as a human being to human beings. Remember your humanity and forget the rest. If you can do so the way

[4] For some debate of the moral significance of Westphalia see Michael Donelan (ed.) *The Reason of States*.

lies open to a new Paradise; if you cannot, nothing lies before you but universal death.[5]

Although this expressed forcefully a widely shared aspiration, it does not show Russell at his best. He has forgotten that the human being is inescapably a political animal. There is no separable 'human nature' or 'humanity' which makes it possible to forget politics. The struggles in which we are embroiled would hardly be quarrels if we could forget the differences between us.

Theory, which in 1949 was still the preserve of an amateur few, burgeoned in the period 1949-62. We expound certain of its principal ideas while avoiding most of its hermetic vocabulary.

By the early fifties, the US had committed itself to a policy of military containment. The notion of containment was that Russia was an expansionist power bent upon moving into any vacuum which it found anywhere on the globe. This tendency to expand had to be resisted at all points as a matter of American self-interest and/or in the interests of those ideals of liberty and democracy that the best part of official America wanted to protect and extend in the world. George Kennan, author of the celebrated article which first gave public currency to the idea of containment, has claimed that he did not favour *military* containment. However that may be, it is unquestioned that for many years the notion of containment (including military containment) provided the official US understanding of the political world within which nuclear strategy developed.

The idea of containment is often associated with the rather different notions of aggression and defence. Much was made of these terms before World War II and they were much used in Allied declarations of policy and in the Nuremberg and other war trials that occurred in the forties. They have received an immense amount of time at the United Nations and have an inescapable, if shadowy, ethical importance. The part they have played in Western thinking about relations with the USSR can be summed up very briefly. It is argued that Russia desires to change the current world political and strategic order, whereas the West desires merely to preserve the status quo. Hence, it is inferred, if there is war between East and West then it will be initiated by the Soviet Union and not the West. Since the initiator of war is 'the aggressor' while the power which responds to such initiation is 'the defender', Russia is inherently aggressive while the West is inherently defensive. People who talk in this way are sometimes prepared to add that they are speaking from a Western viewpoint and that from the Kremlin it may well appear that the West

[5] *Portraits from Memory* 238.

is revisionist and aggressive while the East is conservative and defensive. Lurking, of course, in the background to the argument is the nuance that aggression is morally reprehensible in a way that defence is not. (In pre-war theory, every state retained the right of self-defence while aggression was often denounced.)

At this point in the argument, we wish to make only one observation about the aggressor/defender theories of international relations. In the early fifties, when US preponderance in nuclear weapons was still overwhelming, there was much American talk by among others Secretary of State John Foster Dulles of 'roll-back', the idea that American or Allied military efforts should go further than merely *containing* Soviet military power, should – if the opportunity presented itself – be devoted to freeing from Soviet domination some of the states of Eastern Europe. The significance of 'roll-back' is controversial. Some commentators would dismiss it as merely popular politicking without any roots in serious Western deliberations; some of those who take a different view wish to argue that the US has been the aggressor in the post-war world, the culprit for the Cold War and the main threat to peace.[6] Our intentions are more modest. It seems too soon to be sure either way about the place of 'roll-back' in Western strategy. We therefore wish to qualify the statement above that the touchstone of American policy in the period 1949-62 was containment (including military containment). Containment, certainly, together possibly with the desire to drive the Soviet Union back, provided the context for the evolution of American nuclear theory.

3. Analysis of deterrence theory

Political and military theory, however abstract, is usually developed in response to specific contemporary problems. One of the main formative problems in nuclear theorising has been, how to contain Russia in Europe? In the late forties a number of regimes in Eastern Europe had been installed which were friendly and/or subservient to the Soviet Union and this had been done by the undermining of what were to Western minds potentially more democratic governments. In the early fifties, impoverished West European states had demobilised or were demobilising; American troops were being withdrawn from Europe in large numbers and demobilised; Soviet force levels remained extremely high. It seemed possible (some thought it certain) that the USSR wanted to expand further into Europe and would seize West Berlin if it could do so with impunity. Berlin lay inside East

---

[6] For a level-headed brief discussion see S.E. Ambrose *Rise to Globalism: American Foreign Policy 1938-70.*

Germany, had been used by the West as a propaganda centre to embarrass the Soviet Union, and was indefensible if subjected to military attack. One need not think Russia an especially 'aggressive' power to believe that she would take over West Berlin if at all possible. The US and her European partners therefore faced at least two strategic problems (in fact, of course, there were innumerably many more). How to protect Western Europe? And how to protect Berlin? It is an oversimplification, but not grossly misleading, to say that nuclear strategy was an answer to these and similar questions.

In the early fifties, nuclear weapons seemed to represent a relatively cheap option for the defence of Western Europe. Instead of trying to raise armies comparable in size with those of the Soviet Union and her allies in the Warsaw Pact, NATO placed its reliance on the nuclear deterrent. An early version of the NATO plan is known as the doctrine of massive retaliation. In this version NATO threatened that if a single enemy (e.g. Russian) soldier crossed certain well-defined lines (e.g. into West Germany or West Berlin) then the US and its allies would strike massively, at times and places of their own choosing, against the heartland of the enemy.

But what if the enemy hit back with his always-increasing stock of nuclear weapons? The answer was that he would not hit back. He would not cross the prohibited lines in the first place. For the possibility that NATO would carry out its threat would dissuade him[7] from doing so. However much he wanted to seize Berlin or Europe, he wanted to avoid nuclear devastation still more and NATO could therefore rely on its nuclear threat to check his efforts at expansion.

The basic idea in this scheme is what one might call, to coin a term not current in the literature of nuclear deterrence, the strategy of the overriding risk. One has a quarrel with a fellow-participant in the international system. By one's own efforts one can create a risk so appalling to one's antagonist that he will want to avoid the risk more than he will want to do the thing, whatever it is, over which one is at odds with him. If all the major participants in international relations can do this, one has a *system* of overriding risk in that each power has the ability to settle quarrels by creating overriding risks. Between World War I and II, states had to rely on the increasingly discredited League of Nations, on power-political diplomacy and on war to obtain satisfaction in their quarrels. But here is a new mechanism of international order, made possible by a new technology and the spread of that technology to all of the great powers. Assume that in the fifties there were only two great powers and it can be seen how it

---

[7] We are using 'dissuade' here as a stylistic variant of 'deter' and not in the technical sense employed by the French theorists discussed below.

could be thought that nuclear deterrence underpinned the system of international relations at that time.

If the system is to work, the risks that are being created must be real, appreciable risks. The Soviet Union will not be prevented from seizing Berlin unless the Russians believe that there is a real possibility that NATO will resort to nuclear war as a result. This gives rise to the celebrated problem of credibility. No doubt the US is strongly attached to the preservation of a free Berlin. But is it reasonable for NATO to expect the Soviets to believe that there is any appreciable risk of the US waging nuclear war, at the risk of vast destruction to itself, for the sake of faraway Berlin? Theorists have come forward with numerous answers to this and related questions. Some answers are more plausible in relation to Berlin, others in relation to Yugoslavia, others in relation to Hamburg, others in relation to Norway or Israel, etc.

One reply is that the problem is unreal: deterrence at current technological levels is semi-automatic. Pretty well whatever the US and her allies do, the Soviet Union will not persuade herself that the risk of nuclear war is insignificant. A second type of theory is that NATO can improve the credibility of its threat by developing the forces needed to fight (and win, or at any rate avoid immediately losing) a holding action in Europe. Suppose, for example, that Warsaw Pact forces cross into West Germany and suppose the credibility problem is that NATO cannot expect the USSR to believe that the US will wage nuclear war, risking its own devastation, to protect Germany. Then, so the theory goes, if we develop in Europe forces capable of fighting a holding action in Germany then the Russians will have reason to believe the nuclear threat and will not initiate the military action, or will desist when faced with resolute resistance. There are many versions of this argument. One holds that what is important is the presence of large numbers of US troops, because these demonstrate the US interest in what happens in Europe. ('We cannot let our armies be defeated'; 'They are killing American boys out there'.) Another claims that what is needed is a range of so-called tactical nuclear weapons. These are relatively short-range systems, designed for use on a so-called nuclear battlefield rather than for firing at the heartland of the enemy and equipped with relatively small explosives. The smallness of tactical nuclear weapons is strictly relative: some theorists see the nuclear battlefield as embracing all of West Germany and large parts of France; some of the 'small' explosives have the yield of the bomb dropped on Hiroshima. The argument is that the use of these weapons would delay the progress of enemy armies and give time for thought and negotiation. It would demonstrate US resoluteness in face of Soviet doubts about the reality of the US commitment to wage intercontinental nuclear war on account of Western Europe. Another theory on the preservation of credibility holds that in some situations the threat is credible because the US can be seen to have no alternative to fighting a nuclear war (Berlin), that in some situations the presence of so much dangerous technology would render massive nuclear war all but inevitable once the most limited of hostilities began (Europe), and that in some cases NATO can credibly *threaten to lose control* (e.g. threaten to wage a non-nuclear war in defence of Yugoslav independence whose likely outcome would be a military and political crisis in which the US had little or no alternative but to use nuclear weapons or in which nuclear war would be all but inevitable).

It is sometimes said that nuclear deterrence is no longer as important as it was in the period 1949-62. This statement finds ready acceptance among those who have long since become jaded by the incessant, futile-seeming convolutions of the technical debate, and among those who have grown up in a world in which other things than nuclear crises have occupied the headlines. But it is seriously misleading for the uninitiated. What is true is that official thinking and efforts in recent years, and to a considerable extent what new theory has been forthcoming, has been focussed on other things than intercontinental nuclear war and such grand problems as the protection of West Berlin. The reason for this, however, is that the largest-scale weapons systems are already in place, happen for a number of years not to have been subject to theoretically drastic change, and until recently have seemed to present few new problems for theory. It has therefore been possible to direct attention to subtler questions, such as the nuances of tactical nuclear weapons and the deployment of conventional forces. All engaged in the technical debate agree that these lower-level problems presuppose the grand outlines laid down before 1962. NATO addresses itself to problems that arise within the context of strategic nuclear deterrence. Discussions of tactical nuclear weapons and conventional forces take place in terms of credibility, a term whose current meaning was established in the formative years before 1962. It is arguable that the strategic stability of the past ten years is unlikely to last indefinitely: new techniques of anti-submarine warfare or anti-ballistic missile defence could give rise to new problems of theory. But these interesting possibilities are beyond the scope of the present argument. What is vital is that the reader should not imagine that pre-1962 thinking about nuclear strategy is anything but urgently contemporary.

In terms of the historical cartoon sketched in the foregoing pages, it is possible to highlight certain leading characteristics of current deterrence theory, considered as an aspect of relations between the US and USSR and their allies.

Deterrence is a theory. No one knows whether deterrence works because, given the historical data currently available, it is possible to challenge at each crucial point in post-war history the claim that the great powers were deterred from actions they would otherwise have engaged in. Some people appear to erect this empirical, historical fact into a universal law by arguing that deterrence is unverifiable because it is concerned not with what happened but with what did not happen. It is possible, such people think, to find out about what happens in history (e.g. to find out who is defeated in battle) but not to find out what does not happen (e.g. to find out who would have done such-and-such but for the operation of the deterrent). Such scepticism seems to us unjustified and intriguingly mistaken. Human thought is inescapably involved in both defeat and deterrence: roughly speaking, an essential part of defeating an army is persuading its commanders (or, in case of mutiny, its men) that the army is defeated – the thought that the army cannot go on is an essential part of the 'process'. This thought is not different in kind from the thought that one cannot take such-and-such a risk, e.g. cannot risk the possibility that the US will wage intercontinental nuclear war. If it is currently impossible to know whether deterrence works, that is not because such things cannot be found out but because the evidence is not available to us. If it never will be the case that we shall find out whether deterrence works, that will be because the evidence never becomes available rather than because defeat and deterrence are of different logical kinds.

4. Deterrence and conditional intentions

Deterrence, then, is a theory. It is a theory focussed upon certain conditional intentions. For several reasons, the contention that deterrence is a matter of conditional intentions is often denied. It is very important for ethics to establish the place of conditional intentions in deterrence, so we now examine the objections in order.

(a) All agree that deterrence depends on the issuing of certain threats, in particular on what we called above the threatening of overriding risks. One deters an opponent from some course of action by threatening him with something which he would rather not risk, even if he must abandon his desired course of action. Threats are of two kinds: some are bluffs, others are conditional intentions. If I threaten a child that it will get no pudding unless it finishes its cabbage I may be merely bluffing, or I may be expressing the conditional intention to deny the child its pudding if it does not finish its cabbage. Some who have been troubled by the morality of nuclear deterrence have taken comfort from the thought that one can bluff one's way in the deterrence system.

If I try to bluff the child, what am I doing? I am threatening to withhold the pudding, but I do not really mean to do so; indeed, I mean *not* to withhold the pudding if it comes to it. If the child calls my bluff then I intend to give it the pudding; otherwise, I am not *bluffing*. Whenever it can truly be said that I am bluffing, there is a way available to the person I am trying to bluff to call my bluff and thereby defeat me.

There is no possibility of bluffing in the deterrence system for several reasons. The superficial point is that if one merely bluffs one will be found out. For example, if one issues certain nuclear threats when in fact one (secretly) possesses no nuclear explosive then one will be found out, spies detecting the trick. But there is a deeper point than this. What people tend to mean when they suggest that one should bluff in the nuclear arena is not that one should issue threats which one lacks the military capacity to carry out, but that one should issue threats *without* meaning it. What, if we understand them aright, they mean by this is not properly describable as 'bluffing'. They do not mean that we should issue the threats intending not to carry them out if the bluff is called, but that we should issue the threats without *at the time* intending to carry them out. The analogy is not with the intention to give the child its pudding if it calls the bluff but with the issuing of an ultimatum to the child in the hope that it will give in, where one has not yet decided what to do if the child *still* refuses to eat its cabbage. This is not bluffing.

Its proper description is that it is the declaration of a conditional intention (to withhold the pudding if the cabbage is not eaten) in circumstances where one has not yet decided what to do if the conditional is actualised (i.e. if the cabbage is not eaten). It is vital, if doublethink is to be avoided, to agree that this is not 'bluffing'. For the moral discomfort that leads one to find refuge in the idea that NATO is only bluffing depends on the thought *not* that NATO has not yet decided what to do *but* that NATO has already decided, if the bluff is called, not to carry out the threat.

If deterrence is morally defensible, it must be as conditional intention, not as bluff.

(b) A frequent objection from those with a professional interest in deterrence to the view that deterrence is a matter of conditional intentions is this: what is required for deterrence of the Soviet Union is not that NATO have certain conditional intentions but that the USSR be sufficiently uncertain about what NATO would do in certain future circumstances. Not current fixed intentions but fluid future uncertainties are at the heart of deterrence. This objection is often put forward in the interests not of an easier conscience but solely of accuracy about the subject under discussion. It also has, however, an obvious ethical connotation. For the moral agent stands, or seems to stand, at a greater distance from fluid future uncertainties than from his own conditional intentions.

This professional view of what deterrence is all about is closely related, far more closely than is often realised, to what lies behind the ethically-motivated wish to see deterrence as bluff. What the professional is claiming is not that the future fluid uncertainties can be left to take care of themselves. He is emphatic that their existence depends on what 'we' (e.g. NATO) do now and in the immediate future. He sees the deterrent as dependent as much on Soviet perceptions of Western political will as on perceived Western military capability. That is, it is very important for the deterrent that Russia should take a certain view of current Western conditional intentions, e.g. intentions to act in certain ways if certain things happen in Berlin or Yugoslavia. What we in the West do is, on this view, important for deterrence if only because it is what the USSR will look to in trying to determine Western intentions.

The professional sometimes wants to draw distinctions within the field of deterrence. Consider a pair of rather crude examples (the strategist will no doubt wish to be subtler with his instances, but the logic of the argument will be the same). (i) There was perhaps a time when Western political and military leaders had the conditional intention that if the USSR and her allies crossed certain lines then NATO would strike massively, at times and places to be chosen according to circumstances, against the 'aggressor'. (ii) But now the situation is far more complex. Take just one of the several threats currently available, namely the threat to lose control. In making this threat, NATO is expressing the conditional intention to engage in certain kinds of non-nuclear warfare, knowing and wanting Russia to know that such activity may well result in a loss of control in the West and the uncontrollable onset of nuclear war. Can the professional not urge that the first example (i) is an instance of a conditional intention to use nuclear weapons whereas (ii) is not?

We propose to consider this argument alongside another, which is often put.

(c) It is frequently said that, whatever may be the case with the

USSR, we in the West desire peace and the point of deterrence is the preservation of peace. We are aiming to avoid war and if war occurs deterrence will have failed. To represent deterrence as a matter of conditional intentions to wage nuclear war is to ignore unfairly the laudable objectives of our deterrence posture.

We now proceed first to dispose of argument (c); secondly to consider the possibility that our criticism of argument (c) provides the proponent of argument (b) with an unassailable defence; thirdly to show that argument (b) is indefensible; and finally to ask what significance is to be attached to the complications into which we have been drawn in discussion of the simple-looking contention that deterrence is a matter of conditional intentions.

Argument (c) is easily disposed of. We have no wish to question the widespread and very understandable desire to avoid nuclear war, nor have we any doubt that this wish plays some part in the thinking of those who maintain the deterrent. The question at issue, however, is how to describe current efforts in the direction of preserving world peace. Insofar as one is considering NATO efforts in this direction one must mention the deterrent. The correct description of the situation is that NATO has certain conditional intentions which, it hopes, will keep the peace. NATO intends to do certain things if certain conditions arise and the hope is that, because NATO has these intentions, peace will be maintained and the conditions in question will not arise. One has to put the point in this way because it is NATO's conditional intentions which differentiate the NATO method of promoting world peace from other (e.g. utopian) methods. The reference to NATO's conditional intentions cannot be refused merely on the strength of what NATO hopes those intentions will achieve. If there is a serious case against talk of conditional intentions, therefore, it arises from argument (b) rather than from argument (c).

Does this demolition of argument (c) give comfort to the proponents of argument (b)? A little symbolism may serve to show why it might be thought to do so. According to argument (c), the point of deterrence is to keep the peace. Let us represent this as Y. We replied that the way deterrence purports to keep the peace is that NATO has certain conditional intentions, intentions to X if P. We claimed that the only way to differentiate deterrence from other methods of keeping the peace was by saying that the practitioners of deterrence intend to X if P and hope thereby to Y.

Look at argument (b) in this symbolism. Can its proponents not make two assertions? First, that what deterrence consists in is all those activities (e.g. the sending of certain submarines to certain points on the globe, or if you will the conditional intention so to do) which, it is hoped, will preserve sufficient fluid uncertainties to deter the Soviet Union. Schematically, Y is to preserve the uncertain future and what the practitioners of deterrence intend to do is X (e.g. send submarines to certain points) if P (e.g. there is major international crisis), the hope being thereby to Y. This first assertion applies to all deterrence.

Second comes the assertion which is specific to such threats as the threat to lose control. Here, the conditional intention in question is the intention to wage non-nuclear war under certain circumstances, the hope (Y) being thereby to avoid those circumstances and keep the peace.

It might be thought that both of these arguments are just as cogent as our argument against argument (c). Hence, a dilemma for us: if we are right about the untenability of (c) then we can have no answer to argument (b).

This is not a genuine dilemma. There is a decisive difference between the cases. In arguing against (c), we argued that there is a certain description of deterrence which cannot be refused, namely the description of it in terms of conditional intentions. It cannot be refused because the conditional intentions are what differentiate deterrence from other ways of trying to keep the peace (e.g. the utopian). But a proponent of argument (b) has to proceed in a very different way. He has to show that a certain description of deterrence can be refused and *cannot* be accepted. No one wishes to deny that a great deal of what goes on in the deterrent can for some purposes some of the time be described in terms of efforts to maintain future uncertainties. The question is whether reference to conditional intentions can be eliminated altogether: this is what (b) must show if it is to be interesting. And this cannot be shown. For that which holds the deterrent together is the concept of conditional intention. Officials from day to day can perfectly well proceed without reflecting on the intellectual structure underlying their activity, and do this in terms that make no reference to conditional intentions. But NATO activity is the enacting of a theory and that theory is inextricably wedded to certain ideas about conditional intentions. This must be agreed by all except those who believe deterrence to be semi-automatic. For there is a reason (and only one reason) in deterrence theory for thinking that political will matters in addition to military capability: this is that, according to the theory, the opponent is deterred by future uncertainties of a certain kind, namely, uncertainties as to one's intentions and capabilities. The dilemma, therefore, which is genuine and which is finally disastrous for all versions of argument (b) is this: either deterrence is a matter merely of military capability and the strategic agonisings over credibility are fundamentally mistaken or political will is a vital part of deterrence and – whatever officials in their day-to-day activities may think – reference to conditional intentions is an essential part of deterrence.

This discussion of the simple-looking idea that deterrence is a matter of conditional intentions has been long and complicated. The length and complexity require some comment. They are an example of a difficulty which can only increase as our book proceeds. There are two very widespread attitudes to defence issues. One sees defence as an impenetrably complicated technical subject, properly the preserve of experts. These experts cannot be expected to engage in extended discussions of ethical issues because morality is a matter of individual opinion and there are no moral experts. The other attitude sees defence debates as sick with amorality and in need of a bracing moral tonic, perhaps a few good blunt moral principles. Both views contrast technical expertise with morality, assuming that morality is or should be simple. There is much to be said for the view that moral principles should be relatively few and relatively simple; if they are not, they are likely to die the death of a thousand qualifications because we will be unable to avail ourselves of them in practice. But what there seems to us no reason whatever to believe is that the consideration of ethical issues will involve no intellectual complexity. We are not here referring to moral dilemmas – of course there are moral dilemmas, a fact pondered below. What concerns us at present, however, is the possibility, which many people without a philosophical training find unfamiliar and suspicious, that the most straightforward of moral judgments might involve intellectually difficult and complicated argumentation. Our discussion of the objections that can be brought against the idea of nuclear deterrence as a system of conditional intentions is an apt example. It is important for ethics to know how deterrence and conditional intentions are related. Both casual conversation and the technical literature generate doubts, often propounded with considerable tenacity, about this relation. A serious moral consideration of deterrence cannot but follow the argument where it leads. In the going, some are likely to drop away because they suspect the objectors are in bad faith or that the critics (ourselves) are arguing for the sake of arguing. The reader can only be left to draw his own conclusions.

In asserting that deterrence is a matter of conditional intentions we are not making a moral claim or working within ethics. Our argument involves no ethical premises and advances no ethical conclusion (though it is a necessary preparation for ethics). Our contention purports to admit of no doubt, whether moral or non-moral. We are arguing that, appearances to the contrary, there is no intellectually respectable alternative to this view of deterrence. Our analysis rests firmly on the meanings of the words 'bluff' and 'intention' and we do not think that a dissenter will obtain any support for a different view in the difficult literature on the philosophical analysis of intention: the issues in that literature are different.

Deterrence is a theory of conditional intentions, then. More especially, it is a theory of the conditional intention to inflict nuclear devastation upon the civilian population of one's adversaries. Several objections are often brought against a heavy emphasis on civilian population, and these must be considered.

(a) Much thinking, especially since 1962, has been concerned with other technologies than those of intercontinental nuclear war. It might therefore be thought anachronistic to concentrate on so-called counter-city strategies.

(b) Furthermore, NATO possesses the nuclear option to wage either 'counter-city' or 'counter-force' warfare: i.e. the decision to aim our missiles at cities rather than hostile forces lies with a very few people, and is a closely-guarded secret subject to revision in the light of new circumstances. Is it not therefore dogmatic to harp all the time on those options which relate to civilian populations?

(c) The supposed moral distinction between civilian and soldier has been subject to very considerable erosion in this century of total war. Douhet is quoted in Chapter One, for example, declaring that 'in a war between nations the damage cannot be restricted merely to paid gladiators'. Is there not, therefore, the grinding of out-of-date axes to be heard in heavy emphasis upon civilian populations?

The main thrust of (c) will be considered later. Of course, our interest in the distinction between cities and forces is as a prelude to ethics. But this is not to say that the distinction is alien to the literature on nuclear deterrence; the distinction is freely used there.

Our attitude to (a) has already been made clear. Of course, with the stabilisation for a time of the strategic deterrent and with anxieties about credibility, official attention has fairly widely shifted to other areas. But current thinking presupposes the large-scale deterrent, and many of the so-called tactical nuclear weapons would very probably be used against cities, as well as showering them with fall-out. The deterrent as a whole would not be what it is without the very substantial ability and commitment against cities.

To say this is not to deny the facts appealed to in argument (b). A good deal of thinking and preparation has gone into nuclear warfare against hostile armed forces. But there are several difficulties here, of varying degrees of interest. At present, some of the enemy forces –

specially his submarines at sea – are impossible to hit. Even if one had some chance of hitting a very large segment of his nuclear forces, the very great damage that he could still do to us with only a very small part of his force would be one of the things against which it was necessary to guard; and the only available guard would appear to be his cities, considered as hostages for his good behaviour. Somewhat less dependent on the vagaries of current technology is the importance *theory* attaches to threats against cities. Theorists feel a good deal more certain that the USSR would regard the destruction of its cities as an overriding risk than that they would take this view merely of their forces. Unless the Soviet Union has to reckon with political will (conditional intention) to attack its cities, the threat will lack credibility – or so it is thought.

The imaginative appeal in argument (b), the impression of options left open, requires attention. One of the most important aspects of the argument is the view it invites us to take of what manning the deterrent is like. It suggests that the deterrent is to be seen fundamentally as a machine being worked by a very small group of people making decisions in times of extreme crisis, on their own to wrestle with appalling dilemmas which could affect the future of human life in every country in the world. It is a modern variant of the great man view of history. But whereas Tolstoy in *War and Peace* assailed the notion that the hero can stamp his personality on history, what we have to think about here is the notion of a few little men with a *great problem*.

There is indeed something heroic in the background. It is stirring and deeply moving to talk with persons responsible for nuclear bombers on regular duty during the Cuba missile crisis and thinking about what they should do, recalling colleagues who in earlier political crises had refused to fly. But it is one thing to recognise and feel the poignancy of their situation, another to know how to describe it. To have the correct characterisation is, once again, a necessary preparation for ethical thinking about the deterrent.

Suppose that, in some future crisis, a handful of men have to decide whether to target cities or to target forces (or, equally, have to decide whether to initiate nuclear war). Is it correct to say of these persons, without qualification, that the decision is theirs? The belief that this is correct is what is important in the argument which invites us to dwell on the fact that NATO's options are still open, for it is the description of the choice as a future choice by a handful of persons other than ourselves, the readers and writers of this book, that makes possible a distancing of ourselves from the choice: the decision is theirs not ours.

Whatever the handful do, it is quite wrong to describe their action as theirs alone. This is not a moral but a pre-moral point. In describing what the handful do one is making sense of it, indicating the background against which alone it can be understood. Why is that person speaking those words into the telephone receiver? The only possible answer to this, unless something is merely question-beggingly taken for granted, will refer to the NATO deterrence posture, its history, and the events that have led up to the present time when that person is speaking the words that he is speaking into that telephone. His utterance is an inseparable part of the enacting of the theory of deterrence. There is no way of understanding what he is doing, and very many ways of misunderstanding it, unless all the background of deterrence is assumed. This is a logical not an ethical observation. The understanding that one has of what is going on among our supposed small group of people presupposes deterrence; without that presupposition there is no reason to give the explanation or description we in fact would give, and no reason to credit such an explanation or description if it is proferred. Whatever view is taken of morals, regardless of what one thinks about individual and collective responsibility, the activity of our supposed handful of men is logically inseparable from the theory in practice of deterrence. It is therefore radically incoherent to believe that 'the decision is theirs alone'. In a pre-moral sense, the decision cannot be theirs alone; it is part of a thing, namely deterrence which necessarily involves lots of other people in addition to this handful. The ethical questions of who is responsible for what will be considered later; at this stage we are concerned only with the correct description, as a prologue to ethics, of deterrence in its various forms.

So far in this chapter we have been concerned with nuclear deterrence between the US, the Soviet Union, and their allies. We have been working within a sketch of post-war political relations between these powers and have discussed only issues which have had or currently possess some currency. In that sense, our approach has been historical. But we have not tried for a balanced historical view of the period: such a perspective would require far more space than is here available and we doubt whether the time is yet ripe. We have taken up those issues which appear to us most important for ethical thinking about deterrence and have worried at them in an intuitive unsystematic way. The focus of our attention has not been upon nuclear *weapons* considered as a specially significant sort of hardware but upon nuclear *deterrence* considered as a theory of international relations which has been practised for many years by the US and its allies and arguably by the USSR and associated states. One reason for this approach is that, unlike thinking about airpower up to 1945, deterrence is or purports to be one of the principles of such order as pervades the international system in the post-war world.

We turn now to two phenomena which are interestingly but obscurely related to nuclear deterrence between the superpowers: one is the spread of nuclear weapons, the other terrorism. It does not require any great gifts of imagination or prescience to see that these may in the future come to be inextricably intertwined if nuclear weapons become available not only to more and more states but also to non-state groups, e.g. to insurgents, liberation movements, freedom fighters, terrorists.

An historical rooting for one's thinking is still more difficult in the case of the spread of nuclear weapons and the case of terrorism than it is with superpower nuclear deterrence. The central deterrent, as one might call it, has a history of a sort which is by now relatively stable, however unpredictable the future is and however likely to upset our view of the deterrent's history. But the spread of nuclear weapons and terrorism belong so much to the future, and their immediate past appears to depend so much on the future for any order that may come to be visible in it, that one feels decidedly at sea. If one is to discuss the subject at all, therefore, it is necessary to be even more speculative here than in the treatment of deterrence between the superpowers.

5. The spread of nuclear weapons

In a trivial sense, the spread of nuclear weapons began with their acquisition by the US or by the USSR. In a more interesting but unacceptable sense, it is often said, at any given moment to have its beginning with the power which has not yet acquired nuclear weapons but will be the next one to do so. This tendentious thought is usually expressed using the long word 'proliferation' instead of the short word 'spread'. Proliferation is usually divided into 'vertical' proliferation, i.e. the acquisition of new weapons and weapon systems by states who already have some nuclear capability, and 'horizontal' proliferation, the acquisition of nuclear weapons and weapon systems by powers which previously had none. Critics of the conduct of nuclear powers in the period since the signing of the Non-Proliferation Treaty in 1968 are apt to blame them for the spread ('horizontal proliferation') of nuclear weapons because non-nuclear signatories always expected that their self-denial would be parallel to the containment of vertical proliferation, the growth and qualitative improvement of existing nuclear armouries.[8] The charge is that those

[8] See, e.g. John Maddox 'Prospects for Nuclear Proliferation'.

who have nuclear weapons are doing nothing of any significance to stop the spread of nuclear weapons. The tendency to use the term 'horizontal proliferation' to refer only to those who do not yet have the bomb is a symptom of this failure to act. Since we have a good deal of sympathy with these critics, we propose to avoid such usage of the word 'spread'.

What we have in mind in our discussion of the spread of nuclear weapons is this. The central deterrent between the US and the USSR and their allies has by now a . long history and considerable complexity. It is arguably a principle of world order. The acquisition of nuclear weapons by any other power, given the ambitions and perceptions of the two superpowers, complicates in fundamental ways the central deterrent. It is useful for analytic purposes to have a word for such complicating processes and the word we have opted for is 'spread'. This refers to the acquisition of nuclear weapons by all other powers than the US and USSR, including non-states.

The spread of nuclear weapons began well before the central deterrent was as well entrenched as it now is. The first states involved were the United Kingdom and France, both in varying degrees allies of the US. China, as her relations with the Soviet Union deteriorated, developed a considerable nuclear capability whose future extent and quality is thoroughly unpredictable. India, by exploding what her government has been pleased to describe as a peaceful nuclear device, has served notice on China, Pakistan and other interested parties of her nuclear status. Israel is widely thought to have the. components of a nuclear weapons system ready for assembly should occasion seem to demand it. We have no reason to believe that the catalogue will not be longer by the time this page lies before the reader.

Perhaps the best starting-point for thinking beyond the central deterrent is to notice that what is spreading is nuclear weaponry and not necessarily nuclear deterrence. The full meaning of this proposition cannot be made plain by reference to what has already happened, but let us begin by considering briefly the cases of France, China and Israel before turning to some of the indefinitely many possible future developments.

The case of France, which we will consider somewhat abstractly and without reference to the historically important nuances of internal French politics and tradition,[9] highlights an aspect of deterrence between the superpowers which has so far been ignored in our exposition. We have spoken so far as though the problem of credibility is built into the very notion of deterrence between the US and USSR,

---

[9] On which see Wolf Mendl *Deterrence and Persuasion*.

but our examples have all been of credibility problems arising not from the security of the US but from the security of Western Europe, i.e. not from the protection of the US itself but from the protection of its allies. It is impossible to decide how important it has been that the most influential US and European thinking about deterrence has been preoccupied with the integrity of allies rather than of the superpower. Would the problem have been different, or differently perceived, if certain parts of Western Europe had been parts, states of the US? The answer is by no means obvious. On the one hand, in a world of sovereign states, there is a deep difference in kind between a (perceived) threat to one's own state and all other kinds of threat. On the other hand, the question of whether it would be justifiable to engage in nuclear war for the protection of Alaska or some still more remote and notional portion of one's own state is by no means rhetorical. Had it been the case that strategic Western thinking had been forced to cope with the possibility of Soviet incursions into peripheral parts of the very US, the nature of our thinking about the deterrent, and hence of the deterrent itself, might have been very different or might have been very much the same as it is.

The proponents of an independent French deterrent express in a particularly cogent and practical way anxieties about the nature of the central deterrent which are widely shared in varying degrees. 'The' French view is (or was) that France cannot rely on the US to protect it: in a crisis of vital concern to France, it is too likely that the US would remain inactive, paralysed by the prospect of overriding risks to itself. France cannot hope to establish a deterrence system capable of threatening the USSR with the kind of devastation which the US could inflict if so minded, but (it is argued) France can do two things: it can develop nuclear forces sufficient to give the Soviet Union reason to believe that France might possess a nuclear catalyst, capable of embroiling the US even against the Americans' will in any European conflict of vital interest to France; and it can equip itself to 'tear off an arm',[10] that is, to inflict damage on the USSR or its allies which, though not disastrous, would be sufficiently severe to outweigh any gains Russia might hope to obtain at French expense. For our purposes, what is as important as the question of whether this argument is cogent in the case of France is the much less widely discussed issue of whether it might be plausible in the case of some state or other at some stage in the spread of nuclear weapons. Far from certain that 'the French' are wrong about their own situation in their own terms, we are still less convinced that their arguments are

---

[10] Phrase used in Mendl.

devoid of systematic importance for the future. It seems very hard indeed to resist the view that if nuclear weapons continue to spread then there will not be cases even more like that envisaged by the French than the French case itself. Some French thinkers[11] have gone so far as to consider the implications of the idea that France might be as much threatened by the US as by the USSR, and therefore have as much occasion for deterrence against its post-war ally as against what might appear outside France to be its principal potential enemy. We do not find this a particularly persuasive view in the case of France, but considered more generally as an idea about the spread of nuclear weapons it seems rather important. If future political alliances and allegiances are fluid, there is the very real possibility that lesser nuclear powers will – in their own terms – have occasion to plan if possible for deterrence against their current allies. What this will mean for the character of alliance politics is utterly unpredictable.

The case of China, unlike that of France, leads to very serious doubts about the continuation of the central deterrent and raises some unsettling questions about the future of all deterrence. The place of China in the world is currently a matter of extreme uncertainty. Perhaps it will become necessary to understand the world as divided between three 'superpowers' instead of two, at least in the sense that China, like the US and USSR, might develop the capacity and desire to take an interest in what happens politically and strategically throughout the world and to be in a position to intervene in very many places. China, although far behind the US and Russia in the development of nuclear weapons and (more important) nuclear delivery systems, might also become capable of threatening these two with that kind of devastation with which they can threaten one another. Were this to happen, it would undoubtedly complicate the central deterrent very considerably. A good deal of work has been done by the US and USSR to make crisis management easier and thereby to make nuclear war through mistake less likely. The differences between a crisis involving two powers and a crisis involving three are a matter of kind, not merely of degree and crisis management in a world of three (or more) superpowers would involve problems which have never been faced, let alone coped with adequately.

China has made very considerable efforts to protect its population from nuclear war by means of deep shelters. This is a thing that France, given its resources, economic system and strategic position in the centre of Europe, could not reasonably contemplate doing. It is a

[11] Mendl 83.

measure which neither the US nor the Soviet Union has embarked upon. In terms of established deterrence theory it is a deeply unsettling move. For many of the problems (so-called 'scenarios') which most impress strategists suggest that it is very important for deterrence that each power be able to threaten to kill a very large proportion of the opponent's population. Without this, the strategy of overriding risks might find itself without any overriding risks: if a state stands to lose only its military forces in a nuclear exchange, it might well have occasion to take the risk. There is no way of knowing what view Chinese leaders take of these strategic implications. It is, for example, possible that their development of deep shelters is a response to current problems: they have many and sharp quarrels with the USSR and are massively inferior in nuclear forces. They are in the short-term powerless to present against the Soviet Union anything more than a French deterrent (the threat of tearing off an arm) but at the same time have had the ability, very impressively exercised, to protect their cities in another way. In a situation of very marked nuclear inferiority, a combination of formidable non-nuclear defences, shelters against nuclear attack, and long-term nuclear preparations would make very good military sense. But long-term it threatens to undermine some of the orthodoxies of nuclear deterrence.

The example of Israel challenges the stability of deterrence in a different way. It is very easy to see why Israel might have a use for nuclear weapons. A very small population facing overwhelming military odds has been able to win a succession of wars only by technical and military innovation and remarkable qualities in personnel and morale. These wars have progressively sapped the resilience of the Israeli economy. Nuclear weapons and weapons systems can seem to be cheap: this played a very important part in the decision in the early fifties to rely on nuclear weapons for the protection of Western Europe and the apparent relative cheapness of nuclear weapons in labour terms is especially important for such a small and outnumbered country as Israel. Indeed, it can be argued that the spread of nuclear weapons to Israel has not already occurred only because the diplomatic leverage on the US made available to Israel by the threat to go nuclear has outweighed marginally the advantages of the actual deployment of nuclear weapons.

What seems to us of most general interest about the case of Israel is that Israeli nuclear weapons would not necessarily mean Israeli nuclear deterrence. Much would depend on the kind of weapons acquired and the context. It does not seem impossible that Israel, or some other state, should have occasion to acquire not the kind of weapon and delivery system that makes for deterrence but a system whose main utility would be as an adjunct to a non-nuclear battle. Such a prospect is not technically straightforward, since the manufacture of truly small nuclear weapons requires greater scientific and technological sophistication than the development of larger bombs of, say, the yield used against Hiroshima and Nagasaki. But in a desert battle many miles from the nearest towns, a rather large bomb might have a 'tactical' use without any very great deterrent implications and its delivery might be no great technological problem. Whether Israel (and every other state in an analogous situation) would have a greater interest in deterrence than in defence by means including nuclear weapons is a question about which generalisation is impossible.

The possibilities that we have drawn out from current examples alarm the popular imagination less than two developments of a more speculative kind. These are the case of the suicidal state, and the prospect of nuclear terrorism.

Deterrence as we know it rests on the value-systems of those people who determine state policy. The risk of nuclear devastation is an overriding risk, and reliably so, only because the leaders of states tend to be rather firmly attached to the kinds of things that one can destroy with a nuclear bomb: such things as people, material civilisation (houses, hospitals, roads, paintings, pianos, etc.), political and social institutions. But it is not everything that can be destroyed in this way. Certain things, for example honour, are not subject to the vicissitudes of mere devastation. The man who does justice though the heavens fall or puts his honour before all things is not, when it comes to the decisive choices, to be impressed by the mere prospect of the destruction of the material world. If nuclear weapons should spread to a group or individual, whether or not a state, whose values have this sort of heightened spirituality (and thoroughgoing dualism between spirit and matter) then the inhibitions that underlie deterrence would be predictably unreliable. Hence the possibility of the suicidal state.

People who are worried by this prospect often link it to another. The existing nuclear powers, especially the US and USSR, have given much thought to the problems of avoiding nuclear war by mistake. Many kinds of possibility have been uncovered and (up to a point) removed. A fanatic or group of fanatics might occupy the positions of authority, or a leader might go berserk. In a crisis, failure of communications or the panicking of advisers might result in catastrophe. Random failure of command and control systems might result in a launching of nuclear weapons subject to no one's will. And so on. People who find the US and USSR more impressive in their ability to cope with such problems than some potential nuclear states consider that the possibility of nuclear war by accident is increased very greatly by the spread of nuclear weapons and weapons systems.

Nuclear terrorism clearly involves both of the risks just mentioned, and in addition a third risk: deterrence rests upon one's ability to identify one's opponent. Only if one knows one's (potential) enemy is one in any position, short of a doomsday bomb to destroy us all, to threaten him with overriding risks. (This is one of the reasons why some possible developments in climatic warfare are so unsettling. It seems that a state might find itself experiencing extremely damaging climatic changes without being in a position to establish that this is the work of an enemy, or who that enemy might be.) When one tries to imagine nuclear terrorism, one is not always able to be sure that one will know one's enemy. This might give him an impunity to act which would be troubling in itself and a threat to peace.

We defer the discussion of nuclear terrorism for consideration below when we turn to terrorism in general. For the moment, we want to consider the general implications of the possibilities just sketched for the spread of nuclear weapons. What is quite certain is that as the weapons spread, so the work of military and political leaders will become still more desperately complicated. For more crises will have a nuclear dimension and some crises may involve more powers than any nuclear crisis hitherto. This is a grave threat to peace because deterrence requires those who administer it to be in full control of the problems facing them, and not swamped with information.

It seems very likely that the spread will continue because there are many states with a considerable interest in acquiring nuclear weapons and – to put the point very mildly – the existing nuclear states have done very little to limit the growth of existing nuclear armouries which in the eyes of many potential powers is a quid pro quo of self-limitation. ('Vertical proliferation' certainly provides a *pretext* for 'horizontal', if not a *justification*.) It is not clear that in every instance the spread of nuclear weapons will be harmful: it is just possible that new balances of deterrence will make for peace as many people think the central deterrent has kept the peace in (most of) Europe since 1945. But nor is it certain that the spread of nuclear weapons will always mean a spread of deterrence, or that all cases of deterrence will be cases of peace.

The worrying aspect of nuclear weapons without deterrence is closely linked to certain controversies about developments within NATO. These discussions have been conducted in terms of one of the more memorable and apt items in the vocabulary of nuclear strategy: the issue is the 'nuclear firebreak'. Just as in a forest one requires firebreaks over which no flames will leap, so – in the view of many but not all strategists – it is vital to keep nuclear weapons on the further side of a firebreak, so that there is the sharpest possible separation between non-nuclear and nuclear war. This assertion has been challenged within NATO by those who favour the deployment of very low yield nuclear weapons which might be used in circumstances which left the enemy in some doubt as to whether one saw oneself as having carried the war to a nuclear level and which left relatively low-ranking commanders at liberty to introduce nuclear weapons into the battle on their own discretion. The arguments are extremely technical and complicated but the points with a bearing on our theme are relatively simple. Forces equipped with instruments for the detection of radio-activity will always know whether an attack which they have undergone (and survived!) is nuclear or non-nuclear. It is in many circumstances far easier to know this than to establish the yield or type of nuclear or non-nuclear weapon used against one. Hence *any* use of nuclear weapons on the battlefield is likely to convey a very simple message – 'The enemy has gone nuclear!' Action on the battlefield is, as Clausewitz never tired of stressing, action on very incomplete information so that the difference between simple and complicated messages is one of systematic importance. The likely question with which an enemy will be faced by any nuclear attack, however small, will therefore be the question of what to do now that he has been attacked with nuclear weapons. That is, he will necessarily be impressed *not* by the possibly very low yield of the weapon *but* by the fact that it is nuclear.

Those who argue, quite rightly, that there seems to be no moral difference in principle between nuclear and non-nuclear weapons – the only moral questions being as to numbers and categories of people suffering what sort of death or injury – are apt to overlook this technical fact about nuclear weapons which has moral implications. Given the exigencies of battle, one's opponent is likely to have no option, if one uses any nuclear weapon, but to re-consider the whole of his and one's own nuclear armoury. The likelihood of more and more damaging nuclear weapons is thereby enhanced. This has implications for the present in Europe and for the future in any situation (e.g. the Middle East?) in which a state deploys for nuclear defence as distinct from nuclear deterrence.

One occasionally hears people say that of course nuclear weapons have never been used. One knows what they mean. The only two occasions on which nuclear weapons were used were in a very different world from the present. There is no way of knowing (as yet) how important it is that nuclear weapons have been used (so that people know they can be, and have some poignant appreciation of what they can do which is not culled from mere computer scenarios) but only in a world whose order, pre-dating the emergence of deterrence, was quite different from the contemporary order. Should it one day happen that nuclear weapons are again used (perhaps by a group of terrorists) or that a nuclear war is fought between minor nuclear powers, what will it mean for world order? There is no way of finding out except to wait and see, but certain conjectures may be worthwhile. Suppose that there is an explosion in anger or a (small) war in which a few thousand (or hundred thousand) people are killed but in which no state is destroyed and no large-scale political and social change occasioned. Such an event would of course seize the headlines, curdle the blood, etc. But more important, it might liberate the imagination from certain limits to which it has been (mercifully) subject since 1945. It was pointed out in Chapter One that inter-war air theory far outdistanced experience and that the limited experience of World War I was arguably misinterpreted. All agree that most of our post-war thinking about deterrence vastly outruns our experience. But the experience of Hiroshima and Nagasaki, and a certain continuity in post-war developments, structure contemporary debates about deterrence. The Japanese bombings, if not the worst raids of the war, were at any rate appalling and ever since the size and sophistication of the world nuclear armoury has increased. We have no option today but to think about nuclear war as like the Japanese experience only far, far worse. But a (relatively) small nuclear war might change all this. It might give reason for saying 'After all, nuclear wars are not necessarily so bad'. No one, of course, will infer from this that nuclear holocaust would be anything but thoroughly appalling. But it would make it possible to argue, on the strength of something popularly accessible and more solid than computer print-outs, that it is possible to fight a nuclear war without catastrophe. This could very readily weaken the position of those who argue for the importance of the nuclear firebreak. A small, far-away war could in this way alter things at the centre and increase the likelihood of a war at first waged with very small nuclear weapons, but increasingly and uncontrollably tending towards holocaust.

The reader will have noticed that we are alarmed at the implications of the spread of nuclear weapons, but our argument is not meant to be merely alarmist. We will be well satisfied if our sketch serves to call into question an attitude to nuclear problems which appears to be widespread both in popular and in official thinking. Many people profess themselves relatively untroubled about the central deterrent and about Europe but very worried about what they style the proliferation of nuclear weapons. The calm with which the central deterrent is contemplated is in itself unsettling. John Kennedy expressed the view during the Cuba missile crisis that the odds of nuclear war then were evens.[12] All proponents of the deterrent attach great importance to the relatively volatile nature of politics, viewing the strategic balance of terror as at any rate more stable and dependable than the vagaries of political détente. There appears to us to be no guarantee in deterrence theory or in politics that the world will be spared indefinitely crises as acute, and at least as likely to result in major nuclear war, as that over the Cuba missiles. Perhaps next time one will not be so lucky.

Our dismay is deepened by reflection upon the spread of nuclear weapons for, as we have tried to show, this is not a separate phenomenon quite apart from the central deterrent but inextricably bound up with that principle of world order, modifying it and modified by it in ways that seem to make nuclear war and even holocaust more likely.

One further remark on the spread of nuclear weapons. We have pointed to the more troubling implications of nuclear weapons used on the battlefield rather than in deterrence. One should add that the weapons so used may not be indiscriminate. Much depends on the battlefield, on the weapon, and on one's definitions. If the battlefield is well away from centres of population, if the weapon's nuclear yield is rather small and if one excludes the effects of fall-out from the direct effects of the weapon's use, then it may be arguable that the weapon's use is far more discriminate than any of the strategic bombing of Germany in World War II was, or was capable of being.

6. *What is 'terrorism'?*

We turn now from nuclear weapons to terrorism. The definition of the word 'terrorism' has been the subject of some ingenious, even helpful debate.[13] The word has of course a pejorative connotation: we have freedom fighters, groups to whom we are indifferent have guerrillas, our enemies employ terrorists. This emotive aspect of the term is separable from it: there is no paradox in the English language in announcing (as we have no intention of doing) that one proposes to defend terrorism and argue that it is a good thing in some circumstances. We are going to use the word without any vague pejorative implication in a sense that we hope to define rather sharply.

A convenient starting-point for the task of definition is to be found

[12] Graham Allison *Essence of Decision* 1.
[13] A good guide is Paul Wilkinson *Political Terrorism*.

in J.C. Slessor's remarks quoted in Chapter One above about the analogy between control of the air and control of the sea. Slessor, it will be recalled, argues that one should speak not of command of the air but of control of the air and this for the same reason that one speaks of control and not command of the sea:

> The reason is to be found in the same quality, the capacity for evasion, at sea of the submarine, in the air of the aeroplane.

In both cases, according to Slessor, 'the cubic area of the battlefield is so immense that absolute command is hardly ever practicable'. The analogy to which Slessor draws attention extends further, to a certain kind of *land* warfare. In very many military operations on land 'the capacity for evasion' is crucial, and frequently understood as being crucial by those who stand to gain from it, as also sometimes by those who stand to lose from it. Sometimes the capacity for evasion is attributable to geographical vastness, as readers of *War and Peace* will readily understand. Sometimes it derives from other sources: Belfast is a small place but the opportunities it affords the gunman for evasion are very great. It is often the will of (some segment of) the population, together with the political situation, that affords one's opponent such opportunities for evasion that absolute command is not practicable; hence Mao's celebrated remark about the guerrilla swimming in the sea of the people and the desire of some counter-insurgents to land the fish by drying up the sea.

The context we propose for thinking about terrorism derives from the notion of the capacity for evasion. We argue that this is the best currently available context, and provides an intellectually satisfying, practically significant understanding of terrorism. The warfare of evasion is not new. Kutusov used it to draw Napoleon on to his doom in the Russian winter; ragged forces loosely co-ordinated with Wellington used it against Napoleon in Spain. But in the post-war world, for reasons that cannot yet be expounded without question-begging but can be guessed at without prejudice, evasive warfare has acquired a radically new importance.

A good deal of contemporary (Western) interest in the warfare of evasion can be traced back to the idea, outlined earlier, of military containment. The USSR, and later other communist states which broke with the USSR, were seen as threatening to expand into every vacuum in the world and to require among other things a military response. In Europe the response was deterrence. In Asia, Latin America and Africa deterrence was thought to be decidedly unpromising because of problems of credibility and the unsuitability of the tactics developed in Europe to many terrains and enemies. The opponent in these areas appeared in many cases to be waging evasive war. The West therefore developed a considerable practical interest in understanding and countering evasive war, in developing techniques of counter-evasive war.

Related to this aspect of containment in ways about which it would be premature to attempt to generalise has been the use of the warfare of evasion against states with colonies. Many of these states, of course, have been allies of the US, and the rhetoric of the Cold War has coincided at many points with the rhetoric of anti-colonialism. We have no wish to attempt to establish what the reality is of the relation between East-West confrontation and the collapse of empires. It is sufficient for our purposes to note that the two have occurred at much the same time and have been seen as connected.

The great political changes of the post-war world in the aftermath of the withdrawal from empires have occasioned a number of civil wars and other fighting in which considerable use has been made of the warfare of evasion. There are thus at least three, no doubt interrelated, sources of the frequency and importance of evasive (and counter-evasive) war in the post-war world.

Widespread revulsion against various aspects of Western dealings with other states has occasioned considerable sympathy, not least in the West, for states and non-state groups who find themselves in anti-Western postures in a wide variety of different types of conflict. Very often these states and groups have had occasion to resort to the warfare of evasion, and there is therefore a widespread tendency in the West and elsewhere to see such warfare as, in our time at least, the characteristic method of armed liberation. Although some of the pioneers of such warfare have been staunch Westerners (T.E. Lawrence is a striking example) there is nevertheless much to be said for seeing counter-evasive war as characteristically Western in the post-war world and evasive war as typically anti-Western. This often preconditions popular thinking and feeling about the warfare of evasion and counter-evasion.

One other remark about evasive warfare is required before we turn to the definition of terrorism. One very good reason for waging evasive land war is because one lacks the military strength to wage the kind of land war that employs large concentrations of military force fighting from time to time decisive battles. Very often, if not quite always, the reason for the inability to fight battles is military inferiority in numbers or fire-power to one's opponent. There is therefore built deeply into the warfare of evasion the likelihood that the practitioners are in a tolerably clear sense the military underdogs. Wherever there is a predisposition to sympathise with the underdog, this too preconditions popular thinking about evasive and counter-evasive war.

In our view, terrorism is a species of evasive war and counter-evasive war. It is, quite simply, indiscriminate war of evasion and counter-evasion. We believe that this understanding accords well with the common use of the word 'terrorism' and the direction of interest that guides it, and we argue that it clarifies common usage considerably.

In some cases it is rather obvious that acts or campaigns of terrorism fall within the sphere of the war of evasion and counter-evasion. Take, for example, the practice of widespread assassination. Before one is prepared to call this 'terrorism' one assumes, or seeks to establish, that it is not mere criminality, e.g. merely gang killings carried out for purely private material gain: one connects terrorism with war as contrasted with crime. There are borderline cases, as when one speaks of gang warfare, but these serve only to establish the claim we have just made: the doubts that one has about whether gang warfare is warfare support the view that by and large a rather sharp distinction is drawn between war and crime. Some have suggested that certain brutal crimes should be described as criminal terrorism,[14] but this appears to be a modification, in extension of ordinary usage rather than in conformity with it. Insofar as it is correct to say that war is politics by other means, the common use of the word 'terrorism' appears to classify terrorism as political and in particular warlike, rather than as merely criminal, and in particular violently criminal.

Assassination, however widespread, is not part of that kind of warfare which is centred upon the concentration of force in battle. The assassin characteristically relies on evasion to continue with his activity. (This is why he is often, often unfairly, regarded as a coward.)

It might be thought much less obvious, even appear very doubtful, whether aeroplane hi-jacking could be regarded as belonging to the warfare of evasion; but is this not one of the things that most occupies the popular imagination when one thinks about terrorism? Some hi-jackings, we think, are not terrorism at all – they are mere crime. When people link hi-jacking with terrorism, they seem to have in mind not all seizures of aircraft but specifically those which are 'political', warlike. This will probably be agreed without much demur; what might seem much more open to question is the view that aeroplane hi-jacking is part of *land* warfare: does it not tend to occur in the air? This question is not of merely pedantic interest. Our point is

[14] Wilkinson 32.

that aeroplane hi-jacking is one weapon (more strictly, one tactic) in the armoury of groups powerless to wage sea war (no boats) or air war (no planes) or the land war of concentration and battle (inferior forces) but capable of waging the land war of evasion. Hi-jacking is not an isolated phenomenon but part of a larger whole, of which most of the other constituents are quite obviously aspects of land war; and, to be pedantic, all the hi-jacker needs in the way of equipping himself is the ability to move on land to the point where he boards the plane.

Probably the main objection to the view that terrorism is to be equated with indiscriminate land warfare of evasion derives from the natural belief that terrorism has something to do with terror. For example, is not terrorism to be equated with military operations aimed to induce terror, or to be effective via terror? We are resistant to this view because it makes it imperative to describe some of the bombing operations described in Chapter One as 'terrorism'. We have no objection to the accurate, if somewhat emotive, descriptions 'terror bombing' and 'terroristic methods' for those raids, but we think that when people usually speak of 'terrorism' they have in mind something a little more restrictive, often thought of not without reason as a largely post-war phenomenon. We think that there is a very widespread tendency to connect the word 'terrorism' not with the bombing by one state of the cities, towns and villages of another but with that cluster of contemporary phenomena which includes guerrilla war, counter-insurgency, wars of national liberation, struggles against colonialism, peasant wars, and so on. We think that it is useful to have a word for some of the things in this field and the word 'terrorism' is the obvious one.

There is another reason for refusing to connect 'terrorism' with terror by definition. One is often much more certain that an act or campaign of terrorism has been conducted than what the objectives or ideas of the terrorists have been. In the common use of the word, a person may be a 'terrorist' regardless of his objectives. Our definition preserves this feature of the word, in that a person's activity may be a case of indiscriminate warfare of evasion regardless of his attitude to the inducement of terror in his opponents or victims. All of the ambiguities and uncertainties pointed out in Chapter One concerning the limits of area bombing and the dividing line between it and other things are repeated here in the case of terrorism, for in both cases definition turns on the idea of indiscrimination which, as pointed out above, admits of a variety of interpretations.

What is, and what is not, an example of terrorism? A campaign of widespread assassination in which careful efforts are made to kill those, and only those, engaged in the fight against one is discriminate and therefore not terrorism. An assassination campaign in which no effort is made at discrimination, or in which the killing is deliberately indiscriminate, is a campaign of terrorism. An aeroplane hi-jacking in which the lives of uninvolved passengers are put at risk is terrorism; the hi-jacking of an enemy's military aircraft would not be terrorism. A campaign of indiscriminate killing as part of the warfare of counter-evasion is terrorism. We believe that these distinctions correspond quite well with 'common sense'.

7. Terrorism and political theory

Given the importance in the post-war world of the warfare of evasion, it is unsurprising that terrorism has assumed considerable importance. (Notice that we, unlike many commentators, are able to say this without taking sides in the debate about the causes of contemporary violence.) What is perhaps more puzzling is the apparent tendency of terrorism to spread like an epidemic. The explanations of this with which we are familiar are profoundly unsatisfying (e.g. 'I blame the media') in that they quite fail to come to grips with the relation between terrorism and the imagination; they are thoroughly external accounts which do not give one any intuitive or sympathetic understanding of terrorism. This is worrying because it sets up a very marked asymmetry between the understanding of war and deterrence between states that is available and the understanding of terrorism. An ancient, well-elaborated and highly respectable set of traditions about the background to war is available in Western political theory. War is unmysterious, a part of the human condition. No doubt there is much still to be understood, but at least at a superficial level (a level at which much practical thought operates) one knows where one is with war. A person who has never thought much about war and suddenly receives call-up papers knows in his bones a good deal about what war is: he learnt it in learning the word 'war'. Terrorism, on the other hand, is a deeply obscure phenomenon, shrouded in mystery. The terrorist is the fearsome or glamorous stranger, of whose activity our theoretical understanding is very poor, extremely thin. We may know anecdotes about terrorists, but the interstices between the stories remain to be filled. This gaping hole in our understanding is partly responsible for both the repulsion and the attraction of the terrorist.

We offer, no doubt over-briefly, some reflections on the nature of terrorism. Let us begin by assuming a world divided into sovereign states, the issues between which are political in one sense or another of that chameleon word. (Our remarks can be adapted, without much difficulty, to a world in which there is an over-arching religious order, such that the deepest struggles are to be described as much in religious as in political terms; similarly with a world of empires, a world of suzerainties, etc.) One characteristic of the existing world of sovereign states is that interstate war tends to occur within it, for reasons (or from causes) which need not detain us here but which are at least in part political. Interstate war is one of the principles of order in the interstate system. (As we have pointed out above, another principle in the post-war world is arguably deterrence; but this point need not complicate the argument at present.)

Western political theory, despite some exceptions, has been overwhelmingly interested in the state and interstate system viewed from the standpoint of the state. This is clearest in what might seem the best disproof of it: very many theorists have taken the fundamental problem in political theory to be 'Why should I obey the state?' It might seem that this question represents the outlook not of the state but of the subject or citizen, and of course there is a sense in which this is true: the imaginary speaker of the question is the subject, not the state. But more important for present purposes is the fact that the question generally asked is 'Why should I obey the state?' rather than 'To what extent should I obey the state?'. The question asked sees obedience as an all-or-nothing matter, and theorists who wish to make exceptions have to swim against the tide of their own questioning. There is a dominant consensus throughout Western theory that the natural, the first question to ask is one that presents obedience as an all-or-nothing matter. The state is seen as resting upon obedience, which is indivisible. The first question which any attempt to limit the state's legitimate powers has to answer is 'Where will this limitation stop? Are you not threatening the state itself with this proposed limitation?' The answer may be yes or no, but the question is invariant. This is as true of medieval Christian theorising as of the more overtly statist theorising from Hobbes to the present.

It seems to us that the best understanding of terrorism is to be obtained by a questioning of this traditional perspective of the state. Michael Walzer has outlined very vigorously an imaginative and illuminating version of the theory that political obligation is a matter of consent.[15] In this sketch, political life is characteristically a matter of divided allegiances. The individual is viewed not as having his political being within one frame-of-reference (the state and interstate system) but simultaneously in a number of different frames of reference (he might have ties to a certain state, a certain church or

[15] *Obligations: Essays on Disobedience, War and Citizenship.*

sect, a certain political party, a certain trade union or manufacturing group, and so on). Whereas the picture that is usually taken for granted, accepted without examination, suggests that the individual human being is either unequivocally a subject in a state or a person totally without human society (and therefore as Aristotle said either a beast or a god),[16] in Walzer's analysis the citizen is a natural rebel: there is every reason to expect that he will be a rebel against the state for he has from the first divided allegiances. The possibility of a clash of loyalties and of his deciding against the state is evident from the first.

If the interstate system had been for a long period stable, undergoing none but slow and undrastic change, then Walzer's picture of divided political man might be rather surprising. Suppose, for example, that for a long period people had been born into a world of sovereign states and international churches. There would of course be the possibility of a clash of loyalties between these two but equally, given the stability of the system, it would be rather likely that one would find a well-understood, widespread consensus about the division of powers between state and church. The meaning of the word 'politics' would be quite likely to reflect this division, representing politics as something located within but not significantly troubled by a wider context of religion.

But of course the contemporary world has undergone rapid and drastic change. Many states are very recent and it is in no way surprising that for many people in many different political situations the image of political man as an essentially divided being is a compelling self-portrait. The need for nation-building is therefore quite unsurprising. Despite the great weight of Western political theory, the idea of the political individual as typically a person with a multiplicity of political loyalties only too likely to find himself at odds with the state in which he happens to find himself is at least as plausible as the much more entrenched view that the only alternative to anarchy is political existence within a single frame of reference. Historians of, among other things, the multiplicity of groups involved in the English Civil War make it clear that the situation is not uniquely modern.

No one finds it in the least surprising that states resort to war: whether one thinks war sometimes justifiable, never permissible or merely a brute and inevitable fact of life, we none of us usually find it remarkable that states wage war. *Resort to the warfare of evasion by divided political man is neither more nor less surprising than resort to war by states.*

---

[16] *Politics* 1253ª, tr. J.A. Sinclair 29.

Everything that can be said for and against the employment of war by states can equally be said for and against evasive war on the part of divided political man.

Consider one crucial aspect of the matter. It is, we saw in Chapter One, often difficult to answer the question whether war is useful or not. To look at the Allied bombing campaign as though it were *a priori* obvious that it was engaged in as a means thought to be useful in the pursuit of some well-defined goal is, we argued, a very dubious proceeding. Many other explanations of the campaign are possible. The same is true of terrorism. One is apt to think of the terrorist as, however sympathetic, a ruthless figure prepared to use indiscriminate violence in pursuit of a well-defined goal. But there appears to us to be good theoretical reason to doubt all such stereotypes. Often, states wage war because they believe that they have no alternative; similarly with the terrorist. States frequently consider that resort to war is the only way of showing that they are in earnest; the same may very well be true of politically divided man. To wage war because one thinks one has no alternative, or because one believes that war is the only way to show that one is in earnest is not necessarily to do something which one assumes is understandable, or justifiable, as means to some end.

This may explain the epidemic spread of terrorism. One of the things that requires explanation is the occurrence of many acts of terrorism which appear to be utterly hopeless and unpromising when considered as means to any remotely conceivable political end. Such actions will be readily understandable if the parallel we have been suggesting is accepted. For no one finds it surprising (though they might find it movingly heroic or infuriatingly foolish) that states wage hopeless (and often indiscriminate) war when they think they have no alternative. (Even in the just war tradition, the insistence that war be waged only when there is a reasonable hope of success is sometimes qualified to permit hopeless wars of self-defence.) Similarly with interstate war aimed at showing oneself in earnest. If the terrorist is typically Walzer's politically-divided man, and if war of evasion on his part is as natural as war on the part of states, then terrorism will be equally unremarkable even where it seems unlikely to be productive.

This supposed explanation of the epidemic of terrorism invites at least two questions: why associate the divided man with *evasive* war? and why equate the terrorist with Walzer's politically divided man? The first question is easily answered: in a world of states, preponderance of military power on the part of the state is to be expected. This is partly a trivial matter of definition in that some (but not all) states use as their criterion for recognising something as a state its ability to exercise effective coercion over a certain territory. That the possessors of an effective preponderance of military power should be the states of the world in a world of sovereign states is therefore as natural as the parcelling-out of the world into territories. If one's opponent enjoys military superiority one has no military alternative but the warfare of evasion; hence, evasive war is to be expected as the resort of the politically-divided man who takes to arms.

But why equate the terrorist with Walzer's politically-divided man? Our answer is that we very much doubt whether closer study of terrorists will be able to remain content with merely psychological analysis supplemented by the politics of ruthlessness, the politics of means-end. Suppose, for example, that a certain terrorist has engaged in activity extremely unlikely to achieve any of the serious political goals that he desires. (He has massacred certain Olympic athletes at an airport in Europe and it seems inconceivable that this will bring any nearer the establishment of socialism in a certain Asian country, for example.) In what terms are we to understand what he has done? One might say that he has miscalculated to a lunatic degree, or that he is venting his rage against the system and his inability to bring about change in the world. These are characteristically psychological explanations and invite·an examination of his psyche. This might prove illuminating, revealing (say) that he does indeed have a very poor grasp of the differences between likely, unlikely and hopeless means to ends. But it is equally possible that examination of this kind will result in puzzlement: he seems entirely rational, we say. His rage must be very great! So we file him away under the psychopathology of rage, an example of the appalling effects of frustration.

We have no wish to ridicule such an approach. Erich Fromm has developed a psychoanalytic notion of certain types of aggression that promises to be deeply rewarding[17] and other psychological studies may be worthwhile.[18] All we wish to suggest is that a psychological approach, however well carried-out, is necessarily one-sided. Whether he knows it or not, the terrorist's activity is analysable also in strictly political terms. There is a clear sense (non-moral) in which warfare of evasion on the part of politically-divided man is as much a principle of order in the interstate system as is war or deterrence; and terrorism is as much a principle as is indiscriminate war or deterrence that threatens indiscriminate war. This is easily shown: war is politics by other means; the politically-divided man is just as predictable a

[17] *The Anatomy of Human Destructiveness.*

[18] See e.g. Norman Dixon *On the Psychology of Military Incompetence.* Although somewhat crude in its use of history, this gives reason to hope that one might carry analysis down below the level of those high rankers studied by Fromm.

participant in the interstate system in time of drastic change as is the state itself; evasive war is the type of warfare to be expected from the politically-divided man.

The epidemic of terrorism is therefore not to be attributed merely to the media, nor even to be studied in merely psychological terms. If it is true that the occurrence of terrorism, as distinct from its reporting, has increased very considerably, there is good theoretical reason to expect that the explanation lies deep in the evolution of the state and interstate system. We are not, of course, in a position to substantiate this assertion in the present chapter; and maybe the time is not yet ripe for its confirmation or refutation. We are content to point out that there is some reason to think that the possibility is there that the terrorist is not an utterly alien, mysterious individual to be consigned to students of abnormal psychology, a figure romantic or repulsive on account of his strange difference from all that is most familiar in politics. It may be, on the contrary, that his violence is neither more nor less understandable than the belligerency of the state itself. It should be noted that our argument makes no assumption that the world is divided into two parts, with the terrorist viewed as the freedom fighter of the oppressed.

One corollary of our view of terrorism and comparable discriminate violence as a principle of such order as is to be found in the world of international politics is that in many situatiòns it can happen that what requires explanation is not that a group resorts to violence but that a group does *not* resort to violence. If it is true that in our world resort to war is for state and divided political men alike, the natural final resort for showing that one is in earnest, it will often be the absence of terrorism that should surprise us.

8. Nuclear terrorism

This is a troubling thought already at current levels of violence, but all the more alarming when one ponders the possibilities of nuclear terrorism. The development of nuclear weapons by certain states has given rise to an ordered set of relationships distinct from that of war. As we have tried to show, deterrence is an extremely precarious ordering, with very many possibilities of collapsing into major nuclear war. But while it lasts deterrence is a theory in practice which requires to be distinguished from the theory in practice which is war. Is it to be expected that nuclear terrorism, too, might give rise to some distinct ordering of the world? Already in, for example, hi-jackings the terrorist relies upon threats of violence as often as upon violence. It might therefore seem plausible to suppose that in the future deterrence or something like it will spread from the state to the politically-divided man.

It is, of course, particularly rash to try to predict such things, but there seems to us rather strong reason for doubting that nuclear terrorism alone could alter radically the principles on which world order rests. The point is worth pursuing both for its intrinsic interest and for the light it sheds on non-nuclear terrorism. A clue is to be found in the kind of demands that terrorists characteristically make when they are in a position (e.g. during a siege or hi-jacking) to attempt blackmail. Very often the things for which they ask fall into three categories: tactical demands (e.g. that troops be withdrawn from nearby positions, that an aeroplane and bus to the airport be provided, etc); immediately concedable political demands (most notably, the release of political prisoners); and long-term political demands (ranging from the closing of transit camps for Jews travelling from the USSR to Israel to independence for the South Moluccans). The distinction between on the one hand tactical and short-term objectives, and on the other hand longer-term goals, appears to have systematic importance. Contemporary examples of terrorist blackmail vary in duration but last a very short time relatively to the time required for the attainment of their longer-term political goals. Those demanding independence for the South Moluccans, for example, were in no position to keep their action going until such independence was granted, and irreversibly established. Those demanding the closure of transit camps could sustain their action long enough to see that the camps were closed but not long enough to see that they were kept closed. The relation between the duration of a situation in which the terrorist can enforce blackmail and the duration of his longer-term political objectives is a crucial determinant of the kind of military power of which he is capable. Because the individual incidents he can sustain tend to be relatively brief, the terrorist is apt to rely less on individual incidents than on convincing his opponents of his ability to sustain a campaign of evasive warfare, sometimes including, but always outlasting, well-publicised blackmail incidents. Given the kind of political objectives which the terrorist very often has, a week is very rarely a long time in politics and his need is to show that his military pressure can be sustained as long as his goals require.

It seems to us exceedingly improbable that the mere spread of nuclear weapons to terrorists would change this equation. A group which became able to threaten to use a nuclear explosion, e.g. against a major city, would certainly seize the headlines. Its capacity for blackmail would probably be very greatly enhanced in that its tactical and short-term political objectives would be very much harder to resist than most of the analogous demands made to date. The bomb would enable the terrorist to get more political prisoners out of the country. But how deep would consequent changes in world order go? We doubt whether the implications of such a change would be very great. For the terrorist is not enabled, merely by the acquisition of a bomb and delivery system, to alter radically the length of time that he is capable of sustaining his opportunity for blackmail. To take a very modest example, he may be able to extort the closure of transit camps and the promise to keep them closed, but unless he can keep up his blackmail indefinitely he cannot enforce the keeping of the promise. The point is still clearer in the case of more ambitious political goals. For example, a change of régime in some country requires time and the terrorist alone is unlikely to win enough time merely by obtaining nuclear weapons.

The consolations for those unsympathetic to terrorists and disappointments for sympathisers consequent on this limitation of the possibilities opened up by the spread of nuclear weapons require qualification, of course. If the military-political situation in some area of crisis is on a knife-edge, terrorist nuclear blackmail might prove crucial. (Suppose a Middle-East war in which Israel finds itself in desperate need of American supplies. A terrorist group could presumably enforce a delay in such supplies which would turn the war decisively in favour of Israel's opponents.) But this is a somewhat different point. We have been mainly interested less in the prospects of terrorism as an adjunct to military-political struggles deriving mainly from other things than the warfare of evasion, than in the status of divided political man as distinct from the state. Once introduce the state into the argument and the usual finely balanced possibilities of deterrence require introduction. (If terrorists threaten New York with destruction by nuclear attack, perhaps they can be deterred by threats of nuclear reprisal against those states in whose interest they are plainly acting. It would be a very calm, steady-nerved manager of crisis who would be capable of thinking this way, but that is nothing new in the psychology of nuclear deterrence.) Leaving aside nuclear terrorism as an adjunct to state politics, we see little reason to think that the mere spread of weapons will alter radically the terrorist's leverage on the political world because, quite simply, time is still against him.

This is not to say that nuclear terrorism is not alarming. Our view that the terrorist is as likely to act out of necessity or to show himself in earnest as in pursuit of goals to which war is the means implies that the use of nuclear weapons by terrorists will be entirely unsurprising. The status of nuclear weapons is very important here. Many commentators have stressed that the spread of nuclear weapons among states has been partly determined by the status of these weapons: they are an emblem of political rank and importance. Such considerations are as likely to weigh with politically-divided man as with the state. And one can go further. The fame or infamy of being the first since 1945 to use nuclear explosions in anger will be very great. Few acts in recent history would be so certain to declare one in earnest about one's politics (however powerless to attain one's goals). If our account of the parallel between indiscriminate war on the part of states and terrorism by the politically-divided is correct, it would not be mere exhibitionism or psychopathy to work for this black honour: its attraction can be understood in terms of the soberest political theory.

It should be remembered, too, that if terrorists make their own nuclear weapons and delivery systems and do not steal them then at least the first terrorist explosions are likely to be large (on the Hiroshima-Nagasaki scale) and 'dirty' (i.e. involving large quantities of fall-out). The making of very small tactical nuclear weapons and of weapons whose fall-out is small are relatively speaking extremely sophisticated activities, unlikely to be within the scope of any but the most technologically advanced states. There is, therefore, the very decided possibility of large (though not vast – truly enormous bombs are hard to make and harder to deliver) dirty explosions of a declaratory kind and of nuclear blackmail capable of securing tactical and short-term political objectives. But we have given some reason to believe that these wretched possibilities do not promise a change in world politics comparable with that which can be attributed to the emergence of deterrence between the superpowers. As pointed out earlier, the possibility is there that nuclear war on a minor scale would change everyone's thinking and feeling about deterrence itself, with unpredictable long-term consequences. Ever since Nagasaki 'The Bomb' has had a magical status which may not last for ever.

In this chapter we have examined the bombing of cities at the highest and lowest levels. Whereas Chapter One looked at the bombing by one state of the cities, towns and villages of another state, in this chapter we have looked at nuclear deterrence, which in the contemporary world provides a context within which area bombing is constrained, and at terrorism, which is the characteristic resort not of states and alliances but of those who for whatever reason are unable to wage war in the ways that states are capable of. In our chapter on the Allied bombing campaign of World War II we pointed out in a historical example some of the debates and options that are possible at the middle level, i.e. at the level of non-nuclear war between states.

We noticed that there was no clear consensus or imperative concerning the waging of indiscriminate war. Given the job they had to do, some of those concerned with the campaign are to be found some of the time arguing for indiscrimination of various kinds, others at other times against various sorts of indiscrimination. In the present chapter we have not followed with similar closeness any one debate. Instead we have examined the consensus theory about deterrence and have offered some theoretical reflections upon terrorism. We pointed out that deterrence between the superpowers involves a deep commitment to threats of indiscriminate war, because only such war poses risks which all concerned (or almost all) confidently expect the opponent to regard as overriding. There are, however, possibilities of discriminate nuclear war. It is arguable that these threaten deterrence and could make major nuclear war more likely. In our discussion of terrorism we made very little reference to indiscrimination. We defined terrorism as indiscriminate warfare of evasion and counter-evasion, but our examination of the place of the terrorist in the contemporary political world made no reference to the distinction between discriminate and indiscriminate warfare. We discussed merely the person whose political life is to be understood in terms not of the creature of traditional political theory whose only options are life in the state and life without society but in the powerfully suggestive image sketched by Michael Walzer: that is, a life of divided political loyalties in which political rebellion is as likely, for political and not merely psychological reasons, as political obedience. We suggested that the celebrated dictum 'War is politics by other means' applies as much to the politically-divided man as to the state. He is just as likely to use the means of war, just as likely to think that he has no option but to go to war, just as likely to feel that only by war can he make it clear that he is in earnest. The kind of war to be expected from him is the warfare of evasion.

What is one to say about the divided man's use of indiscriminate warfare? Here, perhaps, the analogy of the World War II bombing campaign is suggestive. It would seem to us likely that the same kind of arguments to be seen there will be found also in the deliberations of non-state warmakers. Some examples follow. Suppose a group of guerrillas have decided, for whatever reason, on a campaign of assassination. A question of interest to the student of war if not to the guerrillas themselves is what decision they will make as between discriminate and indiscriminate assassination. They are rather likely to resemble the practitioners and theorists of the Allied bombing campaign in seeing themselves as men with a job to do, namely to wage and if possible win war with the least possible losses and uncertainties to their own side. They may also, like the airpower theorists, be concerned about moral questions including that of discrimination; they may have to consider the effects of the moral opinions of others. (For the World War II commanders: will religious leaders criticise the campaign and demoralise the troops? For the insurgent: will the population be shocked by indiscrimination into siding with our enemies?) And, like the practitioners of airpower, they may have occasion to weigh what Sir Arthur Harris was apt to call 'operational factors'. In the early years, Bomber Command could only hit large targets. One has no control over whom one hits with a letter bomb. In debating the relative merits of area bombing and pinpoint bombing, US and British commanders were repeatedly forced to weigh the losses to be expected. If the decision is between shooting the moment the door is opened, at the risk of killing the butler, and shooting only after one has established that the person opening the door is indeed an enemy in some narrowly defined sense, it may be necessary to consider how many losses will and can be sustained when the door is opened by an armed security man, guns blazing. Finally, the declaratory function of the campaign may in both cases be very important. In the early years, Bomber Command enabled the UK to tell Hitler, the Soviet Union and itself 'We are still in the war, we are fighting back, we are using all possible means because this is a war of survival.' Given what he is trying to do, the insurgent may have very strong reasons for a declaration by means of indiscriminate war. His killing may be meant to say: 'You think this kind of killing terrible; agreed, but see how important our cause is, that we find ourselves having to over-step even such inhibitions as those against indiscriminate killing to obtain our objectives.'

In short, it seems to us very likely that for the insurgent as for the theorist or practitioner of Allied bombing, the question of discrimination is a *professional* matter, inextricably bound up with the task and values that he has accepted in taking on the job that he is trying to do. Indiscrimination is not part of a general theory within which the insurgent is constrained to move, and therefore terrorism is not indiscriminate in principle in the way the nuclear deterrence is. But there may be plenty of professional reasons for indiscriminate killing.

III

War and Pacifism

1. Wright's legal definition of war

The two words 'war' and 'pacifism' are very hard to define, but they are necessary for any sustained discussion of the ethical aspects of war. It has been suggested[1] that war cannot be defined because it is so all pervasive, invades so many areas of human experience in so many different ways, that it transcends the categories in which we seek to organise the world and our experience of it. When at the beginning of his monumental *A Study of War* Quincy Wright attempts to define war 'in the broadest sense' he sees it as 'a *violent contact* of *distinct* but *similar* entities' and in this sense of the word

> a collision of stars, a fight between a lion and a tiger, a battle between two primitive tribes, and hostilities between two modern nations would all be war.[2]

It was presumably something as broad as this that the pre-Socratic philosopher Heraclitus had in mind when he said that 'war is the father of all and king of all'.[3] It seems doubtful, however, whether such wide definitions have any utility in the study of war: Quincy Wright uses his widest definition only to narrow it down, giving a thrilling sense of homing-in on the subject in hand from a vast cosmic distance as though one's viewpoint were that of God, but hardly advancing the analysis. In practice, Wright employs a very narrow definition of war in his study of contemporary phonomena, equating what he calls 'modern war' with 'the legal condition which equally permits two or more hostile groups to carry on a conflict by armed force'.[4]

The first edition of *A Study of War* was published in 1942 and stands very clearly within that inter-war tradition of thinking about international relations which relies on international law for its

[1] W.B. Gallie Wiles Lectures 1976.
[2] *A Study of War* 8.
[3] G.S. Kirk and J.E. Raven *The Presocratic Philosophers* 195.
[4] Wright 8.

fundamental concepts. The second edition of his *Study* appeared in
1965 and one experiences a great sadness in reading it. Wright
struggles to accommodate deterrence to his analysis, but it goes
against the grain of the system of ideas underlying his work; evasive
warfare on the part of politically divided man receives scant attention.
It is arguable that the most important part of inter-war and World
War II data relating to war can be understood admirably in terms
derived from law. To take one difficult example, it has been argued
that resistance movements in World War II should be considered not
as autonomous groups but in their relation to the Allied war effort.[5]
That is, they are to be related to that legal condition specified by
Wright rather than to the model of politics which we derived in
Chapter Two from Michael Walzer. But however this may be, the
post-war world has generated an international order which outruns
contemporary or any likely legal order. Nuclear deterrence is widely
regarded as illegal in terms of such law as exists,[6] but this appears to
call in question the status not of deterrence but of law: for a legal
system so at odds with the vital practices of the great powers looks
unreal. If the reality of international law derives from agreement then
the relevant agreements look decidedly thin and cosmetic; if
international law is to be understood by analogy with common law
and the rules of conduct implicit in practice, the course of post-war
history suggests that deterrence is legal and that any view to the
contrary has quite lost touch with what law is. (Like Quincy Wright,
we are naturally thinking of legal law, lawyers' law rather than
natural and divine law, which is considered later.)

Terrorism is just as unmanageable in any likely legal system as is
deterrence. For international law is produced by states and it seems
wildly unlikely that states will agree together to the view that the
international order includes other actors than states, and in particular
actors whose natural tendency is to political rebellion. States are
resistant enough to the view that multinational companies are
autonomous actors in the system; the politically divided man poses an
altogether more deep-seated challenge to their sovereignty, legitimacy
and dignity. It is possible that the international community will evolve
legal regulations giving certain rights to, and imposing certain duties
on, the terrorist. But this will be a matter of humanitarian concession
to a phenomenon whose theoretical significance is exceedingly
unlikely to be admitted by any state, let alone by all states. Thus,
although law may regularise the treatment of terrorists, it is most

[5] Henri Michel *The Shadow War*.

[6] Guenter Lewy 'Superior Orders, Nuclear Warfare, and the Dictates of
Conscience'.

unlikely to generate concepts suitable for the understanding of terrorism. This is not necessarily a criticism of the law *qua* law, but it casts serious doubt on the adequacy of legal notions as an appropriate framework for thinking about war in general, or in ethical terms.

It can also be argued that even within his chosen, inescapably rather narrow, field Quincy Wright's legal definition of war is somewhat misleading in that it assumes too uncritically that all states take a Western view of international relations. There is a long tradition in the West of regarding world politics as a matter of relations between states which are legally if not militarily equal. In this tradition, there is very strong resistance to all attempts to discover some deeper reality underlying the international order. But students of comparative law and jurisprudence have long been aware that the Western view of the relation between the state and the international order is not universally shared. To take only two prominent examples, in Islamic theory the world of sovereign states is regarded as a strictly transient phenomenon,[7] while in Marxist theory it is held that world revolution will bring about the vanishing of the interstate system. The relation between theories of jurisprudence and day-to-day practice is variable, of course, but there is reason to believe that some states, given their dominant intellectual traditions, take a thoroughly un-Western view of international law and accordingly wage war in a way that is not readily described from the practitioner's viewpoint in the legalistic terms deployed by Quincy Wright. To take an obvious example from World War II: it seems quite likely that the marked contrast between the mutual forbearance in the treatment of prisoners of war on the western front in Europe and the unbridled fury in the east derives in part from the different views of law taken in eastern Europe. Viewing war in the way that he does, Quincy Wright is ill-equipped to explain such things.

For some purposes a sharp definition of the word 'war' is required. For example, where the waging of inter-state war is an orderly proceeding involving explicit declarations of war and the observance of complex conventions in the conduct and aftermath of war, there diplomats and lawyers need a clear and workable definition of the state of war and its (legal and diplomatic) consequences. But for other purposes it is not obvious that a clear definition of the word 'war' is necessary. Is a definition needed for the purposes of this book? It is tempting to try and proceed without a definition, relying on ordinary language as a guide to thought and guarantee of mutual comprehension between authors and readers. But we think that the ·

---

[7] Majid Khadduri *The Law of War and Peace in Islam* 44.

temptation has to be avoided and that a definition is necessary. There are several reasons for this, all deriving from the obscure relationship between war and that nebulous word 'violence'. Some examples follow. Many people are impressed by the idea of structural violence, and consider that because the world is pervaded by structural violence there is no separate problem about the understanding or justification of war: war is merely violence by another name. Some people are impressed by the supposed bearing of animal studies on war, believing that animal analogies reveal the human species as innately violent ('aggressive') and therefore naturally disposed to war. Pacifists are frequently seen by other people as being opposed to violence while understanding themselves as opposed to war, with a great deal of consequent mutual incomprehension. Perplexities about the relation between 'violence' and 'force' can readily generate paradoxes for the understanding of war.[8] And so on.

In our view it is possible and desirable to meet such difficulties head on by means of a definition that makes the meaning of the word 'war' as explicit, and as distinct from muddier terms, as possible. For reasons that will emerge shortly, we propose to define not the word 'war' but a related phrase of our own coining, namely, 'the military dimension'.

2. *The military dimension*

Very many phenomena have a military dimension. That is, in the understanding, explanation, study, etc, of many phenomena it is necessary to refer to a cluster of rather general facts about the world, namely:

> the fact that people fight each other in a certain way; the fact that people threaten to fight each other in that certain way; the fact that people prepare to fight each other in that certain way; the fact that people threaten to prepare for such fighting and prepare to threaten such fighting; and so on.

The kind of fighting we have in mind has four characteristics:

(a) It is always likely to be fighting to the death, i.e. to the death of individual human beings. At the beginning of his great treatise *On War* Clausewitz compares war to a wrestling match and to a duel.[9] No doubt there is the risk of death in even the best organised of duels and wrestling matches. But it makes sense to think of wrestling matches

---

[8] Cf. Hannah Arendt *On Violence*.
[9] Clausewitz I.I.2. tr. Howard and Paret.

and even duels as surrounded with rules designed to guard against fatalities. With war it is different. There are many instances in military history of the evolution of practices aimed to limit fatalities, but fighting whose rules were aimed to preclude fatality would not be war. When Clausewitz insists that war is an act of force,[10] one of the things he has in mind is the vital fact that war is about killing people.

(b) The fighting, very likely to the death, that we have in mind is fighting between groups organised for such fighting, or between such organised groups and disorganised or unorganised opponents. Individual combat, except in the context of a wider fighting between armies, is not an example of what we have in mind. The fighting between armies is; so is the fighting between insurgent forces and their organised opponents; so is the pathetic and one-sided fighting that has always occurred when an army is permitted to sack a city, battening down on disorganised groups of citizens or unorganised resisters against rape and torture.

(c) The fighting we have in mind employs weapons designed for the purpose. If there are tribes somewhere who fight each other (to the death) with their bare fists, it is not war that they are waging. The history of warfare is inseparable from the history of weapons and weapons designed for the fight have a central place in the military dimension.

(d) The fighting we have in mind is inseparable from quarrels over matters relating to whatever the fundamental categories are in which the people living in that world understand their social, political, religious, economic, etc., life. Lethal group fighting with purpose-made weapons over issues that all regard as concerning merely private profit do not enter the military dimension. Consider gang warfare in Chicago. Insofar as this was concerned solely with private power and private profit, it does not enter the military dimension. But if the gangs can plausibly be seen as the rulers of Chicago and arbiters of such law as pervaded its life, and if this rule was one of the issues in the armed struggle, that struggle has a military dimension. (After all, no less a political theorist than Augustine develops with great erudition the view that most of human political life has been the rule, rise and fall of bandits.)[11]

What we are trying to define is the military dimension. We say that something has a military dimension if and only if it can be understood, explained, justified, etc, only by reference to fighting which has the four characteristics just mentioned and/or by reference to threat of such fighting, preparation for such fighting, threat of

[10] *ibid.*
[11] *The City of God.*

preparation and preparation for threat of such fighting, and so on. We wish to argue that this notion of the military dimension provides such clarification as is possible of the difficult but necessary word 'war'.

Arms races clearly have a military dimension, in that they are preparation for fighting of the kind mentioned or preparation for threats of such fighting (a nuclear arms race aimed to improve the deterrent will be of the latter kind). Nuclear deterrence, being the threat of fighting of the kind indicated, has a military dimension. Gunboat diplomacy, since it involves a threat, no matter how delicate, of fighting of the sort indicated, has a military dimension.

On the other hand the war of the sexes does not appear to have a military dimension: the person who brains his or her lover with a glass ashtray – however conscious of solidarity with other embattled members of the sex – is not employing a weapon made for war. Trade wars do not, as such, have a military dimension for in their economic definition they do not involve any of the things mentioned above. (Of course it is very important that a trade war might turn out to be more than that.) Class struggle does not as such have a military dimension, so that talk of class war where this is used as a synonym for class struggle is for us merely talk by analogy: there is no real war involved. *But* Marxian analysis at its best reveals how likely it is that conflicts which are described by the protagonists, and in particular by the economically dominant protagonists, in strictly, antiseptically economic terms will in fact have a military dimension. What our definition is aimed to do is to provide a guard against loose terminology and highlight the empirical content of the most cogent Marxian analysis. Structural violence identified solely in statistical terms by reference to the relative deprivation or absolute need of some population does not as such have a military dimension. It can be shown to have a military dimension if, but only if, it can be shown to involve fighting, threats or preparations of the sort mentioned. (Police intimidation alone may not be sufficient: much will depend on the nature of the intimidation.)

Our definition of the military dimension does not purport to provide any key to the underlying causes (if such exist) of war. In this it is much less ambitious intellectually than such definitions as those offered by animal watchers, economic theorists of war, and those who claim to derive war from the international system. On the other hand, our definition provides a systematic safeguard against oversimplified explanations of war. An example may serve to make this clear. One aspect of 1914 that has been widely discussed has been the readiness with which people flocked to join up (the animal analogy is unsurprising, if also unenlightening). If one thinks that people are innately aggressive then one might think this flocking easily explained, the crisis of 1914 providing an excuse for a fight. But any such view fails to answer the question of why the desired fighting took the form that it did: why the kind of fighting which we have taken as definitional of the military dimension? If people were simply spoiling for a fight after a long period, why were there not many outbreaks of lethal brawling devoid of political connotations?

Such unanswerable questions are damaging for more important theorists of war than those who operate with an ill-defined notion of individual aggression.[12] Rousseau is often credited with great insight for his argument that war is inevitable in a system of sovereign states. His argument is indeed ingenious. He points out that in any enterprise involving the exercise of a plurality of wills, there is almost certain to be a clash between individual and collective interest in the absence of any way of guaranteeing in advance against such divergences. Unfortunately for those who consider that he gives a complete explanation of the way in which war is endemic in international relations, there is a gaping hole in the argument. All that Rousseau explains is the existence of conflict in the system; he gives no indication whatever of why conflict should have a military dimension.

One cannot remedy this deficiency by invoking human nature. For, as has been pointed out above, explanation of war in terms of individual aggressiveness is thoroughly unconvincing. Another possibility is that one should take the view that the system necessarily generates conflict; human nature involves an adeptness in the discovery of means suitable to the pursuit of one's goals; war is a useful instrument given that one is involved in conflict; so that the system and human nature together explain the existence of war.

Such an argument overworks the notion of means to an end. There is no reason whatever to assume that war has developed by being refined as a means to clearly envisaged ends. For some purposes it is desirable to try to think about war in the means-ends terms, though as we saw in Chapter One it is by no means easy and not obviously good history to do so. What is known is that at some stage in the history of human development, things came to have a military dimension. Whether this happened quickly or slowly is a question for historical and archaeological enquiry. There is no reason to believe that it will ever be possible to show that war was an invention in the way that the bicycle was an invention, i.e. a thing brought into being by human ingenuity consulting certain objectives and striving for appropriate

---

[12] For a critical review of many theories about the causes of war see Kenneth Waltz *Man, the State, and War.*

means. It is at least as likely that the military dimension has emerged, that war has happened to the human race, as that men invented or discovered war.

This is rather important both for the expectations which are brought to the study of war's aetiology and (for our purpose more salient) for the kind of sense that one expects history in general, and the history of war in particular, to make. In Chapter One we pointed out that the origins of nuclear deterrence are to be located in something that has very little to do with deterrence, namely, the fear that Hitler would obtain nuclear weapons first and the unexamined conviction that it would be better if this did not happen. That strongly felt conviction is responsible for the availability of nuclear weapons in World War II and the subsequent development of nuclear deterrence depends on it. One should not expect nuclear deterrence to make too much sense, having these blind antecedents in something other than that Reason which first envisages its objectives and then casts about for means. The same is true of war. Knowing what we do (and do not) about it, we have reason to expect that it will not make too much sense. For it is probably something that befell us like a fatality rather than an instrument which would make perfectly good sense if only we could re-discover its forgotten point.

Many who have tried to understand war appear to have overlooked its historical contingency. This applies as much to those (e.g. Clausewitz, Quincy Wright) whose interest has been practical as to those who have desired merely to understand war, without necessarily wishing to do anything about it. If war were an instrument for some discoverable purpose, perhaps one might hope to improve its conduct (Clausewitz) or abolish it (Wright) by calling its objective to mind and acting accordingly. But if war is not even an instrument but merely a pre-rational fact of human history and the human condition (like perhaps language and sex), the hope of perfecting or abolishing it seems as likely as not to be defeated by the kind of thing war is. In making this suggestion, we are not hinting that the struggle against war should cease. We are merely pointing out that war may well be more resistant to the human will than our everyday thinking would suggest. From the fact that statesmen and terrorists think about war every day in means-ends terms it is fallacious to infer that the military dimension can be conceived adequately in those terms; and the difficulty is rooted not in supposed individual aggressiveness but in the likely history and origins of war.

This gloomy story of the non-instrumental character of war is capable of taking a remarkable twist. Just as there is no guarantee of our being able to comprehend, perfect or abolish war, so there is no

guarantee of our being unable to do these things. Were the causes of
war truly rooted in invariant human nature or in the character of the
political world, the prospects for abolition without changing ourselves
or our world would be bleak indeed. But by the same token that
makes it right to view war as something that happened to the human
race in large measure independently of human will, so there is in
principle no reason why the curse of war should not simply leave us.
In these dark times it would be absurd to pretend to any knowledge
about how this might happen but- it cannot be excluded *a priori*.
Human beings stumbled into war and we can see no guarantee that
they will not just as inexplicably stumble out of it again.

This discussion of the causes of war is not meant as mystification.
We see no reason to think that war is mysterious or inconceivable.
There are many ways of thinking about it and many questions
concerned with it are both worth asking and answerable. Among
these are strategic questions, economic, political, historical and – as
we hope to show – ethical questions. The reason that we have laid
some emphasis on the hidden and in a sense probably impersonal
origins of war is that we agree with those who believe that war in a
way defies definition and overrides all categories. There is good
historical reason why it should do so. As we will see, the pre-rational
origins of war are important for another reason too: they matter if one
is to do justice to what is to be said in favour of pacifism.

Before we turn to pacifism, one more remark is needed on the
definition of war. In the first two chapters of this book we stressed the
great uncertainty of the historical present. Our way of defining war is
closely linked to this sense of uncertainty. Those who think they know
where they stand in history cannot be expected to take the same
interest as we do in the kind of definition of war that eschews all
particular historical involvements and sees war as a part of human
history in general. As an example, consider once more Quincy
Wright's definition of war as 'the legal condition which equally
permits two or more hostile groups to carry on a conflict by armed
force'. Wright's *A Study of War* is informed by a very different
perspective from that of the authors of this book: he knows who are his
allies and who his opponents. This emerges very clearly when he
explains at the very outset what he takes 'the problem of war' to
be. He thinks that 'war is not a problem' for people who take it as

> an adventure which may be interesting, an instrument which may be
> useful, a procedure which may be legitimate and appropriate, or a
> condition of existence for which one must be prepared.[13]

[13] Wright 3.

War is a problem, in the sense that interests him, only for those who see it as

> a plague which ought to be eliminated ... a mistake which should be avoided ... a crime which ought to be punished ... an anachronism which no longer serves any purpose.[14]

Behind this dividing of the world into two camps one feels the weight of the inter-war crusade against war.

We find ourselves unable to rely on any such set of polarities, whether that suggested by Quincy Wright, or that to be found in Marxism, or in popular ideas relating to colonialism and containment. It might be concluded that our argument, like much of our language (e.g. our frequent use of the word 'complex') represents a typical liberal or bourgeois evasion. We are uncertain about this. Our argument appears at certain points to diverge very sharply from much of what passes as liberal thinking. For example, the kind of political sympathy extended in Chapter Two to terrorism is not likely to be found in typically liberal 'evasions'.

Speaking about our alignment in our own terms rather than the terms of potential critics, we see ourselves as standing in a certain uneasy relation to the just war tradition. We consider this tradition to have a contemporary value which it is the task of this book to bring out. At the same time, we are conscious of the very important proof by a recent historian of the tradition[15] that the idea of a just war is subject to the vicissitudes of ideology. What one says about just war, if anything, is inseparable from one's ideology; and this is as true of the present book as of other treatments of the subject. So far as we can see, the appropriate response to this fact is to try and make as explicit as possible the viewpoint and range of sympathies and identifications from which we are writing. To a large extent this is a task for the book as a whole. What is important at this point in the argument is to stress the very unusual set of interests informing the book. What we are doing, in effect, is as follows.

We assume that there is some truth in the view that military personnel and thinkers of all ideologies have much in common. In particular, they face certain common problems, including those outlined in Chapters One and Two. Pretty well whatever their ideology, the practitioners of war are likely to face from time to time choices between discriminate and indiscriminate warfare. We have elected to concentrate on this choice rather than upon social, political

---

[14] *ibid.*

[15] James Turner Johnson *Ideology, Reason and the Limitation of War: Religious and Secular Concepts 1200-1740.*

or religious analysis of the context within which this choosing, and the rest of the military life is lived. We are far from claiming to be free of ideology either in this choice of subject-matter or in our treatment of it. But what is perhaps more important than the fact of our ideology is that it should become visible to the reader, and call into consciousness his or her no doubt different outlook.

3. Pacifism defined

We turn now to the discussion of pacifism. Pacifism has been more often ridiculed and condemned than understood, so we begin by attempting to define it and to draw a few distinctions within it. An eminent American sociologist of the military is to be found claiming – seemingly without tongue in cheek – that the professional American officer is pacifist.[16] One sees what he means: US officers would very much rather not be involved in war. But, on any usable definition, pacifism will mean somewhat more than merely 'preferring peace to war'. Even Hitler would have preferred a (temporary) peace with the UK! The difficulty in defining pacifism lies in establishing the something that makes it up, over and above the preference for peace.

A person is presumably a pacifist in virtue of what he or she *thinks*. But it does not seem that any useful purpose is served by trying to delimit the range of beliefs that make someone a pacifist: as we will argue in a moment, the diversity of view is too great. What seems to us worth pointing out is a certain relation between the beliefs which make someone a pacifist and that person's actions. A person is a pacifist if and only if they have beliefs such that, if they acted in the way those beliefs require, they would refuse all participation in war. This is a rather undemanding formulation. It does not require the pacifist to be a conscientious objector (perhaps he is lucky enough never to be subject to conscription, perhaps he lives in a country at peace). Nor does it require that all pacifists act as their beliefs require: there is ample room within it for cowardly pacifists who give in to the recruiting officer, pacifists torn between their beliefs and the desire to avoid humiliation for their wives and persecution of their children, and so on. This seems to us only right. There is no reason to make pacifists or any other human group into moral heroes of a single-minded kind by definition.

In terms of our definition, the Jehovah's Witness is a pacifist. This is not because of any beliefs he has about war as such or about violence as such. The reason he is a pacifist is that he believes God to

---

[16] Samuel P. Huntington *The Soldier and the State* 79.

have forbidden him to serve in the kingdoms of this world. He is quite ready to fight at Armageddon (a battle unlikely to exhibit what we have termed the military dimension) and has no special objection to war or violence. But the implication of his beliefs for what he should do plainly makes him a pacifist. For our purpose, the Jehovah's Witness is of interest mainly as an illustration of the great varieties to be found within pacifism.

Very many sorts of pacifism have something to do with beliefs that the pacifist has about war or about violence. The Shorter Oxford English Dictionary gives 1905 as the first use of the word 'pacifism' and offers a short definition:

> The doctrine or belief that it is desirable and possible to settle international disputes by peaceful means.

This definition is what one would expect in a dictionary first published in 1933.

A distinction to which many people give credence is between on the one hand religious pacifism or pacifism in principle and on the other hand prudential pacifism. The distinction appears to reflect, as much as anything, the experience of many people in the 'thirties. Having begun as pacifists and then changed their minds with the increasingly ominous threat from Hitler, many have had good reason to distinguish their own views from the less changeable outlook of, for example, some of the intellectual and religious heirs to the 'old grave pacifist Quakers'.[17] The trouble is that such a proceeding tends to distort the nature of that pacifism which was not moved by fascism. For example, description of it as 'pacifism in principle' makes it appear to be a matter of solely simple moral principle; while the term 'religious pacifism' makes the thing appear to be an axiom rather than a conclusion of religious understanding. A good deal of so-called religious pacifism appears to us to be informed with views about history which have been carefully pondered; the difference between it and 'prudential pacifism' is as much a matter of the view taken of history as of the difference between secular pragmatism and religious or moral intransigence.

An example adapted from discussion with pacifist friends may serve to make the point clearer than any of the usually polemical literature for and against pacifism seems to do. In Western society, despite many areas of borderline doubts, there is a tolerably clear distinction to be made between engaging in activities of the kind mentioned in our definition of the military dimension and very many other types of

---

[17] See SOED definition of 'pacific'.

activity. Those engaged in fighting of the kind indicated, and those engaged in threats of and preparation for, fighting of that kind, and those engaged in threatening such preparations, etc., form a relatively small and readily definable part of the population even in wartime. To say this is not to say that the efforts of this group can be separated for all purposes from the rest of the community's life, still less to claim that this group can do its work without the 'support' of the rest. All that is being claimed is that 'fighting' of the kind indicated, 'threatening' such, and so on, are activities limited to a small part of the population.

'Central to' the activities of this group (which includes soldiers, civil servants in the ministries concerned with the military, politicians with authority in matters of military security, workers in arms factories, and the managers of these factories) is fighting to the death in organised groups using weapons designed for the purpose. One point that often impresses pacifists is the loss of control of one's own actions that is involved in taking any part in the activities of this group, a loss of control different from that involved in pretty well any other of the innumerably many sorts of activity engaged in in our Western society. No single person, unless perhaps a Frederick the Great or a Napoleon, is in any position to assess and control that fighting which is 'central to' the activities of this group. The weapons are designed for, the training tailored to, fighting which no individual can bring under his control. Although those involved may be able to hide this fact from themselves, by describing their activity to themselves in terms that conceal its true point, the pacifist is often arrested by the significance of this group of activities. He notices that it is only definable, distinguishable from other activities, by reference to a certain sort of killing. He may be prepared to concede that those who participate in the military dimension are many of them motivated by high idealism ('We hope to keep the peace by means of deterrence'), but his attention is riveted by the defining characteristic of this branch of human art: he is mesmerised by the killing, and the commitment to engage in this killing in circumstances where one can guarantee that one will not know what one is doing.

It can, of course, be pointed out that there are spheres of activity in our society where one is hardly in a position to know what one is doing: how many motoring accidents does the worker in a car factory contribute to each week? But what differentiates the military is to some extent the degree to which control of one's actions is assigned to others (the soldier's duty to obey orders, to engage in coordinated activity under conditions where much is secret from him, etc.) and to some extent the matter in which control is surrendered: others and not I are to decide when I shall kill! The pacifist who finds himself refusing all·participation in such activity need not believe that it is possible to settle international disputes by peaceful means – he may be agnostic or deeply pessimistic about that. The beliefs that make him a pacifist may be: that killing human beings for whatever purpose is a deeply problematic proceeding; that in doing things which are deeply problematic one should be very sure about what one is doing; that no one participating in war is capable of such assurance; and that therefore such participation is wrong.

The beliefs just mentioned do not include anything specially religious or remarkably a matter of principle. They consist in part of moral platitudes to which many non-pacifists would agree and partly of reflections upon war which are factual: if it could be shown in a particular case that the loss of control which is usual in war can be avoided then the beliefs just indicated would not entail pacifism. (Readers of Clausewitz or of *War and Peace* will not expect that such an example can be found: the dust of battle is too thick.)

The pacifism just sketched is perhaps most aptly termed a pacifism of scruple. For someone who finds himself debarred from activity with a military dimension because in problematic areas one should not act unless one is certain of what one is doing is a person peculiarly circumspect about what he or she is doing, peculiarly *scrupulous* about the precise character of his or her own actions. Let us consider the relation between a pacifism of scruple and some of the better known criticisms of pacifism.

4. Miss Anscombe's objection

Elizabeth Anscombe, writing from within a form of the just war tradition, says:

> It is so clear that the world is less of a jungle because of rulers and laws, and that the exercise of coercive power is essential to these institutions as they are now – all this is so obvious that probably only Tennysonian conceptions of progress enable people who do not wish to separate themselves from the world to think that nevertheless such violence is objectionable, that some day, in this present dispensation, we shall do without it, and that the pacifist is the man who sees and tries to follow the ideal course, which future civilization must one day pursue. It is an illusion, which would be fantastic if it were not so familiar.[18]

Miss Anscombe is very far from believing that all forms of war are

---

[18] 'War and Murder.' Quotation is from *War and Morality* (ed.) Richard Wasserstrom 42.

permissible or inevitable. The paper just quoted contains a passionate denunciation of the Allied bomber offensive against Germany and Miss Anscombe campaigned actively against the award of an honorary degree to President Truman by Oxford University on the ground that he was responsible for the use of the atom bomb against Japanese cities. She holds that

> The policy of obliterating cities was adopted by the Allies in the last war; they need not have taken that step, and it was taken largely out of a villainous hatred, and as corollary to the policy, now universally denigrated, of seeking 'unconditional surrender'.[19]

But she does not infer from this view (which is rather far from that taken in Chapter One above) that indiscriminate warfare is unavoidable in contemporary conditions: considering the assertion that 'the "old conditions for a just war" are irrelevant to the conditions of modern warfare' she writes:

> People who say this always envisage only major wars between the Great Powers, which Powers are indeed now 'in blood stepp'd in so far' that it is unimaginable for there to be a war between them which is not a set of enormous massacres of civil populations. But these are not the only wars. Why is Finland so far free? At least partly because of the 'posture of military preparedness' which, considering the character of the country, would have made subjugating the Finns a difficult and unrewarding task. The offensive of the Israelis against the Egyptians in 1956 involved no plan of making civil populations the target of military attack.[20]

The examples Miss Anscombe deploys are not to us persuasive. There is reason to believe that were Sweden to attempt to join NATO, a less remote possibility than is popularly believed, then the Soviet Union would move into Finland, the bitter winter campaign of 1939-40 notwithstanding. And the Israeli policy of reprisals against refugee camps for terrorist outrages in the periods between her wars with Arab states is surely inseparable from her conduct of those wars. (The pressure Israel might come under to protect herself with nuclear weapons was pointed out in Chapter Two.) But we have no wish to labour the point: Miss Anscombe shows great courage, rare enough among philosophers, in being prepared to come down to cases, and one is grateful for the concreteness of her argument. Strategies of inoffensive deterrence currently receive a good deal of attention and give strategic substance to her argument.

What is more important for our present subject is that she feels

---

[19] *ibid.* 50.
[20] *ibid.* 52.

entitled to change the subject. She is dismissive of the problems of 'the Great Powers' in a way that is not available to those who serve these states. Her insistence on the 'villainous hatred' informing the Allied bombing offensive ignores the job the pre-war strategists and wartime commanders had to do; her statement *à propos* of the Great Powers today that 'these are not the only wars' is, unless backed with an argument to show that NATO, or its members, can adopt a different strategy (violent or non-violent), of little help or even interest for NATO's servants. It might be replied that this is hardly the point. One does not expect a moralist or moral philosopher to be ready with helpful advice for concentration camp guards, except perhaps the counsel that they should resign. Perhaps Miss Anscombe is writing in, so to speak, a prophetic manner, calling on the Great Powers for repentance.

We consider this possibility below. For the moment, notice the apparent tension in Miss Anscombe's argument. On the one hand, she is plainly wishing to address those who 'do not wish to separate themselves from the world'; on the other hand, it is far from obvious that she is speaking to the condition of those whose job it is to preserve the perceived security of the Great Powers of the world. There is some sort of difficulty, still to be sought, in holding these two things together.

Miss Anscombe's criticism of the pacifist assumes that he is an opponent of 'rulers and laws', 'the exercise of coercive power', and 'violence' employed in the service of law. Such an argument will be recognised as hitting the target by many who were, or thought themselves to be, pacifists in the early thirties, but who changed their minds as the fascist threat became clearer in meaning and closer to home. Such people will be apt to agree that, perhaps despite lapses including the Allied bomber offensive, the war against Hitler was an exercise of coercive power in defence of law and order against an unbridled destroyer of all civilisation. It was a (very, very) large police action.

But Miss Anscombe's argument in no way touches the pacifist of scruple. His problem is not with rulers and laws as such, nor even with the exercise of coercive power as such, but with the loss of control of one's own action that is everywhere visible in the conduct of *war*. The pacifist of scruple is not necessarily a refuser of all killing (he might be a passionate advocate of mercy killing and a friend to the police). His problem is with war.

Miss Anscombe, and the tradition that stands behind her powerful article, does not come to terms with the pacifism of scruple for a good reason. In medieval thinking about war, the paradigm is the police

action: war is police action by other means. The social world is
pervaded by law and at every point it is possible to attach a precise,
practical meaning to the idea of law enforcement. It is law
enforcement that Miss Anscombe is defending against the pacifist,
with war as a special case. But the pacifist of scruple, for his own good
reasons, does not see war as a special case of anything else. It is an
ancient thing, *sui generis*, in which for good or ill all men with the
conceivable exceptions of such as Napoleon or Frederick the Great
systematically resign moral evaluation of their own actions. Maybe
the world is less of a jungle because of law and law enforcement, but
few will feel so confident that the world is less of a jungle with war
than it would have been without.

5. The garden path problem

It may appear that the pacifist of scruple is merely a figment of our
imaginations, for the idea of a pacifist who is prepared to kill may
seem nonsensical. To consider more closely the truth of this we want
to consider an argument against pacifism of a more popular kind,
cruder than Miss Anscombe's. Suppose an enemy soldier is coming
up the garden path to rape your sister and murder your mother. You
are in the garden shed, where there happens to be a gun. You happen
to be a tolerable shot, but the gun is a rather crude one and the only
options which happen to be open to you are to shoot the soldier dead
or to do nothing to prevent outrage to your family.

Different pacifists respond to this coarse old problem in different
ways. Quite a good reply is that whatever one did one would at least
not cross the Channel to murder the soldier's aunt; but this hardly
goes to the root of the matter. Some pacifists say that they hope they
would have the self-control to do nothing, but think they would
probably be swept away by their feelings. The precise nature of these
feelings is of some interest. The pacifist might be saying that he 'fears'
that certain *moral* feelings would overwhelm him. If he takes this view
he is in effect conceding that in the imaginary case there is a great deal
to be said against refusal to kill and that he concedes, however
reluctantly, its moral cogency. The thin line dividing pacifism from
non-pacifism will be examined at some length later.

Some pacifists are confident that the imaginary case is no difficulty
for them at all and that for two reasons, one interesting, the other not.
The uninteresting reason for confidence is that they are sure the case
is artificial, unreal, and cooked up by enemies of pacifism. Of course
the case is unreal, that is its charm and convenience: the real question
is whether it bears a significant relation to possible realities, and the

pressing of this question should not induce paranoia in a tolerably well-integrated pacifist. The interesting ground for a confident dismissal of the imaginary example is that it misses everything on which the pacifist rests his case.

Now, if the pacifist is against violence, whatever its character, such confidence is certainly misplaced. For there appears to be no guarantee whatever that situations significantly analogous to that in the example will not arise. But if what the pacifist is against is war then the confidence is vindicated. For perhaps the most striking thing about the example once one notices it, the thing which gives the example its immediacy and explains why it is so hackneyed by popular repetition is that in the given situation the person in the shed is so obviously and completely in control of his own actions. The moral problem is clearly laid out before him and the only question he has to consider is the question of whether to kill the soldier or let his sister be raped and his mother murdered. This is very strikingly unlike the kind of problem envisaged by the pacifist of scruple. His problem, to repeat, is not so much with deciding what to do in a clearcut moral situation as with putting himself into a series of situations in which he will be called on to perform or participate in actions whose morality is *prime facie* dubious, cannot be foreseen, and will not be subject to his own judgment. The contrast with the problem of the soldier and the garden path could not be sharper.

This is one part of the best explanation we know of for the (well-founded) confidence on the part of some pacifists that the garden path problem is not their problem. There is another part, with a close bearing on our commentary on Miss Anscombe. It is no accident that the pacifists who are apt to dismiss the example as not their problem are often British, while those tending to be suspicious of it are frequently American. In a British context it is still for many of us possible to accept as a mere unexceptionable setting-up of a deliberately artificial problem the statement that in the shed there happens to be a gun and that the person with the problem happens to be a good shot. But few Americans can regard this as mere decoration: the proliferation of guns in the US is too immediate a problem for the American pacifist for him to accept the proposition that there just happens to be a gun in the shed. For him, the availability of guns is a systematic fact about a certain order of society, as troubling in its way as the loss of control which is characteristic of war. This necessarily infects the typically British complaisance with which we have so far treated Miss Anscombe's breezy assurances about the merits of law and law enforcement. In a British context, despite the regular carrying of arms by certain specialised units and the deeply troubling allegations of widespread police brutality, there is still much to be said for the view that entry into the police does not involve that loss of control of one's own actions which is characteristic of war. The policeman will find himself carrying a gun only under closely specified conditions in which the decision to use it is not taken entirely out of his hands. He may find himself having to apply for transfer from a corrupt police station, to resign the service on account of patterns of prejudice or shady dealings with informers, even driven into dilemmas about the betrayal of the trust of colleagues who have behaved with gross impropriety. But these possibilities are of a profoundly different kind from that loss of self which is characteristic of war.

Consider, as a contrast, the view Tolstoy took of Tsarist Russia. He considered the state to rest upon systematic violence – laws that violated the most obvious and fundamental interests of vast segments of the population were, in his view, brutally and arbitrarily enforced by a police force only partially restrained by the rule of law. Given the society with which Tolstoy had to deal, it would have been extremely artificial of him to try and separate his attitude to war from his attitude to the state. Distinctions which we have drawn in terms of a view of war which owes much to Tolstoy (especially the Tolstoy of *War and Peace*), and a view of civil society determined by a perception of contemporary Britain which many would dismiss as a mere liberal evasion, are not to be expected where domestic society seems so much more of a jungle than we have suggested. Tolstoy was not attached to Tennysonian ideas of progress, though of course it is also true that he never discovered a viable solution to the problem of the land and the peasantry. Miss Anscombe speaks as though the only question to ask about law and law enforcement were a question about the world as a whole, viewed from some place above history. But historical analysis would reveal many points at which there was much to be said for, and less against, the view that 'anything is better than this present order, so that we must overthrow it and then discover what to do next'. Not all would think Luther in the right when, confronted with an anarchistic peasant rebellion, he urged the princes to put it down with what would perhaps today be termed maximum force.[21]

Because of the dependence of pacifism on the view taken of the social reality corresponding to those ideals 'law' and 'law enforcement', we would be surprised if a pure pacifism of scruple was ever to be met with. A preoccupation solely with war, and not at all

---

[21] Roland Bainton *Christian Attitudes toward Peace and War* 140 quotes the charming injunction to 'smite, stab, slay, and kill'.

with law enforcement, would demand a (perceived) law-governed realm so just that it is hardly to be expected in this world. Nevertheless, since our subject is war and not law enforcement, we propose to pursue the pacifism of scruple somewhat further.

6. *Jan Narveson's objection*

In a well-known article, Jan Narveson has argued that pacifism is incoherent. The argument is simple and elegant: What the pacifist is against is violence. It is opposition to violence that sustains pacifism; remove the objection to violence and you no longer have pacifism. Now here is a problem for the pacifist: in some circumstances a person who is genuinely against violence will necessarily use violence as the only available means of opposing that to which the pacifist is opposed. So either the pacifist's opposition to violence is not genuine or he cannot be a consistent pacifist.[22]

We have already tried to indicate a substantial sense of the word 'pacifism' in which it is not the case that violence is what the pacifist is against. What he is 'against' is that loss of moral control which is everywhere characteristic of war plus, depending on his perception of the social reality of 'law' and 'law enforcement', that part of police action which corresponds to the lawless, arbitrary and violent order denounced by Tolstoy rather than the relatively benign set of arrangements which we have suggested are typical of modern Britain.

But this hardly answers Narveson's point, for his argument can perfectly well be re-stated using the word 'war' instead of the word 'violence'. Indeed, Narveson's argument challenges the absolute renunciation of anything whatever. To take a much discussed example, Miss Anscombe has argued vociferously that the killing of the innocent is absolutely forbidden and never to be contemplated under any circumstances.[23] It is easy to see the implications for this of Narveson's argument: in some circumstances a person who is genuinely against the killing of the innocent will necessarily kill the innocent as the only available means of opposing that to which Miss Anscombe is opposed ...

Narveson's argument plainly entails some kind of difficulty for the pacifist, but equally clearly it is not a difficulty which confronts only the pacifist. It will be considered in the next chapter. For the moment, we want to conclude this scrutiny of pacifism with a discussion of another objection which might be thought to present greater

[22] 'Pacifism: a Philosophical Analysis.'
[23] 'Modern Moral Philosophy.'

difficulties for the pacifist than for anyone else.

A thought which is very often expressed is that it is all very well for the pacifist to indulge in the private luxury of pacifism but that this option is not open to the state, which has the interests of others to consider.

We propose to examine this view by considering in outline the example of the contemporary United Kingdom. This is not necessarily the best example, but it has the merit of being a real one well known to many readers of this book. It should be noted that we are not arguing for or against a pacifist Britain; merely seizing on the example as a convenient one.

There seem to be three main reasons for thinking that the UK requires military forces: they are needed for external threats; they are necessary for internal security; and prestige demands them. We consider each of these in turn.

7. Pacifism and the threats to the UK

The nature of the external threat thought to be facing the UK is inseparable from the identity attributed to the UK. For our present purpose, two views of the current identity of the UK are of special interest. At the time of writing, many would agree that both answers are 'in the air'.

One view is often dubbed the 'little Englander' view, a term only too apt to occasion derision in Wales, Scotland and Northern Ireland. The little Englander thinks that 'we' are the United Kingdom of Great Britain and Northern Ireland, a state with a long history and considerable cohesiveness despite efforts going on in Northern Ireland to use armed force to detach that part of the state and despite bewildering pressures for a greater autonomy for Wales and Scotland whose eventual implications for Great Britain are unpredictable. The little Englander is not necessarily selfish: to devote oneself to the welfare of the fifty-odd million inhabitants of the UK is not necessarily selfish. The political implications of the little Englander view are not well thought out if only because little official thinking has been forced to ponder in detail the problems arising out of this view of the world.

The other view of who we Britishers are is that we are the US and her worldwide allies, a group whose membership has changed to some extent in the years since the war but a group many of whose members have gone through a lot together in the last thirty years, and are deeply attached to one another. There remain somewhat peripheral members of the alliance which possess some of the most abhorrent regimes in the world. There is no special point in attempting to draw a sharp line around the alliance, for an important part of its political reality is that it shades off into various sorts of legal inexplicitness, tacit understanding, shamefaced support, and so on. It is perhaps as important for the alliance that it does not have sharp edges as it is for the UK that its borders have been plotted with the greatest precision.

The external military threats to the UK for the foreseeable future are extremely slight. This is not a particularly controversial assertion. Most of the UK's current security problems are seen as being matters of the threat to NATO as distinct from the threat to the UK. There are perhaps some residual problems, e.g. with the protection of North Sea oil rigs from potential foreign interference, but as things stand such problems are of little significance, or cost. What would the effect on the UK as distinct from NATO be if the UK withdrew from the integrated command, as France did, or still more radically withdrew its signature of the North Atlantic Treaty? The question is, of course, unanswerable. It is possible, for example, that Soviet pressure on North Sea oil installations would increase. But one view which seems to us to be as likely as any other, and to command fairly wide assent, is that the effects on UK security would be minimal. The effects on NATO might be very considerable (e.g. damaging the morale of the European partners), but for the little Englander this is a question of residual interest. He would perhaps like to help these European states if the UK could afford it; but, he might argue, withdrawal from NATO might under some circumstances be in the economic interest of the UK, and that interest might be so considerable that the UK could not afford to remain in the alliance. (As pointed out above, such an argument would not be properly called 'selfish'.) The arguments about what conditions would need to be like for withdrawal to be in the substantial interests of the UK are very complicated. For our present purposes, it is necessary to flesh out the sketch only a little. Suppose that: the prospects for re-employment of workers in industries related to defence in the UK made redundant by withdrawal were rather good; the non-military disadvantages of loss of eminence in certain advanced technologies consequent on withdrawal were rather small; the potential costs that UK's NATO partners could inflict as a penalty of withdrawal were relatively slight; and the economic savings from withdrawal were considerable, and capable of being directed to other highly desirable sectors of the economy. Under these not inconceivable circumstances withdrawal might, from the little Englander's viewpoint, be highly desirable, or even imperative.

Were the UK to withdraw and to suffer relatively few adverse effects, then according to deterrence theory the UK would be benefitting from an alliance to which it did not contribute. In this, its position would be analogous to that of Sweden and Switzerland, whose neutrality is seen by the populations of those countries as being defended by formidable national forces but is also widely regarded as resting in part on the central deterrent.

Critics who have argued for UK withdrawal from NATO have been challenged to say what sort of defence arrangements they would envisage for the UK as an alternative to deterrence. They have found themselves at a loss because it is extremely hard to imagine what UK defence needs would be in a situation in which the UK's financial interest lay very heavily in withdrawal. In this respect the UK would be somewhat unlike Sweden and Switzerland. For those states have a long history of neutrality in a world of shifting alliances: their military preparations have developed gradually in response to a situation in which it made sense for them to guard against a variety of possible opponents, none very likely and none successfully resistable if thoroughly determined to impose their will, but each capable, at the cost of some sacrifices of independent foreign policy, of being persuaded not to subject the neutral to military invasion. The UK situation is different for several reasons: the UK is a collection of islands and unlikely to be faced with any threat of military invasion which, alone, it could possibly avoid by dissuading the likely aggressor; equally, perhaps more important, different constellations of opponents for the UK are extremely hard to imagine. The traditional enemies, France and Germany, have not changed their geographical position and have in principle the industrial base from which to threaten the UK militarily. But the political upheavals which would be required before a military confrontation threatening the UK with invasion could arise are utterly beyond the realm of thought taking current and likely immediate futures as its guide.

For the alliance-minded, who identify the United Kingdom for purposes of thinking about military matters with the US and its worldwide alliances, these reflections are decidedly unimpressive. The real question for them is whether the US and its allies could become pacifist. But for the little Englander, the argument just outlined suggests that so far as external threat goes the UK could perfectly well become pacifist in the relatively near future. For present purposes, this is sufficient.

At present, and in our view for the foreseeable future, the UK faces internal threats most notably but not only in Northern Ireland. The nature of these threats requires accurate description. They come from various portions of the political spectrum and cannot be identified (say) with the activities of the left. An inescapable question which would-be pacifists of the left find very hard to face, let alone answer, is how they would propose to cope with race riots instigated and sustained from the far right.

The British dilemma in this matter is one which is necessarily unfamiliar to an American reader. There is at least the myth in Great Britain and even to some extent in Northern Ireland that the police are typically an unarmed force whose use of authorised violence is minimal, and closely circumscribed. The myth has been under considerable attack and no doubt requires qualification, but it seems to us to possess an important residual truth. It is still largely the case that in Great Britain the police are an unarmed force; the military, on the other hand, are basically trained for their work in NATO and their training and equipment have to be adapted, often with great difficulty, for use in Northern Ireland and Great Britain. (Of course, as the Northern Ireland emergency continues, military expertise in counter-insurgency work within the UK increases. Whereas in the early seventies it was largely a product of counter-insurgency experience gained during the retreat from empire, today it has a different quality, largely gleaned from the current internal emergency.)

Given this wide separation of duties, there is considerable disagreement and perplexity over what should be done about the so-called 'third force' tasks – the large variety of functions discharged in some states by a para-military third force but belonging to the repertoire of neither the British army nor the British police. Current practice appears to be pragmatic and institutionally conservative. No new 'third force' institutions are being created, but it would be misleading to suggest that the new functions are being 'shared' between army and police. The two sides are not competing to obtain the new duties; neither wants them, and they are assigned not according to any overall plan but as seems best, case by case, as each new case has to be faced. The context within which this process occurs is, it must be stressed, a context within which the primary duties of the police and, most important, the army, are relatively clearcut. Neither the police nor the army is a force in search of a role.

Suppose the UK withdrew from NATO and proceeded to cut its defence establishment still further, progressively guided by the belief that UK external needs were very slight. Suppose the external environment did not give reason to change this policy, while the level of internal violence calling for something more than unarmed police action continued or even increased. Under these circumstances, the military would be under very strong pressure to seek new internal security roles. The point can be put very gently, without supposing the military to consist either of specially aggressive individuals who require an enemy to fight (or prepare to fight, or threaten) or of specially cynical people who put the interests of their organisation before everything else. Every large organisation has its priorities constantly under review. Remove some of the higher priorities and those lower down the scale will be moved to the top. If it is the case, as presumably it is if a large organisation contains individuals espousing every arguable view in which the organisation has an interest, that some in the military will favour army exercises of the third force functions then the removal of other duties will necessarily move these options towards the top: their proponents will be arguing on matters of higher priority. Should they prevail, the military will be committed to seeking the new functions.

We have stated this point in a deliberately abstract way. The tendency for the military to take a heightened interest in internal security roles is independent of particular historical circumstances. The success of those favouring military adoption of these roles will depend on historical imponderables, including no doubt the full range to be found in Chapter One. Force of character, the options outside the service open to those in it, the interests of others outside the force, etc., will probably all be relevant. But the tendency for the question to come to the top of the organisation's agenda is inevitable, given only the abandonment of other functions and the continuance of internal debate about what the organisation should be doing.

What attitude should the state adopt to problems of internal security in view of this likely pressure from the military to assign at least some of the 'third force' duties to the contracting military sector of an imaginary pacifist UK? We approach this question by taking two examples: the problem of riot control, and the issue of how to deal with terrorists equipped with advanced weapons.

8. Riot control

Any extensive discussion of this topic would be out of place in this book. But the problem of internal disorder plays an important part in forming the view that states cannot be pacifist and some comment is therefore necessary. We venture some brief conjectures which are not well attested in the established literature but may be worth further enquiry.

The state has a considerable interest in controlling riots and violent demonstrations. It has to rely for control on its police, military and any 'third force' which it has established. The police have characteristically to deal with individual and organised group crime;

the army with armies and insurgents. Neither the professional soldier nor the professional policeman is raised on crowds, and each is likely to try to understand crowds by reference to his principal opponents. It is important to be clear from the beginning what sort of problem a riot, or an actually or potentially unruly demonstration, presents. For example, is a riot a small battle in which one's objective should be to 'destroy the enemy's forces'? Or is it a confrontation of a different sort from any other in military and police experience? If the latter, it may be that military and police counsel on riot control would be systematically misleading.

It seems to us that riots and violent demonstrations are significantly different from both battles and warfare of evasion: a crowd is neither an oncoming army nor a collection of practitioners of evasive warfare. There is a simple reason for this. The crowds engaged in demonstrating or rioting are not organised fighting groups. There may be persons in the crowd trying to manipulate its behaviour, but this does not make a crowd into an army. A fighting force operates through a command structure rather than mere manipulation. Doubtless a good commander knows how to manipulate the residual group dynamics of his unit – he is good at morale. But without the prior existence of a command structure he would not be a *commander*.

Since a crowd is not an army there are things within an army's power which it cannot do. It cannot occupy a country or intervene in politics. It cannot preserve itself in being for long periods, endure setbacks and return to the struggle. It can have political importance, but this has different roots from those which make armies important. Those having to cope with crowds act under conditions of appalling uncertainty, as the literature on crowd control stresses constantly. The controller is having to act in situations where he is in no position to know what is going on, who is trying to do what and how. He can know that he is facing a crowd rather than an army, but what if anything the crowd is 'trying to do' is hidden from him. He may be able to recognise some members of it whose general political intentions are known, but the moment-to-moment intentions of such are hidden from him.

A crowd puts the controller under threat of injury and even death. He faces taunts and humiliation. His professional pride as someone capable of 'coping' when called on to do so is at stake when he faces a hostile crowd. The kind of mutual respect that can grow up between soldiers in opposing armies[24] is impossible between a controller and a hostile crowd: for the mutual respect of soldiers is grounded in the

[24] Cf. J. Glenn Gray *The Warriors* 131-48.

perception of a common skill deployed in response to a common set of problems, whereas a crowd has no skill or problems. It is, in a tolerably clear sense, inhuman because those attributes of individuals and organised groups which make it possible for human beings to recognise one another's humanity even in conflict situations are not attributes of crowds.

Because of such facts as these, riot control poses a difficult philosophical problem for the state: the state wants its servants to 'cope with' riots, but there is no easy or obvious answer to the question of what one should mean by 'coping with' a riot. This comes out very clearly in the vexed question of the extent to which the controllers of a disorderly demonstration or riot should rely on *weapons* as against *manpower*.

One rough-and-ready generalisation which seems to emerge from the extensive US studies of crowd control is that the controllers have, in their own terms, far more need of weapons if their numbers are smaller. A force of men large enough, given the local situation, to contain a body of potentially unruly demonstrators by a cordon of linked arms may have no 'need' of any but the simplest and, as weapons go, least lethal kind. At the other extreme, a group of police outnumbered by hundreds – or thousands – to one may be unable to do anything to make its authority recognisable to a threatening crowd unless it possesses an extensive armoury which it is prepared to use.

To be precise about the variables of manpower and weapons is very difficult, less because of the absence of information (a great deal of data of a kind is available) than because adequate organising concepts are lacking. For example, it is often said that the aim of riot control should be to use the minimum level of violence (or 'force'). This formulation is defective because it presupposes a separation of ends and means which cannot be made independently of a consideration of the extent to which violence is to be countenanced. Whereas the aim of conventional warfare is military victory and the aim of police activity is the apprehension of criminals, the aim of riot control is not a datum determinable without reference to the level of force which the state is prepared to authorise.

The indeterminacy of the objective of riot control is especially important because any weapon injected into a riot threatens to become uncontrollable. This is not an alarmist statement, merely a corollary of the point made above that the professional pride of the controller is threatened the moment a riot seems to be getting out of his control. At that point, there is nothing in the notion of minimum force to prevent the controller from making matters worse by using such weaponry as he has to reimpose his authority on the situation.

Unless it is thought that some level of weaponry will enable the controller to dominate the situation without any serious possibility of things getting out of hand, any weapon put into the situation threatens to become uncontrollable. Of course, technologies are available which can in a sense remove all possibility of the crowd's getting its way – one can annihilate the crowd, for example. But that is not the problem.

Is any better norm of riot control possible than the nebulous one of minimum force? One possibility, we think, is that 'coping' consists in obtaining whatever is possible in the way of limiting injuries, deaths and damage by the mere organised, unarmed presence of the security forces. In many situations this will provide the state with a good deal of what it wants since it can often limit or eliminate violence. (One very potent resource of the security forces is knowledge. Recent experience suggests, for example, that it is important to give a crowd several ways out of a confined space if violence is to be avoided or limited. Such knowledge is incrementally available to the security forces and is one of the things that distinguishes them from a mere mindless crowd.)

This norm might be dismissed as hopelessly utopian/irresponsible. It was conceded above that to face a crowd is a terrifying experience; now it is suggested that the security forces do it unarmed. This is, in fact, not the suggestion. There is a great difference between enabling the security forces to protect themselves – i.e. providing that level of protection which is required if the controllers are to cope at all and not to panic – and providing weaponry on which the controllers are to rely for coping with their problems. Suppose, for example, that the controller has to face stoning by a hostile crowd. It is one thing to provide him with a shield for his individual protection, another to equip him with weapons designed or intended to stop the stoning. Is it unrealistic to expect the police or military facing a hostile crowd to endure stoning without doing anything in reply? Would it not be only human for them to want to hurt their opponents, if not to stop them? In reply, one could of course distinguish between what the police or army would like to do and what they can be allowed to do. But a somewhat deeper point can be made. If state policy on riot control is to rely on manpower exclusively and not at all on weapons, the security forces may in fact be doing something, and something very important, by simply enduring a rain of stoning, using their shields as best they can, and waiting for the riot to end, meanwhile doing what is possible to limit casualties and damage. 'They also serve who only stand and wait.'

An analogy may be illuminating here. It used to be said that the

NATO armies would face extreme difficulty in manning the nuclear deterrent because soldiers want action, want to be doing something. Why has this not in fact been a difficulty? For two reasons: first, because manning the deterrent is, if deterrence theory is accepted, doing something of very considerable importance; secondly, because it has proved possible to explain to soldiers what it is that, according to deterrence theory, they are being asked to do. Similarly, a state which adopted a manpower-only policy on riot control (and similar measures) could perfectly well explain to soldiers what they were being asked to do: the theory that there is a range of options, that all weapons-reliant strategies risk the situation getting out of hand, that in being there and doing what he can without weapons except such as are solely defensive (shield and no sword; no training in, and regulations against, the use of a shield as a battle-axe) – this theory is no more difficult to understand than deterrence theory. Of course such measures demand courage and self-sacrifice of the security forces, but then so does every strategy. Weaponless riot control is unable to eliminate all violence, but that also is true of every strategy. Whether it would on balance eliminate more violence than alternate strategies appears to us to be a question that is utterly unanswerable.

We have so far considered a weapon-free strategy of riot control in relation to the limitation of casualties and damage. How is it related to political influence? Two fairly widespread objectives of practitioners of evasive warfare in general, and of the manipulation of crowds in particular are: to persuade the population that the state is not protecting them; and to persuade the population that the state is repressive. The introduction of weapons into a riot situation by those trying to control it makes the latter objective easier to attain, for every use of weapons (except in self-defence most narrowly defined) can readily be represented as state repressiveness; and the general policy of resort to weapons can be pointed out as evidence that 'the state is violence'. Insofar as the state's problem is to avoid a reputation for oppressiveness, therefore, reliance on a strategy of a manpower-only response to riots is clearly advantageous. But what of the other insurgent objective of showing that the state cannot protect its citizens? If the state is able to persuade its citizens to see a manpower-only strategy as a whole, rather than as a series of unrelated incidents, it may be able to counter the claim that it is failing to do all it can to protect its citizens. There are very considerable difficulties here, for a theory is much harder to communicate on a mass scale than a succession of lurid incidents. But this difficulty does not seem totally insurmountable – witness the skill with which deterrence has been popularised.

It does not seem to us impossible that a future UK embarking on the experiment of minimising its reliance on military preparations should adopt a strategy for riot control of the kind just indicated. If it faced extensive threats of internal crowd disorder, it would need a large pool of manpower for its almost unarmed security forces. Whether these would be best organised in police, military or some third structure is an open question beyond the scope of this short sketch. The essential point for present purposes is that riots do not seem to present an insuperable obstacle to pacifism on the part of a state.

9. Dealing with terrorists; prestige

In this section we consider the problem that the UK would face with a terrorist group already in the country, equipped with sophisticated weapons, and in a position to shoot down incoming airliners. It was pointed out in Chapter Two that such a group would be powerless to secure long-term political objectives by means of such an operation. Short-term political aims, e.g. the release of prisoners, might be within its power if it can impose irresistible blackmail. The state has the obligation to protect its inhabitants including, presumably, those in its airspace. It cannot, therefore, simply wait the terrorists out: if possible, it must protect those who stand to suffer in the meantime. It seems to us that in such circumstances distinctively military expertise is required, in that there is very strong reason for fighting or threatening to fight a rather well-defended group of entrenched enemies. A level of technical sophistication to match or out-match that of the terrorists might also be required.

Although conducted by combat units employing sophisticated weapons, the kind of 'battle' we are here imagining is of a peculiar kind. In the first place, it belongs not to conventional land war but to the warfare of counter-evasion. In the second place, within the repertory of counter-evasive war it occupies a peculiarly innocuous place. It is waged against an isolated group of individuals and has a clear beginning and end. There is therefore the possibility of isolating the incident: what precedes and follows it will be activity without a distinctively military dimension. The loss of control of one's own actions which is characteristic of activity with a military dimension will be very considerably less in this kind of situation than it usually is. The usual objections to military activity of the pacifist of scruple might lack force in the special circumstances here envisaged.

It is commonplace that the warfare of evasion and counter-evasion is apt to spill over into all aspects of life, eroding such distinctions as that between military and civilian. Is it not well known that the counter-insurgent has to be prepared, if things so work out, to disregard the normal demands of civil liberty in his struggle against indiscriminate killers who are able to melt away into the population at large?

The answer to this is not straightforward. Of course, some kinds of evasive and counter-evasive war wreak havoc throughout the life of a people. But not all do so. The case we have just been imagining has no such tendency to spill over for two reasons. First, the guerrilla group is isolated. Secondly, we have imagined the state acting against a specific incident and not against the organisation if any that underlies that incident. Insurgent groups have a notorious resilience in surviving the defeat of particular operations and becoming able to mount further operations. But it is an important and difficult question whether the military and police should see themselves as fighting the group that remains in being or whether their perception should be confined to particular crimes and criminal organisations, particular riots, and such particular operations as that against airliners coming into an airport. It is probably true that if a state is forced to see itself as fighting counter-evasive war against an organisation which must be combatted between operations, it is under very strong pressure to extend the war to the entire population. But we are not convinced that a future UK would have to understand the internal threats against it in such a way. Perhaps a weapon-free strategy for crowd control together with the use of military units against isolated guerrilla threats would suffice. If this seems credible, the possibility of a pacifist UK is enhanced.

Such a development might involve considerable reductions in the military establishment. This would bring extensive organisational problems in the re-employment of soldiers. But it would not entail a crisis of identity in principle. There would be a continuity of function with the past which is very important in any military organisation which has not suffered the kind of catastrophe experienced by the German army in 1945. In particular, it would still be the case that military force was directed fundamentally against the Queen's enemies. One would not be asking the force to adopt some new political function within the state but giving it things to do of readily understandable importance in the service of the state. Any proposal to carry military activity more deeply into the life of the people appears to us to threaten this admirable tradition.

Assuming that the state might cope with external and internal threats without resort to any military forces which would be objectionable to the pacifist of scruple, what must be said of prestige?

The state's duty is to consult its citizens' interests: the relation between these and prestige presumably varies. It will depend on how important prestige is to the people (e.g. how much economic leverage is obtained by prestige) and the extent of popular interest in prestige for its own sake. If, as in the UK, the state has to consult on such matters, an additional question for it will be what view of their interests it should commend to popular opinion.

Deeply ingrained in the Western imagination is a theory of the state which makes the idea of a pacifist state arouse scepticism and incredulity. The implications of this for prestige are imponderable. No doubt the experience of a pacifist UK would be watched by other states with suspicious interest: its difficulties would be scrutinised as evidence of 'what happens when a state gives up its military forces'. If things went badly with an almost unarmed UK, it might serve as confirmation in the eyes of other states that the state requires a strong military. If, on the other hand, things went well, this might prompt other states to take the UK as a prototype for similar experiments elsewhere. The gains in prestige might be very great.

10. Gentleness in international relations

It is now possible to conclude these lengthy speculations about a possible future for the UK. We have not, of course, been attempting to provide a realistic analysis of the military options for the little Englander. It will suffiice for our argument if it is granted that the kinds of consideration we have been bringing forward are not too wide of the mark. We have suggested that the UK, free of external enemies and coping with enemies internally by a combination of a manpower-only strategy for such things as riot control and a small, highly-sophisticated fighting force for coping with terrorists who become embattled, is an imaginable state in the modern world. No doubt many of our details are questionable or simply mistaken, but if it is granted that such a strategy is arguable our point can be established. We asked whether a pacifist state was conceivable. Political theory since Hobbes suggests strongly that it is not: for is not the modern world a system of sovereign states, each having to rely ultimately on itself for its security in a situation where force is the final arbiter of events?

Our answer, in the light of our sketch of a possible future for the UK, grants to the Hobbesian something, but far less than he demands. We have imagined the UK benefitting from a balance of power (a balance of terror, if you will) to which it does not contribute and coping with internal disorder and internal enemies by means that do not raise the spectre of uncontrol which makes the pacifist of scruple object to war. Such a UK could reasonably be called pacifist at least in the sense that its security arrangements do not, as a matter of deep principle, run counter to everything that could reasonably be called 'pacifism'. The UK is committed to using force, violence to deal with certain threats, and it is deeply exercised about its own security. That much is granted to the Hobbesian. It may also be extremely touchy about its sovereignty. But it is not a sovereign state bristling with guns: this is the challenge to Hobbes.

It might be replied that even if our sketch of a future UK is granted for the sake of argument, it is exceedingly unimpressive as a challenge to the orthodox view of the relation between the state and military power for at least three reasons: we have not considered what would happen if the external environment changed; we have ignored the fact that pacifism is a matter of principle; and we have shamelessly ignored the rest of the world. We consider these points in order.

What if the external environment changed? It is of course possible to imagine the world changing in such a way that the UK was faced with external enemies, and it would then be false to say that a low level of military preparedness would have the justification that we have been assuming throughout: in a sense, external circumstances would call for a higher level of armament. Because of time-lag, the UK would be ill-placed to respond to this situation as it happened. The question is, what inferences one should draw from the manifest possibility of such a change. To plan for it is in a way impossible, for one has no idea of the quarter from which the threat would come, or of its specific nature. One is arguing from the general fact that political orders are volatile, so that some threat is possible. In practice, what this implies is probably that one should retain a high level of military technology and attempt to keep up with the most sophisticated systems developed elsewhere lest these suddenly become available to states which have suddenly become one's enemies. The cost of doing such a thing would be immensely greater than current expenditure levels, but this might be regarded not as an objection to the argument but as a *reductio ad absurdum* of the possible future we have been imagining for the UK. For, it might be argued, the little Englander is giving enormous hostages to fortune in the way that certain Gaullists did: he is trying to meet every conceivable military threat in circumstances where he lacks the resources to do so. How much better to view the world from the viewpoint of the US grand alliance which, centred as it is on one of the powers at the head of all arms races, can guarantee the avoidance of massive military disadvantage!

Such an argument fails to take Hobbes seriously enough. The point from which the argument proceeded was the recognition that political orders, including the US grand alliance, are volatile. The alliance provides no guarantee against a capacity for coping with its break-up and a subsequent situation of animosity unless within the alliance the UK sustains a level of military technology which in the last quarter of a century it has proved unable to afford. The question, 'How ought one now to respond to a possible future threat whose nature and source is unpredictable?' is unanswerable.

Pacifism as a matter of principle. Our sketch for a possible future UK does not exhibit the British and Northern Irish peoples as becoming a nation of pacifists. Were this UK subsequently faced with an external threat that seemed to call for massive military preparations, our sketch gives no reason to believe that the UK would scruple at such preparations on pacifist grounds.

What is one to make of this? It is of course the case that any group of people for whom pacifism is not the first or only priority will in appropriate circumstances be unlikely to remain pacifist. But what follows from this? It by no means follows that the group cannot reasonably be called 'pacifist'. It may be a group especially congenial to the pacifist, a group in whose life he can find an important part to play and in which he has reason not to despair of persuading his fellows to persist in pacifism even when the going becomes difficult. To refuse to call such a group 'pacifist' merely because it might take decisions in as yet unforeseeable situations which will make it non-pacifist is merely arbitrary. For there may be much to be said for the view that it is pacifist, and little to be said against this except by reference to a remote and unforeseeable future. The point is important because of the gulf that is often seen as being set between the pacifist and the state. If the UK in our sketch is rather proud of its non-reliance on military force and so organised that arguments for future rearmament would have to surmount formidable objections, it would seem arbitrary not to call it 'pacifist' even if at a later time it re-armed.

The rest of the world. Perhaps the most powerful argument against the use we are trying to make of the sketch of the UK's future is that we are challenging a well-established picture of what happens throughout the world by reference to two peripheral islands of no importance to anyone much except their inhabitants. Is it not fallacious to argue in such a way? Perhaps odd states on the edge of the world can escape the normal pattern, but that hardly shows that military force is anything but central and inescapable in international relations.

There is obviously some force in this argument: there are many places in the world where the argument 'They don't need military forces' would be far harder to render plausible than in the case of the future we have been imagining for the UK. But it seems to us fallacious to infer·from this that the UK example is merely peripheral. To think so is to make an equation which was questioned above. It is one thing to argue that resort to war is endemic in the modern world. It is quite another thing to argue that resort to war generally *pays* in the modern world. If the second of these assertions is accepted, the UK example will certainly appear peripheral. But there seems no way of checking its truth. What we can say is that sometimes war has brought disaster and sometimes a kind of success, and the pattern is likely to continue in the future. No one knows how – taken overall – the two sides of the sum relate, whether on balance human happiness is enhanced by the practice of resort to war. There is no way of finding out. In the absence of certainty on this point, the prince does (or fails to do) his best by the people who are his special charge using whatever institutions and guides are available. At present, no example of a pacifist state is available to him because there has never been one. This limits seriously the range of options open to princes. For a state to experiment with pacifism would not guarantee the spreading of pacifism: the experiment might be, or be seen as, a disaster to be avoided for the future. But by the same token it might not be. It might open up a new range of possibilities to princes for the future of international relations, supposing international relations has a future. The first pacifist state could as readily be taking the first steps in establishing a new principle of international order as important or unimportant as the principle of deterrence. To assert this is not to maintain a Tennysonian conception of progress; merely to insist that the political future is, as it always has been, open-ended and unpredictable. The implications for world order of a single pacifist state are unpredictable and by that token capable of having the most serious systematic importance, whether as a warning or as an example to be adapted to a variety of other situations.

It is thus possible, at last, to comment on the frequently heard assertion that it is all very well for the individual to be a pacifist but that states cannot be so. We have traced this argument at some length. No historical example is available so we have constructed an imaginary one which is not, we trust, wholly fanciful. We have tried to show how a particular state, namely the United Kingdom, might have occasion to embark on a policy which can reasonably be described as pacifism. Such an experiment, depending on how it went and how it was perceived, might influence the practice of other princes profoundly or not at all. It does not seem to us reasonable to demand more than this of *any* piece of military-political thinking.

For example, deterrence which in some ways radically alters the

Hobbesian picture of international relations is not criticised on the ground that it fails to displace Hobbes completely. In the Hobbesian picture of international relations, war between states is likely, as likely as rain during a rainy season, to use a celebrated simile that comes very naturally to a political theorist as British as Hobbes.[25] According to deterrence theory, major nuclear war between the superpowers is extremely unlikely. No one supposes that there is some deep tension between Hobbes and deterrence theory because of this qualification: one neither feels that Hobbes is out of date, nor does one feel that deterrence should be able to eliminate the likelihood of war at all levels and between all states and other belligerents. The same kind of view should in consistency be taken of the relation between Hobbes and the pacifism we have been sketching: to argue that some states might have political occasion to rely on pacifism is to challenge Hobbes, but only in the way that deterrence challenges him. One is placing one picture of international order against another. This should surprise no one in a world where the dominant consensus is that international relations is a realm ruled by several different theories, including power politics and deterrence.

And yet it does surprise, for pacifism calls into question something very deeply engrained in our view of international politics. The pacifism of scruple is apt to side with a kind of *gentleness* that one finds neither in Hobbes nor in the threats of mutual annihilation that underlie deterrence theory. This is perhaps the deepest outrage that pacifism, if it were taken seriously, would do to the received understanding of world politics. One can see the difficulty in the kind of disillusioned venom one feels on contemplating the celebrated inter-war image of the international system as a family of nations. A family is one of the places in which, for all the recent gloomy counsel, one might find gentleness. But the first emotional lesson of modern history is that there is nothing between states but brutality and 'force'. The deeply cherished 'message' of that group of English poets characteristically termed 'the war poets' is an instance of this which is encountered by most British school-children: the war poets, notably Wilfred Owen, went to war – so the myth goes – with high hopes and light hearts. All the high spirits and good living of the advantaged classes of Europe before 1914 were poured into the war but the lesson was disillusionment. The first war taught the lesson of the horror of war; the second war taught the even bitterer lesson of the horror of the human heart. That luminous generation of 1914 seem, as one listens to countless retellings of the story, to stagger through the horror of the

[25] *Leviathan* I.13.

first war that leaves idealism troubled but unscathed, through the naive self-delusions of the inter-war dream of a family of nations, through the holocaust against Jews and gypsies, to the prospect of nuclear annihilation. Nowhere in the story is there a foothold for gentleness. The conscientious objectors get their mention as courageous holders-on to principle, and a very few people appear as brave critics of the Allied bombing offensive (often grouped with the holocaust and the Nuremberg trial and the horror images of the enemy in World War I). The correctness or incorrectness of this myth hardly matters for present purposes: what is important is the relation between it and the response to pacifism that it makes natural. So long as one thinks within it, an antithesis between political reality and anything that could be described as idealism is natural. The pacifist automatically is shunted into the idealist camp. He may be praised as a brave man or scorned as a fool, but his place in the picture is the same – he is the outsider, beyond the pale of political reality.

Our discussion of pacifism calls this view into question. It exhibits pacifism as something into which a state might stumble in the very ordinary pursuit of 'its own self-interest', something which might arise as a consequence of the very ordinary processes of a prince trying to do his best by his people. As such, it is likely to displease both would-be realists and certain pacifists. The realist objections have been considered at some length. It remains to consider the pacifist objections.

These are of many kinds and we cannot attempt to consider all the varieties of pacifism.[26] But one particular objection is specially relevant to our argument. Wolf Mendl has developed a historically plausible account of modern pacifism which, unqualified, carries damaging implications for our argument.[27] He divides inter-war pacifists into, roughly speaking, two camps: those who were pacifist for pragmatic reasons, and subsequently abandoned their pacifism; and those who were pacifist as a matter of deep religious or moral principle, and retained their pacifist allegiance. His treatment of the latter exhibits a thoroughgoing attempt to come to terms with the dismissal of all pacifists as unrealistic. What he does in effect is to show the pacifists of principle as inhabiting a different reality from that of the pragmatic pacifists. In this different world the great political difficulties of pacifism are admitted. But, just as the strategist has his commitments, just as it was appropriate to insist in Chapter One that the theorists of air power had a job to do which determined their special perspective with all its difficulties, so the pacifist of

---

[26] For a searching brief examination of *eighteen* types, see John Yoder *Nevertheless*.

[27] *Prophets and Reconcilers*.

principle is seen as having his perspective from which he can no more depart than the soldier under orders.

To argue that pacifism can have creative implications for international order (through the potential to create a new precedent, for example) is not to contradict Wolf Mendl's historical analysis, but it does muddy somewhat the waters that he has rendered clearer. For 'it suggests a return to the pre-war situation of a blurring of the sharp distinction between a pacifism of principle and merely pragmatic pacifism. The more the pacifist attempts to argue with others on their own terms, it might be argued, the less clearly the pacifist can witness to his own stand on matters of principle.

The apparent tension here, though it needs careful handling, can be removed. We have exhibited a state stumbling into pacifism and laid stress on the possibility of its not remaining pacifist. But our story-telling demands no compromise or muting of his witness on the part of the pacifist: for all we have said it may be that his stand on matters of principle, judiciously voiced, has hastened rather than slowed the evolution of a pacifist UK.

What is really at .stake is the pacifist's self-understanding. At present, the British pacifist who is knowledgeable about recent history is forced to see himself in terms of the grand pre-war divide between the idealistic and the realistic, and is forced to explain his idealism not least to himself as a realistic grappling with other problems than those exercising such authorities as the War Cabinet and the Air Staff. Unless he is to ignore history this is an essential part of his self-understanding. What our argument purports to show is merely that this self-understanding is itself historically conditioned, and could change. The pacifist of principle could, in terms of our argument, one day have reason to see his ideas as falling on the side of realism. This would be if one state made the experiment and others took it up and made of it a principle of world order. It is for our purposes important to notice this possibility, though of course the pacifist cannot currently avail himself of it and is likely to be found arguing that his (historical) self-understanding gives a rather different picture.

The same point requires to be made about the profound differences in circumstance between British and American pacifists, and between the little Englander's and the grand alliance's views of the question of UK security needs. If 'we' are little England then our military needs may be relatively small; if 'we' are the US and her worldwide allies then our military needs will be beyond measure greater. The difficulties of arguing in a manner analogous to the above for a pacifist USA are formidable in the extreme: the US is guarantor of too many insecure states and the implication for US security of Soviet strategic nuclear forces is too obscure for one to be able to argue at all persuasively that the US could stumble with its eyes open into pacifism. The possibility of course remains that Americans should agree together to be pacifists, but it seems unlikely that anyone would wish to rest anything on this possibility. The difference between the two cases should not be surprising, or be seen as damaging to pacifism. It is widely believed that a person can be an honest pacifist only by setting himself at a considerable distance from the world. The distance depends in part only on the pacifist: different states are at different distances from pacifism.

We suggested earlier that Miss Anscombe's dismissal of the Great Powers should perhaps be seen as a prophetic call for repentance. The same view is possible of the pacifist. The distance between the prophet and his people depends largely on the people: at times the prophet may come close to being their leader, or their leader's cherished counsellor; at other times he may appear to be the most forlorn of – to put it bluntly – cranks. In terms of the standards which the prophet espouses, the distance between prophet and people is determined by the extent to which the people transgress (in the case of a prophet understood as the mouthpiece of God, the distance will be determined by the extent of the people's apostasy). If the people live (wholly or partly) by other standards than those employed by the prophet (as, for example, in all states where Machiavelli or Hobbes are seen as tellers of bitter truth – this in contrast perhaps to ancient Israel), another view will be possible of the distance and it will be possible for the people to stumble into the ways proclaimed by the prophet and to stumble out of them again. This is true both of the proponent of the just war tradition and also of the pacifist.

In this chapter we have tried to do two things. First, we have offered a definition which comes as close as possible to being a definition of war. We have argued that the military dimension is *sui generis* and in particular is distinct from mere law and law enforcement. The second, and longer part of the chapter has been a critical examination of pacifism. Some of the best known arguments against pacifism have been scrutinised and found wanting, not against all pacifism but against the pacifism of scruple which is stopped short by certain peculiarities of the military dimension. The argument by Narveson against pacifism and all absolute principles has been deferred, and will be pursued in the next chapter. As the argument stands at the end of this chapter the case against pacifism is not proven.

IV

Virtue, Proportion and Discrimination

In the first three chapters of this book we have sought to provide an outline description of the various phenomena which fall under the general heading 'the bombing of cities'. We have concentrated on theoretical aspects, proposing a framework of political theory within which thinking about area bombing, the warfare of evasion and counter-evasion, and nuclear deterrence can proceed. We have sought throughout to take as seriously as possible the viewpoints of those immediately involved in the bombing of cities: in Chapter One, we depicted the pre-war theorists of airpower and the war-time protagonists as men with a job to do; in Chapter Two, we expounded deterrence theory largely in its own terms and tried to show that the terrorist can best be understood as a special case of that familiar participant in modern politics, the person whose allegiances are divided. In the present and the next chapters we examine the bombing of cities from a distinctively ethical viewpoint. So far, we have aimed mainly at description, though guided by ethical interest. We now turn to specifically ethical argument.

We begin by considering some general ethical theories of current interest in philosophy or theology. It is necessary to begin with the very general because different people approach ethics in very different ways and one's substantial moral judgments depend in part on the view taken of ethics. In the present chapter, we assume that there are such things as moral standards, that people are sometimes responsible for their actions, and that there is serious disagreement about what is right and wrong. The implications for ethics of war of a denial of all standards, or a denial that people can reasonably be held accountable for what they do, are examined in Chapter Six.

1. Utilitarianism and other consequentialist systems

According to utilitarianism, it is always right to promote the greatest happiness of the greatest number and always wrong not to do so. This view seems to have been held by Jeremy Bentham and John Stuart

Mill, and has many contemporary adherents.[1] One merit often claimed for utilitarianism is that in every situation where moral claims appear to conflict, the principle of promoting the greatest happiness provides a decision-procedure. Utilitarians often grant that much of the time we are right to be guided by more detailed rules than that of maximising happiness, but they point out that such rules frequently clash with one another. In all such cases, according to the utilitarian, one should promote the greatest happiness. It is argued that a theory enabling one to decide what to do is better than a theory that has no way of settling moral conflicts.

One great strength of utilitarianism is that it is so immediately expressive of the sympathies which a good person brings to morality. It sets explicitly at the centre of things that which surely, in some sense or other, matters more than anything else – namely, the happiness of everyone. There is no sectional interest in it, putting the happiness of Englishmen above the happiness of everyone else, and it goes straight to the heart of the matter by stressing happiness rather than those lesser things, e.g. truth, justice, fidelity, which are so prominent in some ethical thinking but which do not have the same self-evidently valuable ring that happiness possesses. The *generosity* in utilitarianism is to be seen in an especially clear way in the moral concern of Jeremy Bentham and his successors about the treatment of animals. In contrast with the savage indifference of the major Western religions to non-human animals, the utilitarian solicitousness for *all sentient beings* breathes a gentler and more humane atmosphere. This is not a point that utilitarians often stress, and requires to be made against the many detractors of utilitarianism.

The utilitarian morality is exceedingly, some would think excessively, demanding. For the utilitarian, every opportunity to maximise human happiness is to be seized; any idleness from the cause, unless it is required for recuperation, is wrongdoing. The utilitarian makes no distinction between mere abstention from wrongdoing and positive generosity in going beyond the call of duty in the promotion of the good: for the utilitarian, all promoting of happiness is duty. The cruelly over-taxing education of John Stuart Mill is a notorious example of the superhumanly or inhumanly great burdens that utilitarianism can impose.[2] More humorously, J.N. Findlay remarks that the utilitarians make it

[1] For a vigorous debate see J.J.C. Smart and Bernard Williams *Utilitarianism For and Against*. Anthony Quinton *Utilitarian Ethics* provides a straightforward introduction. David Lyons *The Forms and Limits of Utilitarianism* is an important, difficult analysis of the possible varieties of utilitarianism.

[2] See John Stuart Mill *Autobiography*.

obligatory for each and all of us to go as far as we can in the direction of infinity in the sheer multiplication of welfare. Bentham sought to frighten away his ascetic conscience which he regarded as a bogey, but he replaced it by a bogey infinitely more frightening: the horrible haunting fear of having failed to realise a possible throb of pleasure for someone.[3]

Findlay appears to have two points here: one is the triviality to which one can reduce utilitarianism by taking it at its word – how ludicrous to be seized by a 'horrible haunting fear' that one has failed to produce, where one could have done so, something of so little importance as 'a possible throb of pleasure for someone'. Secondly, Findlay is arguing that there is a deep difference between those moral rules concerned with the struggle against evil, which specify our duty, and other rules concerned with pointing out the good to us, which we are *invited* to promote out of generosity and good fellowship, over and above our duty. (In Findlay's view, it is not a *moral* fault to decline the invitation to generosity.)

Other charges against utilitarianism are stressed more frequently than the argument that it is over-demanding. In particular, it is pointed out in all the textbooks that utilitarianism neglects the claims of justice and truth, beauty and excellence. According to utilitarianism, it may – depending on circumstances – be right to kill one innocent person in order to increase the happiness of the many. It may be desirable to replace the criminal law system with a set of arrangements based on preventive medicine, in which there are no offenders, only sick people who are taken into medical care before they do the things which in a system of penal justice would be called criminal: the importance of the loss of liberty which such a revolution would involve is, according to the utilitarian, to be weighed against all the other aspects of happiness. If the happiness of the majority requires a sacrifice of truth, beauty and excellence, the sacrifice may be mandatory. The utilitarian can reply to such examples that they are many of them somewhat unreal, and John Stuart Mill tried to draw a distinction between 'higher' and 'lower' pleasures and to deploy a systematic defence of liberty – two moves which, if successful, would have done much to remove some of the more troubling implications of utilitarianism. It seems unlikely, however, that such defences render utilitarianism immune from the charge that it ignores elementary principles of justice, e.g. that the innocent are not to be killed for whatever purpose.

An argument often pressed against the utilitarian is that the idea of maximising happiness is incoherent. Bentham imagined a calculus of

---

[3] J.Ṅ. Findlay 'The Structure of the Kingdom of Ends'. Quotation from *Values and Intentions* 426.

felicities, in which it would be possible to assign quantities to all pleasure and pain and by means of calculation to arrive at the overall total of happiness and unhappiness in different possible courses of action. Such calculation, if possible, would of course be capable of being erroneous. But the deeper charge laid against the idea is that it makes no sense because any attempt to construe happiness as a collection of discrete pleasures and pains, to be weighed on a common balance, overlooks the fact that happiness is not only an aggregate of mere sensations. This argument does not settle the question completely. Modern utilitarians do not rely on assigning numbers to sensations but on preference orderings among possible states of affairs. The suspicion remains that they are misconstruing happiness, however.

What is one to make of the many criticisms that are advanced against utilitarianism? If the utilitarian were trying to show that his ideas coincide at every point with 'common sense', then the criticisms would be damaging. But Bentham and Mill were not mainly interested in analysing common sense but with clarifying and popularising what they took to be a correct understanding of right and wrong. For all the contemporary efforts to analyse common sense, many utilitarians still follow Bentham and Mill in this regard. Anyone prepared, as they were, to challenge 'common sense' can quite consistently argue that many of the considerations brought forward against utilitarianism represent genuine moral disagreements. An example would be the issue of one man whose death would be expedient for the general interest. In a time when there is a very marked lack of moral consensus, genuine moral disagreements are to be expected. The charge that utilitarianism misconstrues happiness is a more difficult case. If there were some available 'common sense' about what constitutes happiness, and if this could be separated from the widespread disagreements about morality, it might be thought that utilitarianism could be undermined by showing that it seriously misunderstood happiness. After all, we commended utilitarianism above on the ground that it goes straight to the heart, putting happiness at the centre of the system. If it could be shown to misunderstand happiness then much of its appeal would be cut off.

But it is hard to believe that a non-question-begging argument of this kind is currently available. Critics of many kinds allege that the utilitarian, by aiming to *produce* happiness *in* others and *for* others, neglects the vital fact that happiness is to be found, if at all, in *living one's own life*. Utilitarianism is sometimes blamed for the passivity which the welfare state is claimed to encourage. By trying to make people happy, the utilitarian robs them of the initiative, possibly reducing them to the state of mere recipients of pleasure with no independent lives of their own.

What seems to be right about such arguments is that a particular interpretation of classic utilitarianism characteristically runs into very many difficulties whose nature it is too early to determine. This interpretation insists that to have happiness in society we require *fairness*. Where traditionally there have been gross ·inequalities, to maximise happiness there is a need for fair shares. The pursuit of fair shares (e.g. in education) prompts widespread criticism of levelling down. What is difficult is, paradoxically, the impossibility of calculation. The critics of fairness-first utilitarianism claim that standards are eroded; the proponents of such utility argue that it is necessary to pass through a transitional period, that the so-called levelling-down is part of a far wider upheaval in which a new society is being created with its own new criteria of excellence. The critics appeal to standards whose very relevance the utilitarians dispute; the utilitarians promise a new age which by its very nature is not yet visible. It is therefore impossible for the two sides to sit down together and calculate. There are too many things in dispute. Among them is what constitutes happiness: on the meaning of the word 'happiness' there is in this dispute no common sense, no consensus.

The foregoing paragraph attempts to crush a large and complicated debate into a very small compass. There is not space here to elaborate and qualify further, but it is necessary to point out that the critique of utility just reviewed focusses on the effect of the utilitarian's efforts to promote utility on other people than the utilitarian himself. The allegation is that the utilitarian misunderstands other people's happiness. They can be happy, it is said, only if they live their own lives; whereas the utilitarian is disastrously bent on giving them anything but the liberty to live in this way. Sharply different from all such arguments about other people are considerations about the moral agent himself. As pointed out above, doubts have been expressed about the demandingness of utilitarianism – what does it do to someone to be a utilitarian?

The utilitarian has an answer to this question which appears to enlist very wide sympathy. He insists that the costs to the moral agent of being moral must be weighed against all other costs: the ultimate test of an action is its relation to the general happiness rather than anything so sectional or selfish as the agent's own interests. This is a general argument of very wide significance. Suppose someone, not a utilitarian, says that he refuses to do something because he refuses to have blood on his hands; suppose the thing in question (perhaps killing an innocent man in the general interest) would be very valuable in the increments of happiness it would bring to the world at large. What is one to make of the argument 'I was right not to do it, because it would have meant having blood on my hands – I washed my hands of the whole affair'? To the utilitarian such an argument is without any force whatever. For in his terms it amounts to the claim that there being blood on the hands of the person who refused to act counts more in terms of general happiness than there being all the increments which action would have secured. The only explanations the utilitarian will allow are that the agent was in the grip of mere superstition, which blinded him to the proper standards for appraising the situation, and that the agent was being selfish, putting his own lilywhite conscience before the real interests which any decent conscience would be exercised about. The utilitarian is likely to find rather widespread agreement on this point; we consider it further below.

Thus, utilitarianism has something to be said for it but is the subject of numerous criticisms. Some of these are plainly disagreements of a moral kind. The status òf some of the others, in particular the dispute about the nature of happiness, is less easily determined. It seems clear enough that more than merely philosophical issues are at stake: in addition to the current meaning(s) of the word 'happiness', part of the disagreement concerns possible future developments about which there is little or no agreement and about which there can be little discussion in commonly agreed terms. At first glance, the utilitarian appears to be immune from the challenge of the person who washes his hands of some action: the utilitarian will find considerable support for the claim that such a person is being merely superstitious or merely selfish (or both).

Far more modest than classic utilitarianism is a range of systems which resemble it in all respects except in putting forward some other objective than happiness. For example, Marxism interpreted as an ethic puts forward some such thing as the revolutionary triumph of the economically disadvantaged as the ultimate arbiter of value: some brands of power politics and nationalism see advancement of the national interest as the supreme value; G.E. Moore in *Principia Ethica* claims that certain states of consciousness (roughly, the consciousness of friendship and beauty) determine all other values.[4] Marxism and power politics, it is important to notice, cannot be understood exclusively as moral systems: putting the point in a distinctively

[4] On Marxism as an ethic see Eugene Kamenka *The Ethical Foundations of Marxism*. For a discussion of the relation between power politics and ethics see Chapter Six below.

ethical way, they contain – in addition to the moral system – an explanation of why the proposed goal is the only one that should or can be sought. For example, Marxist economic theory purports to show that the promotion of happiness is systematically frustrated by the economic order: only after the revolution will utilitarianism be viable (if then). According to theorists of power politics, the international order makes it impossible to pursue the general happiness: the best that the politician can do is to try to safeguard and enhance his nation's power and security.

Unlike Marxism (and utilitarianism), power politics explicitly confines itself to some aspects of life. It purports to guide the politician but in some formulations presupposes a moral order elsewhere, presumably in the private sphere, where happiness is sought and promises are inviolate.

The systems of Marxism, power politics, and *Principia Ethica* retain the willingness implicit in classic utilitarianism to justify such horrors as the killing of the innocent. If there is something to be said for them, it is that in abandoning the grandiose objective of happiness they opt for something more attainable, more real. (This is said assuming that utilitarianism does capture one's deeply considered wishes, that one genuinely does wish all sentient beings well. There is the darker possibility that morality ought to reflect such things as one's hatreds of people. For example, it could be argued that some parts of Marxism and some brands of nationalism articulate class and national hatred respectively. From the viewpoint that admits hate into morality, it is a positive weakness in utilitarianism that it expresses concern for all sentient beings. The place of hatred in ethics is examined below.)

Utilitarianism and such systems as the Marxist, power political and Moorean ethics are often described collectively as 'consequentialist' or 'utilitarian' systems. The term 'consequentialism' is apt to suggest that these systems pay attention to the consequences of actions at the expense of the moral value or disvalue of actions apart from their consequences. But this impression is rather misleading. Classic utilitarianism can include the intrinsic value or disvalue of an action in its calculations providing that this intrinsic value is derived from happiness: if, for example, one is considering in utilitarian terms the merits of taking a holiday, the intrinsic pleasurableness of holiday-making will appear in the calculations in addition to considerations about the utility of the holiday (making one less anxious, more productive, easier to live and work with, etc.). The same is true of some other consequentialist systems. What justifies use of the word 'consequentialism' is that any distinction which can be made between an action and its consequences is rather unimportant in these systems.

It does not matter for the utilitarian if no clear differentiation is possible between actions and consequences; and if a distinction can be made, it is unimportant within utilitarianism.

2. *Deontological systems*

Often contrasted with consequentialist systems of morality are what might be called deontological moral systems. Deontology is concerned with strict duties. In a way, of course, classic utilitarianism is deontological in that it claims that there is just one duty, that of promoting happiness. But the term 'deontological' is more usefully reserved for moral outlooks which claim that there is more than one duty. An example would be a system founded on a literal reading of the ten commandments. Peculiarly important for ethics of war are deontological systems which insist that the killing of the innocent is absolutely prohibited. A very simple deontological system might claim that the killing of the innocent is absolutely prohibited but that our duty, subject only to the provision that we must avoid killing the innocent, is to maximise human happiness.

Two utilitarian criticisms of deontological systems are very well known. First, such systems are attacked as rule-worship: because duty systems lay down a variety of mutually independent rules without deriving them from human happiness, the utilitarian considers that they make a fetish of the rules. A typical utilitarian question would be: there is an ancient tradition of regarding adultery as absolutely prohibited, but what, apart from the happiness of those involved, does adultery matter? Secondly, the utilitarian is apt to stress the possibility of conflict between the rules in a deontological system. Suppose such a system requires absolute truthfulness and absolute love: what is one to do in a situation in which love demands that one tell less than the truth, or the whole truth? The utilitarian will point out that from his own viewpoint there is an obvious way of analysing such situations: either happiness requires one solution as against another, or utilitarianism enables us to know why the situation is inescapably difficult, namely, because the overall best possibility of happiness is obscure. According to the utilitarian, the deontologist's position is in this regard defective: for the deontologist believes that a right answer to the question of what to do is obtainable but is unable to explain how such an answer is to be obtained.

At this point, a distinction is needed. Some deontologists have attempted to take account of the widespread common-sense belief that many moral situations involve difficult moral conflicts, but have tried to harmonise this admission with the idea that it is possible even in a situation of moral conflict to know what to do. A leading example of such an approach is that of W.D. Ross.[5] Ross elaborates with great subtlety a rather simple core idea. He claims that one recognises a fairly small number of 'prima facie obligations'. In a real situation, one is likely to see that one is under several conflicting prima facie obligations. Hence the common sense of moral conflict. One possesses the ability to ponder these conflicting obligations and to see the right thing to do. One obtains the right answer by intuition. 'Explanations come to an end somewhere'[6] and Ross feels no need for further explanations; there just are a variety of conflicting prima facie obligations; there just is the phenomenon of intuitive insight into which prima facie obligation is overriding; there just is, in a real situation, the ability to see the right thing to do. Ross gives no indication of why it should be that out of conflict comes an unproblematic absolute duty.

Very different in background from such ideas as those of Ross is the kind of religious or theological view of morality that has religious or theological reasons for holding that in any real situation there is at least one right answer to the question of what one should do. For example, there is the theological view which holds that an omnipotent, omniscient, all-loving God requires perfect obedience from human beings and has given the moral law as a code which, if only men will observe it, guarantees such obedience. On this view, there are reasons independent of all considerations about the 'common sense' of morality for believing that it is never the case that there are situations in which 'whatever one does, one is damned'. It is easier to understand religious convictions about the possibility of unproblematic absolute duties than to comprehend the confidence of such a theorist as Ross.

It is easier, too, to oppose the criticisms of a utilitarian from a religious or theological standpoint than from an outlook that relies solely on the analysis of 'moral common sense'. For the religious can refer any difficulties in deriving conflicting principles from a common, reconciling source to the inscrutable will of the supposed maker of all values, but a merely secular analyst has no way of explaining why it should be the case that the difficulties to which the utilitarian refers can be resolved. On the contrary. Any secular analyst who supposes that all moral conflicts can be satisfactorily resolved is bound to face difficulty in explaining how such an amazingly good correspondence obtains between moral consciousness and the demands of morality in

---

[5] See in particular *The Right and the Good.*
[6] L. Wittgenstein *Philosophical Investigations* I, 1.

view of the fragmentary history of morals. We know that the moral allegiances we have inherited have a very various and partly scandalous history,[7] so one would expect to discover ultimate conflict rather than ultimate harmony in the sphere of morals unless the religiously-minded are right in supposing that there is, behind history, some beneficent agency bringing reconciliation to the warring elements. This comment is by no means decisive: Ross apparently feels no need to engage in such metaphysical speculations and would seem to be perfectly entitled to confine his investigations to the moral sphere. Maybe he is right in thinking that it just is a fact that despite the variety of and conflict between our prima facie duties, nevertheless we possess the power to see what is right and our absolute duty. His ultimate appeal (or lack of appeal) is to the moral consciousness of his readers, to that if anything which can reasonably be described as moral common sense.

3. Situation ethics

An ethical idea which appears to have found favour among some theologians in recent years is the notion of situation ethics.[8] The appeal of this seems to be its contrast with utilitarianism and deontology. According to situation ethics, the moral agent faces always-new situations and has to deal with each one on its own merits. Whereas both consequentialists and deontologists concentrate their attention on the rules which in their view should govern men's actions, the adherent of situation ethics considers that reality outruns our rules: for him, the complexity and novelty of new situations is at least as important as the always over-simple categories which we bring to them. What is required according to situation ethics is that the moral agent be open, sensitive and responsive to each situation as it comes.

There is something to be said for situation ethics in certain circumstances. If a moral tradition has dropped into the habit of describing the real world in stereotyped terms that make moral judgment easy but accurate description of the way things are difficult or impossible, situation ethics can serve to replenish one's sense of the overwhelming fullness and abundance of experience. In trying to control the world in thought and action, men are often prone to hammer out some world-picture and then force all future life into it, rejecting so far as possible the suspicion that new patterns are emerging that require new description and new thought. The proponents of situation ethics have often been most exercised about

[7] Cf. Nietzsche *On the Genealogy of Morals.*
[8] Joseph Fletcher *Situation Ethics: the New Morality.*

the moral guidance which should be given to individuals about sexual and related personal problems. It is a commonplace that sexual mores have altered very drastically in this century. Many churchmen have considered that their own traditions have yielded a damagingly stereotyped perception of these changes; whatever its weaknesses, situation ethics insists on trying for an open, full, compassionate description of the states-of-affairs to which the moralist is supposed to be giving his mind.

The case for situation ethics is often stated in terms of the polarity between conventional and unconventional. Thus, it is often said that the churches have responded badly to contemporary shifts of sexual custom because they have been too conventional, contenting themselves with reiterating the conventional wisdom where what is required is some unconventional insight, a break with convention. Gordon Dunstan argues powerfully against such a view:

> Conventions ... embody expectations; they impose limitations, they result in liberation – liberation for the individual and the conditions of freedom for the community. Assurance is itself a liberating force. Where there is a convention of honesty and fair dealing, buyer and seller can negotiate together without crippling suspicion or fear: to have 'a garage you can trust' is the car-owner's dream. An accepted convention of marital fidelity and some sort of domestic solidarity enables friends and neighbours to associate freely without fear of family disruption. If, in their inter-personal behaviour, unmarried people of student age are less strictly governed by the conventions of an earlier generation, they develop conventions of their own, because assurance of some sort, 'knowing what to expect of one another', is necessary for security, even in the communes of protest.[9]

The strength of situation ethics lies not in the challenge to convention but in the appeal to truth: in a situation of rapid social change it is peculiarly difficult to obtain a fair-minded description of the new phenomena to which old rules must be applied, adapted or rejected as no longer viable.

Situation ethics, which appears to be merely a doctrine in ethics, in fact presupposes an epistemology which is hopelessly weak. It is presented as a self-sufficient set of ideas, without realisation of what is involved in accepting the view that the proper and only stance of the moral agent is to accept each situation as it comes and view it in isolation from all other phenomena. If the task of the moral agent is indeed solely to make the best of what comes, it is open to the opponents of morality (whose identity varies from case to case) to determine the limits of thought within which moral thinking is conducted. The moralist is enjoined to address himself to the case-in-

[9] *The Artifice of Ethics* 14.

hand. If that is the only thing he may do, he cannot reflect upon the significance of the case-in-hand for wider issues. An example which plays an important part in our subsequent argument may make this clearer. It is a deliberately fanciful example; its unreality is considered below.

Latin America. An army captain, Pedro, has twenty Indians tied up against a wall. He is about to shoot them when Jim, an English botanist, happens along. Pedro offers Jim a choice: you shoot one of the Indians or I shoot them all. Jim has very good reason to believe that heroics, e.g. turning the gun on Pedro, will save no lives; and knows that Pedro is, though a brute, a man of his word who can be trusted to release the nineteen Indians if Jim will shoot the twentieth. What should Jim do?[10] This question is rather important for several of the ideas sketched in this book, including utilitarianism and the pacifism of scruple. Its bearing on situation ethics is this. According to that theory, *the* thing to do in morality is to give one's mind to the situation confronting one. The moral adviser is to give his mind to the personal problems of the people seeking his counsel and Jim is to give his mind to the problem set for him by Pedro. Some consider that this is a plausible thought applied to the counsellor; but it surely misses something out when brought to bear on Jim's conundrum. *What* is missed out is extremely hard to determine, and will be examined below; but that something is missing will be agreed by many people. Jim is surely in some sense entitled to the thought that 'This is perfectly frightful – the blame for this lies wholly with Pedro – he has fixed this!' Jim would be less than a fully human moral agent if he did not have this thought – or so it seems to us.

This is, of course, an extreme situation as well as a fanciful one. But the point that it puts rather starkly can be made also by reference to more ordinary situations. The proponent of situation ethics is unable to explain how the moral agent singles out 'significant situations' from among the flux of experience, and how he begins to think about the situations that he picks out. Granted that sometimes new thought and imaginative leaps of insight are required; it remains a question how the moral agent even begins to know how to recognise a problem as a problem and, having picked his question, even begins to set about answering it. He is, say, confronted with a woman in her forties who has devoted her life to the welfare of an aging parent whose exploitative demands are constantly increasing and threatening to wreck the health and sanity of the person seeking help. How does he know that there is a problem here, and how does he begin to think

[10] The example is Bernard Williams': Smart and Williams 98-9. See also Barrie Paskins 'Some Victims of Morality' 95-101.

about it? Suppose he has an instinctive nose for misery, and an instinctive desire to alleviate it. Then he may be able to sniff out the fact that there is some suffering going on. But how does he begin to determine the way in which to think about this suffering? How does he know whether to concentrate on the parent's sense of outrage, betrayal, desertion or on the child's miserable plight? Only if it is assumed in advance that there is some proper standard, however rough-and-ready, about what is due to parents and what is due to children can the moral agent begin to understand the situation. In short, concentration on the situation in hand, in the sense intended by proponents of situation ethics, presupposes some idea of justice. Because situation ethics is a theory and not simply an attempt to modify a tradition, this presupposition is extremely damaging. The theory is taking for granted that which is problematic: for the nature of justice is in dispute in those processes of change to which situation ethics seeks to address itself.

An important issue in situation ethics is the question of when to make exceptions. If one accepts a deontological system then one cannot make exceptions unless by altering or abandoning the system. It is presumably part of the point of a system of duties that it is resistant to the making of exceptions. To the person who comes to putative moral rules from a sense of the fulness and overwhelming abundance of experience, the making of exceptions is a natural proceeding: the most he will expect from rules is that they should give one's thought an initial impetus (in the example of the aging parent, an impetus to see things primarily through the daughter's eyes?). Gordon Dunstan comments:

> Convention ... can always be disregarded, of course, in obedience to particular demand; sometimes it must be. But observe the risk: if a convention has a particular protective function in relation to any of the more sensitive areas of human relationship – for example, that which confines sexual union to within marriage or that which attributes the right in a fetus normally to come to birth – every time it is broken at the dictate of a momentary or individualist demand of 'compassion' or 'love' it is weakened, and other persons are left more at risk; and conventions, once eroded by disuse, defiance or ridicule, are not always re-established ... without the social disfigurement of extreme reaction.[11]

For present purposes it is necessary to be as clear as possible about the force which this argument has. It can be taken in various ways. Perhaps the least interesting is to construe it along the lines of the old textbook debate. *A* announces that he proposes to break some

[11] Dunstan 14.

venerated taboo. *B* says 'But what if everyone did as you are proposing to do?' *A* replies 'But they won't!' The good old examination question invites the student to assess the cogency of *A*'s reply. We will not pursue this because Dunstan appears to be more interested in what in fact happens when conventions are breached: does every breach weaken the convention? We are unaware of any extensive body of research on this, and will confine ourselves to some rather speculative remarks.

It is hard to believe that making an exception purely in private can have much general significance, if only because few people can know about it. The widespread making of purely private exceptions could have a widespread significance because the small circles privy to each exception amount in sum to a very large number. The public making of exceptions in private or public affairs can presumably exercise a general influence. Thus, public pronouncements by church leaders and well-publicised conduct by youth heroes are capable of an influence which is not to be expected from the exceptions made discreetly in private by a parish priest or a bank clerk. In the chapter from which we have been quoting, Dunstan refers repeatedly to the international conventions that purport to order dealings between states. The making of exceptions to these is a singularly public act, understandably expected of one another by antagonists in the inter-state system and regularly discovered in stereotyped terms by intelligence organisations. The caution that Dunstan urges about the making of exceptions is therefore quite peculiarly plausible in the case of conventions relating to war and international relations.

So far in this chapter we have been reviewing a variety of general ethical theories of current interest in philosophy or theology. The ethical theory informing this book is distinct from all of the theories so far examined. Its distinctness is of considerable importance since doubts which the reader may entertain about our argument may well derive from a difference of ethical view: it seems unlikely that all parts of our argument could be accepted in terms of classic utilitarianism, any other consequentialism, any deontological system, or in terms of situation ethics. Our attention is focussed neither on the rules that should guide action, nor on the situations to which the moral agent is required to give thought, but on the nature of virtue. We will give some reasons for favouring such an approach but it seems to us to be in the nature of the case that there will be irresolvable ethical disagreements, and consequent moral disagreements, between adherents of the various notions so far sketched and those whose primary interest is in virtue.

4. The ethics of virtue

Our outlook can perhaps best be made plain by reference to Aristotle, Hume and Kant. In a celebrated passage at the beginning of the long work which has come down to us divided into two books called *Ethics* and *Politics*, Aristotle writes:

> Our discussion will be adequate if it has as much clearness as the subject-matter admits of, for precision is not to be sought for alike in all discussions. ... Now fine and just actions, which political science investigates, admit of much variety and fluctuation of opinion, so that they may be thought to exist only by convention, and not by nature. And goods also give rise to a similar fluctuation because they bring harm to many people; for before now men have been undone by reason of their wealth, and others by reason of their courage. We must be content, then, in speaking of such subjects and with such premises to indicate the truth roughly and in outline, and in speaking about things which are only for the most part true and with premises of the same kind to reach conclusions that are no better. In the same spirit, therefore, should each type of statement be *received*; for it is the mark of an educated man to look for precision in each class of things just so far as the nature of the subject admits; it is evidently equally foolish to accept probable reasoning from a mathematician.[12]

This is susceptible of several interpretations. It might, for example, be taken to mean that 'political science' should concern itself with rules of conduct, mindful that such rules are necessarily rough-and-ready, admitting of exceptions in particular cases. The 'mark of an educated man' will then be to refrain from bringing forward merely fanciful examples. The example of Jim and Pedro might then be criticised as just the kind of thing one would expect from the ill-educated.

Such an interpretation does not accord very closely with Aristotle's practice, which is to scrutinise not rules of conduct but virtues. What matters for present purposes, however, is not the exegesis of Aristotle but solely the fact that his remarks admit of a different interpretation. If the proper subject of ethical analysis is virtue, what Aristotle is telling us is that the best one can hope for is a rough outline of virtue. This does not necessarily imply that fanciful examples are to be avoided. Some magnificent examples of the literary celebration of virtue and satire of vice employ exceedingly artificial situations, and it is by no means obvious that the philosopher's approach should be different. It may even be that a decent doctrine of the virtues will enable one to distinguish between fanciful examples that are interesting and others that are merely the ingenious but trivial

---

[12] *Ethics* 1095ᵃ, tr. Thomson 27-8.

products of ill-bred minds. The truth of this should become somewhat clearer as we proceed.

In embarking on his enquiry into 'the true origin of morals', David Hume says that he is going to rely on 'a very simple method':

> We shall analyse that complication of mental qualities, which form what, in common life, we call Personal Merit: we shall consider every attribute of the mind, which renders a man an object either of esteem and affection, or of hatred and contempt; every habit or sentiment or faculty, which, if ascribed to any person, implies either praise or blame, and may enter into any panegyric or satire of his character and manners.[13]

Plainly, this proclaims an intention to analyse virtue and vice rather than principles of action or the situations in which the moral agent finds himself. Hume has an exceedingly powerful general argument for adopting this method. Suppose it is objected to Hume that the analysis of what men praise and blame can reveal at most what is thought to be good and bad rather than what *truly is* good and bad: should not ethics be concerned with what is *in fact* right rather than with what is held to be right? Hume has an answer to this:

> The end of all moral speculations is to teach us our duty; and, by proper representations of the deformity of vice and beauty of virtue, beget correspondent habits, and engage us to avoid the one, and embrace the other. But is this ever to be expected from inferences and conclusions of the understanding, which of themselves have no hold of the affections or set in motion the active powers of men? They discover truths: but where the truths which they discover are indifferent, and beget no desire or aversion, they can have no influence on conduct and behaviour. What is honourable, what is fair, what is becoming, what is noble, what is generous, takes possession of the heart, and animates us to embrace and maintain it. [But] ... what is true procures only the cool assent of the understanding; and gratifying a speculative curiosity, puts an end to our researches.[14]

Thus, if an enquiry into what is *really* good is to be a moral enquiry, it must discover not merely that which is true but also that which is capable of enlisting human sympathies. Hume apparently assumes, with good reason, that the natural place to look for that which is both capable of enlisting human interest and important for ethics is 'Personal Merit'.

This much is well known, but there is a subtlety which appears to have escaped notice. Kant, of course, was prompted by the philosophy of Hume to embark on his own mature work. One deeply obscure

[13] *Enquiries* 173-4.
[14] *ibid.* 172.

matter over which Kant took odds with Hume was the issue of 'the true origin of morals'. Popular expositions of the disagreement see Hume as tracing morality to 'sympathy', whereas Kant is said to argue that mere sympathy is never a moral emotion – morality is always a matter of the exercise of *reason*. Sympathy is merely one of the passions; reason is sovereign over the passions; morality derives from reason. Sympathy is a feeling that comes and goes, and a person cannot be held responsible for feeling or not feeling sympathetic; reason, a steady constant, underlies morality and gives stability to the activity of the moral agent. This well-known antithesis is indefensible. Kant assumes throughout that all human beings desire what Hume calls personal merit, and says as much in an important passage in *The Moral Law*:

> The practical use of ordinary human reason confirms the rightness of this deduction. There is no one, not even the most hardened scoundrel – provided only he is accustomed to use reason in other ways – who, when presented with examples of honesty in purpose, of faithfulness to good maxims, of sympathy, and of kindness towards all (even when these are bound up with great sacrifices of advantage and comfort), does not wish that he too might be a man of like spirit.[15]

If such an example, granted, can confirm the Kantian viewpoint, the same example rejected can call it into doubt. Kant's philosophy presupposes certain wishes on the part of those to whom it is supposed to apply.

This concession of the importance of human interest in ethics is a grave matter for Kant's moral philosophy. The point needs making for present purposes, because we want to use some Kantian material, but taken out of a Kantian context. According to Kant, there is one and only one thing of unconditional value: the good will. A person shows good will in consistently acting out of reverence for the moral law. Kant offers four formulations of the moral law, which he considers to be equivalent. We agree with the consensus of many modern philosophers that the four forms are in fact far from equivalent; for present purposes it is necessary to discuss only one formulation. This is that the moral law is:

> Treat humanity, whether in your own person or in the person of another, always as an end and never merely as a means.[16]

We want to evaluate this principle as a way of thinking about the ethics of war. But the bearing on it of Hume's argument that ethics

[15] *The Moral Law* 114-15.
[16] Cf. *ibid*. 91.

should concentrate on things capable of enlisting human sympathy needs to be made plain from the outset. To try to determine Kant's view of the relation, though fascinating, would take us too far from the present main subject. We will therefore merely try to state the crucial difficulty, and indicate the way in which we hope to solve the problem.

Kant has often been criticised for rule-worship. Some reasons for this can be found in the popular antithesis often drawn between Hume and Kant. If Hume derives morality entirely from sympathy, at least he can be said to have secured that the moral agent is characteristically moved to act by the person whose good he aims to secure. For sympathy is perception of the interest of another person together with the impulse to further that person's interest if occasion presents itself. If Kant derives morality entirely from love of the moral law, as he often seems to do, he apparently makes certain that the moral agent is *not* moved to act by the plight of the person who, if things go well, benefits from his obedience to the moral law. For what makes his action moral is not a thing (sympathy) that he happens to feel towards the person he is trying to help, but his steady attitude as a rational being to something quite impersonal, namely the moral law. Men can fall in love with anything, even an abstract principle, so there is no obstacle in seeing love of the moral law as that impulse which, according to Hume, must underlie morality. But there is a very considerable difficulty in explaining how it could come about that human beings love, of all things, a mere abstract principle.

It is perhaps a symptom of this difficulty that Kant has no even remotely attractive theory of moral *education*: what little he says on the subject envisages the moral law as being stamped on to a passionate being that has nothing remotely moral about it. In Hume's theory, the process of moral education is readily understood as a progressive widening of the agent's sympathies: granted some initial concern for somebody at least part of the time with at least part of the heart, the task of moral education in Hume's system is one of extending the practice of sympathy to more persons, more of the agent's time, and more of his heart. Kant's moral theory cannot allow any such development to be counted as a process of *moral growth*: Kantian beings either are or are not rational beings equipped with a love of the moral law. The only improvement they are capable of is in the direction of giving more practical effect to their love of a moral law that is engraved in, or stamped on to, their hearts from the beginning.

The charge of rule-worship is extremely important in the political criticism of morality. An argument very often put, and examined below, claims that the moralist is merely a worshipper of abstract principle whereas the good politician, for all his faults, is at least trying to serve the real interests of real people. If one is to use a formulation of the Kantian moral law, therefore, it is necessary to be explicit about the question of rule-worship.

5. The man of good wishes

The moral psychology employed in this book is not that which perhaps led Kant into rule worship. It is, on the contrary, rather Humean. Our view is that the moral agent begins his moral life with certain limited sympathies. If things go well with him morally then these sympathies become extended – a process of moral education. Any principles that he embraces are seen by him as codifying the interests which enlist the sympathies of the better part of himself: the principles give clearer expression or order to his sympathies, and perhaps extend them: they do not do violence to his existing sympathies. It is a morally important fact about the good moral agent not only that he has a good will but also that he has good *wishes* towards all men (and all sentient beings – a complication that need not concern us).

Our appreciation of the importance of wishes in ethics owes much to J.N. Findlay. He says

> What we wish or do not wish for fills the interstices and provides the background of conduct, and ... for all developed ethical views, it is as important what we wish for in our hearts as what we do in the market-place. ... Wishes span the gulf between means and ends, between the possible and the impossible, the actual and the non-actual, the practicable and the impracticable, and they are impervious, save as regards grammatical expression, to the temporal distinctions of present, past and future. If wishing provides an unbounded horizon for idle fantasy, it also provides an horizon where rationality may range unfettered.[17]

This is the liberating perspective which we hope to bring to bear on the ethics of war.

Suppose, for example, that the good man is walking in a park and sees children whom he does not know thoroughly enjoying themselves at play. It is in our view a morally important fact about the good moral agent that he is spontaneously delighted for the children, even though this has no bearing on his actions. If in need of a general principle to codify his sense of what one ought to do, then the good moral agent, if well informed, invokes Kant's principle: 'Treat humanity, whether in your own person or in the person of another, always as an end and never merely as a means.'

[17] Findlay 428.

Our man of good will (and wish) may have a darker side. There may be times when the worse side of him, a matter of indifference or hatred towards other people, may be operative in his actions; and a deep nausea or loathing towards humanity may be detectable in his wishes (perhaps through psychoanalytic investigation of his dreams and fantasies). But in our view the good man (morally speaking) typically behaves in a way that is best made sense of by seeing him as often spontaneously motivated by sympathy, frequently responsive to a sense of duty which is codified in Kant's principle, and sometimes falling short of his own better self in ways to be construed in terms of his own understanding of himself as engaged in a struggle with the worse part of himself. There may be black moods in which he does what he takes to be his duty grumblingly, and periods of deadness in which he feels indifferent to everyone and everything, and remains active only from a sense of grinding, onerous duty. But his own best understanding of such times, and the understanding which is most important for ethics, is that in these times he is something less than his full moral self: he is in a kind of moral dream, not to be taken seriously for the analysis of moral psychology any more than dreams are to be taken seriously as a key to metaphysics.

In order to determine the relation between this person of good will and good wish and the ethics of war, we want to consider at some length the problem posed to Jim by Pedro. Let us suppose that the twenty Indians whom Pedro is proposing to kill have done nothing which could be adduced as evidence that they deserve to be killed as a punishment (or even that they deserve some lesser penalty). Let us also assume that the twenty Indians do not know which one of their number will be singled out for execution if Jim accedes to Pedro's offer and that therefore, very reasonably, the Indians implore Jim to accept the offer. Finally, let us assume that Jim knows that the Indians are not guilty of anything for which Pedro is proposing to punish them, and knows that the Indians want him to take up Pedro's terms. What, if Jim is the good man of our last few paragraphs, will he think and do?

Having good wishes towards all men, Jim will wish that the situation had never arisen. He will further wish that Pedro had never embarked on the adventure of wickedness that has created the difficult situation in which he – Jim – finds himself. We have given no reason to suppose that he wishes that, if there had to be such a situation then someone other than himself should be the one facing the problem. The wishes of the better part of himself were, for all that we said, directed entirely towards other people and not at all towards himself. It is possible that the feebler part of himself wishes someone else had the problem, but this is merely a fact about the portion of himself against which he is struggling. It is not obvious that Jim will wish that there had never been such a person as Pedro – if hatred is the desire for the non-existence of that which is hated, the person of good wish will hate the hideous activity of Pedro, but not necessarily Pedro himself as distinct from his action. (Cf. 'Love the sinner, hate the sin'.) It is not necessary that Jim have the wishes just mentioned *at the time when* he faces the problem: at that time, he may be already in, or be shocked into, a state of indifference or nausea towards all mankind; or there may be too much of a practical kind on his mind for it to be significant to say of him that at that time he had these wishes. But it is in our view necessary to say that the good man who is facing the problem is the very same person who has these wishes, so that if he does not have them at that time then some special explanation is required.

So much for Jim's wishes; what of his will and actions? He will be guided by the principle: 'Treat humanity, whether in your own person or in the person of another, always as an end and never merely as a means.' What action does this principle require? Bernard Williams points out that this Kantian principle has anti-utilitarian implications for such an activity as promise-keeping.[18]

It might be thought that a parallel argument could be applied to Jim's unpleasant problem: it is for each of us to avoid killing the innocent; the Indians are not guilty of any offence whose punishment is in question, and in that sense can reasonably be called 'innocent'; it is for Pedro to avoid killing these innocents; if any of them are killed it will be Pedro's doing, even if someone else pulls the trigger; it is for Jim to avoid murder, and it is not for Jim to aid or abet Pedro in his crime. In attempting to save the Indians, Jim would be merely treating himself as a means and sacrificing his own moral integrity.

The place of such an argument in the fully-developed Kantian philosophy is obscure. Perhaps reverence for the moral law would give it force. But we are here concerned with the Kantian principle only in the context of the person of good wish and will. For him, it has no force whatever, as is easily proved. The better part of Jim is concerned not with Jim himself or with safeguarding his (Jim's) integrity but solely with doing the best possible by the Indians. Their interest, given the assumptions made above, is unquestionably in Jim's acceding to Pedro's offer. To do what is in their interest in the given situation is to treat them as ends and also to treat himself as an end: for, by hypothesis, everything that Jim does is best understood as a striving to serve the best interests of others. There is nothing in Jim's

[18] Smart and Williams 88-9.

life which could be pointed to as evidence that in agreeing to shoot one
of the Indians he would be treating himself as a means merely and not
also as an end; there is a great deal that can be adduced as evidence to
the contrary. Treating oneself as an end is living to the full the life that
is in one, and Jim will be doing this if and only if here as elsewhere he
strives to promote the interests of those involved.

Bernard Williams uses the example of Jim to point out that we are
not all of us single-minded utilitarians.[19] The argument just adduced
suggests that non-utilitarian considerations of a partly Kantian sort
yield the same practical conclusion as utilitarianism: that Jim should
agree to shoot one of the Indians. This might appear an exceedingly
unexciting conclusion: what possible interest can there be in an
ethical view that in practice coincides with utilitarianism?

To answer this question, we want to draw attention to a feature of
the example of Jim which is common also to an example discussed
earlier in our critical examination of the pacifism of scruple. We
looked in Chapter Three at the hackneyed question of what the
pacifist would or should do if he sees a soldier coming up the garden
path to rape his sister and murder his mother, if the only two practical
options are to kill the soldier or to do nothing. We pointed out that
this is extremely unlike the kind of problem which the pacifist is apt to
be preoccupied with, in that in the garden path example it would be
perfectly clear what one was trying to do in killing the soldier, whereas
typically in involving oneself in the military dimension one loses
control of one's own actions. Similarly, in the fanciful example of Jim
it is very clear what Jim is trying to do: he is trying to save as many
Indians as possible and trampling on no one's rights in the attempt. In
all such clear-cut examples, utilitarianism and the morality of the
man of good will and good wish are apt to agree, for different reasons,
about what ought to be done in practice.

6. Existential dilemmas

Divergences in practice begin to emerge when we turn from such
clearcut problems to cases in which it is difficult or impossible for the
moral agent to know what he is doing. Consider, for example, the
objection brought against all involvement in war (except perhaps on
the part of a Napoleon or Frederick the Great) by the pacifist of
scruple. His argument is, it will be recalled, as follows: killing human
beings is prima facie wrong; in doing, or preparing or threatening to
do, something which is prima facie wrong one should be very sure
what one is doing; in taking part in war it is impossible to be sure

[19] *ibid.* 108-18.

what one is doing; therefore one should not engage in war. For the utilitarian this argument is not specially impressive: the principles involved in it are to be weighed against the general happiness and merit allegiance only insofar as they are productive of happiness on the whole. The principle 'Be very sure before you act' may be useful or may not be. If, in a given situation, there is a difficulty of knowing what to do, that is solely because it is difficult to see which course of action would produce happiness.

But now consider the pacifism of scruple from Jim's standpoint. Being a man of good wish he wishes if possible to promote the general happiness, and in this agrees with the utilitarian. But is it open to him to engage in activity whose morality he is in no position to assess, knowing only that it is dubious? That is, is it open to him to seek to treat humanity as an end and not merely as a means, knowing only that it is dubious whether he will in fact be treating humanity as anything more than a means?

The reason that this question is difficult is that it arises at a point where one's grasp of the meaning of the idea of treating someone as an end and of treating someone merely as a means *slips*. There are very many sorts of situation in which one knows what is meant by treating someone merely as a means, and by the same token very many situations in which one knows what is meant by treating someone not merely as a means but also as an end. Speaking very roughly, these are the situations in which there is a clearcut choice between a kind of conduct that takes account of the fact that the people involved are moral beings each with a moral life of his own and a kind of conduct which ignores the moral life of some or all of the people involved. One of the great appeals of Kantian, in contrast to utilitarian, thinking is that it attaches utterly central importance to the activity of representing the fact that in a great variety of situations each of the people involved has a moral life of his own. It is this feature of Kantian thinking that makes possible the criticism of utilitarian ideas about replacing the criminal law with a system of preventive medicine that removes from people the opportunity of choosing to respect or disobey the law.

The conceptual trouble with thinking about pacifism from the viewpoint of modified Kantian ideas that we have been proposing is that the pacifist of scruple lays his finger on a special case of a kind of problem that poses an irresolvable dilemma to the Kantian. The pacifist takes one horn of the dilemma; as we will see, there is another horn.

The kind of problem involved can be illustrated from very familiar, ordinary examples. Suppose one has to choose between telling a dying person something which will cause him intense suffering and misery, and maybe kill him, and withholding the information. What should one do? For the utilitarian, this is a pretty easy question: one should withhold the information, since the person will not be made unhappy by this so long as he does not find out what one has been doing. To many people, the very easiness of this answer is a clear indication of the triviality of the utilitarian understanding of human nature: for, they think with at least part of their minds, there is something more to man than the kind of happiness which can be secured by withholding the truth. The Kantian is able to state this problem quite clearly. In withholding the information one has very much the look of someone who is treating the dying person – a person with the capacity to face the truth with heroism or cowardice – merely as a means to the maximisation of happiness. 'What does happiness matter? The truth is what matters, the person is what matters!' Many of us feel the force of such an assertion. But equally many of us feel that it is grotesquely one-sided. The utilitarian is not a mere rule-worshipper, a happiness-fetishist: the utilitarian has a reason for putting happiness at the centre of his system. This reason is often stated to be that happiness is self-evidently *the* important thing. This is a somewhat misleading formulation, for it conceals the rather obvious fact that most utilitarians have a further reason for regarding happiness as *the* important thing: happiness is 'self-evidently important' because happiness is what matters to you if what you care about most of all is people. It is the truth of this proposition that makes utilitarianism such a naturally appealing moral system.

Because what the utilitarian cares about is people, he is well-equipped to point out how one-sided it would be to say simply 'What does happiness matter?!' at the bedside of the dying. Of course happiness is what matters! This assertion would not be acceptable in full-blown Kantian philosophy. According to Kant, the only thing unconditionally valuable is the good will; happiness is valuable only conditionally, as something added to the good man. Happiness appears in Kant's analysis of *absolute* good[20] but not as something which might get in the way of an uncompromising insistence on always respecting the moral life in other people and in oneself. The compassion for the dying that makes one hesitate about agreeing that they should be told the truth even if it destroys or kills them finds no articulation in the Kantian system: such compassion is merely an operation of the passions, a distraction from morality.

But the situation is different in the non-Kantian moral psychology that we have proposed as a context for Kant's principle. In our view,

[20] *Critique of Practical Reason* I, I, II; tr. Beck 114-54.

this principle is embraced as a codification and extension of pre-existing moral sympathies, to which it does no violence. The fully developed Kantian system does cruel violence to one's feelings about the problem of the dying person and the truth. It systematically separates that in the person which cries out for the truth from that which will suffer, and possibly be unable to stand, the truth.

All that is required for the carrying forward of the present argument is that, for a person who adheres to Kant's principle as a non-violent codification of his pre-existing moral allegiances, the problem of whether to tell the truth to the dying or to withhold it is, in a sense, an impossible problem. For his moral outlook gives him reason to speak, reason to remain silent, and no criteria by which to decide between these incompatible choices.

To say this, however, is not to say that the person cannot choose. He must choose – to do nothing is to come down on one side rather than the other. The modified Kantian cannot escape the problem and must somehow cope with it without the guidance of moral criteria: all the guides have been used up and it is necessary to proceed without guidance.

It seems to us that the choice between pacifism of scruple and a certain kind of willingness to go to war is, in an almost exactly similar way, a criterionless choice. Let us, to make the point as clear as possible, leave aside the question of a war's utility and assume that the war to be discussed is in a sense a hopeless one: the persons we are interested in have, let us suppose, no chance of winning or staving off military defeat. If they surrender they will certainly suffer grotesquely humiliating annihilation. This is not the most ordinary situation with a military dimension, but it strikes us as the one which will make the point most straightforwardly; other cases can be considered afterwards.

Let us suppose that a particular person (it may as well be Jim) faces the following choice. *Either* to fight, knowing that the fighting involves something prima facie wrong (killing, perhaps killing the innocent) and unable to know that his efforts will nevertheless be right or at least not wrong, and in fighting to share in the last heroic act of resistance of a doomed people. *Or* to refuse to fight, thereby setting himself apart from the life of his people in the hour of their greatest glory.

The question is not whether he shall let his people down when they *need* him: they are past needing anyone.

WESTMORELAND:
O that we now had here
But one ten thousand of those men in England,
That do not work today.

HENRY V:

… No, my fair cousin.
If we are marked to die, we are enow
To do our country loss …
Rather proclaim it, Westmoreland, through my host,
That he which hath no stomach to this fight,
Let him depart; his passport shall be made,
And crowns for convoy put into his purse.
We would not die in that man's company,
That fears his fellowship to die with us …
Thou dost not wish more help from England, coz?

WESTMORELAND:

God's will, my liege, would you and I alone,
Without more help, might fight this royal battle.[21]

Shakespeare is here commemorating in a patriotic play a battle which was in its effects very far from being merely a shout of defiance in the face of fate. But the view taken of hopeless odds is the one that we require.

It is not for present purposes necessary to decide what fate will come to our hapless Jim if he decides not to fight: whether his own side will kill or abandon him, or protect him with that reckless generosity of Henry's proclamation so that he dies a sordid death in a ditch when the enemy finally triumph, or whether he will somehow escape altogether to write his memoirs of his (perhaps brave) conscientious objection.

The point we wish to make about Jim is that if one views him straight, and preserves one's caring about people from such systematising simplifications of the emotions as utilitarianism and Kantian philosophy, he plainly has an impossible problem. As some would put it, whatever he does he is damned. Of course he must be with his people in the greatest struggle; and of course, as the pacifist of scruple points out, he must refuse to fight. (Let us suppose battlefield conditions offer no other options – stretcher-bearers are not much use in a war of annihilation.) It is also obvious that Jim must do something. His choice, which is inescapable, is criterionless.

It seems to us right to describe Jim's problem as, in a much-abused word, existential. The same is almost but not quite true of the choice between telling the truth to a dying man and withholding it. In the present context, an existential choice can be defined quite easily in a way that coincides fairly closely with Sartre's usage. If, in terms of his own values, a person must make a choice in circumstances where all

[21] *Henry V* IV, 3.

the criteria available to him have been used up, and if what choice the person makes will determine to a significant degree the kind of person he is, then the choice is existential. Jim's choice is plainly existential in this sense: if he opts to fight he becomes a warrior, a moral category with its own distinctive content; if he opts not to fight he becomes a conscientious objector, another distinctive moral category. Sartre explains the use of the word 'existential' by claiming that according to existentialism a person's existence precedes his essence, i.e. what kind of person he is is determined by the choices he makes and not vice versa.[22] Our formulation does not permit this sweeping claim: Jim was and remains an adherent of the Kantian imperative, and this partly determines *who* Jim is. He would not have the problem he does have if his values had not forced him to face a question which they make it impossible for him to answer by the application of rules for action. But Jim's essence (warrior or conscientious objector) is partly determined by his choice: his existence partly determines his essence.

The reason why Jim's choice is existential whereas the choice to tell the truth to the dying person or withhold it is not existential is that Jim's choice partly determines who he is whereas the choice with regard to the dying man is merely an episode in one's life, harrowing and impressed on one's memory perhaps, but not decisively determining the kind of person that one is. There is, it seems to us, no other significant difference between the two cases: they are examples of the same dilemma. The pacifist of scruple embraces one horn of the dilemma, warrior Jim the other. There is no choice but to choose.

It might be thought that the example just brought forward is unduly *romantic*, that it is too far from *realistic* thinking about war to merit any ethical weight being put upon it. To answer this criticism one faces a desperate difficulty of *tone, atmosphere, style*, which in various ways is present throughout this book but becomes especially acute here.

The kinds of things about morality that can be said in philosophical prose are many, but there are certain things that must be *felt* and the language of philosophical analysis is not an apt instrument for saying these things. This would not matter too much if we could suddenly break off the analysis and write with the outrageous humour to be found in *Schweik* or *Mash*, the encyclopaedic psychological evocativeness of *War and Peace*, the high seriousness of Wilfred Owen, Isaac Rosenberg, David Jones. But of course such skills are beyond our powers.

On the whole we have merely ignored this impossible problem, but

---

[22] *Existentialism and Humanism.*

when a question-mark is set against the example that we have used to suggest that the choice between pacifism and participation in war is existential then we are forced to meet part of the problem head-on. For part of what is in question is this: how can one have the face, in this anti-heroic, anti-rhetorical age to refer without irony to the idea that it might be morally important to be fighting alongside one's people in their hour of greatest glory? Is not Churchill's judgment on Britain's continued resistance to Hitlerite Germany 'This was their finest hour' (18 June 1940)[23] to be understood as inspiring rhetoric rather than as the sort of thing that requires to be taken account of in ethics?

The best way that we have been able to hit on of dealing with such questions is to return to the 'very simple method' announced by David Hume and quoted above:

> We shall analyse that complication of mental qualities, which form ... Personal Merit.

In particular, we shall consider something that might enter into a panegyric of a man's character and manners.

7. *Sarpedon as an example of virtue*

What would it mean if one praised a man as being 'like Sarpedon'? We turn to his creator, the very *un*romantic poet Homer, in the glorious Elizabethan translation by George Chapman, for an answer:

> He spake to Glaucus: 'Glaucus, say, why are we honour'd more
> Than other men of Lycia, in place; with greater store
> Of meats and cups; with goodlier roofs; delightsome gardens; walks;
> More lands and better; so much wealth, that court and country talks
> Of us and our possessions, and every way we go,
> Gaze on us as we were their Gods? This where we dwell is so:
> The shores of Xanthus ring of this; and shall we not exceed
> As much in merit as in noise? Come, be we great in deed
> As well as look; shine not in gold, but in the flames of fight;
> That so our neat-arm'd Lycians may say: "See, these are right
> Our kings, our rulers; these deserve to eat and drink the best;
> These govern not ingloriously; these, thus exceed the rest,
> Do more than they command to do." O friend, if keeping back
> Would keep back age from us, and death, and that we might not wrack
> In this life's human sea at all, but that deferring now
> We shunn'd death ever, nor would I half this vain valour show,
> Nor glorify a folly so, to wish thee to advance;

[23] A.J.P. Taylor *English History 1914-45* 491.

But since we must go, though not here; and that, besides the chance
Proposed now, there are infinite fates of other sorts in death,
Which, neither to be fled nor scaped, a man must sink beneath;
Come, try we, if this sort be ours, and either render thus
Glory to others, or make them resign the like to us.'[24]

This passage enacts the drawing of a thought's consequences in action. Sarpedon reflects on the reputation and honour that such as he and Glaucus enjoy. He recognises that this may be a mere appearance ('noise', 'look') or that they may give it the reality of action. If they act then it is against the backdrop of the knowledge that it is impossible that they should not 'wrack/In this life's human sea'. Knowing that they must suffer some disaster or other, Sarpedon faces the death of battle without fear. This is not rash courage – for him there is nothing to fear because of the certainty that disaster must be undergone at some time and the knowledge that if it is experienced now the encounter will have all the ennobling quality of making real the social glory in which he has lived: there is nothing to be afraid of. (One might be tempted to add: 'except fear itself.' But such a thought, and the possibility behind it, is quite alien to the world of the *Iliad*.)

H.A. Mason makes an aesthetic criticism of Chapman's translation that has a moral significance: he says 'Chapman's parallels and antitheses are too insistent: "and shall we not exceed,/As much in merit, as in noise? Come be we great in deed/As well as look; shine not in gold, but in the flames of fight" '.[25] This is indeed a deeply important limitation of Chapman's achievement for the significance of these antitheses, read in the inescapable light of Shakespeare's liberation in the succeeding years of English poetic diction, is the incongruous suggestion that Sarpedon is dwelling with pleasure on his own words, is delighting in *thought* and *talk* about action where the whole point of the speech is that it shows us, not a man contemplating action but a man drawing the consequences of thought in action as he strides to meet his fate, urging his fellow warrior on.

Subject to this qualification, we see this passage about Sarpedon as a fit expression of something so 'honourable, fair, becoming, noble, generous' that it 'takes possession of the heart, and animates us to embrace and maintain it'.[26] As such, it is an appropriate item for the kind of enquiry Hume proposed into the 'true origin of morals'.

An ethical enquiry which takes as its starting-point not the dogmatic certainties of utilitarianism or the Kantian philosophy but a range of human sympathies capable of being moved by Homer *has* to

---

[24] *Iliad* XII; (ed.) Shepherd 148.
[25] *To Homer Through Pope*.
[26] Hume 172.

find some place for the 'personal qualities' celebrated in Sarpedon's speech. Sarpedon exhibits toughness of mind in his recognition of the relation between action and his honour's reality and of the impossibility of avoiding 'wrack/In this life's human sea' and he shows prodigious courage in drawing the consequences of what he knows in what he does. These are formidable virtues and require their recognition. Let us now see how they relate to Jim, caught in the dilemma between war and pacifism.

Three points require clarification before we proceed. Sarpedon is inescapably a warrior with no scruple about war-making, whereas Jim is not. Sarpedon is an aristocrat, utterly unashamed about the social distinction that he has enjoyed; Jim is not necessarily that. Sarpedon is already unequivocally committed to the view that disaster is humanly unavoidable; what view is Jim to take of that?

The shameless bloodiness of the protagonists is taken for granted in the *Iliad*, and any calling of it into question would result in a view of the Trojan war utterly different from Homer's: Homer celebrates certain qualities in his heroes on the assumption that killing in battle is not the sort of thing that calls into question any personal quality worth mentioning. The whole balance and stress of his argument rests on this assumption. But the qualities in Sarpedon that are enacted in the speech we have been discussing do not rest on the assumption: the Homeric celebration of these qualities, but not the qualities themselves, presupposes the non-questioning of mere bloodshed. There is therefore no reason to suppose that Jim might not possess the very same qualities, though of course Jim could not possibly be a Homeric hero: no one in the *Iliad* entertains good wishes towards all men and all sentient beings – the question cannot arise. Jim, given his good wishes towards all men and his adherence to Kantian principle necessarily has a scruple that is necessarily not found in Sarpedon. But he may nevertheless be 'Sarpedon-like', in the sense that implies praise.

Personally, we have little time for aristocracies (and that not only because of the little time aristocracies have for us). But what is important about the relation between Sarpedon's lordliness and Jim is not the question of whether Jim can be an aristocrat but the question of whether he must be if he is to be seriously compared to Sarpedon. If the aristocratic tendency of Sarpedon's thought is an essential feature of his celebrated qualities the possible ethical significance of those qualities is seriously affected – for it becomes an important question what one is to make of 'virtues' that can be exhibited only by some members of some social orders – the relation between ethics and politics becomes acutely problematic. If, on the other hand, the lordliness of Sarpedon is merely a part of Homer's story rather than of that which this part of the poem celebrates, these difficult problems do not arise.

To settle this issue it is necessary to establish the logic of Sarpedon's argument. Roughly speaking, his argument is a practical syllogism: (1) 'The renown of such people as you, Glaucus, and me, Sarpedon, exists merely in look unless we now realise it in deed'; (2) 'We must sometime wrack in this life's human sea'; *therefore* (3) 'Come! Into battle!' The problem is to determine just what (1) amounts to. Sarpedon invokes the social status of himself and Glaucus, but how important is it?

Sarpedon is saying: We receive the people's praise. This is praise either for something real or for something which is mere appearance. If we go and fight now it is praise for something real, otherwise it is praise for mere appearance. The reason that he mentions the inevitability of somewhere suffering disaster is that he wants to save something from the wreck ('wrack'). The something that can be saved is either the praise of something unreal or it is that which makes the people's praises into praise of something real. Not the least of Sarpedon's virtues is his desire to save from the wreckage something real. He does not retreat into dreams or fantasies but goes out to make something real.

It is for our argument vital to get the nuance right here. It is not that Sarpedon is saying: 'We have received the people's praises and now is the time when we must act in such a way as to deserve them.' That would make him out to be repaying a debt: the people have lent him meats, cups, goodlier roofs, delightsome gardens, etc., and now is the time to pay them back, maybe even with interest. In Homer, there is no hint of owing anything to the people; it is not even suggested that these aristocrats owe it to themselves to be really brave. There is a glory in what Sarpedon is doing (and putting into words) which any such hint of debts would obscure. He is, entirely as a matter of course given the person that he is, making real that which stands against time's wrack. He is not obeying the law of his nature, but fulfilling it.

Let us suppose Jim to be a thorough pleb. It will be recalled that an essential part of his moral psychology, distinguishing him from the Kantian moral hero, was that his times of indifference to or hatred of mankind were at most bad patches in which, as in a dream, he lost sight of the reality that normally sustained him. Another way of expressing this is to say that he is characteristically not sunken in a despair or listlessness from which he is saved only by a sense of duty that takes no delight in the good enjoyed by others or by himself. We assume, here as throughout, that Jim is rather intelligent.

If he is both characteristically rejoiced by the good enjoyed by others and by himself and also intelligent, it will hardly escape his notice that he has something good to thank others for. However miserable his background, he will necessarily have received much good from others, if only the enlivening joy of watching the self-absorbed delight of children; and he must know this. Furthermore, if he has been happy enough even in the rootless twentieth century to live among persons to whom he had good reason to refer as 'my people', 'the people to whom I belong', he will have to reckon these people, and the good he has received from, with and among them as a part of the good he has known.

Two attitudes towards the good he has experienced are interestingly possible for Jim: he may see it as either internally or as merely externally related to his own actions. The jargon here can perhaps best be made plain by reference to a related matter which has been discussed by Peter Winch.[27] Winch points out that someone who undergoes punishment can interpret their suffering either in a merely external way as such-and-such a quantity of pain, deprivation of liberty, loss of money, etc., inflicted by such-and-such a person or agency for such-and-such a reason of their own; or can interpret it as the very meaning of what they have done. In the latter but not the former case, the criminal will typically think, 'This is perfectly frightful but no worse than I deserve.' In that case there is an *internal* relation between the crime and the punishment.

A thoroughly unendearing internal relation between the good that one has experienced and one's own actions is the thought, 'That was very nice but no better than I deserve.' Often more appropriate is the internal connection that comes out in the thought, 'That was so good – in such sharp contrast with what I deserve.' But the internal connection which interests us is neither of these. Suppose that Jim, reluctantly perhaps, reflects upon some morally fine action that he is performing while he is doing it and blushes to realise[28] that the thing he is doing is a fitting complement to the good that he has received: it would be not inappropriate if such good as he has received should be added to the author of such actions. Such a thought would not be unduly or falsely modest for two reasons: no one is a self-made moral

---

[27] 'Ethical Reward and Punishment.'

[28] We suggest that modesty is a necessary part of the good man. This might be disputed on the ground that the good man of all people has nothing to blush about. Our reply is that the good man is necessarily *astonished* at his own moral excellence, necessarily regards it with *amazement*. If this were not the case, the good man would be a being without any anti-moral tendencies in himself: he would be hardly human – what Kant calls a 'holy will'. Cf. *The Moral Law* 78.

man and the good Jim has received is part-author of the good action he is doing – he cannot claim all the credit; and the impersonality of the thought is appropriate to the impersonal form of the Kantian imperative, 'Treat humanity, whether in your own person or in the person of another, always as an end and never merely as a means.'

Now it is of course possible that it should never enter Jim's head to consider the relation between the good that he has received and his own actions. (Similarly, Sarpedon might never have thought about the relation between praise and the person praised.) But suppose he does, as is not impossible. One thought is not available to Jim as it is available to Sarpedon: praise, that Sarpedon receives, is necessarily praise for something; and realisation of this fact about the logic of praise readily leads on to Sarpedon's reflections that his people's praises are praise for something real, or merely an appearance. But good, which Jim receives, is not necessarily good *for* something. It is not, for example, a loan: it is gratuitous. It would not be the good that it is if it had been given with strings attached.

8. The virtue of gratitude

Closely connected with this is the paradox that although gratitude appears to have something to do with morality there is nevertheless something odd about the idea that there is an *obligation* of gratitude. In terms of the Kantian philosophy, the oddity of any such obligation can be explained by saying that gratitude is a feeling and mere feelings lie outside morality. But this hardly gets to the bottom of the matter. Of course we will sometimes think none the worse of someone if they do not *feel* grateful (perhaps the benefactor is an ungracious person about whom it is impossible to feel anything but irritation and confusion). But this does not mean that it is ever all right for someone not to *be* grateful when they have received some gratuitous good.

What is meant by *being* grateful? It seems to us that gratitude is neither more nor less than recognising that one has received good from somebody and, should occasion present itself, returning good for good. Returning good for evil (e.g. in Christian terms), returning evil for good (e.g. in the manner of Lucifer), returning evil for evil (e.g. according to the maxim of an eye for an eye) have all received extensive discussion in ethics. But returning good for good has, in Western moral philosophy, been seen mainly as a matter of doing justice, that is, returning for good received that which is a due return. The reason gratitude is a conceptually tricky notion is that gratitude is what is appropriate when there is the possibility of returning good for a good received which was gratuitous. To accuse someone of being ungrateful towards oneself is peculiarly humiliating because it is uttering a moral reproach in circumstances where nothing is due: one gave a gift, one did not make a loan and so one has no claim to vindicate in uttering the reproach. The returning of good to oneself can, under such circumstances, only be spontaneous; but if the reproach is effective, that for which one is calling is impossible. One is under the extreme humiliation of asking the impossible.

Gratitude requires *thoughtfulness* in a way that mere justice does not. If you have made me a loan it does not require any insight on my part to know that sometime the loan is due for repayment: there is nothing my thought can contribute once I understand the transaction. But if you have given me a gift, the possibility of my returning good for good is not written into the transaction: since a gift is without strings, there is nothing about that which I have received and nothing about your having given it to me that tells me that there might be occasions on which it is for me to return good for your good. This is something I have to see for myself. It is morally important for me to see it: if I do not, I shall be thoroughly ungrateful or only incompletely grateful and ingratitude is a serious moral matter. This is one of the reasons why it is so important that the developing moral agent should be reproached for ingratitude: unless they are naturally grateful, they can learn to be so only by recognising in their own lives cases in which they have failed in this regard.

Jim is a fully-grown moral agent and as such capable of gratitude. Gratitude can play the same part in his plebeian life that aristocratic reflections upon the people's praise played in Sarpedon's speech. For if Jim is to be grateful he will consider the good he has experienced as internally related to his actions, not as externally related to them. For he will necessarily be asking himself: what actions of mine would be a fitting expression of gratitude for the good that I have received? As a person in whose life gratitude is operative, he will necessarily be thinking as follows: I have received good from my people. This good is either met with a grateful return of good or it is met with something less than gratitude. If I do such-and-such now I shall be returning good for good; otherwise the good I have received will be met with something less than gratitude. This argument is precisely parallel to that which we found in Sarpedon's speech. In drawing the consequences in action from the argument by doing the act that shows gratitude Jim, like Sarpedon, will be not obeying but fulfilling the law of his nature. It is therefore possible for Jim to be in a serious sense Sarpedon-like without being an aristocrat: he might be a grateful pleb.

9. The tragic sense of life

This brings us to the third point requiring clarification about the relation between Jim and Sarpedon. We have examined the difference between the two in their attitude to killing, and the relation between Sarpedon's clear-eyed attitude to praise and Jim's gratitude. We noted that Sarpedon is unequivocally committed to the view that disaster is humanly unavoidable; what view is Jim to take of that? Nothing that we have so far said about Jim warrants any particular view of this question. To answer it, it is necessary to add something to what has gone before. The addition that we suggest is this. We have been assuming throughout that Jim is a mature moral agent, with the intellectual qualities and strengths of character that maturity brings. Now, it is surely a part of maturity to have had acquaintance with the disasters that characteristically beset human beings: the mature moral agent has seen the best of men suffer irrevocable defeat in things on which the best part of his heart was set, and has seen death and deformity destroy and mar otherwise undefeated lives. An otherwise admirable moral agent may, through inexperience, have not yet faced these things either as afflictions of other people or as facts of his own life. But not to have faced them, and faced them out, is not virtue, merely lack of experience. An essential part of fully developed personal merit is surely to have seen, in others and in oneself, failure in the most important of things and the disastrous onset of death and disease. These things, which in the Greek imagination distinguish men from gods and entail a certain triviality in the lives of the gods, are inseparable from the way the world is.

To say this is not to imply any particular philosophy or theology. It is quite consistent to agree that death and failure are inescapable in human life and yet to give all one's efforts and hopes to the attempt to hasten economic revolution. One can admit the facts and yet argue, as Kant does, for an afterlife in which the good in the individual human being is slowly brought to perfection. To assert the facts is to deny the perfectibility neither of society nor of the individual. Admitting the facts is not yet assigning to them any particular significance: *that* they have some importance is a necessary part of their being truly recognised; but *what* importance they have remains to be determined – one view of the world might demand their contemplation, as a way of ·humbling an over-proud heart (*memento mori*); another might require that they be admitted only with the profoundest of suspicion (any harping on them being a liberal evasion); another might give them the prominence they have in Sarpedon's speech – the backdrop that gives to individual life its urgency and glory, regardless of what if anything may follow this life for the individual soul and follow this present social and political order in the world.

The kind of urgency found in Sarpedon's speech is important for our theme. Even in Chapman's Elizabethan translation, haunted as it is by the Elizabethan consciousness of 'fell, decaying time', Sarpedon is not saying, 'Hurry, for death is at our heels.' His movement towards the fateful encounter is quite without anxiety or mere hurry: his being is coming to fulness, fruition, ripeness. The urgency is not in his actions or thoughts but in the context that requires such actions and thoughts: it is simply that, given the situation, now is the time when action is required. Such a thing is impossible for the Greek gods: because they are immortals with an undifferentiated endless future in front of them there can be no urgency in their circumstances. However badly things go with them in the short term, they always have more time in which to re-group and fight back. There are no final battles for the gods. Their situation becomes poignant only when they fall in love with mortals and are touched by the finality of mortal time.

Precisely Sarpedon's kind of urgency is possible, and in a way necessary, for Jim. His wishes, like those of the gods, are entangled with mortal men: given his starting-point, the emotions of which all else is but a codification, Jim cannot but recognise that now is the time. The gratitude which underlies his action, as aristocratic pride underlies Sarpedon's, does not have an indefinite god-like future in which to play. Those to whom he is grateful are dying: if the grateful man is to come to fruition, now is necessarily the time. Of course, Jim may also be anxious and rushed – for we have allowed a great deal of latitude in respect of Jim's psychological make-up. But the urgency in his actions cannot be solely a matter a merely psychological (as Kant would say 'pathological') anxiety, worry and hurry. If he is to be a mature and intelligent moral agent at all he must be acting with knowledge of the urgency of the situation: either he acts now, time being what it is, or the gratitude that is in him cannot become real.

10. *War as the last flicker of humanity*

So much for the comparison of Jim and Sarpedon. Let us now return to the question: how can one have the face to suggest, in this anti-heroic age, that there is a moral problem facing Jim in the choice between pacifism and fighting in company with his people in their hour of greatest glory? We were imagining Jim's people to be facing annihilation, at the hands of an enemy who would grant no quarter to those who tried to surrender. The options facing the people are to die like sheep or to die fighting. To die like sheep is to die apart, each lonely and passive, doing nothing that might be regarded as a flicker of human life. To die fighting is to die together, even if each is bleeding in his own separate ditch: for overriding the physical separation is the unity of a common action and purpose; to fight when there is nothing else to do is at least to show a flicker of life.

Why is the prospect of thousands of people trudging quietly to a passive death in the extermination camps so deeply oppressive? It seems to us to be not only the cruelty of their oppressors but the deadness of the victims that makes one long to turn away one's eyes. Why are the few inhabitants of the camps who, set to guard their fellow-prisoners, turned their guns on their captors so moving? Here at least is a flicker of life: without hope of bringing about a better state of affairs in the world, without any purpose that is readily comprehensible in most systems of ethics, these few at least fought back. The Kantian principle enjoins reverence for the humanity in other persons and in oneself. In the trudge to the gas chambers humanity has already been extinguished; in the forlorn fighting back it is still visible, just.

These remarks about the camps might be thought to offend against Jewish and against Christian tradition. It might be thought that the Jewish notion of Israel as the suffering servant provides an understanding of the camps different, and deeper, than that just suggested; and that the image of Christ on the cross is outraged by our interpretation. It is possible here to offer only the briefest response. The suffering servant is *serving*: he is active in his master's business. It makes excellent sense to understand the observation by Jews (and Jehovah's Witnesses?) of their prescribed form of life in the camps in terms of the suffering servant: this is life lived in obedience. But, unless it can be shown that the submission to Nazi oppression is part of the ordained life, the notion of the suffering servant does not there apply. We do not believe that the link can be established: of course, there are connections between the non-resistance of so many victims of the holocaust and the history of Jewish life. But obedience is life according to law, not history.

A similar point can be made about the application of the Cross. The passion of Christ is a revelation not of passivity but of activity: Jesus is actively obeying his heavenly father. His crucifixion is not to be considered in isolation from the larger whole of which it forms a part: it is but a part of the challenge to Jerusalem, in which Jesus is active and on the offensive. To see the passion as passivity is to trivialise it. For where, without obedience, is its victory?

These remarks must serve to suggest that a hopeless fight may be *good*. Where no other flicker of humanity is possible, and there is at least the possibility of a fight, combat on the part of the people may be good.

If this is granted, Jim's problem emerges more fully. On the one hand the pacifism of scruple constrains him to avoid action with a military dimension. But on the other hand, he is under the urgent necessity of returning good for good. His people, from whom he has received good, are now engaged in a final fight. It is not that they need him ('would you and I alone,/Without more help, might fight this royal battle'). It is that the fight is good and how can he, grateful as he is to these his people, stand aside? He cannot be one of those who 'fears his fellowship to die with us'; he necessarily desires to die in that people's company.

It is possible that a person might face something like Jim's problem without understanding it, and without its being quite the problem that Jim faces. If, for whatever reason, a person judges that fighting would be absolutely wrong, he cannot have Jim's problem: for to override one's conscience is hardly doing good, and therefore cannot be an example of returning good for good. But let us remain with Jim, who has not yet made up his mind whether to fight.

Jim's problem has a rather direct bearing on the Allied bombing campaign against Germany. We pointed out in Chapter One that an important element in the bombing effort, particularly in the early part of the war, was the desire to hurt the enemy. In Chapter Three we quoted Miss Anscombe to the effect that the campaign was prosecuted 'largely out of a villainous hatred'. Miss Anscombe's opinion is widely shared, and will be seen by many as finding unequivocal support in any reference to a desire to hurt the enemy when one can do nothing more effective. Now, no doubt there is something to be said for Miss Anscombe's view; but it is surely one-sided. Many, including some of the leading protagonists, saw the situation facing the UK in 1940-41 as having precisely that desperate urgency into which we have put Jim. They thought of themselves as a people fighting for its survival in a war which, if it crossed the Channel, would be one of extermination. Perhaps they were mistaken about the facts, perhaps their judgment was too hasty. For example, there was at this time a group including Lloyd George and Basil Liddell Hart which favoured a separate peace with Hitler.[29] We now know that Hitler too desired such a peace. How long it would have lasted is a moot point: Hitler seems to have intended it to last only until the defeat of Russia when he would turn his reinforced energies

[29] Paul Addison 'Lloyd George and the Compromise Peace' in *Lloyd George: Twelve Essays* (ed.) A.J.P. Taylor.

to a final and perhaps annihilating onslaught against the UK. But it is facile to attach much moral significance to such factual judgment. If the UK experience seems unconvincing, the most perfunctory reflection on Russian suffering will furnish an incontrovertible example, from a few months later, of a people literally and without any need of qualification fighting against an enemy bent on individual annihilation.

What is the significance of this? Are we saying that the bombing, insofar as it was a matter of trying to hurt the enemy in circumstances where it was impossible to do anything more constructive, was *justified morally*? This is not what we are saying. Our claim is being made from within a different context of ethical thinking. It is this: there is good moral reason, which we have set out at length, for interpreting this least productive of the bombing as an exercise of virtue in a situation demanding existential choice from the best of men. The only way of fighting at this time was by means of bombing, which given the available technology was necessarily indiscriminate. To fight in what were taken to be the circumstances was, if our analysis of Sarpedon and Jim carries conviction, one of the two options in a situation requiring from the best of men (Jim) existential choice in a moral dilemma.

So, to put the question again, was it justified? It may not have been, in the sense that as a matter of fact all the individuals concerned were motivated by nothing but the desire for revenge. But insofar as those concerned were facing Jim's problem, and resolving Jim's dilemma in action, someone who condemned them as doing something unjustifiable would be missing the point.

It has to be added, however, that one aspect of doing the right thing is necessarily absent. For it was, and remains the case after he has chosen, that Jim is acting in a morally impossible situation. He will doubtless put this out of his mind for much of the time and exhibit the jauntiness of one who has come through a difficult decision. But it would require special philosophical explanation if, after the decision, there were no facts about Jim which supported the view that he has not lost sight of the impossibility of his decision. A good example of what such facts might be is the well-known contrast between the spirit of many in 1914 and in World War II. For the many who were later to suffer disillusionment, the moral skies were clear in 1914: there was an exultation of spirit, an expansiveness, no occasion to wear blinkers. But in 1939 the characteristic feeling in all countries was that one had a grim, unpleasant job to do.[30] One had to make the best of it. The

---

[30] D.C. Watt *Too Serious a Business* 110-34.

soldier's cheerfulness went in blinkers: certain questions were not to
be raised, there were many things to be laughed off (either you laugh
or you cry). Jim, if he opts for fighting, must go in blinkers: the
decision has been made and it would be worse than useless to keep
brooding on it; but the impossibility remains. It cannot be sloughed
off, for an existential choice only partly makes the man: he is already
part-formed; otherwise he would not be in a moral dilemma. The
clear skies of doing the right thing, which are perhaps implied in the
notion of justified or justifiable action, are absent from Jim's virtuous
waging of war, as from his virtuous pacifism.

So far, we have been examining only the most difficult and elusive
case of war, namely, war which has little or no chance of bringing
about any desirable state of affairs in the world. It might be thought
that this case is irrelevant because of Clausewitz's insistence that war
is an instrument of state policy. Politics, it might be suggested, is
forward-looking and concerned not with the heroics of the individual
soul but with the creation and maintenance of a frame for living. The
example we have been studying may make for good novels and poems
but is irrelevant to politics.

This is seriously mistaken. Clausewitz is of course right that the
politician must understand the peculiar properties of those
instruments of state policy which have a military dimension; but
equally important is that he should understand what *politics* is. If he is
any good he is no doubt adept at politicking, but that is no guarantee
of an understanding of the nature and possible variety of politics. The
idea that politics is in all circumstances an activity of bringing about
good states of affairs in the world is seriously misleading. For one
thing, as we shall now try to show, it has the serious consequences of
rendering terrorism incomprehensible.

The essential point is that Jim's resort to war is, among other things,
a political act. He acts, if this is the choice he makes, in solidarity with
his people. His people may be a polity, or they may be one of those
other orderings of human relationships which in the modern world
result in politically-divided man. Suppose, for example, that Jim is an
East Ender: he is quite unmoved by Winston Churchill's speeches
invoking Britain. For him, Churchill is the man who used the troops
against the workers and Britain is a fictional entity used to exploit the
working class in general and the East End of London in particular.
For good or ill, such views of the state in which one and one's people
are doomed to live are characteristic of our time (maybe of all times).
What poses a moral problem for Jim is not the battering being taken
by the United Kingdom ('Those nobs wanted taking down') but the
fact that Hitler is hitting the East End: one's own people are being

threatened with annihilation. If, as suggested in Chapter Two, it is right in general to see politics as the activity both of states and of persons whose allegiances are divided, then Jim's warfare will be political. He will be quite right to say 'I'm fighting for the East End.' If he is not to be an ungrateful wretch, of course it is the East End he is fighting for. Similarly, many a German was fighting for Hamburg rather than Hitler. This is the nature of political action: a chaos of loyalties finding expression in political action whose only contemporary ordering is the order of the interstate system. The very process of nation-building, which seeks to abolish divided loyalties, attests the fact: the loyalties are there, and strongly resist abolition.

Terrorists are often dismissed as people 'merely craving publicity'. The possibility of dismissing something on the ground that it is a search for publicity is a symptom of the inadequacy of political theories that disregard the politically-divided man. 'Seeking publicity' suggests the essentially trivial and non-political action of trying to get into the newspapers and on to television. But, more soberly, publicising something is bringing it into the public arena, making it a public matter, bringing it forward for public rather than merely private consideration.[31] The terrorist intent on obtaining maximum publicity is not engaged merely in the private search for notoriety (as some *murderers* appear to be). Although there may be strong within him, as within many of us, the desire for public exposure and attention, what he is trying to do (regardless of motivation) is to bring a certain grievance into the public arena. Often, he may hope that once it has arrived there something will be done: such hopes are sometimes realistic, sometimes look even more far-fetched than the British hope in 1940 of eventual victory. But bringing the grievance into the public realm may have a moral significance apart from all productiveness: the moral significance of the last faint flicker of humanity in resistance to an oppressor. 'They destroyed us, but at least we told the world, and that hurt them.' This may be revenge talking, or the last spark of humanity, or a mixture of both. The terrorist search for publicity can be dismissed only if the bombing to hurt, and Sarpedon's heroic throw, are also dismissed out of the political realm.

11. Simmons' account of his pacifist stand

To conclude this long discussion of the relation between pacifism and non-pacifism, we want to examine a most interesting account of his

---

[31] Hannah Arendt *The Human Condition.*

own history by Clifford Simmons, who became a conscientious objector and then joined the army:[32]

> By the time I was three years old, both my parents were dead – my father was killed at Passchendaele in 1917 and my mother died soon afterwards from an illness brought on by grief. I have always supposed that my ensuing bewilderment helped to form in me an obsessional interest in the problem of war and the conditions which cause men to resort to violence.
> ... Although I had received formal religious education, the Church of England, as I knew it, before I reached the age of twenty, meant nothing to me ... I was at a loss to understand how it was possible for the voice of the Church to reconcile the Christian way of life with the picture of war which I had formed in my mind. How could the lines of dead, in khaki and field grey uniforms, lying side by side on a field of mud and tangled barbed wire be reconciled with the gospel of good-will to all men which Christianity had preached for nearly two thousand years?
> ... In my early twenties I left my job in the Midlands and became a social worker in London. I was fortunate in being associated with the church of St Martin-in-the-Fields, a place where, at last, I found, in practice, a living Christianity nearer to my own beliefs.
> ... When fighting began in Spain I found that I had great sympathy for the Spanish government and with those who went from this country and many others to fight against Franco. If there were any justification for war the struggle of the Spanish people against the forces of Fascism was surely it. However, believing that one should not take life in any circumstances and that violence would beget violence, I could only stand miserably aside and watch the departure of some of my friends.

On being conscripted, Simmons claimed unconditional exemption from military service and on appeal got it. During the Blitz he worked with the Civil Defence Services and 'felt that I was making some contribution to mitigating the effects of war ...':

> When the bombing stopped I started to worry about the comfortable circumstances in which I lived. The war had hardly touched me at all. I knew that I was involved in it whether I liked it or not – after all, some of the food I ate came from overseas in convoys protected by armed ships, and I was alarmed by the thought that men were losing their lives in order to feed me. It seemed to me that, professing Christian beliefs, I could not stand aside from the experiences of others. I remembered my time in Germany and thought of what was happening to the Jewish population and to those who were in opposition to Hitler's government. I had been made aware of the existence of the concentration camps ... I still believed that the position of the pacifist was ultimately right but I was beginning to realise that, at the same time, I could not stand aside from the struggle which was engulfing my contemporaries ...

[32] Clifford Simmons (ed.) *The Objectors* 7-27.

In May 1942 I became a trooper in the Royal Armoured Corps. I had no illusions that this action would resolve my doubts, but I found comfort in allying myself with those who were actively struggling against Fascism ... I felt that I had won my own freedom and that my reasons for becoming a soldier were entirely my own, not those of any external authority. My original stand against war still had for me great validity, since I felt that I had protested against the right of any government to exact unquestioning obedience in matters which touched upon human conscience or the moral law. Even after joining the Army, from time to time I found myself in opposition to those in authority over me, especially when their attitudes were unnecessarily brutal – Fascism was what I had joined up to fight and I could not tolerate its appearance amongst a few of those who were training me ...

Simmons took part in the Normandy landings and after the war spent five months as a staff officer in the Ruhr, a job which brought him into 'constant contact with the German people'. Among those he met

A German officer – a Roman Catholic, who was never a Nazi – regretted the fact that Germany had lost the war, because he himself was a German. His remark emphasised for me the dangers of nationalism. I had been right to be suspicious of the teaching that one's highest duty was to one's country ...

This narrative is disarmingly modest and honest. It is a sympathetic example of an attitude to war which is widely shared. The argument turns on a polarity between two sets of allegiances. Simmons is committed throughout to 'a living Christianity', to 'not standing aside', to 'allying myself with those who were actively struggling', to 'conscience' and 'moral law'. He is against 'the voice of the Church', 'the government' if it tries to encroach on conscience, 'those in authority ... especially' – but presumably not only – 'when their attitudes were unnecessarily brutal'. Above all he wants to do things for reasons 'entirely my own, not those of any external authority'. The polarity imports certain contradictions into the argument: in a passage not quoted he praises the provision for exemption in the British legislation and the generosity with which the law was administered; yet he congratulates himself on having made a protest against the right of governments to exact unquestioning obedience. But this is perhaps on the surface, merely an effect of a polarity of rhetoric.

A somewhat deeper correlative of the polarity is the pathos which pervades the story – 'I could only stand miserably aside', 'I found comfort in allying myself ...' etc. – one gets the impression of a prodigious moral loneliness. From the viewpoint adopted in the present chapter, this is not surprising. There are two features of

Simmons' story which attest our emphasis on the moral importance of gratitude. He brings to mind the fact 'men were losing their lives in order to feed me', but the response he reports is not gratitude: 'I was alarmed.' And his discussion of the German officer is too brisk: maybe the man was simply a victim of 'nationalism'. But it is just as possible that the man was reflecting on the defeat of *his people*, a disaster that could not but sadden beyond measure anyone with deep ties to (let us say) the Ruhr.

The only people apart from the narrator in the story are isolated individuals who show brutality or kindness (e.g. the second in command of the regiment who learns that Simmons had been an objector but still respects him and recommends him for a commission). Simmons happened to be in London during the Blitz, but there is, understandably, no sense of what is being done to *us*, what *we the East End* are going through. The kinds of corporate being which represent the most formidable threat to nationalism, and which nationalism necessarily seeks to mobilise in its own interest, are absent. The solidarity that Simmons seeks is not corporate being but an alliance of separate human atoms. His enemy, 'Fascism', is naturally an abstract thing for there is no palpable body politic to be fought for. He is distressed so long as he has to 'stand miserably aside', but his comprehension of that from which he is standing aside is extremely selective: we see his friends going off to fight in Spain, but there is no hint that he is also standing aside from the tense struggle to administer the United Kingdom in peace and war.

Finally, notice his idea of the dead. He never mentions the possibility, even to dismiss it, that his father died for him and his generation. (It would, of course, be a bit much to expect him to do so.) Other dead are viewed in a very external way: all we see is the corpses 'on a field of mud and barbed wire', etc. The question of whether these were men who lived well and died well is not raised. In seeing the dead in this way, Simmons is at one with some (but not all) of the war poets and with much of the anti-war literature of the twenties and thirties. 'The poetry is in the pity.'[33]

There seems from the narrative to be no doubt that Clifford Simmons, like Jim, has good wishes towards all men. But what relation does he assume between wish and action? And what does he take the good for man to consist in? His understanding of the connection between good wish and action is immediately practical: in London he 'found, in practice, a living Christianity nearer to my own beliefs'. By helping people he lives what he believes: he is engaged in

---

[33] Wilfred Owen *Collected Poems* Preface.

doing, in producing good. This impulse is like that of the classic utilitarianism: the good is believed to be a certain thing and the natural expression of the belief is in efforts to bring as much as possible of the good into being. This is certainly one way in which good wishes can be translated into action. But it is not the only, or necessarily the best form. A different one is the Kantian, and another the modified Kantian, concept of the good will sketched in this chapter. The Kantian accepts systematically that each person has his own moral life to live and, as has been pointed out above, has sometimes to do some other thing than maximise the good. From within a drastically modified Kantian framework we have studied at length two non-utilitarian constraints which there might be upon the man of good wish: the pacifism of scruple; and the necessity, arising out of gratitude, to fight alongside one's people. We have suggested that these two constraints can create an existential dilemma. Jim is as much a pacifist as Simmons, though for different reasons.

For Jim, the Anglican attitude to World War I may be even more appalling than it is to Clifford Simmons. For the church was preaching war as 'the lesser evil', thus condemning brave soldiers to be seen as doing (however lesser) *evil*. For Jim, on the other hand, some of these soldiers may be doing *good*, at least so far as their grasp of the facts of the situation allows: for they may be self-sacrificingly giving their lives for others in a situation where there is no choice but this and mere passivity. The difference is that whereas Clifford Simmons is analysing the situation in utilitarian terms (what did it all lead to? what was the good of it?) Jim's eyes are fixed on the personal merit, to use Hume's term, of those involved. He can see such merit, Sarpedon-like, even in the showing of 'vain valour' and the 'glorifying' of 'a folly'. In his eyes, talk of 'the lesser evil' is the preaching of a lie.

Lying behind this is a perception of death and the meaning of death which is richer and less abstract than that which is found in the narrative quoted. One has only to compare 'the lines of dead, in khaki and field grey uniforms, lying side by side on a field of mud and tangled barbed wire' with

O friend, if keeping back
Would keep back age from us, and death, and that we might not wrack
In this life's human sea at all, but that deferring now
We shunn'd death ever, nor would I half this vain valour show,
Nor glorify a folly so, to wish thee to advance.

The modern passage has us look at the mute dead; Homer, Chapman evoke the living who are intimate with death and with life's disasters. In the *Iliad* one sees men living and dying, but not dead. The detail is graphic, but death is always an inseparable part of the life of which it is the end. The desecration of Hector's body is not the grotesque mangling of some anonymous corpse, but monstrous outrage to both religion and the mighty hero whom Homer shows to us in battle, debate and in the most private of family scenes. It is not merely a literary convention that Sarpedon delivers his speech to somebody: his world is a public one, in which friends face out death together, not a private one in which men make alliances against 'isms' and come together only when their bodies are laid low together in battle, or laid out for burial.

Is it unfair to suggest that one aspect of 'wrack/In this life's human sea' is the recognition, enforced by experience, of the final impossibility of a utilitarian, a merely practical, attitude to one's cherished wishes towards mankind? The utilitarian impulse to produce as much good as possible receives constant checks, and is incessantly embroiled in perplexities of its own making, partly because it is an adolescent or a young man's system of values. It has built into it no systematic acceptance of the necessity that each should live his own life. Whatever the safeguards one attempts to build into it (e.g. Bentham insisted that in his calculus of felicities each person was to count for one), the utilitarian system is against one. Again and again, any remotely rigorous formulation of utilitarianism is forced back to the idea of happiness as a universal, something like the sea, which is to be maximised. If good wishes towards all men are given a form that aims always at maximising the good, the form works against the initial impulse to cherish each separate man. The same is true of such a thing as that social work which enables Simmons to find 'a living Christianity'. The social worker cannot give any but the most fragmentary expression to his good wishes: the dead weight of human misery is too great. He is forced to choose those cases which are most hopeful, avoiding too much personal anguish over the others; he is forced to maintain a professional distance, so that he can live his life as a social worker and as a human being who is not just a social worker; he is forced to recognise that he cannot live his clients' lives for them; in short, he is forced to accept instead of a practical direct pursuit of the good, the Kantian maxim of striving to treat the humanity in himself and in other people as an end and never merely as a means. It may seem laborious to stress this obvious point, which is, perhaps, only important when an individual painfully discovers it for himself. Such criticism would be fair if one were discussing utilitarianism as a system, apart from that in virtue of which it 'takes possession of the heart, and animates us to embrace and maintain it'. But, as pointed out above, there is good philosophical reason for avoiding such abstractions.

12. Pacifism and the ethics of virtue

The general reasons for preferring a Kantian, or modified Kantian. view of the relation between wish and action to a utilitarian one are also reasons for rejecting an argument, glanced at above in Chapter Two, against pacifism and absolute scruple. Jan Narveson, it will be recalled, argues that pacifism is incoherent because what the pacifist is against is violence and in some situations the only way of being against violence is to use violence. We pointed out that the same argument could be deployed against the pacifism of scruple and against an absolute refusal of killing the innocent. What can now be said in reply to Narveson is this: there are more ways than one of being against or for something. If one is for something then one wishes it well. One way of translating this wish into action is the utilitarian one, but this is not the only way. Another is the Kantian, yet another the modified Kantian. These latter reflect, in a way that utilitarianism does not, the general fact about the human condition that it is for each to live his own moral life. This is a reason for preferring them to a utilitarian outlook. The charge of incoherence is tenable against a utilitarian pacifism, but not against a Kantian one.

If it is true that the Kantian recognition of the autonomy of each moral being is part of the felt tragedy of human life, the co-presence of the several contrasts between Jim and Clifford Simmons which we have pointed out is no accident. For Simmons' vigorous, touching and honest narrative is systematically innocent of that weight of experience which informs Sarpedon's speech. The considerations, for example, which would make it natural for Jim to be grateful if there are men losing their lives to feed him are simply not available in the Simmons narrative: he only sees the dead bodies; he misses the greater intimacy with life and death that shows that what matters is not the corpses but the life (e.g. the altruism) lived by the sailors.

In this chapter we have been feeling for an appropriate starting-point for ethical reflection. The one that we favour is that which concerns itself not with the search for principles or the analysis of situations but with the outline of virtue. We agree with Aristotle that in ethics and politics one must be content to have the truth 'roughly and in outline' and we follow Hume in examining that which may enter into a panegyric. The quality that we study is that of being 'Sarpedon-like' and this turns out to reveal a thoroughly unmodern intimacy with the meaning of death and the tragic quality of life. It does not imply an unreflective lack of scruple about war-making or an unashamedly aristocratic attitude to lofty social position. On the contrary, our pleb Jim is capable of being Sarpedon-like, and this generates the possibility that he, unlike Sarpedon, may be drawn into an existential dilemma. That he has such problems is, of course, conclusive proof that Jim has a conscience. In Chapters Five and Six we seek to draw out the implications of this moral starting-point for the idea of a just war.

In conclusion, we want to examine the suspicion that our analysis has done less than justice to pacifism. There seem to be three outstanding issues. First, our treatment of pacifism has been extremely selective. We make no apology for this: we have not essayed a general survey of pacifism, several of which are available.[34] We have taken up only those types and features of pacifism that seemed to bear most closely on our argument. Secondly, we have been silent in face of the massive inter-war insistence that any ethical concession to the idea of military heroism is exploitable. Thirdly, we may appear to have underestimated the Christian objection to taking life.

Exploitation. The search for a moral system resistant to all misunderstanding and abuse is an ancient and understandable one. It is also pretty hopeless. Words are weapons, so it is naturally desirable to take what precautions one can against articulating values in ways that can lead to abuse. But there is no reason to believe that any but very qualified success is possible, and good reason to doubt. Because words are susceptible of tendentious reinterpretation, their exploitation is only to be expected. There is only one commodity which is resistant to exploitation, and that is the good man, who requires all his cunning and character for the struggle and is quite likely to be defeated. This is perhaps one of the things Aristotle had in mind in insisting that ethics and politics must remain satisfied with outlines. The law necessarily seeks safeguards against abuse and is nevertheless constantly frustrated and hamstrung in its search for fool-proof and knave-proof formulations. But in conversation among friends, as ethical and political discourse is,[35] there is not the need for such safeguards: we who are neither fools nor knaves but free men seeking to know our own minds do not require, as we cannot obtain, a guarantee against the exploitation of our ideas.

The inter-war criticism of the idea of heroism was in large part *self*-criticism: the writers were people who had been taken in and who could not, even as they were writing, quite trust themselves to give their due to honour and heroism. Such things, having misled, were not to be trusted. It was therefore inevitable that in attacking the false use of the language of honour, writers about World War I should ridicule *all* thought of honour. But their work is done now only too well. The

[34] See e.g. Bainton *Christian Attitudes*; Yoder *Nevertheless*.
[35] This Socratic concept of ethics and politics is elaborated in Chapter Six below.

difficult thing now is to give any credulity at all to the notion of the hero (witness the staggering contrast between the very great excellence of many recent productions of Shakespeare comedies and the paucity and feebleness of almost all productions of the tragedies). This is a dangerous situation. It results in an absence of any educated alternative to the crassest kinds of hero-worship, and it cuts us from our roots in the Western tradition that begins with Homer. It impoverishes our sense of the meaning of death, forcing us to see only the corpses and not the persons for whom death is the end of a good, or less than good, life. It weakens the guides and props which the tradition furnishes for the making and encouraging of free men. It diminishes us in the struggle for life and there is no good ethical reason for it. It is for others to determine whether there is good economic or historical reason for it, as Marx and Hegel respectively seem to suggest.

Christianity and the taking of. life. Is the taking of life always un-Christian? Our understanding is that Jesus brought men not the immortality enjoyed by the Greek gods, life unending in which nothing is finally urgent except the love of mortals, but *salvation.* The question is what Jesus is thought to be saving men from. Not, surely, from the fact that sooner or later each of them is reduced to a stinking corpse, but from the tragedy of life: its incompleteness, its lack of fullness, generosity, gratitude, kindliness, scruple, love.

There is a tenacious belief among many Christians that some moral system is God-given; that perfect obedience to God consists in living according to some lofty and demanding moral code and that Jesus saves us from the fact that, through sin, we are unable to make the grade. Some Christians who are mistrustful of systems and (often) of the cerebration they involve substitute for this the view that guidance in situational thinking is God-given – perfect obedience, once again, consists in doing this well and the hell from which men require salvation is the hell of doing it badly, or not at all. (Some Christians, of course, rely on a fundamentalist reading of the New Testament for, among other things, their pacifism or anti-pacifism.)

We are unable to see the cogency of any of these views. To speak in theistic terms for a moment, it is no doubt the case that among the many good gifts men have received from God is the gift of morality. But the crucial question, which is not theological but ethical and political, is how this gift is to be understood. Theologically speaking, the gift of morality like other gifts is presumably given to man for him to perfect in perfect obedience to the will of God. But what does this mean? From the ethical standpoint adopted in this chapter, the meaning should be fairly plain: what man receives from God is the capacity and opportunity for a virtuous life; what it is for man to do is to (simply) be virtuous. The human incapacity, lack of opportunity and sheer practical distaste for virtue is (part of) that from which men require salvation. What a saviour brings is not new virtues but a new understanding of the life of virtue. If virtue demands the taking of life, the saviour hardly gainsays this.

To render these somewhat abstract remarks more precise, let us consider once more the dilemma in which we placed Jim. One side of it was the moral demand that he should share, out of gratitude, in the glorious fight to the death of his people. One thing that might be said against this in New Testament terms is that Jesus founded a new community, a new Israel, so that for the Christian all men are his people. But to adduce the new Israel against our argument is a confusion which is a matter not of theology but of ethics and politics. The idea of the new Israel certainly implies that, after Paul, the Christian must have good wishes not only to every Jew but to every human being, because all are equally children of God, circumcised and uncircumcised alike. It also implies some sort of communal reality corresponding to these wishes. But it does not imply that the gratitude which is due to one's own people is due to all men; it does not *as such* obliterate the distinction between peoples. The community between peoples may be that, when at war, they remember one another's humanity in the solemn ritual before or (more likely) after battle. The inter-war idea of the interstate system as the family of nations has been swept into oblivion by war; but its religious counterpart, which supposes that direct political effect can be given to the common humanity of all children of God, still appears to sustain some sorts of Christian pacifism. Such ideas appear to us to rest on a mistake not of religion or theology but of ethics and politics.

The basic question is, does virtue demand the taking of life?

V

The Idea of a Just War

Clifford Simmons felt during the Blitz that he was 'making some contribution to mitigating the effects of war'. Many proponents of the idea of a just war have seen this, too, as a way of mitigating war's disasters. In this chapter we propose a different interpretation, which gives a deeper and more coherent basis to the idea.

When people speak of *the* just war tradition they mean something to which Augustine and Aquinas, Vitoria and Suarez contributed, and on which such modern writers as Father John C. Ford[1] and Paul Ramsey[2] have drawn. Either there is just one coherent thing which fits into this specification or the term 'the just war tradition' is a misnomer. But no one doubts that there is more than one just war tradition. For example, the 'aggressor-defender' theory of war is a rival to the classic tradition. According to the aggressor-defender theory, it is possible in real situations to distinguish between aggressors and defenders and the kind of conduct which is permitted to the defender is quite different from that to be expected of the aggressor. The aggressor-defender theory was widely held between the wars, and not always distinguished clearly from the classic just war tradition. But in the aftermath of the collapse of the League of Nations, there is good reason to make a sharp separation between the two. In this chapter we are mainly concerned with the classic just war tradition.

1. The Christian and the non-Christian

One important and difficult question about the tradition is: what is it? To give a short account of certain doctrines is useful for some teaching purposes but for philosophical purposes is most unsatisfactory, for one cannot read the classic authors without noticing contradictions between them. If it were possible to point to some agreed body of

---

[1] 'The Morality of Obliteration Bombing.'
[2] *War and the Christian Conscience* and *The Just War*.

gradually progressing doctrine, free of all internal contradiction, as 'the tradition' then the problem of identity would be simple; but such a ploy is impossible.

In view of this difficulty we suggest that the tradition is most readily identified by reference to certain perennial questions. In particular, the classic authors characteristically address themselves to the following two questions:

1. May the Christian, without sin, wage war?
2. What constraints are there upon the activity of the Christian in the waging of war?

These questions do not necessarily exhaust the tradition, but they appear to us to pervade it and to give to it its characteristic direction.

The idea of perennial questions is, of course, viewed with intense suspicion by many historians of ideas. But we do not mean to suggest that they are characteristic of the human mind or the human condition. Our belief is the more modest one that wherever Christians have had occasion to think about matters seen as having a military dimension, these two questions have presented themselves for consideration. It is to be expected that Christian thinking at all times and places will attempt to grapple with them as long as there exist such things as war and the enforcement of law, and as long as Christians attempt to live the Christian life in the world. Our two questions therefore suggest the kind of continuity that is to be expected in the classic tradition. (They are, of course, not the questions to be expected in the aggressor-defender theory.)

If it is right to see the tradition in this way then one rather obviously pressing question, given the frame of reference adopted in this book, is this: what significance has the classic tradition for the non-Christian? Karl Barth has argued that the theologian's primary responsibility is to speak to the Christian community as distinct from the non-Christian world, including so-called Christian civilisation.[3] By no means all theologians would agree with Barth, but it is clear that the non-engagement of theologians with the significance of the tradition for the non-Christian is at least understandable. But in this book we have assumed no particular religious premises, so the question is rather obviously pressing in a world where many do not regard themselves as Christians. The problem is discussed at length in this chapter.

A more general question of great practical importance is: what lies inside and outside the classic tradition? A very powerful orthodoxy

---

[3] For a brief and relatively mellow statement of Barth's position see *The Humanity of God*, especially the essay 'Evangelical Theology in the Nineteenth Century'.

about this has recently been called into question. Roland Bainton developed an influential typology which sees ethical thinking about war as having three distinct strands: the crusade/holy war tradition; the just war tradition; and pacifism.[4] This has been the basis for much of the sociological analysis of the ethics of war.[5] It also has a direct practical suggestiveness in that it depicts the just war tradition as a mean between two extremes. J.T. Johnson has now argued that the typology is highly dubious on historical grounds because, to mention just one point from a complex argument, the classic just war thinking of Vitoria and Suarez is inseparable from certain holy war ideas which were endemic in Europe at the time, and to which the classic formulation is a corrective.[6]

Johnson's argument is closely connected with a difficult question of theory. If the two perennial questions proposed above furnish the underlying principle of continuity in the tradition, what explains the contradictions which are manifest in it? Johnson in effect answers this by pointing out that different Christians have approached the two perennial questions from within different 'ideologies'. In sixteenth-century Europe, one ideology impelled Christians in the direction of holy war ideas, another ideology in the direction of the classic just war formulations of Vitoria and Suarez. Our purpose is not the historical one and we do not employ the notion of ideology, leaving it to the reader to determine what ideology governs our argument. Instead, our approach is more piecemeal: we analyse certain factors which might be ingredients in an ideology and suggest that these predispose different people to give different answers to the two perennial questions. Our analysis supports Johnson's historical findings and carries them further: not only is the well-entrenched division between holy war and just war artificial and misleading; the same is true of the division between just war and pacifism. But this is to anticipate.

So far we have suggested that the classic just war tradition is to be identified in Christian terms, hence raising the question of the interest in it of the non-Christian; and that it is to be understood as a dynamic historical entity containing many contradictions. We have indicated what we take to be its principles of continuity and hinted at the principles of change that we find within it. One further point: not all of the change comes from within. An essential part of the just war tradition is its changing *agenda*. As the world alters which the tradition seeks to comprehend, so the agenda changes for meetings of those who

---

[4] *Christian Attitudes*.

[5] Cf. in particular David Martin *Pacifism* and Michael Walzer *The Revolution of the Saints*.

[6] *Ideology, Reason and the Limitation of War*.

gather from time to time to ponder the two perennial questions 'May the Christian, without sin, wage war?' and 'What constraints are there upon the activity of the Christian in the waging of war?' For example, conditions since 1945 place the issue of war threats (deterrence) and the issue of non-state wars much higher on the agenda than they could possibly have been in the inter-war period.

The tradition is often stated in terms of a series of moral principles. Sydney Bailey has drawn attention to the crucial fact that these principles are largely negative in form, expressing prohibitions and restraints rather than permissions and mandates for war.[7] For example:

The waging of war is just *only if* there is a just cause, all peaceful channels have been tried and have failed, and there is a reasonable chance of success.

War is waged justly *only if* the principles of proportion and noncombatant immunity are observed, and there is a right intention.

Such principles enable one to identify many wars as *un*just but do not tell one when, if ever, a war is just.

Before examining such principles in detail, we want to consider the question of what significance they could possibly have for the non-Christian. This can be done most conveniently in terms of the analysis of some types of ethical theory contained in Chapter Four above. For the utilitarian, the principles will be valuable insofar as their observance maximises human happiness and/or minimises human unhappiness. For the consequentialist who is not a classic utilitarian, they will be valuable insofar as they promote his chosen goals. For example, the revolutionary will value them insofar as they enhance the chances of the revolution, or ease its birth-pangs. For the adherent of some version of power politics, they will be valued insofar as they are useful for his state and/or the interstate system. And so on. For the deontologist, they will be valuable insofar as they state or approximate or conduce to the observance of those principles which the deontologist regards as absolutely binding. For example, one who considers that the principle that innocent human beings are not to be killed is absolutely binding might value the principle of noncombatant immunity as a precise or approximate statement of an absolute obligation, or as a useful instrument for guiding public attention in the direction of absolute principle. For situation ethics, the principles may be valued as a stimulus to thought, guiding but not determining the analysis of real situations. Given the fact that adherents of these

[7] *Prohibitions and Restraints* xi.

various types of ethical outlook are some of them Christian and some non-Christian, it is to be expected that non-Christians will have an interest in the just war tradition. It is equally to be expected that the status of the principles will be the subject of widespread disagreement. Instead of tracing the many ensuing lines of thought one by one, we propose to argue solely from the modified Kantian viewpoint sketched in the last chapter. Some of the other outlooks will receive consideration when we turn to specific principles. The position of one who rejects all moral alignments will be examined in Chapter Six.

2. *Plato's discussion of war*

When we left Jim in the last chapter he was facing an existential dilemma between pacifism and joining his people in their last glorious hour of armed struggle against an oppressor who would grant no quarter. Let us now pull him back from this extremity and consider from his viewpoint the more usual kinds of problem that have a military dimension. He comes to these problems with good wishes towards all men: the killing of any human being is morally problematic for him because his good wishes extend to all human beings. In this regard his outlook contrasts sharply with that implicit in a passage from Plato's *Republic* which is often regarded as a precursor or early form of the just war tradition:

> And next, how will our soldiers deal with enemies? ... First take slavery. Is it right that Greek states should sell Greeks into slavery? Ought they not rather to do all they can to stop this practice and substitute the custom of sparing their own race for fear of falling into bondage to foreign nations?
>
> ... Certainly. Then they would be more likely to keep their hands off one another and turn their energies against foreigners.
>
> And what of ravaging Greek lands and burning houses? How will your soldiers deal with their enemies in this matter?
>
> I should like to hear your opinion.
>
> I think they should do neither, but only carry off the year's harvest ... It seems to me that war and civil strife differ in nature as they do in name, according to the two spheres in which disputes may arise: at home or abroad, among men of the same race or with foreigners. War means fighting with a foreign enemy; when the enemy is of the same kindred, we call it civil strife ... Is it not also reasonable to assert that Greeks are a single people, all of the same kindred and alien to the outer world of foreigners?
>
> Yes.

Then we shall speak of war when Greeks fight with foreigners, whom we may call their natural enemies. But Greeks are by nature friends of Greeks, and when they fight, it means that Hellas is afflicted by dissension which ought to be called civil strife.

I agree with that view.

Observe, then, that in what is commonly known as civil strife, that is to say, when one of our Greek states is divided against itself, it is thought an abominable outrage for either party to ravage the lands or burn the houses of the other. No lover of his country would dare to mangle the land which gave him birth and nursed him. It is thought fair that the victors should carry off the others' crops, but do no more. They should remember that the war will not last for ever; some day they must make friends again.

That is a much more civilised state of mind.

Accordingly, the Greeks being their own people, a quarrel with them will not be called a war. It will only be civil strife, which they will carry on as men who will some day be reconciled. So they will not behave like a foreign enemy seeking to enslave or destroy, but will try to bring their adversaries to reason by well-meant correction. As Greeks they will not devastate the soil of Greece or burn the homesteads; nor will they allow that all the inhabitants of any state, men, women, and children, are their enemies, but only the few who are responsible for the quarrel ... They will pursue the quarrel only until the guilty are compelled by the innocent sufferers to give satisfaction.

... I agree that our citizens should treat their adversaries in that way, and deal with foreigners as Greeks now deal with one another.[8]

Historically, this passage is expressive of Plato's adherence to pan-Hellenism as a remedy for the internecine wars which, in his view, were diverting the Greek city-states from the essential struggle against barbarian Persia. But the passage has in addition an enduring interest as the statement of an analysis with universal relevance. We will examine it for the ideas operative within it, ignoring the difficult question of whether these articulate the most deeply cherished ideals of Plato or Socrates or represent some concession to popular attitudes. The argument turns on a contrast between two types of phenomenon each having a military dimension. One type is located within a context of natural friendship. The other type occurs in a context in which war is natural.

Plato's specific use of this fundamental polarity is to see all 'civil strife' as occurring in a context of natural friendship and all wars against barbarians as natural. Furthermore, he sees belligerency that

---

[8] *Republic* 466d-471c, tr. Cornford 168-70.

occurs within a context of natural friendship as the responsibility of a few. Each of these specific points is variable according to changing historical circumstance. If the perpetrators of rebellion or civil war are seen as threatening the over-arching structure of natural friendship then they will necessarily be seen as natural enemies. (Under such conditions they are often explicitly equated with murderers of their parents for they are said to be trying to kill the land which gave them birth and nurtured them.) On the other hand, if states see themselves as bound together by ties of natural friendship then providing they maintain Plato's 'much more civilised state of mind' they can be expected to see themselves as engaged in something more like 'civil strife' than 'war'. Thus, the civility observed to some extent in eighteenth-century warfare can be accounted for largely by reference to the over-arching sense of friendship (community of interest) among the states of Europe.

The distinction between the few responsible for civil strife and the many who are its innocent victims is often thought to be more closely and inescapably related to Plato's fundamental dichotomy, but this is not the case: some of those who insisted that nothing less than unconditional surrender on the part of the Third Reich could be accepted as a successful outcome of World War II thought that the many in Germany were responsible for the war *but also thought* that Germany and the Allies were natural friends. They therefore supported the programme of denazification after the war but were in no way inclined to favour mass expropriation of the German population, the payment of crippling indemnities, or the application to Germany of the kind of measures envisaged in the Morgenthau plan of 1944, which proposed the breaking-up of Germany into a variety of tiny, rural states incapable of taking any leading part in the post-war interstate system. It is coherent to hold that the many sometimes are responsible for war but are to be spared for the sake of 'natural friendship'.

Plato is vague about the relation between owing allegiance to Hellas and owing allegiance to individual Greeks; the passage is innocent of any good wishes towards barbarians. The points need to be taken in connection with the treatment of natural friendship and natural war if the passage's relation to Jim on the one hand and to Christian and non-Christian attitudes to just war on the other is to be spelled out.

Is it in Jim's terms morally all right to leave the relation between Hellas and the individual vague? The answer is plainly No, since Jim's interest in Hellas is determined not by the consideration that it gave certain people birth and nurture but by the fact that human life is social, and the good life for human beings cannot be separated for good or ill from entanglement with such entities as the Greek city state and Hellas. Jim's involvement with Hellas is limited to the question of what contribution Hellas makes to the public and private happiness and misery of individual human beings. To leave the relation vague is from his viewpoint intolerable.

In theory, Christianity is everywhere in agreement with Jim on this point, since the fundamental concern of Christianity at all times and places is with individual salvation, the relation between God and the individual human being. Not, of course, that this makes Jim a Christian. The Christian's special reasons for having the good of the individual at heart may not be Jim's reasons, if he has any.

From the fact that Christianity is fundamentally concerned with the individual soul, it does not follow that Christians should, in their own terms, wish all men well. For an historically important possibility is that Christians should come to see some human beings as evil incarnate, as devils. Johnson points out that the spread of this perception was an important factor in the prevalence of holy war ideas in sixteenth- and seventeenth-century Europe.[9] If the Christian sees himself as having to wage war against fellow Christians, he will naturally say masses at the end of a battle and give the bodies of his enemies a sorrowful burial: for underlying the earthly quarrel was Christian brotherhood. If, on the other hand, the Christian sees himself as fighting against human beings who are wholly evil, the giving of quarter, the showing of mercy, the bestowing of an honourable burial, etc., would be not only unnatural but blasphemous. The Christian is required to fight unremittingly against evil; evil in a human form is no exception. It is a commonplace in our relatively tame Christian communities that one should love the sinner and hate the sin. Behind this commonplace lie intense theological struggles to affirm that every human being is a sinner capable of repentance rather than an embodiment of evil. Centuries of bloodshed founded on the contrary premise are also a part of the Christian heritage and a kind of tribute to Christian singlemindedness. Is it possible for Jim, as it is for Christianity, to see human beings as evil incarnate? There is a rather obvious sense in which this is not possible, in that Jim's good wishes are to all men, by definition. Unless Jim ceases to be the person he is (which of course is always a possibility) he is incapable of the demonic perception of human beings as devils.

But this rather cheerful observation requires qualification. There is a sense in which the Christian, especially the Christian with a

[9] Johnson Ch. 2.

propensity to perceive human devils and wage holy war, can do no wrong: he knows, or thinks he knows, what is required of him by God and so long as he does it (no doubt an arduous business) he need not fear the ultimate horror which in his view is alienation from the will of God. Jim's moral universe is less comfortable. This is perhaps plainest of all in the existential dilemma sketched in the last chapter. In fighting alongside his people, if that is what he elects to do, Jim is necessarily alienating himself from his deepest attachment, namely, his good wishes towards all men. For he is fighting, with utterly uncreative ferocity, against an enemy to whom, in the real situation, he is powerless to show any glimmer of good *will*. The situation is so described as to preclude all hope of giving any practical effect to his good wish to others than his own people. If the Christian faces a problem of evil in war it is merely the general problem of reconciling evil with the God of love. But Jim faces, and knows it, a more intimate problem of evil: whatever he does, he is necessarily separated from that life of good wishes towards all men to which he is most deeply attached. (Of course, if Jim happens to be a Christian then he may be able to resolve this tension by referring it to his God – the coherence of such a move is a difficult subject and would take us too far from the present theme.) Hence, although Jim is incapable of seeing human devils, there is the possibility of a darkness engulfing him in which he is separated from that to which he is mostly deeply attached.

The attitude of Jim to the ideas of 'natural friendship' and 'natural war' in the passage quoted from the *Republic* will necessarily be determined by his good wishes to all men. He will not necessarily approve all natural friendships: there is friendship among thieves, and Augustine gives ample reason for seeing most of political history as the history of natural friendships among swindlers and brutes at the expense of the populace.[10] Jim will want to know what kind of friendship is in question: if it is a friendship of princes who see interstate war as a convenient means of settling disputes among friends while viewing rebellion in any state as a threat requiring the most ferocious suppression, he may be very hostile to a natural friendship. But he can never accept the idea of natural war in any circumstances. For an essential part of what this phrase implies is that it is all right to wage war against certain human beings quite without all pity or regret – since good wishes towards them do not exist and are never so much as thought of.

A stark example of what is at stake here can be found in David Hume's *Enquiry*, whose method we indicated and adopted in Chapter Four above. Hume sides against Jim when he writes:

[10] *City of God.*

> Suppose ... that it should be a virtuous man's fate to fall into the society of ruffians, remote from the protection of all laws and government; what conduct must he embrace in that melancholy situation? He sees such a desperate rapaciousness prevail; such a disregard to equity, such contempt of order, such stupid blindness to future consequences, as must immediately have the most tragical conclusion, and must terminate in the destruction of the greater number, and in a total dissolution of society to the rest. He, meanwhile, can have no other expedient than to arm himself, to whomever the sword he seizes, or the buckler, may belong: to make provision of all means of defence and security: And his particular regard to justice being no longer of use to his own safety or that of others, he must consult the dictates of self-preservation alone, without concern for those who no longer merit his care and attention.[11]

This gives a very reasonable picture of what the virtuous man must do in a situation of natural war if he is not to suffer very soon a death in all senses futile. But it concludes with words which are natural to Plato and Hume but alien to (Kant and) Jim. No doubt the stupid wretches of this dystopia do not *merit* care and attention; but their meriting or not meriting care and attention was not the overriding consideration in the first place. Jim had good wishes towards all men (in Kant it is good *will*): they had no need of merit since they had his good wishes. Even if the man of good wish finds himself having to do what Hume suggests, he cannot do it with the easy heart that Hume's words indicate: his involvement with human beings does not cease when they cease to merit his care and attention. Thus, Jim's estimate of natural friendship will depend on his judgment of its relation to the interests of those involved; his attitude to natural war can never be one of acceptance, except a practical acceptance of facts that go against his deepest wishes.

The attitude of Christianity admits of a wider range of variety. Doubtless, some Christians have just the wishes that Jim has, related to natural friendship and natural war in the way that Jim's wishes are. But this is not the only possibility within Christianity: it is not demanded by the logic of Christian ideas and experience and is by no means ubiquitous in Christian history. An example may serve to make this clear. The deepest Christian allegiance is loving obedience towards God. It is a question not in religion or theology but in psychology what the nature is of those creatures to whom our love must be directed if we are to love God. It is perfectly possible for someone to attach extremely little importance to 'mere wishes' and yet be a devout and consistent Christian. In the Lutheran tradition, as is notorious, the political *status quo* has very often been accepted

[11] Hume 187.

without question as a datum within which to live the Christian life, rather than as something to be subjected to Christian questioning. Only when the state appeared to threaten the Protestant and Catholic churches before and during World War II did any sizeable proportion of either regard themselves as having religious reason to criticise the state.[12] At another extreme, some contemporary Christians interpret the New Testament as a gospel of social and political revolution in which the whole point of the Christian life (or its whole point in certain historical conditions) is a certain kind of challenge to the social and political order. Jim is at neither of these extremes. Not that he is a 'moderate': his extremism takes a different form. Instead of making *any* particular stance on the political order a question of principle (whether the principle of massive state autonomy from religion or the principle that religion is politics or some other equation), Jim makes wishes the basis of everything: in this lies his extremism. If Jim is a Christian, he stands for a particular stance within Christianity – a stance which has critical implications with respect to politics, and is capable of alignment for or against reform or revolution, but which nowhere interprets politics as an issue of *deep* principle. In this he differs from many perfectly coherent Christians.

We are now in a position to answer the question raised above: if the just war tradition is identified in Christian terms, what interest can it have for the non-Christian? A general answer to this question is impossible, since the significance for the non-Christian of a holy war variant on the tradition which sees some human beings as incarnate evil is necessarily different from the significance of the just war according to Jim. The specific answer we propose is this. Jim's understanding of the just war stands midway between distinctively Christian and distinctively non-Christian attitudes to the world. On the one hand, it is perfectly possible that Jim is a (devout and coherent) Christian, but it is equally possible that Jim is not a Christian at all. To take only the most obvious instances, it may be that Jim's good wishes towards all men are embedded in Christian ideas about all men being children of God; but in our somewhat abstract presentation of Jim it is equally possible that his wishes are devoid of all Christian or religious connotation – maybe he is a tough-minded and aggressive (so far as the good man can be aggressive!) humanist. Jim's view of just war belongs in the tradition if he is a Christian because in thinking about war he will necessarily be asking himself the questions 'May the Christian without sin wage war?' and 'What constraints are there upon the activity of the Christian in the waging

---

[12] Of course, the classic just war theory is an instrument for examining state policy. But the ecclesiastical inhibitions against its vigorous deployment are often very great.

of war?' But equally, Jim's view is accessible to those outside the realm of Christian allegiances, since if he is not a Christian he will be asking himself the different questions 'May the man of good wish, without betraying humanity, wage war?' and 'What constraints are there upon the activity of the man of good wish in the waging of war?' These questions are different in that they make no reference to Christ; but it is equally important to notice that they are also the same questions Jim would be asking himself were he asking them as a Christian in the sense that he would, in trying to answer them, be bringing to bear the same considerations for the same reasons. The backgrounds of Christian Jim and non-Christian Jim are different, but they are so much in the background that all operative considerations are common to the two. They can, without distortion, speak the same language even though there is a sense in which they inhabit different worlds.

3. Against natural law

What we are arguing for here is not a version of the idea of natural law. An historically influential notion which is still widely accepted is that the relation between Christian and non-Christian is founded on natural law. The natural law is recognised by all men, or by all men except those whose judgment has been perverted. Because Christ came to fulfil the law rather than to change it, natural law is as binding on the Christian as on the non-Christian. The Christian may also be subject to an extra discipline, and may have new reasons for obeying natural law or may bring to it a new spirit. But the natural law is already there, a common possession of the non-Christian and the Christian. The just war idea is often seen as falling within the realm of natural law. It is pointed out that Greek and Roman authors are a leading source of just war ideas as of so much natural law; what more natural than to see just war in the light of natural law?

This formulation is, of course, exceedingly simplified and our response to it, based on the simplification, will be similarly simplified. Unless we have misconstrued the notion of natural law, such simplification does not do violence to an idea which has taken on many extremely sophisticated forms.

As we understand it, the idea of natural law sees world moral order as divisible into two parts. One part is that moral order in which the natural man lives. The other part is that moral order in which the Christian finds himself. Perhaps in some historical circumstances, such an analysis is instructive and avoids over-simplifying the world in which the Christian and the non-Christian find themselves. But we do not believe that it is adequate for the analysis of the contemporary moral world, or the best contemporary understanding of moral and religious history. Far nearer the truth, we think, is this: the non-Christian finds himself in a world of competing (non-Christian) understandings of the world which constitute or imply incompatible moralities. For example, various forms of utilitarianism, of Marxism, of liberalism, of 'my station and its duties', of aestheticism and mystical personal religiosity surround him; and he is even quite likely to find himself torn between them. Similarly, the Christian finds himself in a world of competing (would-be) Christian understandings of life which again constitute or imply incompatible moralities. For example, various sorts of fundamentalism, of Christian liberalism and Barthian orthodoxy, of Christian rationalism and rejections of reason in favour of the omnipotence and inscrutability of God are present in the Christian world or history; and again the Christian is quite likely to find himself torn between them. Finally, the best publicised part of this familiar story of divided loyalties is that the Christian may find a vigorous non-Christian in himself, and vice versa. In this context of divided loyalties, the natural law is an artificial construct. It represents at most a raft of consensus between certain Christians and certain non-Christians rather than something characteristic of the natural man whom Christ came to perfect. It is this context which impels us to draw a picture of Jim which spells out rather fully a large variety of kinds of fact about him, meant to make clear his relation to many if not all of the competing world-pictures which are operative in the contemporary world. And it is this context which renders the idea of natural law unavailable.

Take an example. One fairly good candidate for consideration as a piece of natural law is the convention governing the treatment of prisoners-of-war, forbidding cruelty to them and in a variety of detailed ways spelling out how a modicum of mercy is to be shown to people who are within our power and hopelessly dependent on us in a situation where we may be sorely tempted to torment or kill them. On the western front, though not in the war between Germany and Russia and not in the Far East, the convention was widely observed throughout World War II. Some would try to argue against the natural law idea applied to this example that it ignores history: the humane treatment of POWs is a relatively recent phenomenon whose history can be charted, so it cannot be part of the natural man. This is not our difficulty. We are prepared to accept that the natural man may have a history, his law changing with time and perhaps (though not necessarily) progressing. Our difficulty is quite different.

The idea that kindly treatment of POWs might be a moral

imperative having universal validity would appear in the context of holy war as nothing short of blasphemous. For it would imply that there might be something to be said for being kind to devils! There is thus at least one version of Christianity which is forced by its own logic to reject 'the natural law'. Similarly, when Nazi leaders rejected the idea of any mercy towards prisoners on the eastern front, they were forced by the logic of their own ideas into the rejection: in their own terms there was much to be said against, and nothing for, mercy.

This example, which might appear fatuous at first glance, should be considered together with another. Miss Anscombe plainly regards the killing of the innocent as prohibited in natural law; someone who was prepared to consider it in any circumstances would be showing, she claims, a corrupt mind.[13] Many admirable people appear to reject this piece of 'the natural law' – what is one to make of that?

What appears to us to link the two examples is that both are instances having urgent practical importance of the collapse of consensus (if consensus ever existed) on morality. To describe the holy war idea, or Nazi cruelty, solely in natural law terms is to fail in self-understanding. Of course it is true that one of the appalling things about the proponents of holy war was that they saw some human beings as devils and showed them no quarter. But where *precisely* is their error to be located? The natural law tradition identifies it in a moralistic way, telling us in effect that a religious viewpoint which makes the denial of quarter imperative must be wrong. It has to be wrong because it implies action contrary to the natural law, and Christ fulfils the natural law without reversing it. Such an argument may be the best that can be done on the spur of the moment, but it gets things the wrong way round. It is alien to Christian thinking in that it fails to make God the centre of the analysis. To put the point very crudely, it fails to locate the blasphemy which is involved in seeing a human being as a devil. It concentrates on the moral error while ignoring the prior intellectual mistake. It makes things too easy.

The US experience in Vietnam has made popularly familiar the importance of the way in which the enemy is understood. Once grant that the enemy are 'gooks', subhuman, and you have already given away all moral restraint. Natural law concentrates on action at the expense of understanding. It gives some sort of basis for criticising action, but when the underlying consensus is denied, natural law can reply only that the objector has a corrupt mind. Ultimately, this is a dehumanising argument. For 'the corrupt mind' is an unanalysed thing, as mysterious and fearsome as the human devils in holy war or

---

[13] 'Modern Moral Philosophy.'

the gooks in Vietnam. It is something that takes possession of a man, depriving him of his humanity – it reduces him to a thing.

The view adopted in this book is different. Maybe there is some use for the notion of the corrupt mind, but it is not in the field of thinking about such things as the holy war idea or Nazism. Rather than dismiss these as 'corruptions', our approach is to bring them into the light so that their human characteristics can be seen. The holy war mind is as analysable as the mind of Jim. It is in the first instance to be taken in its own terms, so that the drawing of cruel conclusions is humanly comprehensible. Only after this has been done is it appropriate to relate this cruel but human mind to something better, for example the mind of Jim.

There is a close connection between this need to bring evil ideas into the light and psychoanalysis. In Freudian analysis, the fantasy life is treated as a guide to unconscious thoughts and actions which are making the patient ill but which, once he becomes conscious of them, the patient can struggle to control and overcome. What we are arguing for is an analogous approach to the intellectual life. We are not suggesting that the proponents of holy war and the Nazis were mentally sick, as many of Freud's patients were, still less that people in the grip of contemporary demonic ideas can be expected to submit to analysis: Freud's patients knew they were sick; a person in the grip of a demonic idea thinks the world sick, or evil. What we are claiming is that the dark places of the moral life can and should be brought to light, for only in that way can they be combatted in human terms, tracing them back to the point where they diverge from the viewpoint of the good man. The trouble with the natural law idea is that it suggests that there is no problem: one knows in advance what the natural law is, all that is needed is to dismiss as corrupt the mind that disagrees.

What seems to us a more realistic view in a world of collapsed consensus is that one knows in advance (very often) *one's own mind*: one knows what one takes to be the truth, and the task is to discover the point at which the demonic departs from the truth. In the process of analysis one might discover something about oneself (equally, one might not – it is not every value system that yields insights into oneself); one might be changed; one might be able to convince by means of argument alone, without any force but the force of argument, a person in the grip of some demonic idea (or one may not – one may know in advance that persuasion is impossible). But whatever the individual case, the world in which we live, properly understood, calls for the carrying-out of the analysis. Any idea that can legitimise itself demands the recognition that it is a human idea humanly arrived at. However corrupt, it is never merely corrupt. This is not a moral assertion, aimed to articulate the general desire to treat people with respect. (Many ideas merit no respect.) It is an assertion about what is intellectually imperative: evil ideas have the intellectual right to an answer and the general form of the answer is an identification of their point(s) of departure from the best available perspective.

We gave two examples of the kind of objection we have to natural law thinking in the contemporary world. One, the example of holy war and Nazi ideas, was of ideas likely to have no sympathetic response in the reader. The other, Miss Anscombe's contention that any consideration of the killing of the innocent evidences a corrupt mind, will receive a different response in many readers: for many of us are, with all or part of our minds, utilitarians. This illustrates another part of the collapse of consensus; it is a part often confused with the whole. There are some issues on which people who have had good reason each in his own terms to regard the other as thinking morally in terms which are unexceptionable are suddenly brought up short against some massive moral disagreement – for example, about abortion, politics, or the criminal law. To say this is not of course to say that there is no moral consensus between them: they experienced surprise or distress partly because of their consensus and the rude discovery of its limitations. But it is to point up the elusive character of the natural law. Look where we will in the modern world and we are unable to count on finding consensus.

The discovery of the lack of consensus in the most intimate groupings, together with a frequent undecidedness about moral issues in one's own mind, tends to engender moral scepticism. Out in the world one sees all manner of horrors justifying themselves as legitimate views of the world, and there is no circle of acquaintances on which one can rely for a countervailing consensus to which one expects to be able to assent unequivocally. From this it is fallacious but entirely natural to infer that there is no such thing as moral knowledge, that morality is just a matter of opinion, that one view is as good as another, that all moral discourse is just propaganda, and so on.

The idea of natural law fuels such scepticism. For it embodies in a very forceful way a philosophical picture of morality which is an essential ingredient in such scepticism. The natural law tradition tacitly assumes that the *reality* of morality depends on consensus: to know what morality is, look at the consensus view taken by natural man and consider the ways in which Christ completes and perfects nature.

We see no reason to accept that morality depends on consensus in any such disastrous way. Of course things would be easier for our hero Jim if there were extensive moral consensus; doubtless Jim desires that certain sorts of consensus should be strengthened and spread. But there is nothing in our analysis to suggest that the consensus which is so important in natural law has any importance except as a way of realising more fully those wishes which underlie Jim's moral life. Consensus would make his life fuller and more rewarding, but no more real.

One more point to conclude this already lengthy general discussion of the relation between natural law and the moral analysis attempted in this book. Many people whose interest in war has a historical bent feel profoundly at sea with the ethics of war. There are many reasons for this which receive attention elsewhere in this book. But one decisively important consideration, often vaguely felt but not always clearly stated is this: the historical mind tries to see the past and even the present as it really is, avoiding all mere wishfulness in the interests of contemplating objective reality, what really happened. There are several reasons for doubting whether this desire can ever be gratified, but what is most important here is to consider the implications of the desire itself, doomed to frustration or not, for ethics. One great difficulty with the natural law tradition applied to the modern world is that it has a smeary effect on modern history: the politics of great events in this century appear in this tradition as the product of merely corrupt minds. The historical understanding knows very well that there is more to say but the grand ethical tradition of natural law renders it unsayable. In our analysis it is not necessary for ethics to put on such blinkers: ethical analysis proceeds via the identification and scrutiny of moral personalities and intellects. None are tabu – the historian is at liberty, if he is interested in ethics, to look at whatever value systems happen to interest him, and to construe them in their own terms.

The contemporary world is living with the aftermath of what Nietzsche termed 'the death of god', that is, the collapse of all consensus on an authoritative political, social, moral and religious order. One aspect of the death of god is the rise of the politically divided man, discussed in Chapter Two above. Another is the need for ethical analysis that assumes no particular consensus in the natural man (or the Christian). It is against this background that we are writing outside the natural law tradition.

Accordingly, we do not see the just war tradition in general, or the species of it that we are mainly interested in, as belonging to natural law. Instead, we see the tradition in general as circling around the two perennial questions 'May the Christian, without sin, wage war?' and 'What constraints are there upon the activity of the Christian in the waging of war?'. What the non-Christian is to make of the tradition is a question that does not admit of any general answer: it depends on the outlook of the particular non-Christian and the Christian reference-group in which he interests himself. More specifically, if Jim happens to be a Christian then the meaning he gives to the two perennial questions will entail that he is in effect facing the same intellectual and practical problems as certain non-Christians. In short, it is not that the just war is natural law and common ground between Christian and non-Christian but that there is a certain overlap of mind between Christian and non-Christian.

4. Can Jim be a Christian?

Before we turn from these general issues to a detailed consideration of the just war tradition, there is one other matter that requires some attention, however inadequately brief. We have so far been assuming in this chapter that Jim may happen to be a Christian. But it is often thought, for good if not finally conclusive reasons, that the Kantian philosophy is deeply inimical to Christianity. It is often claimed that Kant deifies the moral law, committing himself to an exceedingly sophisticated version of rule worship. It is therefore important to stress that Jim is a *modified* Kantian. An example: it is possible that Jim believes that there is some spark of divinity in every human being and that in wishing men well his wish for each is that he should live, realise in his own life, the divine that is in him. It is consistent with all we have said about Jim to suppose that his understanding of man is thoroughly christocentric: he may perfectly well believe that the only complete fulfilment in this world of his good wishes towards all men is in the life of Jesus. He may consider Jesus the only truly happy, truly human man, and may understand the shortcomings of other human beings in terms of Jesus' perfection. This is said to point out how Christian Jim may happen to be: to take the matter further in a pro- or anti-Christian direction would require another book. For present purposes it is sufficient to notice that whereas the Kantian moral hero has his eyes fixed on the moral law and is therefore possibly a victim of rule worship, Jim is most deeply committed to good wishes towards individual human beings. His thought is necessarily directed towards individual human beings: he finds God there or nowhere.

We turn now to the elucidation of certain parts of the classic just war tradition from Jim's viewpoint. According to Aquinas, there are four questions about war: Are some wars permissible? May clerics engage in war? May belligerents use subterfuge? May war be waged on feast days?[14] All such divisions into a small number of discrete questions are to some extent artificial, but we find it convenient to organise our remarks under five headings.

(a) To what does the idea of a just war apply?

(b) What is the meaning of proportion?

(c) What substance have the demands for the trying of all peaceful means and for a just cause in an age of structural violence?

(d) What is the moral standing of the principle of noncombatant immunity?

(e) Is deterrence different?

It has to be admitted that some of Aquinas' questions receive no attention in our argument.

5. *To what does the idea of a just war apply?*

A notorious contemporary problem in the just war tradition is often expressed in the statement that the churches have developed workable ideas on just *war* but find themselves at a loss over just *rebellion* and *revolution*.

We see the idea of a just war as applying to all activities having a military dimension. As such, it covers unequivocally all 'wars' and much that is described as 'rebellion' or 'revolution'. (Though it does not cover, for example, general strikes that have no military dimension.)

This is, in some ways, a new thought in the tradition. Earlier writers do not, so far as we are aware, essay anything like the definition of the military dimension proposed in Chapter Three above. On the whole they proceed in a more piecemeal way, or via assumptions about the nature of the political order. That is, they discuss specific wars, or assume some notion of what 'war' is or what 'rebellion' is which presupposes particular historical conditions. Writing in a time when the fundamentals of political order are contested (i.e. when different people give different accounts of political order, and some challenge all order) and when a historical consciousness of the very great changes contained within the received tradition is inescapable, we employ the descriptive notion of 'the military dimension' sketched above.

Thus, we see the just war idea as regulating all fighting of a certain kind – namely, fighting very likely to the death, between groups organised for such fighting, using weapons designed for the purpose,

---

[14] *Summa Theologica* Vol. 35 81-93.

involving in one way or another quarrels related to the fundamental categories in which people understand their lives – and all preparation for and threat of such fighting.

Furthermore, we see the just war idea as applying at all levels of command and control. One sometimes gets the impression from even the most perceptive of just war writers that the criteria impinge on practice at only two points – at the level of government and at the level of individual confessional. For example, John Ford draws a sharp line between the question of official policy on Allied bombing and the question of the priest's attitude to the individual in the confessional. Such a move is understandable in the circumstances in which Ford was writing, but implies an undue limitation if generalised. We see the just war ideas as claiming attention not only from Churchill and Roosevelt, Hitler and Stalin, but also from Liddell Hart and Douhet; Sir Arthur Harris, Carl Spaatz and Erhard Milch; group captains, pilots and navigators, and the lowliest aircraftmen. Not only from the IRA high command but also from the individual terrorist who claims to be acting on orders. Not only from those politically responsible for the adoption and development of the policy of nuclear deterrence, but also from those officials and academics who advise and engage in controversy. In this chapter, we are concerned with the tradition's *claim on their attention*. The question of responsibility – of what follows if the just war ideas are rejected or the just war criteria flouted – is reserved for Chapter Six.

In this chapter we are considering the just war idea from Jim's viewpoint. In this chapter, therefore, we evaluate some familiar just war principles to determine the extent to which they are the natural and inescapable beliefs of someone whose thinking is guided by good wishes towards all men and whose understanding of 'war', 'rebellion', etc, is essentially that indicated in the foregoing chapters and especially in our definition of the military dimension.

Accordingly, our analysis is against the grain of all contemporary ideas that see war as an automatic or semi-automatic process. The developments of modern military technology doubtless alter the instruments to be thought about and possibly make thought more difficult. But they do not remove war from the realm of thought altogether. War is something that people do, not something that happens: activity with a military dimension is activity, not mere blind process and event.

6. *What is the meaning of proportion?*

Among the large number of criteria which, according to the classic authors, must be met if a war is not to be unjust, the requirement of proportion is apt to strike many modern readers as the most obvious, least problematic, and most tautological. To those of us with a utilitarian or consequentialist outlook, the meaning of 'proportion' looks obvious – the striking of a balance between means and ends such that the overall outcome of the chosen course of war is better than all available alternatives. To the utilitarian, proportion appears a platitude: it merely re-states in picturesque metaphor the fundamental demands of utilitarianism. A more interesting interpretation is possible which is very much closer to Jim's interests. To demand that people engaged in activity with a military dimension secure and preserve a sense of proportion is to ask for something difficult and strenuous which Jim necessarily desires. It is to require that people think what they are trying to do, remember what they are trying to do, avoid being side-tracked into doing something else instead. Writers as diverse as Clausewitz and Tolstoy constantly stress the muddle and indirection of war: no one knows what is going on, so no one is capable of a sense of proportion.

When Clausewitz urges politicians to realise that war is an instrument of state policy, he is urging them to do something immensely difficult. For the task of ensuring from moment to moment and month to month that military activity is neither more nor less than an instrument of state policy requires vigilance, cunning and good luck. Bernard Brodie offers an admirable account of some of the deficiencies and difficulties of twentieth-century US conduct in this regard.[15]

The just war demand for proportion includes Clausewitz's insistence on political control, and goes beyond it. During World War I especially, people repeatedly forgot what they were trying to do and started trying to do other things instead: as the casualties mounted, new and ever more grandiose war aims were proclaimed. Clausewitz rightly states that as a war progresses there may be good military and political reason for an alteration in military objectives.[16] But the slide of policy during World War I was determined not by an estimation of what, in changing circumstances, was required if one was to attain one's continuing aims; rather, policy was the product of the incoherent feeling that such losses must mean monumental objectives.[17] Clausewitz understood the tendency for military

[15] *War and Politics.*
[16] On War I.I.11, tr. Howard and Paret.
[17] For the fluctuating war aims of the two major belligerents in World War I see Fritz Fischer *Germany's Aims in the First World War* and V.H. Rothwell *British War Aims and Peace Diplomacy 1914-18.*

developments and political passion to interact, but did not demand any resistance to such loss of control. He saw the interaction as a blind and irresistible force, beyond the control of men, and he was uninterested in the question of what one should do when faced with such a process. His attention was confined to the politician and the military commander who accepted that it was his duty, whatever political forces were doing behind his back, to continue with the job in hand, trying to make the best of things.

Always more comprehensive, Tolstoy in *War and Peace* worried at the problem. His account of the 1812 campaign depicted it on the Russian side as a massive and irresistible force sweeping men up beyond their comprehension into a great popular war. But another part of his mind was grappling with individuals outside the mighty blind machine. Pierre attempting to kill Napoleon, and the patience of the peasant Karatayev, embody perspectives on the war which were quite outside the range of Clausewitz's interests. Jim may be in the machine trying to do his best or he may be one of the outsiders: his position in the edifice of war is not determined by his values. Accordingly, his wish of good to all men necessarily goes far beyond the Clausewitzian demand for political control. Jim wants politics to be informed by memory: the interaction of passion and mounting losses to produce political forgetfulness is necessarily something contrary to his wishes and therefore, given the opportunity, something against which he struggles. Jim never can see the enemy as gooks or devils, and necessarily opposes such perceptions in others. An important factor in the spreading of forgetfulness between 1914 and 1918 was the view of the enemy as subhuman or as devilishly superhuman. Jim is necessarily against such developments in a way that Clausewitz necessarily cannot be.

One can go still further. Jim's sense of proportion and feeling for what is and is not disproportionate is determined by a wish of good to all men and also by a deep intelligence about what the good for man consists in. In Chapter Four, it was for this reason that we exhibited him as being a modified Kantian: unlike the utilitarian, we said, Jim draws systematic conclusions from the consideration that each human being has to live his own life. For the man of good wish, there are limits set to making people happy – limits which find expression in the Kantian formula 'Always treat humanity, whether in your own person or in the person of another, as an end and never merely as a means'. Given this focus on the individual, Jim is necessarily committed to a particular kind of view of the states, or other groups, involved in activity having a military dimension. He necessarily regards such formulae as 'war in defence of national honour' with suspicion, for he requires to know the significance of the supposed 'national honour' in the lives of individual moral beings. This does not necessarily mean that he is dismissive of all appeals to honour. Aquinas says that war purely for its own sake would be stupid.[18] But we argued in Chapter Four that a war without hope of success, merely a last flickering of humanity, might confront Jim with an existential dilemma. A war in defence of national honour might be just such a fight, though of course it is likely not to be.

The meaning of proportion for Jim is therefore complex but a predictable necessity. To obtain and preserve a sense of proportion is to see activity with a military dimension in terms of the individual moral beings involved in it, to retain a sense of one's own and the enemy's humanity, to remember what the point of the war is, to practise Clausewitz's maxim that war is an instrument of state policy. Proportion is therefore something intensely difficult.

Why, given the great difficulty of proportion, should it have a special interest for Jim? We have tried to show that if he thinks about the matter then he will necessarily desire a sense of proportion for himself and others, but this does not explain why his attention should become focussed on the cluster of things surrounding proportion in the first place. There are two reasons for regarding Jim as deeply committed to proportion. First, unless Jim is fortunate enough to be spared all involvement in war, he will certainly be faced in a practical way with some of these phenomena. For example, if he does agricultural work as a conscientious objector then he will doubtless be faced with statements by others that declare or imply that the enemy are less than human or fiendishly more than human. If he becomes Chief of the Air Staff and subsequently a minister responsible for war then he will face in very acute form the dilemmas of political-military relationship studied by Clausewitz and Brodie. Jim will find the struggle for a sense of proportion practically speaking inescapable.

Secondly, if Jim can find any sort of consensus on the importance of proportion in the world of collapsed consensus then it will be very useful to him in challenging people to justify their actions. One very striking aspect of the brave efforts by a few somewhat isolated individuals to criticise the Allied bombing offensive was the absence in both official and public circles of any consensus on how the war was to be thought and fought morally. The official debate studied above in Chapter One is almost wholly innocent of any sense of proportion that could conceivably satisfy Jim. This emerges at numerous points in our narrative, but perhaps most strikingly in the impossibility to which we

[18] Vol. 35 195 cites *Contra Gentes*.

drew attention of arriving at any historically just generalisation about what those conducting the offensive were trying to do. Naturally, each of these powerful and strong-minded men was pressing his own view and listening to his opponents hardly at all. One would expect that. What is more surprising, perhaps, is that nowhere does one find any pressure for discussion of the question 'What are we trying to do?'. The understandable practice of trying to hurt the enemy when one can do nothing else gives way by imperceptible degrees and a great quantity of muddle and crossed-purpose to the endeavour to obtain the speediest possible victory with the least possible loss of Allied life. But this is about as far as one can go in describing what those involved were trying to do. Even as an ideal, the notion of proportion was completely absent. Had there been a consensus that proportion was required, the result might have been mere hypocrisy and cant. But other voices would have been empowered to claim a right to speak in a required discourse: it might even have strengthened the hand of those favouring the selective bombing of oil installations against the proponents of area bombing.

We do not wish to suggest that the calculation of consequences has no place in the idea of proportion. Given a due sense of proportion, one is well placed to see how very important the calculation of consequences is. But the concept of proportion is richer than anything derivable from utilitarianism alone. For it sums up those tendencies to drift against which the moral intelligence is necessarily embattled.

7. *Peaceful means and a just cause in an age of structural violence*

According to Aquinas, a private person has no business declaring war since he can seek redress by appealing to the judgment of his superiors.[19] In Aquinas' historical context, with a considerable practical problem of organised violence employed for private profit and as such often lacking in certain necessary features of the military dimension, this remark makes good sense. But taken more generally, it invites a question of central importance in the just war tradition: what if judgment by 'superiors' in the political order is impossible or unjust? There would then appear to be only two possibilities: that the 'private person' must do without redress and without justice; or that he may be entitled to declare war.

Many people believe that the political order throughout the world or in large parts of it, is characterised by 'structural violence', one of the consequences of which is that the authorities' judgment on

[19] Vol. 35 81-93.

questions of justice cannot be relied on. Something like the notion of structural violence is to be found already in Tolstoy's later writings. Tolstoy argued that the Tsarist state was a perpetrator of unholy violence at all levels from the most modest of law enforcement to all-out war. The exploitation of the peasantry was but a part of the general pattern. Tolstoy's favoured remedy, the reversal of all values and the foreswearing of all will to power,[20] is one possible response to structural violence but not the only one. Perhaps the most widespread current view of structural violence is that it entails a war of all against all: the 'system' renders it impossible for anyone to obtain satisfaction by appeal to his 'superiors' and so no one can be criticised along the lines employed by Aquinas for waging war: the private realm, presupposing as it does a rule of justice to which appeal can be made, vanishes if structural violence is all.

The idea of structural violence seems to appeal most to people who find the traditional notion of just cause anathema. One frequently hears people declaring that the idea of a just war is nonsense, a mere ploy on the part of the exploiters to engage in violence that they desire for other reasons, and the same people insisting that structural violence is endemic and must be resisted and destroyed at all costs. What is one to make of the idea of structural violence? We argue that it is an inferior substitute for the more precise and articulate concept of just cause.

Vitoria and Suarez worked to attach to the idea of just cause a very specific and clearly workable meaning. As James Johnson shows,[21] they were trying to counter the spread of holy-war thinking that had come to pervade the just war tradition. In response to a large number of wars fought partly or wholly over matters of religion, they insisted that a war was just only if waged to correct some perfectly definite secular wrong. In their now vanished world there was a consensus about the general character of such wrongs as they had in mind and it made perfectly good sense to think of the causes that they intended to claim as the only just causes of war as being precise enough to be adjudicated in a law court.

In the eighteenth century, the consensus about what kind of thing it was that could be thought of as a just cause for war had broken down: the concept had lost its agreed *content*. But it had not been rendered unviable, for there was agreement that every prince was entitled to judge in his own cause. In place of the earlier consensus about content there was agreement on *procedure*.

---

[20] See in particular R.V. Sampson *Tolstoy: the Discovery of Peace*.
[21] Johnson Ch. 3.

The difficulty at the present time is that there is consensus neither about the content of the notion of just cause nor about its procedure. After many years of deliberation, the United Nations has produced a kind of definition of 'aggression' but one which lays down neither a workable content nor a workable procedure whereby the justice of particular causes can be determined: anyone can say that they are resisting aggression, but there is inadequate agreement on what 'aggression' is.

In this 'death of god' situation, what is required if talk of just cause is to be anything more than mere empty rhetoric is that each should make plain precisely what he takes a just cause to consist in, and why he takes that to constitute a just cause. If this were done, although we might not agree we might at least have the chance of understanding one another.

In terms of just cause, it is perfectly possible for those who use the concept of structural violence to state their case. They consider that 'the system' results in certain sorts of desperate absolute need or relative deprivation for certain sections of certain populations. They believe that this situation warrants resort to measures having a military dimension.

The approach to such an argument from the viewpoint adopted in this book should be clear. The case has not yet been established. Given Jim's interest in the moral life of individual human beings, what he requires to know is who is being authorised to wage war and against whom. Once an answer to that question is forthcoming, he will then want to know how the proposed measures relate to established just war criteria: e.g. whether proportion is being observed, whether the immunity of noncombatants is being cherished, and so on. Then, but only then, will he be able to form an opinion on the proposed action.

Perhaps the most important weakness of the concept of structural violence from Jim's viewpoint is that it blurs the distinction between a description of events as they are and a proposal for action. It short-circuits the demand for justification. In discussing proportion, we stressed that the insistence on a sense of proportion is the requirement of an alert and energetic striving to see war not as something that happens but as something that one is doing, subject to all the normal constraints of action. Like earlier descriptions of the interstate system which suggested that states were impersonal atoms whose impersonal interactions caused the events of international relations, the notion of structural violence used in the way that it often is used reduces the human to the non-human: structural violence and counter-violence is seen as something that happens, not something that is done.

This weakness in the notion of structural violence is not readily removed. For implicit in the idea is a doctrine of something like responsibility which is deeply ingrained in the modern imagination, vital to the impetus of the concept of structural violence, and indefensible.

An example of the doctrine can be found in the passage by Clifford Simmons discussed above in Chapter Four. Simmons says

> When the bombing stopped I started to worry about the comfortable circumstances in which I lived. The war had hardly touched me at all. I knew that I was involved in it whether I liked it or not – after all, some of the food I ate came from overseas in convoys protected by armed ships, and I was alarmed by the thought that men were losing their lives in order to feed me.[22]

Gordon Dunstan comments vigorously on such thoughts:

> Social concern ... literally trades in guilt: it lays the burden of responsibility for the world's ills on Christian people whose only offence, most of them, is to live in an industrialized society whose corporate potential for growing richer far exceeds that of the poorer countries, and which undoubtedly used and exploited those countries to make its own industrial expansion more rapid. The guilty conscience of Christians in the industrialized countries today over social and economic conditions for which only the tiniest few of them ever had actual personal responsibility – and therefore even the possibility of moral fault ... is exploited, partly to raise money for Christian Aid and the rest, partly to provoke to a largely ineffectual anger against 'the system' and 'the structures' which appear to frustrate all attempts at reform.[23]

We wish to lay the ghost which haunts people via such concepts as that of structural violence. To do this, we want to explore some directions in which one might want to disagree with Dunstan's strictures – to see whether coherent disagreement or qualification is even logically conceivable.

One point can presumably be agreed at once. In one sense of the words, 'guilt', 'responsibility', 'bad conscience', etc. are possible only if the individual feeling guilty had some measure of control over that for which he feels guilty. 'Ought implies can.' Simmons' 'alarm' does not assume that he could somehow have stopped the sailors from dying to bring him food and the guilt which many feel regarding the developing countries goes far beyond the suspicion that they personally are not doing all that they could to alleviate the world crisis. Some other idea of responsibility – coherent or incoherent – is at work.

[22] Simmons 16.   [23] Dunstan 2.

An obvious thought is that Dunstan rather under-states the case: he grants that 'we' used and exploited the developing world in the past but omits to point out that those who are tormented by guilt on social questions are firmly convinced that 'we' are still engaged in this cruel exploitation. In the terms of his argument, this makes no difference to Dunstan's case: whether the exploitation is past or present is irrelevant; his crucial point is that it is beyond the control of the individual who is prey to bad feelings.

One thought that seems to emerge in Simmons' remarks is that he is currently the beneficiary of things that he deplores. People who are losing their lives – he isn't asking them to do that! – and perhaps doing things (waging war) which he (a pacifist) wants them not to do are benefitting him: more concretely, they are *feeding* him. Given the centrality of 'feeding' as an image of the divine will in Hebrew and Christian thought, and given the intense physical intimacy of it, there could be few acts of benefaction so inescapable by the imagination. The word 'alarmed' can hardly do justice to the smothering sense that the individual is receiving, against his will, good that in all conscience he does not want. The moral humiliation is intense. A person who pauses over a meal to reflect on the world economic order cannot, if he is well informed, escape a closely related moral nausea. (A good digestion and freedom from any of the physical effects of nausea only makes it worse.) One is eating and drinking good things, which are pleasant and are of a kind which is necessary – one needs food and drink, if not these foods and these things to drink – but in doing so one is receiving benefits from people doing things (being exploited) which one did not ask them to do and which perhaps one wishes they would not do (perhaps one desires from them armed rebellion, or strikes, or something, one knows not what, to bring down the unjust order).

These remarks are merely psychological, and go no way at all to showing that there is any viable sense in feeling guilty about 'the system'. But, properly considered, they can be seen to have a certain moral force. They fall within the ambit of that elusive notion 'gratitude'. If one has received good from someone one is bound to them in a special way. It is not, as was pointed out in Chapter Four, that one becomes obliged to them in specifiable ways but that gratitude demands of one watchfulness for opportunities of returning good for good.

The distress that Simmons felt at the thought of people dying for him in naval actions and the distress that many feel in thinking about the third world is readily understandable in terms of gratitude. For one has received a great good, gratitude demands that one return good for good, and yet one knows that there is nothing one is ever going to be able to do to express, to make real one's gratitude. The largely ineffectual anger to which Dunstan refers is a natural expression of this consciousness of doomed gratitude.

This is our personal view of the matter. It seems to us that viewed in this way, certain feelings which otherwise appear merely irrational can be seen as making sense. Considered in this way, the feelings are rendered relatively immune to exploitation, for the individual who understands his feelings thus is well placed to assess critically all appeals to his feelings about the third world. Suppose, for example, that he is asked to give money to be used by guerrilla organisations. If he understands his rage against the system as an expression of gratitude, the first question that he will naturally ask himself is whether the guerrilla activity is good, and whether his support of it is good – for his desire is to return good for good.

We labour this point because there is another understanding of rage against the system which is current and powerfully influential. It focusses attention not on the good that one receives from the third world but on the injustice that is suffered there. It typically operates not with images of feeding but with images of conflagration, justice and judgment. It expects destructive war to engulf the world, it grimly anticipates disaster for those whom it sees as living in the foci of injustice ('There's going to be a terrible time in South Africa sooner or later' uttered not on the strength of detailed analysis of local conditions but out of a sense of what morally has to happen). It reminds the individual at the breakfast table not of the good in the food that he is receiving, but of the injustice. It deals in doublethink – when one reflects one is angry, one cannot reflect all the time, one relapses into unthinking pleasure in the products of injustice. It takes a remorseless delight in reminding one of one's two-mindedness. ('We too often forget ...')

This doom-laden picture of the world aims to persuade the individual to see himself as 'deserving' justice, judgment, disaster. If the now disadvantaged suppliers cut off vital resources, it claims, that would be no more than 'we' deserve. 'We' have been living too long on borrowed time and exploited labour. The crux of the matter is that one is to interpret frightful things that happen to one as punishment for 'us'.

This gloomy understanding of the world employs ideas which are readily found in Hebrew and Christian sources: the sense that we are all members one of another; the Hebrew conviction that the individual is inescapably and deeply bound up with the life of Israel; the struggle to interpret suffering in terms of the will of God. But it falls disastrously into incoherence. There may be much to be said for interpreting one's own suffering as a kind of ethical punishment ('No better than I deserve').[24] There seems no special reason to deny that we collectively should see ourselves as accountable for what we collectively have done. And doubtless no man is an island. The incoherence comes in the step from 'we' to 'I'. If it is the case that three people A, B, C must each admit that 'Yes, I did it' but must add that it was not an individual action but a collective one, it is appropriate to hold A, B and C collectively responsible for what they have done. For example, if A, B and C have practised torture on someone – each contributing to a collective action which none could have carried out on his own – it is perfectly sensible to hold them collectively responsible – requiring them to undergo collectively some punishment which none could undergo alone.

But from this it by no means follows that 'collective guilt' can be extended to persons none of whom can truly say: 'Yes, I did it; I played my part in the activity.'

It is on this point that the notion of structural violence founders. It depends on an interpretation of rage against the system that relies on the view of violence as judgment not gratitude, and as pointed out above it avoids the question of individuals. (If it enters into that question, it becomes merely a circumlocution of just cause ideas.) If absolute need and relative deprivation in the developing countries are interpreted in terms of gratitude, the question will be 'What if anything can I do, as an individual and in collective activity, to express gratitude?' But this is not the question asked, and does not suggest the kind of analysis engaged in by those who are guided by the concept of structural violence. The question that is asked, in effect, is 'What is the case against us, calling for judgment?' In some ways this is an admirable question, but only if asked within a coherent philosophy. Thinking about structural violence goes beyond all defensible notions of responsibility and as such collapses into incoherence.

To sum up. It is agreed that we live in an age of structural violence in the sense that absolute suffering and relative deprivation on an appalling scale are among the consequences of the world political order. Disgust and rage against the system are therefore to be expected in people who have good wishes to all of their fellow men. But there is a question about the way in which such feelings should be understood. In terms of strict moral obligation, they go beyond all bounds, making the individual feel guilty about things for which he cannot reasonably be seen as having any responsibility. Our

[24] Cf. Peter Winch 'Ethical Punishment and Reward'.

submission is that they make good sense if seen as natural expressions of a gratitude that knows that it cannot find expression. But this is not the view which underlies analysis in terms of structural violence. That notion relies on an incoherent version of the ancient doctrine that suffering is to be interpreted as just punishment.

From the viewpoint adopted in this book, therefore, the idea of just cause is a vital one even though it is often abused and currently possesses neither agreed content nor an agreed procedure. It represents a practical question which Jim will necessarily face from time to time and renders explicit the demand for justification of action in face of the widespread acquiescence in war as something that just happens.

8. The moral standing of the principle of noncombatant immunity

Noncombatant immunity has been the subject of some interesting controversy. Miss Anscombe sees it as an instance of the prohibition of killing the innocent which, she thinks, holds whatever the consequences.[25] Jonathan Bennett contests the claim that there are things which should be done whatever the consequences[26] and James Cargile suggests that there may be right actions which the good man cannot do.[27] John C. Ford argues against the view that modern war renders noncombatant immunity anachronistic.[28] Michael Walzer tries to show the doctrine's humanitarian utility in modern conditions.[29] Thomas Nagel tries to give the principle an 'absolutist' grounding; R.B. Brandt and R.M. Hare to accommodate it to utilitarianism.[30]

Many absorbing questions are raised in this literature; we confine ourselves to three:

a. are there noncombatants?
b. if so, do noncombatants require special moral protection?
c. if so, is the killing of noncombatants always forbidden?

a. Are there noncombatants? We attach a somewhat unusual meaning to the word 'noncombatant'. Traditionally, a combatant is a person engaged in war, war preparation or war threat and a noncombatant is someone who is not a combatant. But the notion of being 'engaged in'

[25] 'War and Murder.'
[26] 'Whatever the Consequences.'
[27] 'On Consequentialism.'
[28] 'The Morality of Obliteration Bombing.'
[29] 'Moral Judgment in Time of War.'
[30] In *War and Moral Responsibility* (ed.) Marshall Cohen et al.

war is somewhat too loose for our purposes. An example may make this plain. John Ford grants that even children

> buy war stamps, write letters of encouragement to their brothers in the service, and even carry the dinner pail to the father who works in the aircraft factory.[31]

The whole point of war stamps is that their sale raises money for the war effort, so in purchasing them the child appears to be 'engaged in' war. The older child may know this, and even experience a certain thrill as a result.

The refinement we propose to the notion of noncombatancy is this. It is one thing for a person to do something whose point relates to war, but quite another thing for a person to be engaged in such activity as one of those parts of life in which, if anywhere, the meaning of his life is to be found. The purchase of the war stamps is merely an episode in the child's life, not an activity constitutive of whatever meaning the child's life contains. By contrast, work as a volunteer soldier or an unwilling conscript is activity of the kind that confers meaning (or meaninglessness) on a person's life. Similarly, the activity of a guerrilla or freedom fighter in their hours off work is the kind of thing that confers meaning on a person's life in a way that the child's purchase of war stamps does not.

In our use of the word, therefore, 'noncombatant' has a rather narrow meaning. A noncombatant is a person who is not a combatant, and a combatant is a person who (i) is engaged in activity which has a military dimension which (ii) is among the activities which confer, if anything does, meaning on the person's life.

The issue is fraught with such confusion that a few further examples may be required. The growing of food, whether or not described as 'digging for victory', is not an activity with a military dimension. Mere membership of a government which is prosecuting a war does not entail combatancy. Taking an active part in the determination of military police in war *or peace* does make a person a combatant. The irregular who is a peasant by day but a guerrilla by night is a combatant. The child buying war stamps is a noncombatant.

John Ford's classic article adopts a different approach to the problem of defining noncombatancy. He offers a long list of occupations and says 'If you can believe that these classes of persons *deserve* to be described as combatants, or *deserve* to be treated as legitimate objects of violent repression, then I shall not argue further'.[32] Such an argument involves an incidental difficulty. For

[31] Wasserstrom 22.
[32] *ibid* 21.

example, Ford's list includes 'telephone girls, advertising men ... typists'. Such people may be engaged in activity with a military dimension, e.g. as military telephonists and typists and as practitioners of psychological warfare. This weakens Ford's argument through under-description – a person's occupation does not always tell one quite enough to determine his combatancy or noncombatancy. But, as indicated above, the deficiency is remediable.

A somewhat deeper difficulty is that Ford confuses the essentially descriptive issue of whether someone is combatant or noncombatant with questions of morality. In our view, combatants *are* to be described as such; it is not that they *deserve* or do not deserve to be so described. Ford's practice in this regard is well-entrenched in the tradition. A classic instance: Is killing lawful, Vitoria asks, when the people concerned may be expected to cause danger in the future? 'For example, the children of Saracens are guiltless, but there is good reason to fear that when grown up they will fight against Christians and bring on them all the hazards of war.' He answers that it is 'in no wise right ... it is intolerable that any one should be killed for a future fault'.[33] This runs together two distinct assumptions: (i) that there is a difference in kind between killing someone where there is some present or past activity on their part which can be adduced in justification and killing someone of whom such justification is impossible; (ii) that the activity in question always entails a fault on the part of the person concerned. So far, we have been concerned only with the question of whether there is a distinction between combatant and noncombatant. To see whether the distinction has moral importance, we turn to the next question.

b. Do noncombatants require special moral protection? Several considerations might be brought forward in the attempt to show that noncombatants do not require special protection. The unhealthy animosity between the western front and the home front in World War I[34] could be contrasted with the sense that 'we are all in it together' which characterised World War II to suggest that a situation in which the whole population is at risk is healthier. It can be pointed out that in some cases the combatant might be the innocent, the noncombatant the person who is far from innocent: this will be the case if, for example, the combatant is a young man living in the Third Reich, an opponent of Nazism who accepts conscription only because the alternative would be to have the Gestapo torture his family and who resolves to fire over the heads of Allied forces unless his fellow soldiers are immediately at risk; and the noncombatant is a fervent supporter

[33] Vitoria 180.   [34] See e.g. Marc Ferro *The Great War 1914-18.*

of Nazism who avoids the fight merely from cowardice. It has been suggested that noncombatant immunity is a cover for apathy, so that in certain situations people can be noncombatant only through some moral or political fault.[35] Finally, it might be urged that every human life is equally valuable; that if a distinction is to be made the soldier's courage makes his life more valuable than that of a civilian who is immune from danger.

On the other side, Michael Walzer points out that of the various lines one might draw to try and limit the destruction caused by war, the line between combatant and noncombatant is a useful one despite difficult borderline cases and regardless of one's feelings about some combatants and some noncombatants.[36] It can be made clear that in the just war tradition 'innocence' does not mean moral innocence but absence of any specific causing of harm, and that the demand is not for sympathy but for justice.

In many cases, a divergence of view is to be found between Walzer's humanitarian perspective and the traditional demand for justice. For example, if overall casualties can be reduced by the killing of noncombatants, the humanitarian impulse is presumably to waive the claim for immunity; but the tradition's stern insistence on justice permits of no such waivers.

As elsewhere in this book, our approach is via our earlier analysis of virtue and our outline sketch of the good man, Jim. For one who is concerned, as Jim is, with treating people as ends there is a very important distinction between two kinds of death in war. Some people, in virtue of what they are doing, can regard death in battle as, however terrible, neither more nor less than suffering the consequences of their own actions. Some other people who might be killed in war do not have this thought open to them. The distinction coincides pretty closely with that between combatant and noncombatant. For the combatant must recognise that death in war would be a fate internally connected with the activity in virtue of which he is a combatant. But, except in very special circumstances, this does not apply to the noncombatant.

The special case has a certain interest. Consider the problem facing the wife of a military man who is about to go on a dangerous posting. She very often has the choice of accompanying him, or not. If she does so, although she does not therefore become a combatant she does embark on a course of action with an internal connection to death in war: what she is setting out to do is to *share the dangers* facing her husband. If, on the other hand, she decides not to accompany him,

[35] Peter Edwards and Oliver Leamen 'Justified Terrorism and Unjustified Apathy'.
[36] 'Moral Judgment in Time of War.'

she is *ipso facto* deciding against the attempt to share the dangers that he faces. (It might, of course, require greater courage to stay at home than to go, depending on the case.)

The internal connection between combatancy and dying in war that we have in mind is a very obvious one, but very often overlooked. To engage in activity that has a military dimension is to involve oneself in fighting very likely to the death, or in the preparation for or threat of such fighting: death through such fighting is part of the job. This applies as much to the worker in a munitions factory or to the Minister of Defence as to the infantryman carrying a rifle, but it does not extend beyond the realm of the combatant. The wife of a serving man who decides to accompany him has a different internal relation to death in war, but one which serves only to underline the point: the internal connection in her case is between her activity of sharing the dangers and the nature of the dangers (viz. death in war) that she is trying to share.

Because of the internal connection between combatancy and being killed, a combatant has the option and opportunity to regard the prospect of death in war as meaningful: written into what he is doing is a connection with being killed that gives his own death a meaning. The same is true of the death of a woman trying to share the dangers of her soldier husband's life. But the death in war of a noncombatant does not have any such guaranteed meaning: it may be something better than a meaningless episode but if this is so then that is for some other reason than that the relation of the person's activity to war makes it so.

This difference is crucially important if not from every viewpoint then certainly from Jim's. For what matters to him above all in virtue of his good wishes towards all men and his Kantian understanding of the good for man is that people should find meaning in their lives and that their suffering and death should not be meaningless episodes but should be redeemed by their part in a larger whole which removes their absurdity. Jim desires that the individual should find meaning in his own life.[37] The relation between combatant and death guarantees the option of finding such meaning; the relation between noncombatant and death furnishes no such guarantee and ensures that in one regard – the activity in virtue of which he is not a combatant – the noncombatant cannot find in his own life the meaning of his death.

In considering the principle of noncombatant immunity, Jim

---

[37] Cf. Nietzsche: 'What really arouses indignation against suffering is not suffering as such but the senselessness of suffering.' *On the Genealogy of Morals* II, 7 tr. Kaufmann and Hollingdale 68.

necessarily contemplates the individuals to be killed or spared, combatant and noncombatant, from the viewpoint of those who are to kill or to spare. This is a viewpoint of very limited information. One is unable to know that one's individual opponent has, or has not, recognised or realised the meaning that is present or absent in his life. One cannot know whether the enemy has made his peace with death. But one can know that if he is a combatant then he has the option of such peace, so that if he fails to find it then that is the fact to be explained, but that if he is a noncombatant then there is no guarantee that his death is anything better than a meaningless episode, a mockery of life. To the good man, possessed as he is with good wishes towards all men and mindful (Sarpedon-like) that the good for man consists in living well and dying well rather than in mere pleasure and freedom from pain, this necessarily renders the killing of noncombatants still more problematic than the killing of combatants.

The lofty tone of this argument invites suspicion. It seems to ignore the essentially squalid facts of war, to look down from an Olympian height of indifference on the suffering and pain of death, and to fly in the face of the belief that in death at least all men are equal. We consider these points in turn.

It is of course true that war is a foul and dehumanising business. If it brings out the best in some people (as it does) equally it is the corrupter and destroyer of many people. It is nevertheless the case that in war some manage to live and die well. The concept of dying well is a difficult one, and requires brief discussion. One case of dying well is where the person dies serenely and with courage, proceeding from this life to nonexistence or the next life with calm assurance as to the meaning of what is happening and good reason to believe or hope that there is nothing to fear. For an essay in philosophy, the most obvious instance of a good death of this kind is the death of Socrates.

Were this the only kind of good death, it would be a cruel mockery to try and expound the notion of a good death *in war*. Nothing could be more remote from the battlefield than the melancholy calm in which Socrates among his friends drinks the hemlock. But at least one other paradigm is compellingly available in Western tradition. According to Matthew and Mark, Jesus dying on the cross called out 'My God, my God, why hast thou forsaken me', gave a loud cry, and died.[38] The other gospels, of course, relate his death in different ways, and it is possible that the words attributed to Jesus by Matthew and Mark are an allusion to a psalm that begins with them and ends with triumph.[39] But the vital point is that at a central place in Christian

[38] Mark 15[34]; Matthew 27[46].
[39] Psalm 22.

tradition the possibility is present, preserved and not contradicted, that a human being truly man and truly god died in utter despair and rout of the faith and conviction that had sustained his life. Read in this way, Mark does not for one moment seem to suggest that Jesus died badly: rather, one's feeling is that at the deepest level Jesus' state of mind at the last is irrelevant. A good death does not require Socratic serenity. Sarpedon, having made his peace with death, might die howling yet still die well.

The application of this to modern conditions of war is exceedingly direct. In the poetry of Wilfred Owen, the horror of the western front is rendered with directness and without any hint that a redeeming significance might be found in any of the soldiers' deaths. Owen did not survive the war to consider it further but David Jones did. He, who had seen as much, renders the horror as unflinchingly as Owen but his great poem *In Parenthesis* is sustained not by pity but by a vision of the killed soldier as the Christ. The last, dying moments do not matter in *In Parenthesis*. A good death on the western front, as on the cross, is shown to be possible. Jones has the right to make the claim. And naturally it can be made as well in Homeric as in Christian terms. It is writ large in the *Iliad*.

We are not therefore denying the squalid facts of war but insisting that among them are the facts of individuals living and dying well, though in torment. Plainly, then, we are not minimising the suffering and pain of death: the greater the physical and mental anguish and the grief of the survivors, the greater the triumph that compels one to recognise nevertheless a good life and death. Somewhat more difficult to discuss is the view that before death all men are equal.

Very many people feel very passionately that morally speaking each person is equally important, so that each death is to be equally deplored and lamented. By suggesting that there is a difference between the death of combatants and that of noncombatants we appear to be challenging this. Our reply is that, in the only relevantly important sense, people are equal if and only if they each have open to them the real possibility of living a good life (including or excluding a good death). A death that deprives a life of its meaning, as is intrinsically likely in the case of a noncombatant, is therefore necessarily horrifying in a way that a death which merely ends a good life, as is intrinsically possible in the case of a combatant, is not. Death is no leveller, for one corpse is the dead body of a person who lived well and another is not. Both require honour, but for very different reasons.

This account of noncombatant immunity differs from what appears to be the normal one in the tradition. There, we take it, the killing of combatants is seen as the killing of people who in some sense or other deserve to be killed. There is an easy but not perhaps very illuminating way of interpreting this traditional view. If it is assumed that war is essentially assimilable to law enforcement, and that those who may justifiably be killed are to be seen as offenders who have to be fought to the death in the enforcement of the law, the notion of deserving to die has an unproblematic application. Our difficulty with the idea is that it seems so incredible when applied to modern if not to all war. Suppose, for example, that the war against Germany 1939-45 was a just war. Does it follow that every German soldier was in some sense at fault and deserving of death in a way that no German noncombatant was? We find this impossible to believe.

A further defence of the traditional position might claim that those German soldiers who could not be regarded as at fault should be on the conscience not of the Allies but of their German leaders; similarly with Allied soldiers killed in the just prosecution of a just war. Such a view certainly salvages much of the traditional view's plausibility but it still seems to us too precarious. It depends heavily on the view that whenever there is war someone somewhere is at fault. We understand that historical circumstances (e.g. those in which Vitoria and Suarez found themselves) might make this a plausible view, but it does not strike us as universally valid. The good man might find himself drawn into war in a context where he can attach no plausible significance to the view that somewhere, someone is responsible. Unlike the traditional view, ours provides for the moral force of noncombatant immunity even in those circumstances. It is therefore less dependent on the vicissitudes of history.

A version of our interpretation which may commend itself to the utilitarian, and which requires mention to show that our interpretation is as closely connected with Jim's good wishes towards all men as with his modified Kantianism, is as follows. Wherever activity with a military dimension is well developed, there is a well-established practice of giving honour and respect to soldiers. War memorials, the tribal memories of regiments, solemn parades, etc, make clear the people's respect and gratitude. Accordingly, it is easier for the soldier before death and his survivors to reconcile themselves to the fact of his death than can be the case with the death of civilians. Thus, taking the leading cases of combatant and noncombatant, the death of the latter is even more terrible than that of the former so far as any generalisation is possible.

There is some truth in this. Ritual very often facilitates the finding of meaning in one's life and serves where there is no meaning to hide the fact. For the utilitarian what matters is the individual's state of mind, so that if a meaning can be *given* that is sufficient, regardless of whether what is given is really there. But for the good man the truth matters more deeply. Unlike the utilitarian, he is necessarily torn by the dilemma (examined above) of whether to tell the truth to the dying man. Faced with the bereaved he will doubtless seek to assure them that the death they are mourning was not absurd regardless of his own view of the matter. But if he is in doubt, he will carry through the pretence with a desperate sadness. What matters to him is that meaning should be found, not given. He will value ritual as a facilitator of the discovery and as a necessary mask. But his desire is necessarily elsewhere.

The case for noncombatant immunity which rests its case on social and psychological facts (e.g. the availability of ritual, the belief that soldiers will have steeled themselves against death where civilians will not) is profoundly unstable. It is all very well noncombatants being thrown off balance for a while by the bringing to them of war but if that is the way things are going then they should surely soon begin to adapt. The genius of the human species is its ability to adapt to changing circumstances. If modern war typically engulfs the noncombatant there is nothing for it but acceptance, on pain of irrationality. This is a compelling argument against the defence of noncombatant immunity which relies on the psychological and social facts of shock and distress. (And of course, pre-war predictions to the contrary, those who underwent aerial bombardment in World War II adapted astonishingly fast, as have other noncombatant populations since.) The man-must-adapt argument can make no headway, however, against the in-principle argument advanced above: to suggest that Jim needs to adapt in the sense of abandoning his good wishes to all men and its consequences is merely to misunderstand.

This, therefore, is our case for noncombatant immunity. Many see the just war ideas as a worthy effort at limiting war: war is something given and the task is to do what one can to mitigate its disasters. But for Jim this is to begin at the wrong end. His problem is not how far war can be limited, but how far it can in conscience be extended. He has, as we have seen, great difficulty in accepting war at all. But his difficulties with the killing of noncombatants are still more formidable. This is because in fighting against combatants one is struggling to the death with people whose activity guarantees the possibility of their seeing their deaths as meaningful – the most that the man of good wish can hope for in a combat where the last thing he can do is actively cherish his enemy's good. In extending the battle to noncombatants even this guarantee is removed: a new inhibition has therefore to be overcome. It is now necessary to consider the question of whether this inhibition is absolute.

c. Is the killing of noncombatants always forbidden? The word 'killing' is often used very broadly to cover all cases where an action results in someone's death, but controversy about principles concerned with killing turns about a much narrower range of examples. The dispute is not about cases in which the death of human beings is an unforeseen consequence of action, and not about the difficult subject of what a reasonable person would or should have foreseen. The issue is action (and avoidance of action) a part of whose foreseen outcome is the death of human beings. A number of controversial topics are in question, including abortion, mercy-killing, the treatment of the dying and of course the ethics of war. A simplified exposition of a very complicated debate must suffice.

The utilitarian, and more generally consequentialist, view is that the value of an action is determined by the total state of affairs to which it gives rise. In utilitarianism, therefore, a person is responsible for all the foreseen consequences of his actions. An influential non-utilitarian view which is to be found somewhere in the just war tradition holds that there is a morally significant distinction between direct and indirect consequences of action: a person is responsible for the direct consequences but not, or not in the same way, for the indirect. Often, the distinction is carried over into the characterisation of the action: the direct consequences play a part in determining how the action is described, but the indirect do not. For example, in medicine a distinction is often made between killing a person and letting a person die. This is sometimes seen as a difference between two types of action, sometimes traced back to the distinction between direct and indirect consequences. If death is a direct consequence, the action is killing; if indirect, it is a case of permitting the person to die.

The idea of double effect is regarded by Miss Anscombe as

> absolutely essential to Christian ethics. For Christianity forbids a number of things as being bad in themselves. But if I am answerable for the foreseen consequences of an action or refusal, as much as for the action itself, then these prohibitions will break down. If someone innocent will die unless I do a wicked thing, then on this view I am his murderer in refusing: so all that is left to me is to weigh up evils. Here the theologian steps in with the principle of double effect and says: 'No, you are no murderer, if the man's death was neither your aim nor your chosen means, and if you had to act in the way that led to it or else do something absolutely forbidden.' Without … this principle … the Christian teaching that in no circumstances may one commit murder, adultery, apostasy (to give a few examples) goes by the board. These absolute prohibitions of Christianity by no means exhaust its ethic; there is a large area where what is just is determined partly by prudent weighing up of

consequences. But the prohibitions are bedrock, and without them the Christian ethic goes to pieces.[40]

This plainly raises numerous issues of great difficulty. Instead of addressing ourselves to it in general terms, we want to consider it from the modied Kantian viewpoint sketched in Chapter Four. That was the viewpoint of a person governed by good wishes towards all men who found the Kantian principle compelling. As pointed out above, such a person is necessarily strongly drawn to utilitarianism, as a peculiarly· direct practical statement of his deepest desires, but is unable to accept it because it fails to take adequate account of the need for each person to live his own moral life.

One very important idea derivable from the principle of double effect is that moral principles govern not so much action as intention: in some sense or other, we are always to look to a person's intentions rather than to their actions for moral assessment. Such a view invites several familiar criticisms. One is that it holds up for admiration the person whose overriding concern is to keep his own hands clean morally. He is an unattractive character who puts purity of 'motive' before the interests of other people. Another criticism, to which Miss Anscombe draws attention, is the danger of doublethink. If directing one's attention in one direction rather than another is

> an interior act of the mind which could be produced at will ... then ... a marvellous way offered itself of making any intention lawful. You had only to 'direct your intention' in a suitable way. In practice, this means making a little speech to yourself: 'What I mean to be doing is ...' ... The devout Catholic bomber secures by a 'direction of intention' that any shedding of innocent blood that occurs is 'accidental'.[41]

John Ford quotes a statement made in July 1944 that 40-50 per cent of the centre of Berlin was 'burned out ... a ruined city' among other statements of the policy of area bombing; he comments

> If these are the facts, what is to be said of the contention that the damage to civilian property and especially to civilian life is only incidental? Is it psychologically and honestly possible for the air strategist in circumstances like these to let go his bombs, and withhold his intention as far as the innocent are concerned?[42]

If it is to be possible for a person to separate his intentions from his actions and secure purity of intention by making himself a little speech, these curious consequences follow.

[40] Wasserstrom 47.
[41] *ibid* 51.   [42] *ibid* 31.

A third, related oddity to which Miss Anscombe draws attention is this: suppose a man is doing something which he knows to have the consequence of poisoning the water supply. His intention is to earn some money by doing what he is doing. If morality inheres in the intention rather than the action then is this man to be immune from moral criticism?[43]

These three difficulties impinge on our ideal moral type, Jim, in different ways. The man poisoning the water is trying to get away with something in a way that Jim could not be. The person preoccupied with purity of motive is, as pointed out in Chapter Four, manifestly not Jim. But the devout bomber is being misled as to his duty by an idea which is philosophical rather than by any moral shortcoming. The question to be asked in our frame of analysis is whether it is a coherent possibility that Jim should be misled in this way.

It is hard to know how far this is a question specifically about Jim and how far it is a question in general philosophy, concerned with the analysis of a concept (the concept of intention) which is independent of particular ethical positions. There is good reason to believe that an intention cannot be an interior act of the mind quite unconnected logically with a person's actions. We will assume without further argument that there is necessarily some logical connection. What is very uncertain is the precise nature of the connection. We are by no means convinced that the utilitarian is unable to give a coherent account of intention. Miss Anscombe insists on double effect as a feature of intention but nowhere shows that it is a necessary feature of every coherent analysis of the idea of intention. Accordingly, we propose to carry the argument forward solely in terms of Jim.

To be capable of living a moral life at all, Jim must be capable of forming binding intentions – for example, of deciding about questions of right and wrong and acting accordingly even in the face of adverse circumstances. It probably follows from this that he needs rather stable moral principles to guide his attention towards morally significant features of his experience. But it does not follow that he needs absolute principles rather than principles that make, in real situations, stringent demands for justification of exceptions. Suppose, for example, that one of his principles forbids the killing of human beings. This certainly draws attention to a salient feature of experience in that people fairly often find themselves in situations relating in one way or another to the death of human beings as a result of human action (though not, mercifully, *very* often). If a person with

[43] *Intention* 41.

good wishes towards all human beings needs this principle, it is presumably because he is under strong moral pressure to slur over the importance of every individual human life. (Not an improbable circumstance: e.g. in the grip of a not very intelligent compassion, Jim might be strongly drawn on a large variety of occasions to kill out of kindness.) Hence if he needs the principle, he needs it to be, in his thinking, highly resistant to the making of exceptions. It must be the kind of principle to make him think here and now rather than the kind of principle which he praises as something which other people need to make them good. But it is, we think, rather easy to show that Jim might have occasion to kill the innocent, knowing what he is doing and, so far as we can see, in such a way as to derive no comfort from the principle of double effect. We give two examples.

a. Suppose Jim is a trained marksman (he might also be a pacifist, as shown above). A gunman has seized a hostage and got into a position from which he is able to decimate a crowd of innocents. The crowd cannot be evacuated; the gunman can be stopped only by shooting him *through* the hostage. What should Jim do? It seems to us plain that he should shoot.

Proponents of the idea of double effect, if prepared to accept this example for discussion, would probably agree that Jim should shoot. What they would probably disagree with us about is the nature of Jim's problem. To us, Jim appears to be having to choose among the innocent, between those in the crowd and the hostage, and being forced to choose against the hostage on the extremely crude principle that in choosing among the lives of innocent strangers one should choose to save more rather than less lives. To the person for whom double effect is important, a decisively important feature of the example is that the hostage's death is 'beside the intention'. Jim is intent on[44] saving the lives of the people in the crowd; a necessary means to this is the death of the gunman; a necessary means to that is shooting through the hostage. The saving of life, the death of the gunman, the bullet passing through the hostage therefore belong to Jim's intention. But the hostage's death is neither an end of Jim's action nor a means.

The distinction is valuable for an analysis of the Allied bombing campaign. Suppose there happened to be civilians working at an oil installation which the Allies were trying to bomb. The Allied purpose would be the destruction of the oil refinery, a necessary means to this the dropping of bombs on civilians, a foreseen consequence the death of those civilians. But their death would not be a means to the end. A

---

[44] We ignore the difficult question of how intent is related to intention.

contrasting example should make this clear. Suppose the Allies are trying to secure German surrender and accordingly bomb civilians in order to force the German government to seek terms or in order to provoke insurrection. In this case, the deaths of civilians are the means by which it is hoped to defeat the enemy. The strategy adopted by Sir Arthur Harris and the British war cabinet (and employed by the US against Japan) is in these terms plainly distinguished from that favoured by British and American proponents of bombing designed to achieve its effect by other means than the deaths of the civilians.

b. A second example may serve to clarify the extent of our disagreement with adherents of double effect. It is the example with which we introduced Jim in Chapter Four. Pedro has twenty Indians tied up against a wall and is about to shoot them when Jim appears on the scene. Pedro offers Jim the choice: you shoot one of the Indians or I shoot them all. Let us suppose that Pedro's motivation, which becomes very plain to Jim, is that he very much relishes the prospect of making the good man squirm. He wants to make Jim suffer. How should the situation be described, and what should Jim do?

We assume that the Indians are innocents and implore Jim to accept Pedro's offer. One tempting thought is that Pedro is wholly to blame and that it would be nice if Jim could say 'On your head be it'. If Jim could wash his hands of the whole affair, that would have the congenial effect of putting all the blame where it belongs, on Pedro. But such a possibility is not open to Jim: he cannot take such a stand on principle because his fundamental interest in the situation is in the good of the Indians. Only a person who put purity and principle before the Indians could wash his hands of the matter, or so it seems to us.

This appears to have damaging implications for the notion of double effect. Jim can save nineteen of the Indians only by killing the twentieth: the death of the twentieth Indian at the hands of Jim is necessarily a means to the end which in our view is morally binding upon Jim. If he does what we think is his duty, then the killing of the innocent is something that he intends.

It should not be inferred from this that the case leads readily to a blurring of the moral distinction that we drew in terms of double effect between the bombing of civilians whose deaths are a means to some military objective and bombing in which the death of civilians is beside the intention. A vital factor in the Pedro example is that the Indians *want* Jim to accept Pedro's offer. Its importance for the ethics of war is the doubt it throws on the principle of double effect as an adequate moral doctrine when viewed from the modified Kantian viewpoint adopted in this book.

The example of the gunman and the shield appears to us more illuminating for the substantial question of how far noncombatant immunity should be observed. In that example, Jim has to choose between strangers to none of whom he has any special ties. If the example is taken seriously as a guide, it suggests the very obvious conclusion that where one has to choose between alternative strategies whose effects are to be considered in terms of enemy losses, one should choose in the light of noncombatant immunity and in the light of sheer numbers. (We have no answer to the question of how these should be 'weighed' should they conflict. No answer is available from the viewpoint of this book and perhaps none should be expected.)

This is a very uninteresting conclusion because it does not tell one what to do when the choice is between enemy personnel and one's own personnel. This choice is a crucial one for any ethical theory. If a military commander has to choose between the lives of his own troops and the lives of enemy noncombatants, what should he do? In terms of the traditional view that sees noncombatant immunity as a matter of the killing of the innocent and relies on double effect to clarify the notion of killing, the direct killing of noncombatants is of course out of the question even to save the lives of people to whom one is most intimately attached. (To mention a different but related part of the doctrine: it may be imperative to let one's wife die if the alternative is to kill an unborn baby.)

Our modified Kantian view agrees with the tradition regarding noncombatants in practice, but from different premises. We accept that the military commander's job is to plan and act for the carrying out of measures determined by the political authorities with the minimum cost to his own force and the state or alliance that it exists to serve. Any ethical theory which is not unequivocally pacifist must come to terms with this duty of the military commander as a moral duty. The question is whether it is subject to any prior constraints. We believe that it is. The military commander inspired by good wishes towards all men necessarily needs to be able to understand his work within a moral framework that accommodates the interests of all men. (Otherwise, he could not do the job for a single day.) The obvious outline of such an understanding is that he finds himself in a world of states engaged in activity with a military dimension. One way of living a decent moral life in such a world is to serve one's state and thereby to serve humanity, one way of serving one's state being military service. In terms of such an outline it must be possible for the military commander to take with moral seriousness the immunity of noncombatants: the same reasons that impel him to understand himself as a moral being serving humanity are reasons for holding in especial horror the killing of noncombatants. (He requires for humanity, both in his own person and in the person of others, the possibility of the good life for man – in his own case this demands a self-understanding in terms of the service of humanity; in the case of noncombatants, it renders their death in battle peculiarly abhorrent from the moral viewpoint.)

Hence, however appalling or unrealistic this may seem, it seems to us a plain conclusion of our moral outlook that the military commander should be prepared to prefer the deaths of his own troops to the deaths of enemy noncombatants.

We are now in a position to answer the question 'Is the killing of noncombatants always forbidden?' In the traditional view, action resulting in the deaths of innocents is not always forbidden, but action of which such deaths are a direct consequence is always forbidden. In our view, as in the traditional one, the crucial issue concerns foreseen deaths. The relevant principle is the Kantian one and it entails (as argued in the previous section) a special moral horror in the killing of noncombatants. In some cases, it is necessary to choose among noncombatants, and then one should of course choose to spare as many of these noncombatant strangers as possible. In other cases, the choice is between noncombatants and one's own soldiers and here the noncombatants should come first even if they are enemy civilians. There is, as very often in morality, the possibility of a conflict between the principle demanding that in cases of difficulty one opts to save as many lives as possible and some principle of qualitative choice (here, that of holding the deaths of noncombatants in special horror). We see no reason to believe that such choices can be anything but criterionless, though in cases of massive disproportion of numbers, the principle of proportion presumably operates.

One great strength of the traditional view, unlike those commendations which urge noncombatant immunity on purely humanitarian grounds, is its resistance to being rendered practically meaningless by means of counter-example. We put the modified Kantian viewpoint forward as having similarly great stability, despite its admission of qualifications. Like the traditional view, it is firmly rooted in Western tradition. It seems to us preferable in having better roots.

9. *Is deterrence different?*

It hardly needs stressing that in terms of the principles of proportion and noncombatant immunity a formidable case can be made out against nuclear deterrence. The very great destructiveness of a major nuclear war, its disastrous effects on neutrals and future generations, the impossibility that it could be waged without large-scale direct attacks on noncombatants, the disproportion between the havoc it would wreak and any likely and attainable objective – all these are too familiar to require extensive treatment. But there are two peculiar features of deterrence which require discussion: first, as long as deterrence 'works', nuclear war is avoided and the horrors just mentioned do not come into being; second, the West is pledged to use nuclear weapons only defensively – is there not some profound moral difference between being the first to bring disaster on the world and being the one who responds to the bringer of evil?

On hoping that deterrence will work. In traditional terms, the argument that deterrence is different because it avoids war is completely untenable. Morality inheres in the intention as well as the action; nuclear deterrence is the (conditional) intention to wage disproportionate and indiscriminate war; nuclear deterrence is therefore straightforwardly and unequivocally wrong.

Our argument diverges in several respects from the traditional one, and might be thought to do so here. Where tradition speaks of intention, we speak of treating humanity as an end. It is therefore necessary to consider at greater length the question of what difference it makes, if any, that deterrence supposedly keeps the peace.

A deliberately artificial example may, once again, be enlightening. Suppose that my family and I live in a very remote place (perhaps because we are a family of miners of some rare material that is to be found only in remote regions). Our house is powered by a highly explosive gas since no other source of energy is available. If I want to, I can explode the gas, destroying the house and all its inhabitants. This fact is very widely known (perhaps I am held in awe among the few people who live relatively close because of the power to cause such a mighty explosion). Bandits are operating in the vicinity who are known to make a practice of kidnapping young children whom they subject to a cruel and revolting slow death. Once a child has been carried off, nothing can be done to protect it: sooner or later, its mangled body will tell us all that we shall ever know of its fate. One night, I surprise one of the kidnappers in my house about to escape with my youngest child. For reasons which we need not go into, I have only one possible hold on the kidnapper: I can threaten to blow the house up, and this cannot be a bluff. A good deal is known about the kidnappers; in particular, that they attach a very high value to their own lives and do not see any important dishonour in failing to carry off a child when surprised. My values and character are such that if the abduction is successful then I shall not subsequently, out of despair or on some principle, detonate the house with myself and my remaining family in it. What should I do?

In practice, there are two alternatives open to me: (i) threaten to destroy the house, my family and the kidnapper in the knowledge that it is extremely likely that, faced with this threat, the kidnapper will relinquish my child and make his escape; (ii) refrain from making the threat in the firm knowledge that my child will then suffer the most frightful death.

Suppose the example is exactly as before except that I know the kidnappers to place honour above life, and to think that honour would be betrayed if they relinquished a child that they had seized. Then the options will be: (iii) make the threat in the firm knowledge that this will very likely result in the death of us all; (iv) refrain.

It seems to us that the choice between (i) and (ii) is different, morally speaking, from that between (iii) and (iv). But the tradition would seem to suggest that they are the same. Utilitarianism, on the other hand, is very familiar with the thought that they are different. What difference, if any, is discernible from the modified Kantian viewpoint adopted in this book?

This is an example of the very difficult subject of the role of *luck* in morality. Machiavelli and Clausewitz, of course, insist on the importance of luck, chance, fortune in the political and military life; and any ethical theory that aims to cope with political issues is forced to grapple at some point with the question of luck.[45] The topic is a particularly difficult one for the modified Kantian outlook because that viewpoint is driven by the conviction of the importance of a life that makes inroads against the mere contingencies of time and mortality, setting the achievement of the good life against all that chance may bring before ill-fortune finally engulfs the virtuous man.

The difficulty that this neo-Kantian outlook has with chance appears to us to be among its great strengths. The man who gives hostages to fortune is the one most likely to lose sight, for systematic reasons, of the importance of treating humanity as an end. In order to give chance its opportunity, he necessarily opens a gap between his actions and the things that he wishes for.

The Kantian can allow one concession to luck. There is a familiar enough category of situation in which luck plays an important part: the class of situations in which there is strong moral reason for doing something with consequences of a hideous sort which are possible but extremely unlikely. To run the risk in such situations is to face the possibility of being desperately unlucky, but it is scarcely to be called

---

[45] Cf. the discussion in Chapter Six below of 'Moral Luck' by Bernard Williams.

the systematic taking of chances, the practice of giving hostages to fortune. The situation in which the choice is between (i) and (ii) belongs in this category, whereas that between (iii) and (iv) does not. We submit that the felt moral difference between the two cases consists in this.

If nuclear deterrence is significantly analogous to the taking of option (i) in the situation sketched above then it will be morally defensible within the framework that we are using. But it seems to us clear enough that the disanalogy between the cases is far more striking than the analogy.

In our fanciful example, the confrontation between the parent and the bandit is a matter of a moment, and in no way alters the general pattern of the parent's life or character. Nothing could be more different from this than nuclear deterrence which, as pointed out in Chapter Two above, is widely seen as a principle of world order. Deterrence employs a very large number of people full time, their working lives devoted to the maintenance of the deterrent. This work is done in the name of the adult citizens of Western and communist states. The parent in our imaginary example is acting on behalf of a child, who cannot be expected to have a view of its own on what should be done. Once one penetrates the level of analysis which sees deterrence as a thing that is practised by states, and notices the human reality below, one can clearly see that reliance on the deterrent is the activity of adults. Understood in this way, reliance on the deterrent imports into the lives of those who man the deterrent, and the people in whose name they act, a deep and systematic reliance on *luck*. Instead of being a marginal matter, as in our fanciful example, trusting to luck becomes the foundation of security on which civilised life is built.

In saying this, we are not taking any controversial view of the likelihood of nuclear war. Of course, if nuclear war were quite out of the question then the morality of the thing would be altered: one would not, under those circumstances, be harbouring a conditional intention. But no one suggests that nuclear war is impossible. The precise probability is beside the point. Whether it has the very low likelihood exemplified in (i) and (ii) or the rather high likelihood of (iii) and (iv), deterrence makes trusting to luck the foundation of security – if only in the sense that if there is a major nuclear war then we will all have been very unlucky.

This seems to us an important finding whose significance is understandably under-rated in the tradition. Even if it is allowed, as in the tradition it is not, that it may sometimes be right to risk morally appalling consequences, it does not follow that all options are to be assessed on some calculus. If the Kantian principle of treating people as ends is taken seriously, then there is a scruple against deterrence which is independent of the particular probability of various options. *But what if the other side do it first?* This question embodies a logical blunder. What is being asked is something like this: If the enemy do something morally frightful to us, are we entitled to do something frightful to them in return? This is the wrong question. If the enemy do something frightful then they do it to certain people living in London, Berlin, Hamburg, etc. If we do something frightful 'in reply' we do it to certain people living in Moscow, Leningrad, etc. The question is therefore: if the enemy infringe the rights of one group of people, are we thereby entitled to infringe the rights of another group? The answer is rather obviously no. What confuses matters is that the action is seen as an exchange between an undifferentiated 'them' and an undifferentiated 'us'. If they do such-and-such to 'us' are we entitled to do it back? But the right of noncombatant immunity, the right to be treated with a sense of proportion, above all the right to have one's humanity treated as an end belongs to individuals not to states.

It might be objected that this argument ignores the political character of human life: if our state is caught up in a situation of military confrontation, we (and all the citizens of the enemy state) are fair game. From the Kantian viewpoint adopted here, such an argument is easily answered. Three examples should suffice.

(a) Suppose that in ancient Athens every citizen had the opportunity and capacity to go every day to an assembly where each voice counted equally in the crucial decisions on war and peace. In such circumstances a citizen could hardly complain if he was among those subjected to direct attack in wartime, even if he had consistently argued for peace. He might reproach his fellow Athenians for what they had brought on the city by refusing to heed his warnings and he might reproach himself for having spoken up too little and too late. But as a member of the decision-making body in time of war he would necessarily count as a combatant. Even in this polis, the argument that we are all members of the state does not make it all right to attack children, slaves, women. But the important point is that modern states are in the decisive respect unlike this Athens: the citizenry does not take the relevant decisions and is therefore noncombatant.

(b) The non-participation of the citizen body is most obvious in the examples of Nazi Germany and Soviet Russia. Set aside for a moment the election which on 5 March 1933 provided Hitler with a shaky confirmation of his position in power and consider the Nazi state as it was by 1939, or the Soviet Union as it is today. It is of course true that the German and Russian people play their part in the drama of war and confrontation in not rising up to overthrow the leadership. It is nevertheless the case that such a rising would require an act of appalling courage, as the July Plot of 1944 testifies. A man or group may reproach himself for falling short of such heroism. But to describe him as a combatant solely because he does not engage in heroic action would be thoroughly perverse.

(c) One has also to consider the liberal-democratic states involved in the deterrent as in the bombing offensive against Germany and Japan. In a liberal democracy there is an electorate which chooses (within pretty narrow limits) (some of) the decision-makers. It might be argued that this makes the people fair game as a target for nuclear attack but the argument would be a bad one. In a liberal democracy the decision-makers are elected to make decisions concerning, among other things, the declaration and conduct of war. To answer the question 'Who is threatening the Soviet Union with nuclear weapons?' by saying simply 'The United States and her allies' would be seriously misleading. Deterrence was decided on by that comparatively small group of people who were in a position, acting in the name of various Western states, to determine Western military security policy. The question is, what follows from the fact that something has been done in our name? There is no one answer to this question. To be relevant at all, the invocation of the American people, the British people, etc., must connect up with something and at different times it may connect up with different things. We are unable to think of any connection between the invocation and the people to override the principle of noncombatant immunity.

In international law, reprisals are prohibited with one carefully delimited exception: if some illegal measure has been used against one, and if there is good reason to believe that further use of that measure can be stopped by use of it oneself, then such reprisal action is licit. The expression 'nuclear reprisal', which plays an important part in deterrence theorising, has no such restricted meaning. Those who believe that deterrence should be organised into a series of different levels of violence hold that the ability to engage in new and ever more destructive reprisals is an integral part of deterrence. One finds in such arguments no consideration of the moral problem that such 'escalation' involves the carrying of the war to individuals not previously affected: it is not that one is hitting 'them' harder but that one is hitting people whose immunity had so far been respected.

An alarming view of the moral standing of 'escalation' is to be found in the article on pacifism by Jan Narveson discussed above. Having argued that pacifism is incoherent, Narveson says 'How much force does a given threat of violence justify for preventive purposes? The answer, in a word, is "Enough".' Suppose, for example, that someone is 'pestering me':

> I call the police and they take out a warrant against him, and ... when the police come, he puts up a struggle. He pulls a knife or a gun, let us say, and the police shoot him in the ensuing battle. Has my right to the prevention of his annoying me extended to killing him? Well, not exactly, since the immediate threat in response to which he is killed is a threat to the lives of the policemen. Yet my annoyer may never have contemplated real violence. It is an unfortunate case of unpremeditated escalation. But this is precisely what makes the contention that one is justified in using enough force to do the job, whatever that amount may be, to prevent action which violates a right less alarming than at first sight it seems. For it is difficult to envisage a reason why extreme force is needed to prevent mild threats from realization except by way of escalation, and *escalation automatically justifies increased use of preventive force.*[46]

Narveson makes plain that he sees this argument as applying to a Hobbesian state of nature as well as to conditions in which the rule of law is operative, and in context it seems evident that he sees states as having the right to self-protection. His argument therefore implies that if a minor nuclear power is able, on having some right trampled upon (e.g. the right of territorial integrity), to precipitate a major nuclear crisis then an ensuing process of escalation might automatically justify nuclear holocaust.

What is one to make of such an argument? An important distinction is that between the individual and the collectivity. It is one thing to justify increasing levels of violence against an offending individual; it is quite another to justify escalation against an offending state, at the expense of overriding the rights of increasingly many individuals (e.g. noncombatants).

The morality of 'escalation' against an offender or group of offenders is itself a difficult topic, far less clear-cut than Narveson suggests. To mention only one elementary point: the treatment of a mere individual *very often* offers to the authorities a variety of courses of action. There could of course be situations like that suggested by Narveson in which those engaged in law enforcement have no option but to choose between saving their own lives or the immediately threatened lives of third parties and killing an offender. But very, very frequently there is a variety of other possible actions. Talk of

---

[46] Wasserstrom 74, our italics.

'escalation' readily obscures the need for a new assessment of the situation at each new level.

A similar obscurity surrounds some doctrines of nuclear escalation. For example, the threat to lose control is a threat to put oneself in a situation where escalation is likely in circumstances in which new thinking about the new circumstances brought about by escalation is impossible. To speak as Narveson does is to lend moral authority to such a strategy: once make sure that your initial grievance over which you threaten to lose control is justified and escalation's automated justification of ever-growing violence will take care of the rest. In any remotely likely case of nuclear escalation, this will bring destruction to ever-widening circles of noncombatants.

In this chapter we have sought to establish a foundation for the just war idea and to consider some contemporary issues in the tradition. The argument advanced in Chapter Two that the modern world is one in which political consensus has collapsed was carried further in the present chapter. We argued that in the aftermath of the death of god, no agreed meaning could be found for the words in which a doctrine of natural law would need to be stated. Accordingly, we attempted something much more modest and appropriate to the time: namely, to draw out the view which our modified Kantian would necessarily take of the just war idea. We suggested that this was a legitimate move within the tradition because just war thinking is a dynamic process containing within itself a mass of historically conditioned contradictions.

The tradition is not, however, an artificial construct. Its characteristic direction is determined by the two questions 'May the Christian without sin wage war?' and 'What constraints are there upon the activity of the Christian in the waging of war?' The meaning given to these questions depends on the Christian's understanding of himself and his world. We tried to show that our ideal type of the good man, Jim, could reasonably be regarded as someone who might happen to be a Christian or might happen not to be: neither hypothesis would result in incoherent thinking on Jim's part. For Jim, if he is a Christian, the two perennial questions in the tradition amount to two questions which would be equally troubling for a non-Christian modified Kantian.

Turning to specifics, we argued that the just war idea applies to all measures with a military dimension and to all levels of command. The requirement of proportion was seen as a very demanding principle enjoining constant mindfulness on the part of belligerents about what they are trying to do. The concept of structural violence was criticised as inferior to that of just cause, and the forlorn demand for the trying of peaceful means was vindicated. Noncombatant immunity was exhibited as powerfully resistant to the uncritical making of exceptions, but we gave reasons for rejecting the traditional just war vision of it as a special application of the supposedly absolute principle forbidding the killing of the innocent. (We tried to show that that principle is not truly absolute.) We considered the argument that deterrence is different and suggested that it is far from defensibly different: in addition to violating the principles of proportion and noncombatant immunity, it introduces an unacceptable quality of giving hostages to fate. Escalation was interpreted as a confused threatening of the rights of individuals.

Throughout this chapter we have been trying to write from one articulate viewpoint, arguing in the process that such a method is necessary. In our next and final chapter, we return to a closer consideration of the bombing of cities. One leading theme will be the fact that those who have thought about this have done so from a wide variety of different moral viewpoints.

VI

Judgment

This chapter contains four main parts. In sections 1 to 4, we draw out some of the implications of the foregoing argument for the morality of the bombing of cities. In the rest of the chapter we examine three aspects of the complicated issues that arise from the fact that our argument has been developed in terms of one outlook on the world among others. Sections 5 and 6 look into the problem of extending moral judgment from the judgment of actions to the judgment of the agents responsible for those actions. Sections 7 to 10 are concerned with the relation between the argument that we have been developing and so-called political realism. Finally, sections 11 to 13 meet head on the scepticism about moral judgment in general and moral judgment about the ethics of war in particular which arises from popular and philosophical ideas of relativism and subjectivism. By the end of the chapter, it should be clear in what sense we are claiming to establish the *truth* of certain moral judgments provisionally formulated in the first section of the chapter on the strength of the political, historical and ethical analysis of Chapters One to Five.

1. Judgment of area bombing

We consider first the Allied bombing offensive against Germany and the use of the two atom bombs against Japanese cities. Chapter One stressed that those concerned with the campaigns saw themselves as men with an unpleasant but necessary job to do. The pre-war strategists saw their task as being not ethical analysis but the construction of a strategy which would obviate the horror and stark prospect of defeat that was anticipated from a repetition of the stalemated trench warfare of the western front. Liddell Hart and Douhet both tried to suggest that their strategy would be more humane in that it would be quicker and cost fewer lives. The British war cabinet, following a bitter controversy between Churchill's two principal scientific advisers, deliberately opted for a policy of the bombing of civilians in order to hasten or secure military victory.

Successive US administrations favoured in Europe another strategy than that of the bombing of civilians, but against Japan exhibited no more scruple than the British did against German cities.

From the viewpoint developed in earlier chapters, one of the most striking general features of this history is the very great unselfconsciousness of those engaged in the pre-war and wartime debates. Secure in their sense of having a job to do, no one appears to have questioned the relation between the carrying out of that job and the moral and political world-order in which the job was created. This may seem a naively inappropriate remark. The profession of arms and the profession of politics are not noted for requiring the typically academic qualities of general reflectiveness from their members – some would think such qualities a handicap if not a disqualification. Doubtless there is much truth in this remark at the level of individual psychology. It is no criticism of the strategists, politicians, and airforce authorities that they were not men of the kind who give much time to pondering the nature of world politics and its bearing on their special tasks.

But this is the least important or interesting aspect of the matter. For just as striking from the viewpoint adopted in this book as the manifest fact that those involved were men of action not reflection, is the point that there was no one whose job it was to consider these practical matters from a general, contemplative viewpoint. We mentioned Sir Archibald Sinclair's explanation to Portal that it was necessary to claim in public that Bomber Command was always aiming at military and industrial installations because otherwise the Archbishop of Canterbury, the Moderator of the Church of Scotland and other religious leaders might come out with utterances that could disturb the morale of bomber crews. But this does not mean that the job of moral watch-dog lay with church leaders. When Bishop Bell spoke out against the bombing of cities he brought the dignity of his office to bear, but it was by no means accepted that to speak thus was his appointed task. No doubt some of the critics of official policy regarded themselves as being called, or being called upon, to speak out. But this is a very different, and much more personal thing than its being one's job to raise the larger questions underlying policy, and in particular the moral issues.

To some extent, this absence of appointed moral critics can be traced to the special historical conditions of inter-war thinking about international relations. As pointed out in Chapters One and Two, the dominant consensus in Britain in the period was that the guarantor of peace was the League of Nations. A great deal of official and semi-official thinking went into that, and military thinking was necessarily a somewhat specialised pursuit without any deep connection with the prevailing theory of the moral world order.

But the absence of recognised critics whose job it was to question the short-term and intensely practical perspectives of the policy-makers goes deeper than this. In the period under discussion it was very widely accepted that moral opinions were a purely personal thing, in no way admitting of the development of disciplined expertise. Only experts could sensibly pronounce on strategy but moral pronouncements were the sort of thing anyone was capable of. If one made certain specific allegiances, one put oneself into the hands of supposed experts on morality: e.g. by joining the Roman Catholic Church one committed oneself to viewing with a special respect if not obedience the moral judgments of the Church's moral authorities. But the public arena was not dominated by any such discipline. Given this situation, it is hardly surprising that there was no one whose job it was to raise the general background questions about war and the preparation and threat of war.

The roots of this situation lie deep in post-Reformation culture. If there is wide religious credence given to the view that the individual conscience is perfectly competent on all moral questions of any significance; if there is wide moral and political agreement that all religious beliefs are morally and politically speaking immune from criticism because 'just a matter of personal faith'; and if there is fairly widespread recognition that all consensus on questions of final value has collapsed – then it is to be expected that the notion that the moral criticism of political and military action is a vital and specialised function will not be accepted or implemented.

Some would hold that the situation demands the formation of a new consensus (or the re-formation of an old one): natural law, the best basis for moral judgment, is a matter for experts. The authority and discipline of natural law should be recognised and if it is anyone's job to raise large background questions about military policy then the appropriate authorities will be those versed in natural law. For reasons that have been given in Chapter Five, we do not accept this view applied to the world as it is. We have no particular view on whether the world needs changing to give new authority to natural law, though a point of great importance for our theme is that if violent change is contemplated then the just war tradition requires consideration, not only in the envisaging of the desired final state but also as governing proper conduct in the period of 'transition'.

We do not infer from this that the pre-war situation, in which it was no one's job to ask the hard general questions about strategy, was inevitable in the aftermath of the death of god. For there is a community whose job it is, in the world of collapsed consensus, to raise the general questions – the community of scholars. For persons with the leisure, expertise and temperament to insist on the facing of these difficult questions are presumably the students inside and outside the universities of subjects which bear in one way and another on the ethics of war – such subjects as international relations, moral and political philosophy, history, law, strategic studies. In the contemporary world these are the people whose job it is to be competent to discuss the general questions which understandably received scant attention from pre-war strategists and war-time politicians and generals.

The Allies in their attempt to pass judgment on the German and Japanese peoples at the end of World War II laid heavy stress on *ideas*: among those arraigned at Nuremberg, for example, was a leading Nazi propagandist seen (reasonably or not) as partly responsible for the ideas which Germany brought to the struggle against the Allies. A point not often made is that the correlative of this insistence on the importance of ideas in Germany was not given effect. Among the many ideas for a new world order current in the late forties, the idea that academics bore a heavy responsibility for the scrutiny of the most general assumptions underlying ideas about military security was not prominent.

The principal considerations which have guided the argument of our first five chapters have been concerned with very general intellectual problems – the breakdown of consensus, the emergence of the politically-divided man, the development of new principles of world order. Reflection on these in relation to the bombing narrative given in our first chapter points to an overwhelming *intellectual* failure as one of the prime issues of moral concern. Between the wars and during the war, as also since, the soldier and strategist, the politician, and the academic have to a large extent pursued what have seemed to each of them separate pursuits with very little bearing on one another. Where experts in the subject called 'international relations' have involved themselves with officials it has largely been in the solving of problems posed by the officials – official questions, unofficial answers. The overall perspective has not been so much as sought by those best equipped to look for it.

One could multiply instances of this at great length but for present purposes all that is required is the manifestly true generalisation that if the pre-war strategists and war-time politicians and military commanders were unreflective about the general principles underlying their action, the fault or nonmoral factors responsible are to be sought in that part of society which is best equipped to remedy the deficiency – presumably the academic community.

This gross intellectual failure affects all more specific moral judgments when applied not to actions but to individuals: if one is seeking people to blame, the university lecturer who confined his attentions to the wrong questions may be at least as important as the strategist who advocated some objectionable measure, the politician who authorised it and the military commander who, having lobbied hard for its adoption, then carried out that for which he had obtained formal endorsement from his political masters. Because of this complication, we confine ourselves in the rest of this section to the assessment of actions, rather than individuals. If there was moral fault in the conduct of the Allied campaign, it was not confined to one level of command. In particular, the strategic bombing of cities was plainly the responsibility of among others the supreme political authorities who, with whatever reservations about its likely success, sanctioned it; the Chief of the Air Staff Portal who, opposing Harris' strategy, failed to dismiss him; and such commanders as Sir Arthur Harris who pressed very vigorously for the measures that he favoured in the face of alternative strategies.

The question of whether one should go further than this and claim that if there was moral fault then it extended to all levels of command is a difficult one. When we urged that the just war idea is binding at all levels in Chapter Five, we mainly had in mind the bearing of just war ideas on the formation of policy at all levels. That is, we were claiming that everyone who has a responsibility for making decisions should be guided in the making of those decisions by the just war principles: this applies as much to a lowly commander deciding on whether to attack a village crowded with noncombatants as to the President or Prime Minister of a powerful state pondering questions of grand strategy. The issue of responsibility for the bombing campaign is rather different from this: below a certain level of command, the realistic question is not whether men should have approached decisions from within the just war framework but whether they should have disobeyed orders representing decisions made by other people. For an understanding of war, it is necessary to insist *both* on the great amount of sharing of decision-making even with those of rather low rank *and* on the operation of mechanisms of obedience in most activity with a military dimension. The moral issue of responsibility for disobeying orders will be considered in sections five and six below.

The two main just war principles which we sought to elucidate in Chapter Five were those demanding a sense of proportion and insisting on noncombatant immunity. A sense of proportion is strikingly absent from the conduct of the Allied bombing campaign.

Perhaps the two most obvious instances of this are the failure, before Portal's memorandum of 1 August 1944, to consider the political aspects of the bombing of civilians and the stubborn unthinking insistence on Japanese unconditional surrender which was such an important factor in the dropping of the atom bombs and which was then effectively abandoned. On the other hand, it is necessary to point out, as many commentators have done, that in Britain and America World War II was fought with markedly less loss of perspective than World War I. The false rumours about German atrocities in World War I appear to have led some to discount the truth about Nazi enormities in the next war.

The clear-cut nature of the struggle against Germany, which could end only in Allied defeat or the unconditional surrender of the Third Reich, presumably combined with the extreme forcefulness and competence of Churchill and Roosevelt to ensure that the usual problem of civil-military relations – that of the relation between political mastery and military thinking – was not a serious issue in the Allied bombing offensive. If Harris enjoyed very considerable freedom of manoeuvre this was within limits set by Churchill. Portal perhaps was too weak to dismiss Harris but no one suggests that the same is true of Churchill.

Because of this clear domination of the political over the military, one of the essential ingredients in a proper sense of proportion was present in the Allied campaign: up to a point, the relation between political end and military instrumentality was secure. But, as we have pointed out, this is far from affirming that the campaign was fought with a due sense of proportion: political thinking about how to use the bombing of cities was absent, as was the finesse required for thinking about the more difficult issue of the treatment of Japan.

All of those concerned with the bombing were apt to see the enemy as an undifferentiated 'they': in bombing German cities one was bombing Germany rather than bombing noncombatants who might possess some well-entrenched right to be immune from military attack. The kind of perception of the enemy which might make one suppose that there was a moral problem about indiscriminate attacks was almost completely absent. And, of course, the immunity of noncombatants was nowhere respected: where some other policy was advocated in preference to the bombing of cities, it was on the ground that the alternative would contribute more to victory, involve smaller Allied losses, and so on. From the Blitz on 'we were all in it together' and that included noncombatant citizens of Germany and Japan.

Thus, on the strength of our examination of the just war idea in Chapter Five, we would criticise the conduct of the Allied bombing offensive as lacking in coherent thought, as lacking in proportion, and as violating the rights of noncombatants. These faults were present at all levels of command concerned with the framing of policy, and their roots are to be sought perhaps as much in the failings of those e.g. the academic community whose job it is to raise such questions as in the failings of the men of action who waged the war.

Similar criticisms apply to the strategy of nuclear deterrence. Philip Green has shown in great detail that those works of social science which purport to have carried through a thorough and 'scientific' analysis of deterrence are in fact thoroughly and obviously unscientific.[1] A good many academics have spent much time on detailed thinking about questions propounded by officials concerned with the deterrent. A small amount of critical work has been done by individuals out of individual concern. The *Bulletin of the Atomic Scientists* is a long-lived attempt to think about nuclear problems but from a narrow perspective. Ethical deliberation and deep questioning of fundamental issues concerning world order have long since vanished from the deliberations of such admirable organisations as the International Institute for Strategic Studies.

If there has been any pronounced change in the intellectual background to military thought and action since 1945 it is that the commitment under certain circumstances to bring war to noncombatants, to neutrals and to future generations has become a principle of world order, a thing on which reliance is placed for the preservation of 'peace'. With the reduction of the Campaign for Nuclear Disarmament to a small band of enthusiasts, nuclear deterrence appears today to be accepted as a fundamental feature of international relations which very few are prepared to question. Such questioning as there is tends to be emotional and above all *amateur* – in the world of the retreat into professionalism, there are very many people in increasingly many countries whose job it is to maintain and extend nuclear deterrence. There is almost no one whose job it is to raise the large issues in terms of which deterrence is problematic – it is therefore inevitable that the case for deterrence is presented with enormous professional expertise, subtlety and fullness whereas the case against is the amateur product of a dedicated few.

2. *Warfare of evasion and counter-evasion*

The warfare of evasion and counter-evasion is in some ways treated with somewhat greater subtlety. It is a commonplace in the Anglo-American literature on counter-insurgency that the fundamental

[1] *Deadly Logic.*

struggle between insurgent and counter-insurgent is a political one. The kind of thinking about area bombing prior to Portal's memorandum which was able to proceed without considering the connection between military and political measures is alien to this literature. But the counter-insurgent regards himself as a man with a job to do: his task is to serve his political masters in their struggles against insurgency. He is alive to the need for a consideration of political measures as an instrument of policy, therefore. But his professional view of politics is necessarily manipulative. It is not for him to ask such vital questions as 'When should we give up?' and 'When must one recognise that there are political concessions which one cannot make?' To some extent, the absence of such questions from the writings of counter-insurgents (as from those of their opponents)[2] is a reflection of historical experience: in the retreat from Empire, military men have not been called upon to decide when to abandon the struggle and in the British case have never been faced with a situation that calls for political concessions which are politically impossible. In the American effort to 'contain Communism', military men as such have had no part to play in determining the political considerations for and against the undertaking and abandoning of military commitments that fall within the realm of counter-evasive war.

An example may serve to clarify this point. The UK and US have mainly fought counter-evasive warfare far from their own shores (leaving aside the special and difficult case of Northern Ireland). This warfare, except in the disastrously entangling case of Vietnam, has not been widely seen by the military as having significant political implications for life in the home country. It has therefore been possible to view politics (i.e. the politics of far-away countries) as one instrument in the armoury available for use in counter-evasive warfare and a good deal of experience has been accumulated to suggest that the use of political concessions and other political tactics is if anything more important than mere military measures. What is such a doctrine to mean to the Rhodesian, South African or Venezuelan counter-insurgent? In the situations facing those countries in the near future, the whole point of counter-evasive warfare may be the preservation of an order whose destruction is the necessary price of the possibility of counter-evasive military success in the Anglo-American style.

Whether or not the dilemmas facing a Rhodesian or South African

---

[2] The failure of Ché Guevara in Bolivia prompted much discussion among those sympathetic to 'the enemies of imperialism' about when the warfare of evasion should not be *begun* but we know of no insurgent study of when evasive war, once begun, should be abandoned.

counter-insurgent enlist the sympathetic attention of the reader, the general point should be clear: although the literature of insurgency and counter-insurgency appears to attach great importance to the political dimension, in fact it does not engage in political analysis but only in a consideration of techniques of political persuasion, coercion and manipulation. Politics is discourse about matters of final importance to those engaged in it, and the discourse is open-ended. What passes for 'politics' in professional thinking about the warfare of evasion and counter-evasion is not this but the trappings of politics.

This is not a criticism of the professional literature as such. We are raising questions about it which it is not the professional's job to raise. It will be his job to consider them only if he is directed to do so. The place where these questions need to be raised in the first instance is in the academic community – it can be no one's job so much as theirs to press the importance of these questions on politician and soldier.

Our insistence on the political dimension of analysis is not directed only at counter-evasive warfare. In Chapter Five we argued that the notion of 'structural violence' was inferior to that of just cause. For all its appearance of precision in some of its more mathematical manifestations, 'structural violence' is essentially an a-political notion. It avoids the crucial political issue of connecting means and ends. As argued above, it fails to raise the question of what kinds of relative deprivation and absolute need justify the employment of what kinds of violent or non-violent measures against whom.

Political analysis is a precondition of that sense of proportion which, as we argued in Chapter Five, is an inescapable demand from the modified Kantian viewpoint out of which we are writing. Without some kind of view of what one is trying to do politically, one cannot go on to raise those larger questions which must be answered if resort to violence is ever to be justified.

We are not, of course, suggesting that all practitioners of evasive warfare are without political analysis. To take the most familiar example, the Marxist insurgent who sees the overthrow of the existing order and the establishment of a regime committed to Marxist understanding of reality as the first priority has his political reasons for taking his stand. By the same token, his is a position about which it is particularly straightforward to raise the broader questions of proportion. From the viewpoint of this book, the most obvious question to raise about him concerns the hostages that he, like the proponent of nuclear deterrence, is giving to fortune. Granted that he has good theoretical reasons for being a little hazy about what the world or his part of it will be like after the success of the revolutionary struggle, the question remains of whether such self-abandon to an unknown future is consistent with a proper respect for the humanity within oneself. Furthermore, of course, if he proposes to wage revolutionary war against noncombatants then he violates a traditional and in our view still-standing prohibition.

It is a mistake to see all warfare of evasion and counter-evasion as committed to the killing of noncombatants. The insurgent who takes good care in a campaign of selective assassination to kill only those engaged in the repressive activities in terms of which he justifies his measures is waging the fairest of struggles. To mark this point, we proposed in Chapter Two to reserve the emotionally and morally charged term 'terrorist' for the practitioner of evasive war whose fighting is indiscriminate. We are in a position now, as earlier we were not, to claim that the opprobrium in the word 'terrorist' is justified.

3. *Warfare of despair, holy war and pacifism*

Special comment is required on the warfare of despair. In our discussion of Jim's pacifism we suggested that our good man might well be confronted with an existential dilemma between a refusal of activity with a military dimension and fighting alongside his people in their hour of greatest glory, in a desperate final struggle without hope of success against an enemy bent on annihilation. Such a struggle might occur at any level of armament: the people with whom Jim identifies might possess a nuclear armoury, a conventional bombing capability, or the capacity for nothing more than the warfare of evasion. Our argument suggested an existential choice for the best of men between pacifism and the fight; by the same token, there might be an existential choice to be made between noncombatant immunity and the last fight. For no one can demand of humanity that it resign its last flicker. But equally no one can demand of the noncombatant that he resign himself to a purely meaningless death. The choice is impossible, but might have to be made.

In political theory, the warfare of despair is a limiting case. There is no such thing as the politics of despair – for that would mean using despair for some political end and despair involves the despair of attaining any political objective whatever. There is no such thing as the politics of despair but there is such a thing as political despair. What happens in the political arena, as elsewhere, can reduce a man to despair. But because there is no such thing as the politics of despair, our concession that there is a moral dignity in the last fight is not morally exploitable. It is not possible to argue from the case to others: there are no degrees of despair, and therefore it would be incoherent to claim on the strength of our argument that in other cases too there is a choice to be made between noncombatant immunity and other things. All except those in despair are capable of moral choices embracing all men, and hence of accommodating themselves to the requirement of noncombatant immunity.[3]

We pointed out in Chapter Five that the received wisdom about the relation between just war, holy war and pacifism was highly questionable. Were the received view which sees these as three distinct traditions correct, then a just war treatment of the ethics of bombing would need to stop at the point that we have now reached, with the argument that certain sorts of bombing and deterrence violate the principles of proportion and noncombatant immunity and have developed in an intellectual climate in which such developments can take place with little but amateur, personal challenge. But if, as we argued in Chapter Five, there is an underlying unity between the supposed three strands then it is necessary to carry the moral criticism of bombing further, into a consideration of the bearing on it of holy war and pacifism.

Of holy war, we have little more to say. Holy war is a demonic form of the just war tradition in which human beings are seen as evil incarnate. Historical examples of such thinking stand as an appalling warning of what the inevitable trend of moral thinking about war is if a sense of proportion is lost. Once forget that war is fought against human beings for purposes which must somehow find their place in the lives of human beings, and holy war is the natural outcome.

The practical bearing of pacifism on our subject is more direct and perhaps less obvious. The place accorded to pacifism in the dominant intellectual ethos of our time is a scandal. Very many people think they know very well in advance of all careful, critical thought what pacifism is and that pacifists are nice, totally unrealistic people who ought perhaps to be tolerated but who can at times contribute to disaster. It is often claimed that British 'pacifism' contributed to the rise of Hitler: when this is asserted, the view taken by pacifists of a just settlement of World War I is ignored and no distinction is drawn between those who held merely that war would be imprudent and people whose scruples about military action went somewhat deeper. Although almost all pacifists are amateurs, from whom the expertise and professionally elaborated thinking of military men cannot reasonably be expected, there is far more to be said for pacifism than many – except convinced pacifists – are prepared to allow.

[3] Of course the word 'despair' is often abused to describe military operations undertaken out of political frustration. This seems to us reason not for abandoning all sympathy with the warfare of despair but for insisting on the word's proper usage.

A good deal of the case for this view has already been stated in Chapter Three. To summarise that part of the case very roughly, those who dismiss pacifism as unrealistic take it for granted that resort to war is a realistic thing to do, and obviously so. Such an assumption is unwarranted by experience: Clausewitz and the pre-pacifist Tolstoy are but two of the many well-informed students of war who insist on the uncontrolled character of war, the reliance on chance, the gift of oneself to luck, the loss of moral control over one's own actions that is an inevitable consequence of engaging in action with a military dimension. In short, the dismissal of pacifism as unrealistic is based on a facile lack of realism.

One further example may serve to confirm the argument. Pacifists often point out that they are not urging people to be totally passive in response to violent repression, that the techniques of nonviolent resistance developed by Gandhi, Martin Luther King and others provide in many situations a real alternative to reliance upon violence. The automatic reply is that nonviolence was all very well against the British in India and in support of Civil Rights in the US but would be hopeless against a more ruthless enemy – look at Hitler's extermination camps and Stalin's murder of millions.

4. The analysis of nonviolence

The automatic reply is at least as naive as the pacifist commendation of nonviolence. We take, as a fair example, a part of Gandhi's 1930 campaign as analysed by an adherent of nonviolence. James Douglass in *The Non-Violent Cross* quotes a report filed from India by the United Press correspondent Webb Miller on 21 May 1930 about the mass attack of 2,500 independence demonstrators on the Dharasana salt works. Their leader instructed them

'India's prestige is in your hands. You must not use any violence under any circumstances. You will be beaten but you must not resist: you must not even raise a hand to ward off blows.'

... The volunteers formed in columns, with their leaders carrying ropes and wire cutters. They advanced slowly towards the salt works ... About 400 native Surat police stood inside and outside the entanglements. Several British officers directed the police, who had orders to prevent the assembly of more than five persons.

... The police ran up and demanded that [the crowd] disperse. The volunteers refused.

... Suddenly, at a word of command, scores of native police rushed upon the advancing marchers and rained blows on their heads with their steel-shod lathis. Not one of the marchers even raised an arm to fend off the blows. They went down like ten-pins. From where I stood I heard the sickening whacks of the clubs on unprotected skulls.

... Those struck down fell sprawling, unconscious or writhing with pain with fractured skulls or broken shoulders. In two or three minutes the ground was quilted with bodies ... When every one of the first column had been knocked down, stretcher-bearers rushed up unmolested by the police and carried off the injured to a ... temporary hospital.[4]

A second wave received similar treatment, the leaders of the demonstration almost lost the crowd, then changed their tactics. They

marched up in groups of twenty-five and sat on the ground near the salt pans, making no effort to draw nearer. Led by a ... Parsi sergeant of police named Antia ... detachments of police approached one seated group and called up to them to disperse under the non-assemblage ordinance. The Gandhi followers ignored them and refused to even glance up at the lathis brandished threateningly above their heads. Upon a word from Antia, the beating commenced coldly, without anger. Bodies toppled over in threes and fours, bleeding from great gashes on their scalps. Group after group walked forward, sat down, and submitted to being beaten into insensibility without raising an arm to fend off the blows.

Finally the police became enraged by the non-resistance, sharing, I suppose, the helpless rage I had already felt at the demonstrators for not fighting back. They commenced savagely kicking the seated men in the abdomen and testicles.[5]

The good old civilised British and their native subordinates do not come out of such typical incidents very well. Douglass comments that

It may be true that a different imperialist power, whether communist as in Hungary or capitalist as in Vietnam, would have raised the cost in suffering even higher in an effort to hold off India's independence. But to those who witnessed scenes such as the above, the British seemed brutal enough ...[6]

He could perhaps have added that the British were fighting what is now known as a limited war: there were good political reasons for their inability to take systematic violence much further than they did.

A vital ingredient in the successful Indian campaigns is hinted at by Douglass without any heavy stress. He says

The British beat the Indians with batons and rifle butts. The Indians neither cringed nor complained nor retreated. That made England powerless and India invincible.[7]

Gandhi and his associates were enabled by historical circumstances

[4] *The Non-Violent Cross* 67.
[5] *ibid.* 68.
[6] *ibid.*
[7] *ibid.*, quoting Louis Fischer *The Life of Mahatma Gandhi* (New York 1962) 279.

and political skill to persuade very many people, including many who were not committed to any particular view of the conflict, to see it as a moral struggle between 'Britain' and 'India'. The imaginative appeal of this vision of a confrontation between two mighty civilisations, one ancient and honourable, subject and resurgent, the other proud, mighty and apparently at the height of its power exerted an influence whose importance it would be hard to exaggerate. In a limited war, such as that which Britain was fighting in India (or the US in Vietnam) the way the issues are imagined necessarily has an enormous impact on the course of events. It gives to the strategist of nonviolence a very great opportunity.

Douglass claims that

> The purpose of non-violence is to move the oppressors to perceive as human beings those whom they are oppressing. Men commit acts of violence and injustice against other men only to the extent that they do not regard them as fully human. Non-violent resistance seeks to persuade the aggressor to recognize in his victim the humanity they have in common, which when recognized fully makes violence impossible. This goal of human recognition is sought through the power of voluntary suffering, by which the victim becomes no longer a victim but instead an active opponent in loving resistance to the man who has refused to recognize him as man. The man of non-violence acts through suffering love to move the unjust opponent to a perception of their common humanity, and thus to the cessation of violence in the commencement of brotherhood. The greater the repression, the greater must be the suffering courted by its victims; the greater the inhumanity, the greater the power of suffering love to begin restoring the bonds of community. Suffering as such is powerless. Love transforms it into the kind of resistance capable of moving an opponent to the act of mutual recognition we have described. The suffering of the victim must be acknowledged by the oppressor as being human before he will cease inflicting it, and it is the love manifested in that suffering undergone openly and voluntarily which will bring him finally to this acknowledgment.[8]

From the viewpoint of this book, this judgment is somewhat overstated but it is far from unrealistic. Our major hesitation about Douglass' judgment concerns its lack of a magnanimous recognition of the great moral dignity of traditional military values. It is simply not true that men use violence against other human beings only insofar as they neglect the humanity of their enemies. Rommel did not under-estimate his opponents' humanity but understood very well the brotherhood of arms: traditionally, soldiers on the battlefield have a deep common bond that is denied to all other men. Their service each

---

[8] Douglass 71.

to his own country and thereby, so the hope is, to humanity in the self and in other people leads them to attempts at the systematic killing of one another, but the strange glory of the soldier's calling can be dismissed only if one is prepared to discount the full range of commitments into which the search for a meaningful life can lead.[9]

Of course, the traditional military code is a difficult and demanding one, requiring moral restraint and self-discipline as great as that of the nonviolent. Western tradition begins, in the *Iliad*, with a poem about an archetypal war crime in which one of the finest of heroes desecrates the body of his glorious enemy out of crazed grief at the death of his friend. The possibility of such breakdowns of self-control is equally present in the practice of nonviolence.

But this reservation aside, there is much to be said for Douglass' insistence on the power of nonviolence and its deep links with practical love. The nonviolent resister gives to his enemy something at least as fine as the brotherhood of arms, namely, the opportunity to give practical effect to the recognition of their shared humanity. Whereas in a battle the man who fires over the head of the enemy out of moral scruple typically achieves no more than to expose his fellows to senseless danger, the nonviolent seeks to trouble his enemy's conscience and typically to enlist his enemy in a common struggle against perceived injustice. (There is, of course, no magic guarantee that every cause for nonviolent action will be a just one. It is currently unlikely, but not beyond the bounds of possibility, that at some time nonviolent techniques should be used to oppose racial integration and the granting of civil rights to minorities.)

Neither being a soldier nor being a nonviolent resister entails abandonment of practical love towards one's enemy: the soldier who upholds traditional restraints on the prosecution of war, war threats and war preparations, and the resister who presses his chosen cause in a way that extends to his immediate oppressors the chance of recognising a common humanity may both be enacting good wishes towards all men.

This perhaps is the crux of our case against the intellectual climate within which war is thought about. Especially in academic circles, it is *chic* to insist on war's brutality, on the 'fact' that war is a brutal instrument of often brutal if necessary policy. Any hint that moral restraint might have a place in war, still more the outrageous suggestion that war might be an expression of love, is thought to be laughably naive. The joke is on the other side. Those whose job it is to give their lives to the maintenance of nuclear deterrence and to the

[9] J. Glenn Gray gives a moving account of the idea of the enemy as a comrade in arms and of its limitations in *The Warriors* 142-8.

preparation, threat and waging of other sorts of war are in no position to adopt such a relaxed, distant, disdainful view. Many, of course, take a relaxed view of the whole subject of what meaning if any there is in their lives – this is as true of soldiers, officials and politicians as of – shall we say academics. If one is untroubled by the question of what, in the largest sense, one is doing then naturally one does not find the issue troubling. But for those who are not thus relaxed about the moral world and their place in it, the problem of the relation between war, morality and even love is inescapable if war is one's job. It is therefore to be expected that a calm, relaxed, easy acceptance that of course war is a terrible thing is least easy to find among those engaged in the management of violence.

The realistic chic of the armchair observer has practical consequences. The full consideration of the full range of options for military and nonviolent political action is a difficult and demanding business. It is not to be expected that the military and their political masters will raise the relevant questions or press their practical importance. Unless the impetus comes from elsewhere, the questions will not be asked and answers will not be found unless by amateurs or serendipity.

To confirm this once again by reference to nonviolence: the proponents of this strategy are a small and dedicated group who cannot be expected on their own to investigate the limits of the effectiveness of their preferred course of action. As a first and doubtless inaccurate approximation, one might suggest that nonviolence is very much more promising in situations of limited war, and especially where publicity is important, than in grimmer struggles. This might suggest that its utility is very restricted – for superior fire-power can always overcome mere publicity, it might be argued. But this is to under-estimate the importance in the contemporary world of the warfare of evasion. We now know a good deal about the capacity of groups whose military resources are strictly limited to avoid decisive military encounters where their inferiority of force would be disastrous. A great deal is known about the considerable frequency with which superior powers are reluctant to bring their full force to bear. The opportunities are there for the seizing.

This is not to suggest that nonviolence is universally promising. To date, it has involved very great problems of organisation and relied on the opportunity for organisers to operate in relative openness. Largely for this reason, in states such as South Africa where individual surveillance is formidably advanced the opportunities for nonviolent action seem scant. Very little appears to be known about the possibility of combining massive nonviolent action with such practices as clandestine leadership and selective assassination.

This book is not a work of amateur strategy, military or nonviolent. What we are concerned to point out is not possible future developments in strategy but the moral significance of the intellectual reception (and non-reception) of strategy. Pacifism is very widely regarded with culpable flippancy. It is only too smart to see the resort to violence as real and realistic and any hesitation as the operation of scruples which, however nice, are an evasion of nasty reality. As against this view, we submit that there are serious questions of a pacifist kind to be asked about the bombing of cities whether with nuclear or conventional weapons, and whether in regular operations or the warfare of evasion and counter-evasion. Not only is the disregard of noncombatant immunity a flagrant violation of deep moral principle, the very resort to military measures of any kind is morally dubious.

To conclude this section of moral judgment on the bombing of cities, we consider a feature of our argument which may have struck the reader as a curious evasion. Although we have written at length about the merits of a sort of pacifism and about the need for restraint in activity which has a military dimension, we have nowhere declared ourselves for or against pacifism. There is, we think, good reason for this. Morality as it is understood in this book has a double life. It addresses the individual in his own particular historical circumstances about his own particular private problems, and it also seeks to pervade and inform the public world which necessarily shapes the self-understanding of each individual. The moral issue of pacifism is accordingly a two-fold problem. There is the question of the existential relation between pacifism and the individual, and the question of the relation between pacifism and the public understanding.

The discussion of any individual's moral questioning about war cannot stop short of a moral decision regarding pacifism, between acceptance however hesitant and rejection however regretful. But such discussion necessarily proceeds from the individual's own starting-point, his own understanding of the world. A good discussion may need to challenge his perspective, but it must begin with it and ceaselessly return to it. Such a course has seemed to us impossible in this book because the individuals to whom we have tried to address ourselves are too various in their outlooks for one argument, however extended, to serve the turn. The moral starting-point of a pacifist who is committed to nonviolent action for the dismantling of the nuclear deterrent and the moral perspective of a devout Christian who happens to command one of NATO's nuclear submarines are too different for a convenient or purposeful argument in one book.

But this does not mean that no public discourse is possible, that all discussion of the ethics of war should take place in the privacy of a man's own soul or the company of a few sympathetic friends. In this book we have been concerned with the public moral ethos in which individuals form their very diverse moral outlooks. One salient feature of this public realm is its systematic undervaluation and misunderstanding of both the just war tradition and pacifism. We have attempted to correct this deficiency and for that it would have been irrelevant and a distraction to engage in the essentially personal task of deciding for or against pacifism. What matters is that the force of pacifism should be felt.

We claim no originality for the moral judgments made in this section. Our main interest is that they should be seen as a logical consequence of the foregoing historical, political and moral analysis. They represent merely certain conclusions which the good man, Jim in our earlier chapters, necessarily draws. We turn now to the question of what business Jim has commenting on the life-and-death issues of war and peace.

5. *Judgment on individuals; the Nuremberg trial*

So far in this chapter we have confined our attention to the moral judgment of actions, arguing that it was premature to judge individuals though suggesting that intellectual responsibility was an important part of the general problem of moral accountability. We now turn to the most impressive and sustained attempt to date to stand in judgment on the conduct of individuals in war – the Nuremberg trial. One of its leading characteristics, often mentioned in criticism of Nuremberg, was that no attention was paid during the trial to the Allied bombing offensive against Germany. For this and other reasons, the trial is often described as 'victor's justice'. Is this the best judgment on the trial?

Many things were done after World War II which are relevant to an assessment of Nuremberg. There were various war crimes trials against German and Allied personnel. In the Far East there was the Tokyo trial of Japanese leaders, closely modelled on Nuremberg,[10] and again proceedings against Axis and Allied personnel. In most of the liberated territories there were acts of summary justice and crude revenge. In Germany there was the official action known as 'Denazification' and in Japan over 200,000 officials were, for a time at

[10] For a searching and damaging analysis of this see Richard Minear *Victor's Justice*.

least, removed from political life. The judicial pursuit of Nazis continues to this day, as does the payment of reparations to victims of Nazi oppression. Out of this tangle of events, we extract the Nuremberg trial for somewhat one-sided scrutiny.

On 25 October 1941, Roosevelt and Churchill warned the Axis powers that retribution would follow their crimes. On 13 January 1942 the punishment of war criminals by judicial process was adopted as a war aim by the Allies. On 1 November 1943, Roosevelt, Churchill and Stalin announced that German war criminals would be put on trial and that the so-called 'major' criminals would be dealt with by a joint decision of the Allied governments. A 'major' criminal was one whose alleged crimes had no particular geographical location: each of the Allies had the legal right to subject each of these men to a separate trial. That would have been cumbersome and perhaps cruel. In the event, the Allies decided on one joint trial – as was their legal right. On 7 May 1945 Germany surrendered at Rheims. On 6 August the atom bomb was dropped on Hiroshima. On 8 August the International Military Tribunal was established by the US, UK, USSR and French provisional government to conduct the German trial. On 9 August the atom bomb was dropped on Nagasaki and Japan capitulated on 14 August. The Nuremberg trial lasted from 20 November 1945 to 31 August 1946 and judgment was delivered on 30 September and 1 October 1946.

Twenty-four individuals had been picked out for trial. One killed himself while awaiting trial, one was found too ill to stand trial. Martin Bormann was tried in his absence. Twelve of the accused were sentenced to death, three to life imprisonment, four to terms of imprisonment ranging from twenty to ten years, and three were acquitted.

The trial has been criticised on many counts. It has often been described as victor's justice. One of the judges at the Tokyo trial went so far as to say that the only war crime he could impute to the defendants before him was the crime of losing the war.[11]

It is certainly true that the Nazis would not have been tried had they not been defeated first; but it is also true that most criminals have to be caught before they can be tried – rather few give themselves up, especially if they enjoy positions of great power and authority in the government of one of the most powerful nations on earth. There has been some complaint that the Nuremberg judges were citizens of Allied states rather than Germans or neutrals. In reply to the suggestion of German judges it is usual to point to the derisory

[11] Minear 59-60.

sentences and ludicrous acquittals that ensued when proceedings against German personnel were entrusted to German justice after World War I. One might also mention some of the more scandalous evasions of the fifties,[12] and ask which Germans are intended. Ex-Nazis? Non-Nazis who had been loyal to the Third Reich? Survivors of the minute resistance to Hitler? German Jews? The suggestion of neutral judges is somewhat less absurd: although there were very few completely neutral states and appointments might have been very difficult to make, neutral judges might have helped some to a more sympathetic appreciation of the trial. But what seems most important is that few are prepared to suggest that the judges who were appointed failed to give the defendants a fair trial. It seems to be widely agreed that within the limits established beforehand the trial was conducted with remarkable fairness. What matters is impartiality, not neutrality.

If the derogatory label of 'victor's justice' is to be made to stick it must be by means of some other argument. There are many available. Some examples:

1. It was invidious to single out some individuals. There were many Nazis, and the punishment of a few was unfair. This seems to us an absurd argument: it is always the case that many criminals go unpunished; no one suggests that this means that those criminals who are caught should be freed. Each criminal is punished for his own actions: the good luck of others in evading arrest or conviction is irrelevant.

2. The rules of evidence at Nuremberg were different from what they normally are.[13] This argument is not to be dismissed as merely a legal quibble. Whatever view one takes of the trial, it is important that it was conducted in a court of law not a court of morals. In a court of law, irregular rules of procedure are necessarily important. In what follows we propose an interpretation of the trial which at once vindicates it in principle and places in perspective the inescapable but limited importance of such objections as that to irregular procedure.

Raising larger issues of principle are the following:

3. The argument that the defendants at Nuremberg were tried for things which were not illegal at the time they were performed.

4. The argument that even if some of the actions tried were illegal, international law is a nonsense.

5. The argument that even if international law has some limited

[12] Cf. Hannah Arendt *Eichmann in Jerusalem* Ch. 2.
[13] Minear 118-23.

validity, it is nevertheless not the case that individuals are accountable under international law.

6. The argument that, though accountable, they are not punishable.
7. The argument that the trial was exploited to pretend that the Allied cause was spotlessly just when it was not, and to cover up Allied outrages including the bombing offensive against Germany and the use of the two atom bombs.
8. The argument that the trial was a search for scapegoats, a contemptible effort at shrugging off the guilt that we all bear or which nobody bears.
9. The argument that the trial did no good at all – e.g. the hangings contributed nothing to the attainment of peace in our time.

As with the history of area bombing, an historically justifiable approach to these questions would need to take as its starting-point the question of what those conducting the trial were attempting to do. A detailed investigation of this would reveal a divergence of purpose at least as great as that indicated in Chapter One in the case of the bombing campaign. But such a detailed analysis is not for present purposes necessary. At the cost of over-simplification, we will concentrate on the common purpose of people who, had circumstances developed differently, would certainly have been at loggerheads. We ignore the Soviet wish to use Nuremberg as a show trial and ignore the differences of approach of various Anglo-American participants.[14]

With the German surrender, high-ranking Nazis became subject to the tender mercies of the Allies. In April 1945 Churchill's view had been that they should be shot out of hand: 'quickly and humanely as one shoots mad dogs' was the way he expressed it to Judge Rosenman, Roosevelt's envoy.[15] But when Churchill saw photographs of the bodies of Mussolini and his mistress, killed by Italian partisans, he wrote to F.M. Alexander (May 1945): 'The man who murdered Mussolini made a confession ... in particular he said he shot Mussolini's mistress. Was she on the list of war criminals? Had he any authority to shoot this woman? It seems to me the cleansing hand of British justice should make enquiries on these points.'[16] The concern here is perhaps to eliminate unauthorised killing rather than to opt for something more enquiring than summary justice. But in 1947, Churchill told Rosenman that Roosevelt had been right to insist on a trial.

[14] A fuller analysis would need to take as its starting-point 'International Conference on Military Trials'.
[15] Minear 9.   [16] *ibid.*

Those who had pressed for a trial saw it as the last act of the war and first act of the peace. As the last act of the war, it would serve to enforce retribution, to give massive publicity not least in Germany to the horrors of the Third Reich, to brand the war onto the public memory, and to be a final vindication of that spirit of justice which some at least thought themselves to be acting on in participating in the Western Allied war against the Axis. As the first act of the peace, the trial was bound up with fond hopes and aspirations for a new world order centred on the United Nations, and having among its principles the conviction that the individual is responsible for his own actions and crimes.

The most obvious success of the trial was in publicising the actions of the Third Reich in a way that admitted of no evasion, that was authoritative and memorable, and that possibly played its part in altering German attitudes in the post-war years. The summary execution of those concerned could not have accomplished these ends.

But Churchill's desire to shoot the offenders 'quickly and humanely as one shoots mad dogs' is understandable. The trial could have misfired and, more important for present purposes, there is a natural desire to avert one's eyes from the depths of evil. Summary execution would have hurried the wretched story into the oblivion that it merits; the conducting of a trial necessarily placed on a fallible human proceeding an intolerable burden. At the best of times, the judicial process is subject to the impossible demand of somehow doing justice to the dark impulses of human nature. The Nuremberg judges were asked to look into the heart of darkness and somehow to bring it under dispassionate critical judgment. It should surprise no one either that many have wished the trial had never taken place or that the trial disappoints one when considered in relation to the immense demands made of it.

It is rather obvious, though the point does not seem to have been made, that the punishments meted out at Nuremberg make very little sense in terms of the most popular general theories of punishment.[17] Usually, punishment in general is understood in terms of instrumental action or in terms of retribution. The best known version of instrumental theory is that which sees punishment as an instrument of deterrence, the punishment of one offender for one crime supposedly serving to deter other criminals from the performance of similar crimes. But there are, of course, other instrumental theories of punishment, e.g. that which sees it as an instrument for reforming the offender and returning him to society. Retribution theory sees

---

[17] For a useful introduction to these see H.B. Acton (ed.) *The Philosophy of Punishment.*

punishment as an end not a means: the offender has done something in virtue of which there is a price to be paid by him and in undergoing punishment he pays the price. (It should be remembered that etymologically 'retribution' derives from Latin with the sense of 'paying back'.)

The Nuremberg punishments as instruments were doomed to failure. The use of punishment to return the offender to society is an altogether too trivial thing for crimes of the enormity of those considered at Nuremberg. A precondition of the effectiveness of punishment as a deterrent is that the potential offender should fear capture, and for this reason if for none other the United Nations system was singularly ill equipped to give effect to a system of criminal (as distinct from nuclear) deterrence. With the worsening quarrel between the great powers in the late forties, the last possibility of a world police force giving bite to world criminal law vanished. As for retribution, it is a fact often overlooked that the crimes were too great – no penalty that one could think of would be appropriate. Retribution theory perhaps makes best sense in the case of the petty criminal: he has not been reformed by a period in jail, no one has been deterred by his example, but at least he has paid the price and having done so must be released. Wherever one thinks the line is to be drawn between offences expungable by the paying of some penalty and crimes that are beyond all price in their awfulness, it is clear that the Nuremberg crimes fall on the farther side of the line.

What, then, is one to make of the Nuremberg proceedings? The Allies had to do something, or by inaction to allow an attitude to emerge. They stood between on the one hand Nazis who were now in their power and on the other hand the victims of Nazi atrocities. They could have resorted to summary executions; they could have used the method of exile, implying neither legal nor moral reproach, that Britain and her victorious allies employed against Napoleon after the Hundred Days; they could have allowed their prisoners to drift back into society, subject no doubt to surveillance designed to guard against political resurgence; they could have conceded the Russian expedient of a show trial. Instead, they opted for a legal proceeding.

It seems to us that morally speaking they had no alternative and did well to act, despite temptations, as their situation demanded. They stood between offender and victim. It was not for them to exact a victim's satisfaction in the form of revenge, but with all their natural sympathy on the side of the victim and their thought guided by the only available canons of judgment, namely, legal rules and procedures, to try and do justice to the victim's case. To say this is not to affirm that it was possible to do justice – we do not think that it was, the evil was too great and transcended normal categories of justice. What was required of the Allies was that they should make their position clear and this they did, despite many incidental deficiencies, by doing the best available justice.

Our view here is determined by the viewpoint developed in this book. We see the victims of the Nazis tried at Nuremberg as being not the states against which the Third Reich waged war and not that always mythical being The Public Interest, but the individual human beings who in their millions had suffered monstrous wrong. Between these on the one hand and the individuals arraigned on the other, the Court attempted to do criminal justice. It was the most the Allies could hope to do and, morally speaking, the least they could do.

In a world of moral consensus, it might have been conceivable that the trial should have been conducted according to sound moral principle (natural law). But in 1945 the best available consensus was represented in the positive international law as summed up in the Charter of the International Military Tribunal. This law was in part open to certain objections, as will shortly emerge.

Certain individuals being picked out for special attention, it was claimed and proved that they had performed certain actions. These fell into three classes called – in legal terminology, of course, given the legal framework – war crimes, crimes against peace, and crimes against humanity.

War crimes were described in the Tribunal's Charter as

> violations of the laws or customs of war. Such violations shall include, but not be limited to, murder, ill-treatment or deportation to slave labour or for any other purpose of civilian population of or in occupied territory, murder or ill-treatment of prisoners of war or persons on the seas, killing of hostages, plunder of public or private property, wanton destruction of cities, towns or villages, or devastation not justified by military necessity.[18]

Prohibition and punishment of such acts was nothing new, though it was an innovation to bring to book high-ranking government officials: previously, only local commanders and their subordinates had been held to account. Notice that the prohibitions which fall under the rubric of 'war crimes' are specific and realistic. It is tempting to think of war or battle as a passionate free-for-all in which there is no possibility of self-control or self-restraint except perhaps in such high commands as those considered in Chapter One above. If war is thought about in this way all rules, even those specifying war crimes, appear to be impossibly inappropriate. This view is mistaken for at least two reasons. The worst of these crimes occur in cold blood,

---

[18] Charter Article 6(b), Calvocoressi *Nuremberg* 132.

far from any battlefield, in the concentration camp and the torture chamber. And even the hot-blooded are capable of a number of different enemy images, some of which (e.g. holy war perceptions) preclude restraint, but others of which leave psychological space for the following of rules, or even necessitate the self-imposed limitation of moral moderation.

War crimes were not the first type of action referred to in the Tribunal's Charter. Pride of place was given to the so-called *crimes against peace*:

> Namely, planning, preparation, initiation or waging of a war of aggression, or a war in violation of international treaties, agreements or assurances, or participation in a common plan or conspiracy for the accomplishment of any of the foregoing.[19]

The Allies attached great importance to the idea of crimes against peace. The Nuremberg Judgment contains the astonishing but characteristic observation that 'To initiate a war of aggression ... is not only an international crime; it is the supreme international crime differing only from other war crimes in that it contains within itself the accumulated evil of the whole.'[20] This is nonsense. Taken as a whole the trial was an insistence that a man is responsible for what he has done, neither more nor less; whereas this statement implies that Hitler was responsible for the crimes other Nazis committed on their own initiative and for the crimes of Allied personnel and politicians.

The notion of crimes against peace has been much and, we think, damagingly criticised. Richard Minear points out that at Tokyo some Japanese leaders were convicted of crimes against peace which the modern historian sees to have been nothing of the kind.[21] Whatever one thinks of the argument put forward by A.J.P. Taylor that even Hitler was innocent of outright aggressive intentions before 1939,[22] many historians would now be inclined to deny that Japan was in any serious sense an aggressor. It is not clear whether this calls in question the very idea of crime against peace or merely the justice of the Tokyo trial. But either way it is very disturbing: one has two main historical examples of the sustained and careful use of the notion of crime against peace – the Nuremberg and Tokyo trials. If in one of these people were wrongly convicted of aggression then that tends to throw doubt on the viability of the very idea of crime against peace.

It would not be so bad if we possessed a workable definition of

---

[19] Charter 6(a), Calvocoressi 132.
[20] 'Judgment' 13.
[21] Minear 125-59.
[22] A.J.P. Taylor *The Origins of the Second World War* 7-27.

'aggression' but we do not. After seventeen years, the United Nations has arrived at an agreed definition but it is impossibly vague. There are many perfectly usable words whose definition is impossible – the word 'love' for example. In pinning down its meaning, one would be pinning love down but a part of the joy and misery of love is that it cannot be pinned down. But the whole point of the attempt to use the word 'aggression' as something more serious than mere idle propaganda was to guide states and international organisations with regard to two supposedly different things called 'aggression' and 'defence'. In view of this and the wrongful conviction at Tokyo, it is hard to believe that the world has any clear idea of what it means by 'aggression'.

A criticism of the notion of crimes against peace which was urged at Nuremberg: it was very difficult to claim that war crimes were not against the law in the period 1933-45, they so obviously were; but the defendants claimed that crimes against peace were not illegal in the period. The issue is extremely complicated, and we confine ourselves to one point. Those who thought that something called 'aggression' was illegal often pointed to the Kellogg-Briand Pact of 1928. Frank B. Kellogg was US Secretary of State at the time. Speaking before the American Society of International Law, Kellogg rejected categorically the idea that the American draft of the Pact 'restricts or impairs in any way the right of self-defense'. What did that mean? The Senate Committee on Foreign Relations reported the Pact thus:

> The Committee reports the above treaty with the understanding that the right of self-defense is in no way curtailed or impaired by the terms or conditions of the treaty. Each nation is free at all times and regardless of the treaty provisions to defend itself, and is the sole judge of what constitutes the right and the necessity and extent of the same.[23]

This is worthy of Humpty-Dumpty. Self-defence is what I say it is, and so is the right and necessity and extent of the same. The words of the Senate Committee suggest that the US, perhaps unconsciously and through self-deception rather than cunning, was from the outset bent on making the Pact meaningless. To point to the Pact as evidence that there were such things as crimes against peace in the period 1933-45 has its difficulties.

How important are these criticisms of the idea of crimes against peace for the justice of the Nuremberg trial? They show the trial to have been less than perfect and perhaps exhibit the Allies as at least as much concerned with their own grievances as states as with the wrong done to individual human beings. If one thinks they were known to the

---

[23] Minear 51.

participants and understood by them as the damaging criticisms that they are then that perhaps shows the trial to have been to some extent a shabby business. But notice that of the accused only one was found guilty of crimes against peace only: he got twenty years. The others, including all those sentenced to death, were convicted in addition of crimes against humanity or war crimes – in this regard, the Tokyo trial was very different, a distinction overlooked in Minear's excellent book.[24]

The third type of action regarded as criminal at Nuremberg was the type described as *crimes against humanity*:

> namely, murder, extermination, deportation, and other inhumane acts committed against any civilian population, before or during the war, or persecutions on political, racial or religious grounds in execution of or in connection with any crime within the jurisdiction of the Tribunal.[25]

There is a complication with crimes against humanity. The Tribunal was careful to restrict its attention to actions which occurred in connection with the war. This may have been in part a discreditable unwillingness to permit or invite examination of the Allied peace-time record (e.g. the Stalinist terror) but it may have been in part a response to a genuine dilemma: prohibit certain peace-time actions as crimes against humanity and you may provide a pretext for intervention by one state in the affairs of another of the kind that the rules against 'aggression' were meant to prohibit.

It is arguable that crimes against humanity were not in any serious sense 'against the law' in the period 1933-45: they were not envisaged, there was no occasion to legislate against them, and there was not even any significant common law on the subject. This issue is legally debatable but perhaps the most interesting question from the present viewpoint is this: suppose crimes against humanity were not 'against the law'. Granted that retroactive legislation is normally an anathema, is it not possible that Nazi outrages were such that in response to them the Allies could not but in conscience resort to the practice of retroactive legislation? We have already suggested that normal theories of punishment do not apply at all convincingly to Nuremberg and that the Allies faced a unique situation. Novel problems may require novel wrenchings of normal legal practice.

At Nuremberg it was established that the defendants (apart from those acquitted) had performed actions of the three types just reviewed and they were subjected to penalties. But conviction and penalty are separated by the very large problem of responsibility.

---

[24] Minear 31.
[25] Charter 6(c), Calvocoressi 133.

Some of the most interesting aspects of Nuremberg relate to this problem.

Article 7 of the Charter declares that

> The official position of Defendants, whether as Heads of State or responsible officials in Government Departments, shall not be considered as freeing them from responsibility or mitigating punishment.[26]

This declaration that the doctrine of act of state was to have no weight at the trial seems to be right in the main but with one reservation. Speaking generally, there is nothing to be said in favour of the view that state functionaries are not responsible for their actions. But the Charter goes further than this, insisting that act of state shall not even be considered as mitigating punishment. Now although the doctrine of act of state is an absurdity, it was very influential in Nazi Germany and no one could rule out in advance the possibility of unreflective individuals coming to trial, who had been brought up to accept unquestioningly that they were not responsible for their state actions and who in consequence became the most hideous servants of Nazism. It would seem to us that their background must be relevant to their punishment: their situation would be recognisably different in any adequate theory of punishment from that of more reflective individuals for whom the idea of act of state was welcome as a cynic's expedient for crime with impunity. The terms of the Charter blur the distinction between the two types of case.

Article 8 says

> The fact that the defendant acted pursuant to order of his Government or of a superior shall not free him from responsibility, but may be considered in mitigation of punishment if the Tribunal determines that justice so requires.[27]

This appears to be sound. Consider a country like the UK, where the only organisation with military discipline is the military. In such a country there is a very marked difference between the pressures on military personnel to obey even manifestly illegal orders and the pressures on anyone else. Formally, there is the stress which a military organisation necessarily lays on obedience as the normal thing, so that the questioning of orders is seen by all concerned as the special or unusual case.[28] Informally, there is the pressure of the mess: military

---

[26] Calvocoressi 133.

[27] *ibid.*

[28] This pressure easily becomes over-stressed. Gerald Draper writes: 'There is no question of "unquestioning obedience" in our military law system. This is one of the TV myths and is utter bunkum. One of the hardest things to achieve as a Prosecutor

organisations do not encourage the development of individual conscience and it is hard to see how they ever could.[29] And we have suggested above that it is hardly the soldier's or the politician's job to see to it that the hard general questions on which moral justification rests get asked and given serious consideration. Hence, there is a considerable difference between the pressures on a military man or woman to obey and the pressures on anyone else in a country like Britain. This does not take away responsibility but it does give rise to the possibility of significantly different cases whose distinctness can be marked only by mitigation. In Nazi Germany, the distinction between military and non-military discipline was blurred, so that in that situation the general provision for mitigation on the ground of superior orders seems rather obviously right.

If it is granted that a person is responsible for actions taken by him under orders then a rather important question concerns the extent of such responsibility. For example, is it his duty to establish the legality of the order? This would be a very stern teaching, often requiring the individual soldier to demand information that was secret to his superiors in order to determine what he is really being asked to do. The Nuremberg Tribunal was vague about this saying merely that 'the true test which is found in varying degrees in the criminal law of most nations is not the existence of the order, but whether moral choice was in fact possible'.[30] This does not make clear what moral choice is. The current legal position seems to be somewhat clearer: it is for the states signatory to international law to see to it that their military personnel are properly instructed in the law relating to war; and what is required of the individual is that he disobey manifestly illegal orders.[31] His state should have taken measures adequate to ensure that he can recognise such, and it is not for him to seek beyond what in actual situations is manifestly against the law. This regime lays a relatively light burden on the individual, but is not completely vacuous. During the My Lai massacre, some of the American troops involved were able to recognise the flagrant unlawfulness of what the unit was doing[32] in spite of the contempt with which international law

---

is a conviction for disobeying a lawful command under the Army Act. There are so many loopholes of fact apart from the vital question of the lawful nature of the order. Letter to Barrie Paskins.

[29] The West German concept of *Innere Führung* attempts to encourage individual reflectiveness, with what success it is too early to say.

[30] Judgment 42.

[31] Morris Greenspan *The Modern Law of Land Warfare*, 495.

[32] Mary McCarthy *Medina*.

was regarded in the training of personnel for service in Vietnam.[33] At Nuremberg, clarification of the issue was hardly required since the defendants were repeatedly proved to have gone far beyond the call of duty in their commission of war crimes and crimes against humanity.

What is the relation between the Nuremberg trial and the moral concerns developed earlier in this book? It seems to us that our ideal type of the good man could not but approve the resort to a trial in preference to other possible lines of action. Having good wishes towards all men and faced with on the one hand the demands for justice of Nazi victims and on the other Nazis who were in his power, he could not but put the interests of the victims first, reserving until later any possible action in the interests of the offenders. He would have first of all to attempt justice on behalf of the victims and only then, if circumstances permitted, to consider what could be done for the offenders (perhaps in the way of encouraging them to realise what they had done and fitting them for a return to society). It does not do violence to the historical record to see the Allies as acting in just this way, though of course with mixed motives and the intrusion of other things including bitter resentment on their part against 'the aggressors'.

Would our ideal type, Jim, approve the categories of offence employed at Nuremberg, the doctrines of responsibility, and the legal framework? Richard Wasserstrom has argued that international and military law is morally abhorrent because unsound when regarded as an embodiment of moral law.[34] For example, it is utterly inconsistent in failing to outlaw with the utmost explicitness all forms of nuclear deterrence that violate noncombatant immunity. It is often replied that, however imperfect, law is the best thing that we possess and is in any case an attempt not to embody the best of human ideals but a second best, a framework within which people can be free and, if they freely choose to do so, pursue moral perfection. A related thought will be considered at some length in the next section. But what requires statement here is that Jim on his own terms would have to side neither

---

[33] Robert Jay Lifton (*Home from the War* 43) quotes a sample of the quality of US teaching of the laws of and customs of war from Vietnam Veterans Against The War *The Winter Soldier Investigation: an Inquiry into American War Crimes* (Boston 1972) 5:

> On the last day before leaving for Vietnam, the staff NCO holds a rabbit as he lectures on escape, evasion and survival in the jungle. The men become intrigued by the rabbit, fond of it, and then the NCO 'cracks it in the neck, skins it, disembowels it ... and then they throw the guts out into the audience'. As one marine explained: 'You can get anything out of that you want, but that's your last lesson you catch in the United States before you leave for Vietnam.'

[34] 'The Laws of War.'

with Wasserstrom nor with those who defend existing law. Jim is not straightforwardly an advocate of a morality of principle: his adherence to the fundamental Kantian principle of treating humanity as an end is but a codification of underlying good wishes and understanding of the human predicament as one in which each must live his own moral life. For him, the law must be viewed as the attempt of those who have made it – lawyers, politicians, the armies which in their adherence to custom have created common law of war, etc. – to live the moral life. For him, the law as it is is not an expression adequate or inadequate of a distinct thing called 'the moral law'. Rather, it is an expression of the moral life of those who have made it. In particular, Nuremberg is for him to be adjudged not by reference to some moral ideal of just conduct in war, but by reference to what those conducting the trial were trying and not trying to do. The piecemeal character of international law viewed as a whole, apart from the lives of those who made it, is not for Jim as it apparently is for Wasserstrom a moral deficiency. The very enterprise of viewing the law as a whole is for Jim necessarily problematic. Committed as he is to an ethic of virtue, the only moral interest he can take in the law viewed as a whole is in it as an attempt on someone's part to make it whole through codification, clarification, amendment, etc. Such an attempt, subject as it would necessarily be to historical circumstance, would be exceedingly unlikely to reflect an admirable abstract entity called 'the moral law'. But equally Jim can give no credence to the idea of the law as a second best, a set of rules within which people are at liberty to be good, mediocre, or within the limits of the law wicked. His desire is for the good of human beings. To opt for second best among available alternatives is necessarily unthinkable for him.

Accordingly, our good man necessarily views the categories employed at Nuremberg and after from a certain critical distance. Knowing that each has to live his own life, Jim will have to recognise that those committed to extending the rule of law in war and international relations are constrained by legal tradition. The question of special rules of evidence at Nuremberg, the legal doubts about the notion of crimes against peace, the jurisprudential difficulty of the question of retroactive legislation will necessarily be relevant and important issues from his viewpoint. The prohibition of war crimes and (if it is legally viable) of crimes against humanity will necessarily commend itself; so too the dismissal of act of state and superior orders as justifying pleas. The undemanding character of current law with respect to illegal orders, limiting the individual's responsibility to the manifestly illegal, will necessarily meet with his disapproval: the considerations that incline him to a pacifism of scruple are reasons for demanding of the soldier that he exercise himself about the legality of orders beyond the merely manifest. The fact of difficult cases is no objection to this view.

Finally, what of the Allied bombing campaign? It could have been brought to trial under inter-war legislation. It violated fundamental moral principles. It is often mentioned in criticism of Nuremberg, as a leading example of double standards.

If our narrative of the campaign in Chapter One is correct, bringing it into the post-war trials would have involved bringing to court Churchill and Truman. Should this have been done? There is an obvious sense in which it should have been done. But perhaps more interesting is a sense in which it could not have been done. The trial was not the work only of the US President and UK Prime Minister on behalf of their states, but the work of a great number of determined and extremely active lawyers and others who, by vigorous lobbying, seized the opportunity to carry out the trial. It is obvious that they could not have got the Allied bombing offensive included even if they had tried. This is important if one is to find the right nuance for assessing the trial. We have been content so far to speak rather loosely of 'what the Allies did' at Nuremberg. It would be more accurate to speak of what a small group of people did on the Allies' behalf at Nuremberg. It would be churlish to suggest that this group 'made compromises' in proceeding against the Nazi leadership but not against those responsible for the Allied offensive. They were in no position to make compromises. They did what they could and refrained from attempting to do something that it is inconceivable that they could have succeeded in doing.

This has a bearing on the question of whether Nuremberg was second best. Considered abstractly as an event that had certain merits but which lacked any reference to the immoral Allied offensive, Nuremberg is less fine than some things that one can imagine. But it would be a blunder to infer from this that the trial was a mixed good, the best that could be expected in the circumstances. At least from the viewpoint of our ideal type, the crucial questions to be asked make no reference to the Allied offensive except in the exceptional case of some few people, e.g. Churchill, who had it in their power to make the offensive relevant or remove it from all practical consideration. If what one is interested in is the achievement of the makers of Nuremberg, the bombing is irrelevant.

This, however, cannot be quite the last word. For in conducting the trial, the US and UK committed themselves to a certain moral position. They took a stand in favour of the application of law, including the creative application of new or stretched law, to international affairs. They are thus subject to judgment in moral terms which they themselves espoused. In these terms, the bombing of cities at all levels of organisation from nuclear deterrence to terrorism stands condemned.

But it is possible to argue, as we indicated above, that there is a case for mitigation. Those who developed and practised the bombing of cities were responsible, but they developed their ideas in an intellectual climate that did little to challenge their conventional judgments of what was permissible when one's job required it. The case for such mitigation is as strong in contemporary circumstances as it was in 1945. If the proponents of indiscriminate war know not what they do, the fault is not all theirs.

6. *Political realism* v. *the ethics of war*

The argument so far has made things very easy for Jim. Although certain mild disagreements between him and the lawyers have emerged, it was to be expected that he would approve of Nuremberg and that it would support something very like his outlook on the world. After all, like him the makers of Nuremberg were men who counted without the demonic presence of power, force, violence in international relations. Like him, their thinking relies on domestic analogies – theirs on the legal order, his on the moral order. But there is a grim old tradition which holds that affairs between states admit of neither morality nor law. It is to that we now turn.

In the late thirties and in the late forties, the notions about international relations that pinned their hopes on the League of Nations and later on the United Nations were subjected to powerful criticism by a number of authors who are now seen as forming a group of 'political realists'. Among them are the historian E.H. Carr, the theologian Reinhold Niebuhr, the diplomat George Kennan, and the political scientist Hans Morgenthau. Although there are important differences of approach, there are certain striking similarities. We take as representative of the group the first chapter of Hans Morgenthau's celebrated textbook *Politics Among Nations*. It is not the latest word on international relations, having first appeared in 1947, but it gives trenchant and succinct expression to ideas that appear to have enjoyed wide currency, and still to be influential.

7. *Morgenthau's* Politics Among Nations

Morgenthau presents himself as the opponent of a certain school of international relations which we will refer to as 'the idealist lobby'. He says that the idealists believe that 'a rational and moral political order, derived from universally valid abstract principles, can be achieved here and now'. The school assumes 'the essential goodness and infinite malleability of human nature', 'blames the failure[s] of the social order ... on lack of knowledge and understanding, obsolescent social institutions, and the depravity of certain isolated individuals' and trusts in 'education, reform and the sporadic use of force to remedy these defects'.[35]

According to Morgenthau, 'the history of modern political thought is the story of a contest between' the idealist lobby and 'realism', of which he is an adherent. Realism 'believes that the world ... is the result of forces inherent in human nature. To improve the world one must work with those forces, not against them. This being inherently a world of opposing interests, and of conflict among them, moral principles can never be fully realised, but must at best be approximated through the ever temporary balancing of interests and the ever precarious settlement of conflicts. ' ... [Realism] appeals to historic precedent rather than to abstract principles, and aims at the realisation of the lesser evil rather than of the absolute good.'[36]

> Intellectually, the political realist maintains the autonomy of the political sphere, as the economist, the lawyer, the moralist maintain theirs. ... The economist asks 'How does this policy affect the wealth of society, or a segment of it?' The lawyer asks 'Is this policy in accord with the rules of law?' The moralist asks 'Is this policy in accord with moral principles?' And the political realist asks 'How does this policy affect the power of the nation?' ...
>
> The political realist is not unaware of the existence and relevance of standards of thought other than political ones. As political realist, he cannot but subordinate these other standards to those of politics. And he parts company with other schools when they impose standards of thought appropriate to other spheres upon the political sphere. It is here that political realism takes issue with the 'legalistic-moralistic approach' to international politics.[37]

While thus insisting on a distinction between morals and politics, Morgenthau insists that there is also a connection: 'Political realism is aware of the ineluctable tension between the moral command and the requirements of successful political action. And it is unwilling to gloss over and obliterate that tension and thus to obfuscate both the moral and the political issue by making it appear as though the stark facts of

---

[35] Morgenthau 3.
[36] *ibid.* 3-4.
[37] *ibid.* 11-12.

politics were morally more satisfying than they actually are, and the moral law less exacting than it actually is.'[38]

This insistence on 'tension' is one of the more appealing features of political realism. We agree with Morgenthau's implication that much 'idealistic' thinking about international relations merely obscures the tension, setting 'the stark facts' in a vague blur of worthiness that betrays the harshness of morality's demands. Morgenthau attempts to preserve the tension by working with 'a pluralistic conception of human nature'. Real man is a composite of 'economic man', 'political man', 'moral man', 'religious man', etc. A man who was nothing but 'political man' would be a beast, for he would be completely lacking in moral restraints. A man who was nothing but 'moral man' would be a fool, for he would be completely lacking in prudence. A man who was nothing but 'religious man' would be a saint, for he would be completely lacking in worldly desires.[39]

Morgenthau offers a theory of international politics. The purpose of his theory is 'to bring order and meaning to a mass of phenomena which without it would remain disconnected and unintelligible'. It must be judged on three criteria: 'Do the facts as they actually are lend themselves to the interpretation the theory has put upon them?' 'Do the conclusions follow from the premises?' and 'Is the theory consistent with the facts and with itself?'[40] His fundamental theoretical concept of interest defined in terms of power

allows us to retrace and anticipate, as it were, the steps a statesman – past, present, or future – has taken or will take on the political scene. We look over his shoulder when he writes his dispatches; we listen in on his conversation with other statesmen; we read and anticipate his very thoughts. ... As disinterested observers we understand his thoughts and actions perhaps better than he, the actor on the political scene, does himself. The concept of interest defined as power imposes intellectual discipline upon the observer, infuses rational order into the subject matter of politics, and thus makes the theoretical understanding of politics possible. On the side of the actor, it provides for rational discipline in action and creates that astounding continuity in foreign policy which makes American, British, or Russian foreign policy appear as an intelligible, rational continuum, by and large consistent within itself, regardless of the different motives, preferences, and intellectual and moral qualities of successive statesmen.[41]

Morgenthau considers that interest defined as power serves as a

[38] *ibid.* 10.
[39] *ibid.* 14.
[40] *ibid.* 3. The formulation of the three criteria is our own.
[41] *ibid.* 5.

'guard against two popular fallacies: the concern with motives and the concern with ideological preferences':

> To search for the clue to foreign policy exclusively in the motives of statesmen is both futile and deceptive. It is futile because motives are the most illusive of psychological data, distorted as they are, frequently beyond recognition, by the interests and emotions of actor and observer alike. Do we really know what our own motives are? And what do we know of the motives of others?[42]

So much for motives; about 'ideological preferences', Morgenthau says that 'Statesmen, especially under contemporary conditions, may well make a habit of presenting their foreign policies in terms of their philosophic and political sympathies in order to gain popular support for them. Yet they will distinguish ... between their "*official* duty", which is to think and act in terms of the national interest, and their "*personal* wish", which is to see their own moral values and political principles realised throughout the world.'[43]

Morgenthau was an outspoken critic of the Vietnam war and later editions of *Politics Among Nations* readily concede the very great divergencies that are possible from 'national' politics conducted in terms of national interest. He goes so far as to suggest as a 'question worth looking into whether modern psychology and psychiatry have provided us with the conceptual tools which would enable us to construct, as it were, a counter-theory of irrational politics, a kind of pathology of international politics'.[44] He does not examine the question of whether several different and competing concepts of rationality might coexist.

The view of international relations that we take belongs to neither idealism as analysed by Morgenthau nor his political realism.

Our concept of rationality may be somewhat less ambitious than Morgenthau's. He appears to believe that there is no problem about assuming that the world of politics is susceptible of rational analysis. But in our view reason must be given for believing that theory is necessary and desirable. Political realism is so reassuring: God's in his heaven (safely out of the way in the hands of religious specialists) and all is orderly in the world. By bringing, or trying to bring, 'order and meaning to a mass of phenomena which without it [theory] would remain disconnected and unintelligible', Morgenthau reassures one when one is feeling low that there is significance in war and international relations. Tolstoy in *War and Peace* conveys a much less

---

[42] *ibid.* 5-6.
[43] *ibid.* 7.
[44] *ibid.*

cosy sense of total absence of intelligible order and meaning, chaos, huge uncontrollable forces at work. We are not suggesting that the world of international relations is so disorderly that theory is completely impossible, but that the possibility should be considered and reasons given for its acceptance or rejection.

In our view, the theory that is possible is a matter of self-explanation, of the exploration of certain ideas of one's own without any guarantee that these will be acceptable, on the strength of shared rationality, to all other rational beings. The breakdown of consensus has gone so far that it is not to be hoped that theory should attain any more ambitious goal than this. It is not clear to us that Morgenthau and other realists would disagree, but what we quoted above about the pathology of international politics leads us to believe that Morgenthau at least believes that there is only one rationally viable view of the international arena – any apparently 'rational' alternative being at best a pathological phenomenon and not something to be taken at face value as a rational viewpoint. In exploring one outlook, as we have tried to do in this book, we are not wishing to hold that it is the only one rationally defensible.

Morgenthau assumes a sharp distinction between 'theory' and 'the facts'. We have no wish to argue in general against the view that it makes good sense to believe that there are 'facts' accessible independent of any particular theory. But there seems good specific reason for questioning Morgenthau's sanguine confidence about which facts are relevant. Implicit in his theory is the assumption that the significant phenomena can and should be traced back to the state. When he speaks of 'national interest' he appears to mean always the interest of the state and never the interest of nations that lack states, or the interest of groups which are neither states nor nations. His choice of 'the facts' is guided by this assumption. All of his examples are drawn from transactions between states. The perspectives of minority nationalisms, insurgent movements, multi-national companies, etc., are systematically ignored.

Instead of concentrating on the state and the statesman, our analysis has proceeded in terms of the individual in a group context who might be a politician, a foreign office official, a guerrilla, the chief executive of a multi-national company, the Secretary-General of the United Nations, or an aggressively insubordinate military commander with passionate views about the way in which a bombing campaign should be waged.

A corollary of this is that there is a clear sense in which Morgenthau and we are talking about different things. Given his belief in the existence and intellectual importance of interstate order, Morgenthau naturally speaks in terms of 'international relations': his study ranges over all aspects of such relations – economic, legal, military, diplomatic, etc. He tacitly assumes a sharp division between interstate and intrastate affairs. Our approach, equally naturally, ranges over all aspects of all activity which has a military dimension. It abstracts from the economic and diplomatic as Morgenthau abstracts from the domestic and trans-national. Where Morgenthau sees the transition from international peace to international war as a matter of what is required by national interest, or as an aberration, we see the transition as demanding justification. Wars in the national interest require just cause just as much as wars against structural violence.

It might be thought that these differences between political realism and our outlook merely showed that one can 'carve up' reality in an indefinite number of ways – that the course of one's thought is largely determined by the questions one asks at the outset. There is some truth in this, but there are also more substantial and specific questions at issue. Morgenthau writes out of special concern about particular historical problems: he is passionately concerned to bring the conduct of US foreign policy into sharp, critical, rational question. In this regard, our concerns are largely the same as his, and the differences are certainly not wholly attributable to the fact that he is writing in an American, we in a British context. Given the common concern about Western foreign and defence policy, Morgenthau finds himself impressed by the order that he thinks pervades relations between states. We, pondering the same facts, are at least as impressed by the disorder in 'the system'. We agree that there are impressive continuities in the policies of many states, but explain these in a different way, and against the background of a different reading of the same facts.

So far, we have been commenting on the descriptive aspect of Morgenthau's theory: i.e. the part concerned with a preliminary demarcation of the subject for study; we turn now to more distinctively ethical issues.

A pivotal word in Morgenthau's discussion of morality is 'abstract'. He assumes without argument that morality is a congeries of *principles* which he several times calls 'universal' which are in constant 'tension' with 'political' imperatives. In Chapter Two we pointed out that many but not all ethical views, or moralities, rest on principle. Utilitarianism relies on one principle; the moralities of absolute duty rely on several. Situation ethics seeks to rely on none. We pointed out the radical weakness of situation ethics in Chapter Two and have no wish to rest much on it here – if foreign policy were conducted in a situational way, its continuity would be incomprehensible. What is important is not situation ethics but that ethics of virtue which we have been developing in this book. Ethics of virtue has at its centre *not* 'abstract', 'universal' principle *but* the good man.

Morgenthau's belief that moral principle always purports to be 'universally valid' may derive from the ambition common in the US and USSR to export values to the rest of the world, and from the intense rivalry of the Cold War. It may also reflect the belief stated by Kant and shared by contemporary philosophers as diverse as Sartre and R.M. Hare that in taking a moral position I am willing that everyone else should think likewise.[45] It is, from our viewpoint, untenable. We argued in Chapter Three that Jim – our archetype of the good man – might become embroiled in existential choice. It is incoherent to suppose that someone making such a choice, and understanding what he is doing, should regard his moral stance as 'universally valid'.[46]

If morality consists of principles, universal or not, then it is to be expected that such principles will be 'abstract': that is, in real situations they will demand that we do one thing where in reality we ought to do something else. Morgenthau's analysis of the tension created by international politics turns on this: the stark and above all simple imperatives of morality pull one way, national interest pulls the opposite way.

The reason for the tension, as Morgenthau expounds it, is that reality is more complex than the moral law knows. In terms of our analysis of morality, the kind of 'tension' provided for by Morgenthau is impossible. For whereas reality is more complex than the moral law knows, it is not more complex than the good man knows. Immersing the good man in ever more complicated problems does not rob him of his virtue or intelligence; indeed, it is a mark of the good man in situations demanding intellectual strength that he can continue to think where others are baffled.

This is not to suggest that the good man can escape 'tension' if he practises politics. In the international arena, as elsewhere, the good man is likely to experience the systematic frustration of his good wishes towards all men, and to be forced into making existential choices which, as pointed out in Chapter Two, are necessarily a matter of regret or remorse on his part. But these are tensions *within* the moral life. They are not tensions between morality *and something*

---

[45] On universalisability, cf. Sartre 46-7, R.M. Hare *The Language of Morals*. On universal ambition, Ambrose 118 quotes a US senator: 'We will lift Shanghai up and up, ever up, until it is just like Kansas City.'

[46] This is well brought out in Peter Winch's discussion of *Billy Budd* 'The Universalizability of Moral Judgments', esp. *Ethics and Action* 163.

else. Where Morgenthau insists on a distinction between ethics and politics, we claim that politics is one of the contexts in which the moral life is lived (and not lived). The context partly determines the kinds of moral anguish that is experienced but it does not turn it from moral outrage into something else, as Morgenthau implies. He is right to reject the slurring over of harsh moral distress that is often found in idealist writing but wrong to see this as a product of a tension between morality and something independent of morality.

This very general criticism has practical consequences. In Morgenthau's theory the task of moral justification is systematically down-graded. Both the practitioner and the student of international relations are required to keep their eyes firmly on the national interest, and there is no hint that they will need to give serious and lengthy thought to moral issues. They will do right when they can, feel torn when they cannot, but the only serious debate about what to do is one to be conducted in terms of national interest. When we look over the 'statesman's' shoulder, according to Morgenthau, 'we think as he does'. In the terms developed in this book, such a view confuses two necessarily different parts of the debate about foreign and security policy. On the one hand, there is the task of understanding what in their own terms politicians and officials are trying to do. On the other hand, there is the task of trying to understand what the good man would do in the given circumstances. In the modern world, it would be profoundly unrealistic to expect officials to engage in the latter task. We have claimed that it is the job of those with the leisure and capacity for more contemplative study, e.g. the academic community. To run the two together is to shore up that moral vacuum in which it was possible, from 1916 onwards, for the detail of strategic thinking about bombing to be elaborated in the crudest and least adequate of moral frameworks, and for the same pattern to be repeated on a larger and much more expensive scale in the evolution of nuclear deterrence theory. Morgenthau implies that 'statesmen' and 'scholars' should engage in dialogue: we agree. He insists that any dialogue which takes place should concern itself with 'the national interest'; we disagree: each side to the dialogue must pursue its own questions in its own way. It is exceedingly likely that officials will attend to short-term, narrow, technical issues whose bearing on the community of all men is non-existent or obscure. But that does not mean that the whole discussion should be conducted in such terms.

So far, we have pursued the argument against 'realism' in terms drawn from Morgenthau. We have contested the view that morality consists of principle, and pointed out that in terms of the ethics of virtue Morgenthau's notion of two realms between which there is tension is objectionable. It would be intolerably one-sided to leave the argument there, however. For there is a part of 'realism' that seeks to show, in terms of virtue itself, that there is a profound tension between morals and politics. We now turn to this. The Western tradition of trying to think about politics in terms of the best imaginable possibility is ancient, dating at least as far back as Plato's *Republic*. In the *Laws* Plato perhaps originated the equally familiar Western search for the second best political option. But it appears to have been left for Machiavelli to try and argue that what politics demands is second-best *virtue*. The fascinating politician who is to be valued in politics precisely because of his lack of moral scruple is thus a relatively late appearance. Two recent attempts to commend it are by Michael Walzer[47] and (perhaps unintentionally) by Bernard Williams.

8. Walzer's 'dirty hands'

Walzer explores the 'conventional wisdom' that in politics dirty hands are unavoidable. He takes the question asked by Hoederer in Sartre's play *Les Mains Salles*: 'I have dirty hands right up to the elbows. I've plunged them in filth and blood. Do you think you can govern innocently?' Walzer is disposed to reply: 'No, I don't think I could govern innocently; nor do most of us believe that those who govern us are innocent ... even the best of them.' He makes the interesting suggestion that 'there may be something to learn ... not merely something to explain' about such unphilosophical judgments.[48]

Walzer envisages the issue as a clash between utilitarianism and the morality of absolute principle: 'a particular act of government (in a political party or in the state) may be exactly the right thing to do in utilitarian terms and yet the man who does it guilty of a moral wrong ... If on the other hand he remains innocent, chooses' to obey some absolute principle, 'he not only fails to do the right thing (in utilitarian terms), he may also fail to measure up to the duties of his office.'[49] Walzer gives two examples.

An example of the struggle for power. Imagine a politician who wants to do good only by doing good, or who is at least 'certain that he can stop short of the most corrupting and brutal uses of political power'. What will we think of him when his conviction is put to the test?

> He wants to win the election, someone says, but he doesn't want to get his hands dirty. This is meant as a disparagement, even though it also means

---

[47] In *War and Moral Responsibility* (ed.) Marshall Cohen et al. 62-82.
[48] *ibid.* 64.
[49] *ibid.* 63.

that the man being criticized is the sort of man who will not lie, cheat, bargain behind the backs of his supporters, shout absurdities at public meetings, or manipulate other men and women. Assuming that this particular election ought to be won, it is clear, I think, that the disparagement is justified. If the candidate didn't want to get his hands dirty, he should have stayed at home; if he can't stand the heat, he should get out of the kitchen, and so on. His decision to run was a commitment (to all of us who think the election important) to try to win, that is, to do within rational limits whatever is necessary to win.[50]

To make the case more specific, Walzer imagines his candidate having to make a deal with a dishonest ward boss, involving the granting of contracts for school construction over the next four years. The candidate 'shouldn't be surprised by the offer' and should accept or reject according to the needs of the campaign. He is 'extremely reluctant' to even consider it. If he hesitates because the very thought of dealing with the corrupt official makes him feel unclean, his reluctance is uninteresting. But he may have other reasons for hesitation: some of his supporters support him because they think him a 'good man', by which they mean a man who won't make such deals; he may doubt his own motives; he may fear that the deal will jeopardise the objectives of his candidacy; he may simply think the deal 'dishonest and therefore wrong'. 'We', his supporters, want him to make the deal

> precisely because he has scruples about it. We know he is doing right when he makes the deal because he knows he is doing wrong. ... If he is the good man I am imagining him to be ... he will believe himself to be guilty. That is what it means to have dirty hands.[51]

An example of the exercise of power. A politician who has won office with an honest pledge to end a prolonged colonial war goes off to the colonial capital to open negotiations with the rebels. The capital is in the grip of a terrorist campaign and the new leader's first decision is this: he is asked to authorise the torture of a captured rebel leader who knows or probably knows the location of a number of bombs hidden in the city and timed to go off in the next twenty-four hours. He orders the man to be tortured 'convinced that he must do so for the sake of the people who might otherwise die in the explosions – even though he believes that torture is "always wrong" '. 'He had expressed this belief often and angrily during his ... campaign. How should we regard him now? (How should he regard himself?)'[52]

---

[50] *ibid.* 67.
[51] *ibid.* 67-8.
[52] *ibid.* 68-9.

Although Walzer does not say so, his examples and analysis appear to be strongly influenced by his earlier insistence on the importance of the politically-divided man, discussed in Chapter Two above. The way Walzer tells it, an important *moral* feature of both his examples is that the politician has given his word, has pledged himself to a group of people who are his political supporters. Ever sensitive to the obligations that arise from such commitments, Walzer leans on them heavily here. Although he asks how the man authorising torture should regard himself, he does so only in parenthesis: the focus is on how we, the supporters, should regard him.

This introduces a peculiar and limiting feature into the examples. The true problem that Walzer points up, but without saying so, is the problem of the politician whose moral understanding advances further than that of his constituency. The man who inveighed against torture under all circumstances in his campaign presumably did so *either* as a political necessity – his followers would accept nothing less sweeping – *or* out of conviction. In the situation Walzer puts him in, he appears to be learning, if he did not know it already, that torture is sometimes justified.[53] Walzer gives no reason apart from the concern at having betrayed trust for seeing the man as torn between contradictory beliefs.

The first example appears to us to carry the same limitation. Walzer's worthy candidate is supported for his hesitancies and disparaged for being too nice when the going gets rough. The use of metaphors implying a game is vital: what the example shows us is a man who has not yet understood *the rules of the game*. The problem confronting him is remarkably innocuous: merely a bit of graft. We have the impression that Walzer would think the case significantly different if the candidate were being asked to contract for a school building he knew would be quite likely to be unsafe, or to authorise in a confidential and undetectable way the carrying out of a few nasty but 'necessary' murders. At some point, we assume, Walzer will want his 'good man' to go over from a campaign to get elected to an anti-corruption campaign, making as plain as possible why he will not and cannot run in politics as currently constituted.

The reasons the candidate in the first example has for hesitation are various. The feeling of uncleanness may be very interesting, in that it may betray an appalling superstition: the good man does not become bad by successfully struggling with, and overcoming, evil in a contest in which he is unchanged and victorious. It would be a fault in

[53] For a discussion of whether it is sometimes justified see Barrie Paskins 'What's Wrong with Torture?'

a 'good man' to think he had been compromised: he would be underrating the beauty and resilience of goodness. Hesitation on account of what his supporters would think we have already discussed in part. We would add that it is part of supporting a man because one believes him to be a good man that one accepts that his moral understanding may outrun one's own. (Of course, one may come to doubt whether he is a good man, but that is not Walzer's point.) Doubt of one's own motives is of course a proper part of the moral life – but Morgenthau is right to criticise a focussing on motive. What a man is trying to do and not his motives is what counts morally as in politics. Fear that the deal will jeopardise the aims of the candidacy is good utilitarian reason for hesitation. 'Dishonest and therefore wrong' betrays an appalling moral naiveté. In sum, we find good reason to doubt Walzer's conclusion that his good candidate 'knows he is doing wrong'. For he knows just what he is doing and Walzer's premiss is that he is doing right.

To respond in this way to Walzer's in our view unpersuasive examples is not to reject his whole argument for the importance of dirty hands in politics. For even if these examples are unconvincing, others might be more plausible. Let us assume that there are such, without enquiring too nicely into what they might be. On the assumption that dirty hands are inescapable, Walzer sketches briefly three views of dirty hands. Each appears to him partly right but he finds himself unable to 'put together the compound view that might be wholly right'.

(a) *The Machiavellian view.* To found or reform a republic, a man must do terrible things, e.g. murder his brother, lie to the people. He must learn how *not* to be good. There are moral standards, which are not to be shrugged off, but the prince must learn to defy them. Power and glory will reward the good man who throws away personal goodness and succeeds in politics. The penalties of failure in politics are not examined.

Walzer thinks it true that the politician must throw away personal goodness but disapproves of the lack of inward life in the 'Machiavellian' hero. That hero is not the sort to keep a diary and we cannot find out what if anything he thinks about his crimes. But 'we ... want to know; above all, we want a record of his anguish'.[54]

(b) *Weber's 'Politics as a Vocation'.* .Here, the good man with dirty hands is a tragic hero. He wants, as Christian magistrates always have, to do good in the world and save his soul 'but these two ends have come into sharp contradiction'. Walzer quotes Weber's essay:

[54] *War and Moral Responsibility* 78.

'the genius or demon of politics lives in an inner tension with the god of love ... [which] can at any time lead to an irreconcilable conflict.'[55]

Walzer dubs this high-minded hero a suffering servant and does what he can to signal respect. But he thinks we suspect the hero 'of either masochism or hypocrisy or both, and while we are often wrong, we are not always wrong'. The trouble being that because the man's suffering is wholly inward 'he himself fixes the price he pays ... sometimes the hero's suffering needs to be socially expressed (for like punishment, it confirms and reinforces our sense that certain acts are wrong)'.[56]

(c) *Camus'* Just Assassins. Out of Camus' play, Walzer extracts the doctrine that just assassination is like civil disobedience. 'In both men violate a set of rules, go beyond a moral or legal limit, in order to do what they believe they should do. At the same time, they acknowledge their responsibility for the violation by accepting punishment or doing penance.' Now of course in 'most cases of dirty hands moral rules are broken for reasons of state, and no one provides the punishment. ... Moral rules are not usually enforced against the sort of actor I am considering, largely because he acts in 'an official capacity. If they were enforced, dirty hands would be no problem. We would simply honor the man who did bad in order to do good, and at the same time we would punish him. We would honor him for the good he has done, and ... punish him for the bad he has done. We would punish him ... for the same reasons we punish anyone else; it is not my purpose here to defend any particular view of punishment.'[57] Walzer thinks that there are no authorities short of the priest and the confessional to whom we might entrust this task, but he prefers this view to (a) and (b) 'if only because it requires us at least to imagine a punishment or a penance that fits the crime and so to examine closely the nature of the crime'. In (a) and (b) there is no 'explicit reference back to the moral code, once it has, at great personal cost to be sure, been set aside'.[58]

Walzer is assuredly right on this last point. The viewpoints that he associates with Machiavelli and Weber set aside moral standards and give no indication of exactly what degree of significance should be attached to them thereafter. But in other respects he appears to us mistaken in a way that is very important for our theme.

All three of the views of dirty hands that Walzer examines focus only on the man of action, without paying any attention whatever to those in whose interests he acts. Now it is certainly correct to hold that

---

[55] *ibid.* 79.
[56] *ibid.*
[57] *ibid.* 81.
[58] *ibid.*

the beginning of any coherent thoughts that one has done wrong is the recognition that something absolutely frightful has happened as a result of one's actions. Guilt by association is a nonsense. In some sense or other, a person must have done something, or have failed to do something, if he is to be accounted guilty. But it by no means follows from this that Walzer is right (especially in his own terms) to focus attention on the men with dirty hands.

Presumably Walzer's characters with dirty hands have always acted with someone's interest in mind. Suppose this person or group tries to soothe the person in authority with the assurance, meant to be morally reassuring, that 'you did it for us'. What is the person with dirty hands who happens also to be a good man to make of this reassurance? The question already arises in the very primitive case examined above in which Jim saves the nineteen Indians from Pedro by shooting the twentieth. Let us continue that story a little. Pedro leaves, Jim kneels sobbing over the wretch he has killed with his own hands. Seeing that the coast is clear, the Indians cluster round him with loud assurances that it's all right, here they are hale and hearty and he isn't to take it so hard – you did it for us! Jim turns on them with bitter contempt and berates them for their shocking – what? Cruelty?

He cannot deny that he did it for them. Is he angry that they are being inconsiderate of his feelings? Surely not. What is so bitter is that he, the good man, must bear the anguish alone because those he has saved are such moral mediocrities that they do not see that the awfulness of the action flows through him to them. One would be suspicious if Jim did not feel dreadful about what he had done. But what underlies Jim's distress is that he did it for them and the killing 'infects' the whole project. It should distress those who are a part of the project in being the willing beneficiaries of it just as it should distress the agent, Jim. Clifford Simmons, in the passage discussed above in Chapter Four, goes still further and feels bad about being the passive beneficiary of activity by others which has a warlike dimension. That view is absurd not because Simmons is not the agent, but because he is in no way a party to the project. (For example, no thought of what he wants or does not want enters the heads of those engaged in the food convoy.)

What is to us unsatisfactory about all three of the views of dirty hands sketched by Walzer is that they ignore the involvement of the beneficiaries in the projects of the good man who gets dirt on his hands. This is especially surprising when Walzer attaches such importance in his examples to the connection between the politician and his supporters. He never suggests that what the supporters should do is not punish the poor man who has done his best on their behalf, but should reflect on what 'we' have done through our chosen leaders. If Walzer is right that there is a deep and inescapable connection between politics and dirty hands then there must be a connection between dirty hands and those who participate, or have the opportunity to participate, not as men powerful enough to get dirty hands but as the supporters of such men. We therefore agree with Walzer that the inward life is more important than is admitted in the view he attributes to Machiavelli. But we think that the inward life of the political actor's followers is at least as important, and as caught up in any dirt that may be inescapable, as the inward life of the politician.

Our attitude to the anguished individual whom Walzer connects with Max Weber's essay is more complicated. We would be suspicious of a man with dirty hands who thought himself able, as Walzer puts it, to 'fix the price he pays'. We suggested earlier in our discussion of Nuremberg that the retributivist idea that punishment was the paying of a price made good sense in the case of the petty criminal who is released unreformed and without deterrent effect because he has 'paid the price' but that in the case of the monstrous crimes tried at Nuremberg no price could be high enough. It would seem to us that if the good man is in earnest in regarding himself as having dirty hands, then he will see his offence as so heinous that no price he could ever pay would be enough. This is not to say that others should adopt this view of him; but to see him as setting a price on his offence is a trivialisation of his anguish. If we are right in general about the requirement that willing beneficiaries should understand themselves in the light of the best self-understanding of their benefactor then it would seem on Weber's showing that they should themselves experience an anguish that regards no penalty as sufficient.

The impossibility of paying the price affects also the view that the man with dirty hands should be punished for the bad that he has done. Walzer appears to mean this as an imaginative picture rather than a realistic proposal. It appeals to him 'if only because it requires us at least to imagine a punishment or a penance that fits the crime and so to examine closely the nature of the crime'. We would prefer that the politician with dirty hands and his supporters should ponder the crime as the kind of corporate activity for which no penalty or penance would be sufficient: such a view would serve as well as Walzer's to concentrate the mind, and be free of the general difficulties that we have pointed out.

Walzer's essay is, we think, to be valued for drawing attention to something that is very often ignored. We agree with him that there is something to learn and not merely something to explain from such judgments as 'No, it is not possible to govern innocently'. But what is to be learnt does not become sufficiently apparent in the essay.

He has not shown reason for thinking that the good man must learn how not to be good. What he has obscurely drawn attention to is what has elsewhere been called 'morality's problem of evil'.[59] This is a problem for the religious and the non-religious alike. Its character can be seen clearly enough in the person of Jim reflecting with horror on his shooting of the Indian. If he is the good man we take him for, a thought that would inevitably come to him is 'How can one engage in a practice that demands this sort of thing?' It is morality that creates the problem he finds himself in – without morality, he would be at liberty to stroll off into the jungle saying to Pedro 'That's your problem, chum'. Just as God is traditionally held to create the world, so morality creates the necessity Jim is under to shoot one Indian in order to save the others. This will necessarily lead him to bitter thoughts against morality, just as the truly religious are apt to be led into situations where they have extremely good reason to curse God.

This is something which is not said by Kant and which is absent from the pages of Morgenthau and Walzer. It is one of the reasons for deep unease about the widely-shared Christian assumption that morality is a perfect gift of God. Kant's reasons for being silent about morality's evil are especially revealing. For Kant, the one thing unconditionally good is the good will. Ought implies can. There is no possibility of serious repining about what morality requires because obeying the moral law determines the values of all other good things, and is not limited by them. We have repeatedly challenged this claim. Jim embraces the Kantian principle that one is to treat humanity in oneself and others always as an end and never merely as a means, as an articulation, in terms of his best understanding of the good for man, of his good wishes towards all men. If morality requires the shooting of the Indian, morality frustrates his good wishes towards the Indian. A Kantian, having shot the Indian, would have nothing of a moral kind to cry about. But if Jim weeps, one knows why: he weeps for the unfortunate wretch he has been forced to kill, as is natural in one whose deepest nature is good wishes towards all men.

What, then, is one to make of it if Jim rejects the comforting thought, proferred by the survivors, that he should not be upset over the dead Indian because 'you did it for us'? The good reason for Jim to

---

[59] Barrie Paskins 'Some Victims of Morality' 103.

reject this is not that he has dirty hands, or that he and the Indians together have dirty hands, but that morality has dirty hands. Morality, which has received such sympathetic attention throughout our argument, proves to be a killer. This appears to us the *realistic* view.

The political realist very often insists that he 'profoundly regrets the necessity' of doing frightful things. Being no cynic but a man well aware that the moral life in politics is a nasty thing, he welcomes Morgenthau's unwillingness 'to gloss over and obliterate' the supposed tension between morality and political necessity 'and thus to obfuscate both the moral and the political issue by making it appear as though the stark facts of politics were morally more satisfying than they actually are, and the moral law less exacting than it actually is'. As a very rough approximation to the truth this formulation, like Walzer's in terms of dirty hands, is to be welcomed. But it is a rough and potentially misleading approximation. The underlying truth, we think, is the scandal of morality itself, which demands such victims as one Indian for the saving of the others at the instigation of a villain.

This characterisation has practical implications. Being realistic about the frightful demands that politics makes on the good man does not require, as is often assumed, any acceptance that there is a deep difference between politics and morality. Any division of the two is dangerous because it gives so many opportunities for doublethink and evasion and because, as Walzer points out, it makes so difficult any reference back to morality when once morality has been – doubtless 'regretfully' – consigned to a place in the background. Healthier, less exploitable and more realistic is the view that morality, which has us inescapably in its grip, shows in some situations the aspect of a destroyer, demanding the deaths of people to whom the good man has nothing but good wishes. Hot, desperate anger against morality and not the cool tearfulness of regret is what moral reality demands. There is no alternative to morality, but it demands its victims. This appears to us an important finding of political realism.

In a footnote, Michael Walzer refers to *Humanism and Terror* by Maurice Merleau-Ponty, in which it is argued that the agony and guilt feelings of the man with dirty hands derive from his uncertainty about the success of his actions. On this view, he will have committed a crime only if his efforts fail; if success crowns his dirty handed activity, he can say that he is justified and the rest of us must agree. Walzer argues this view away as 'a kind of delayed utilitarianism' and for relying too heavily on the anxiety of the gambler which, he suggests, is of no great moral interest. If this were all that needed saying, Merleau-Ponty's argument would have little significance.[60] But Bernard Williams in an examination of some apparently very different examples develops an ethical view that gives some credence to Machiavelli's defiance of morality on the ground that 'history will judge'.[61]

9. *Williams and 'moral luck'*

Two deliberately schematic examples carry Bernard Williams' analysis, simplifications of the life of Gauguin and of the love affair between Anna Karenina and Vronsky. Gauguin has to choose between honouring his moral commitments and trying to become a great painter. Anna's dilemma is between obedience to moral claims towards which she is far from indifferent (e.g. the claims of her son) and her passion for Vronsky. If Gauguin decides against morality and makes a success of his attempt to be a great painter then he will produce something of public value. In Anna's case the relationship must be its own reward: there is no reason to believe that anyone apart from Anna and Vronsky will benefit if it prospers, though some will certainly suffer whether it goes well or badly.

Bernard Williams is emphatic that the moral objections to Gauguin's career and Anna's affair are not to be removed by success or failure:

> There is no ground, whatever happens, for demanding that [those with a moral interest in the matter] drop their resentment. If they are eventually going to feel better towards [Gauguin or Anna], it will not be through having received an answer to their complaints ... They are not to be recompensed by the agent's success – or only if they are prepared to be.[62]

From Jim's moral viewpoint, this view is over-simple. In at least one respect, the two cases of Gauguin and Anna are significantly different. This has important implications, as will shortly emerge, for political realism.

One's sympathy for Gauguin is elicited in part by one's assumption that the kind of thing he is doing – painting – is a thing worth doing, one of the very great variety of things worth doing that give direction and richness to human lives. This assumption does not demand that one attach any importance on one's own account to painting, or that the victims of Gauguin's decision value painting. But it does create some slight presumption of moral right in Gauguin's action. For if the

---

[60] *War and Moral Responsibility* 74 n.16.
[61] 'Moral Luck' 117-19.
[62] *ibid.* 133.

humanity of oneself and others is to be cherished, those activities which give direction and richness to human life must be cherished also, and the possibility of a clash between what they demand and what the moral law demands cannot be precluded.

This might seem to be a paradox. It might appear to suggest that the moral law demands something (that Gauguin paint) which it also prohibits (for he must honour his moral commitments). That the moral law generates impossible problems we have already granted: e.g. it makes existential choice inescapable and puts the individual into situations where he cannot but curse it. But the conflict here is somewhat subtler. Looked at in moral terms, and leaving aside Gauguin's own interest in the matter, the question is whether he shall honour the immediate, obvious, pressing moral claims of his dependents or the remote, problematic, and perhaps slight moral claims on him of those who stand to lose an aesthetic delight in art galleries or an inspiring teacher and reference-point in their work as painters. How such an issue should be resolved is pretty obvious. What is so good about Bernard Williams' analysis is that he makes it apparent that this is not an adequate understanding of the problem. The Kantian moral law itself cries out for an analysis that does deeper justice to the relation between Gauguin and painting, or anyone and those activities other than morality that give meaning and direction to his life. If one is to take seriously the humanity that is in one (and in others) then it is necessary to recognise that the activities in which one lives a truly human life can produce a conflict with morality. But *not* a conflict that can be rendered in *moral* terms. A decently humane moral understanding necessarily recognises that there comes a point where merely moral reflections break down: Gauguin's imperative to serve painting cannot be given proper statement in moral terms, but nor – as ethics has to recognise – can it be abandoned.

This cuts two ways. On the one hand, it implies, as Bernard Williams points out, that Gauguin cannot have an even remotely appropriate moral defence. But on the other hand, it implies that Gauguin's victims must recognise, if their moral understanding is anything like complete, that their moral case against Gauguin is by no means the whole truth of the situation viewed from that viewpoint which attaches the significance to morality accorded in this book. There is therefore a possibility of reconciliation that Bernard Williams ignores.

The case of Anna appears to us to be decisively different. It is an inescapable part of life that if people are truly to live then they must engage in activities other than morality (otherwise, the Kantian notion of 'humanity' will be empty). But this unassailable general proposition gives no reason for thinking that there is any justification whatever for Anna to betray her freely-given commitment to her husband and son in favour of a new love affair. It could happen to anyone that they should be drawn into Anna's appalling situation, but what this means is that it could happen to anyone that they might fall in love and that love might lead them into a defiance of morality. Anna has a very great claim on our pity and compassion but there seems no reason to think that her reneging on her projects of marriage and motherhood should find any sort of justification in a reasonably humane ethics. When Karenin is moved to forgive his wife it is not and cannot be by the thought that after all life is necessarily like that in a world in which each person must live his or her own life; forgiveness can come only through realisation of how much he loves the suffering human being who has betrayed him.

It is important to be clear about this distinction from the outset because Bernard Williams develops a subtle distinction that implies the need for a careful modification of what was said earlier in this book about giving hostages to fortune. Although he does not say so, his argument threatens to reinstate a form of political realism. We argue that, properly understood, such a reinstatement is unviable.

Crucial to Bernard Williams' argument is a distinction between two types of failure. If Gauguin sustains some injury on his way to Tahiti which prevents his ever painting again, or if Vronsky is accidentally killed, then the defiance of morality ends in failure but the failure is a matter merely of misfortune: they were just unlucky. Bernard Williams calls this 'extrinsic failure'. If, on the other hand, Gauguin gets to his island and then the painting will not work, or if the affair with Anna takes a turn which leads to suicide on Vronsky's part then the failure is not a matter of merely external misfortune – Gauguin will have failed, the relationship in which Anna has put her trust will have failed. Gauguin will have to recognise not only that the project has failed but that he is a failure; Anna must recognise not only that the defiance of morality has come to nothing but that 'we, Anna and Vronsky, have failed'. This is 'intrinsic failure'. Bernard Williams asserts that the person risking intrinsic failure has a special claim on one's moral respect because of the depth of the failure that he or she is risking.

The bearing of this on Machiavelli, or Merleau-Ponty, and on the strictures elsewhere in this book on giving hostages to fortune is not far to seek. We have been assuming so far that the person giving hostages to fortune is always risking only extrinsic failure. We have been siding with Walzer's contention that the risk-taker is merely a gambler, of no great moral interest. Whatever one makes of Bernard

Williams' argument, it shows that things are not so simple. We have insisted throughout on the Kantian principle demanding that one reverence people's humanity. The disaster facing the person who risks' intrinsic failure as it is depicted by Bernard Williams would be, from Jim's viewpoint, trivialised if one ignored the risk being taken by a person with himself.

Machiavelli's prince had to choose between the mighty work of building or sustaining a republic and the claims of morality. Failure will mean the failure of himself. Although Michael Walzer is right to assert that Machiavelli is silent about his prince's inward life (if any), the possibility of intrinsic failure is present in Machiavelli's pages and confers a heroic grandeur on his hero.

To determine the implications of this for our argument, it is necessary to ask about the place of one's attitude to intrinsic failure, and the risk of it, in the cases of Gauguin, Anna, and the prince. But before this can be done, the general structure of Bernard Williams' argument must be made explicit.

He claims to be drawing attention to certain formal properties of caring about anything at all. On one interpretation of his argument it is quite irrelevant that the examples he uses – Gauguin, Anna – elicit sympathy in at least some readers. His case could be made as well by reference to a person who risks intrinsic failure in the pursuit of racialist objectives. Yes, the person is trying to murder thousands of innocent people, but at least he has this heroic grandeur, that he is putting himself at risk – taking the risk of becoming a failure.

We do not think that this is the interpretation Bernard Williams intends. He has elsewhere decried the philosophical scrutiny of such dry problems as those of the conscientious Nazi and the universal sadist. What he appears to be doing in 'Moral Luck' is to be arguing, to people with values worth discussing, that regardless of the precise detail of those values, moral respect for the risking of intrinsic failure demands ethical consideration. In the terms developed by G.E. Moore in *Principia Ethica*,[63] he is proposing the risking of intrinsic failure not as something having value in itself, regardless of its wider context, but as a possible ingredient in some larger organic whole which is assumed to be at least sympathetic.

On this interpretation, it is vital for Bernard Williams first of all to obtain the reader's sympathy for the person risking intrinsic failure. In short, unless he is developing a curiously complicated version of the conscientious Nazi problem, Bernard Williams is committed to the assumption that the person risking intrinsic failure commands sympathetic attention.

[63] Chapter Six.

Because of this assumption, it is necessary to consider in each case the ground of the assumed sympathy for the person risking intrinsic failure. We suggested that Gauguin elicited one's moral respect because he was quite sensibly engaged in one of the innumerable activities that gave direction and meaning to human life. In the course of this pursuit, he came into conflict with morality and it emerged that a case could be made out for defiance of morality on his part which could not be stated in moral terms but which had to be recognised as having considerable force by anyone taking the view of morality espoused in this book. In the case of Gauguin, therefore, the risking of intrinsic failure appears to be important as a necessary side-effect of something that is to be expected in anything recognisable as human life.

This is not quite accurate, however. Bernard Williams suggests that success is of final importance to Gauguin and Anna. Whereas in the Kantian system it is the good will that matters above all, so that the consolation of having tried is available to the person who has failed, Bernard Williams sees Anna and Gauguin as staking everything on success. In the case of Gauguin, this seems to us a suspicious claim. If what Gauguin cares about is painting as distinct from his own success or failure then an important consideration with him in deciding between morality and his career will be the thought that he owes it to painting to try and realise his gifts. ('Painting will suffer if I do not try.') And if he fails, an important source of consolation is available for him in the thought that 'At least I did my best in the service of painting'. To say that he might be unimpressed by this thought is merely to point out that he might reject a rational consideration with a close bearing on what his attitude should be, on his own terms, to his failure.

This is a point of some generality. Whenever a person enlists one's sympathy because he is engaged in one of the innumerable pursuits that confer meaning and direction on human life, a relevant consideration is that he is serving some human activity (e.g. painting). If he fails, a consolation of the form 'At least I tried' is therefore always available. The depth of despair that, according to Bernard Williams, is a necessary part of intrinsic failure is therefore absent in all such cases.

The relation between Anna and intrinsic failure is plainly very different. Her claim on our sympathy is that it could happen to anyone in her situation to fall in love and come into collision with morality. The consoling thought in case of failure that 'At least I tried' is unavailable for at least two reasons: her initial attachment is not to an activity (e.g. painting) that survives her defeat but to a person

(Vronsky); and love does not require servants, as painting does. (After all, Anna and Vronsky are not engaged in the social activity of advancing the claims of a more libertarian set of sexual conventions – they are merely in love.) Hence in Anna's case the failure of the relationship is total disaster for her, and the fact of intrinsic failure merely deepens her plight and our pity. This is not a general fact about what is involved in caring about anything whatever, but a consequence of the specific kind of dilemma in which Anna finds herself.

For our purposes, the important case is that of the prince. We have suggested that it is necessary first to consider the ground on which one's sympathy for the prince is elicited, and then the consequent relation between the prince and intrinsic failure.

Is it right to say that the prince is brought into collision with morality in the way that Gauguin is? We think not: of course, as pointed out earlier in this book, collisions within morality are possible that have an important bearing on the moral life. But the argument we are now considering is not that the prince might have to make an existential choice within morality, or have cause to curse morality. It is that independent of all such tensions within morality there is something else, having to do with the prince's risk-taking, that entails some special dignity for his action. What is striking here is the difference between on the one hand politics and on the other the innumerable activities, e.g. painting, which give direction and meaning to people's lives. In the case of Gauguin, something not immediately moral – namely, the activity of painting – gives rise to a conflict with morality. But in the case of the prince, there is no such non-moral thing to give rise to conflict. For politics is morals in a special context, as our earlier argument goes some way to showing.

Is it right to say that the prince comes into conflict with morality in the way that Anna does? Yes, up to a point: for if the prince takes some appalling moral gamble and loses then there is no activity (e.g. painting) to which it is possible to point as a consoling reference point. There is nothing by reference to which one can claim: 'Well, at least he tried.' But the analogy with Anna is imperfect: in her defeat, she has a claim on our pity – it could have happened to anyone. But it is not in the same sense true to assert that the gambler's throw of the prince could have happened to anyone. Love descended on Anna as it were from without, like a fatality. But Machiavelli wants his prince to make the gambling throw entirely out of his own inner pride and defiance.

The price is all sacrifice of one's sympathy. Michael Walzer is correct, despite the interesting distinction between extrinsic and intrinsic failure, to dismiss the Machiavel as a mere gambler. We agree with Bernard Williams that there is the serious possibility of morality generating a conflict with itself which cannot be stated in exclusively moral terms but we have argued that this gives no comfort to political realism.

We have given extensive attention to the arguments of Hans Morgenthau, Michael Walzer and Bernard Williams from a conviction that political realism contains important ethical insights, which it mis-states. We earlier compared our philosophical analysis with a psycho-analytic one that seeks to bring hidden or mis-understood material to consciousness and control. Far too often, moralising about war either ignores as romantic posturing the dignity which some impute to the warrior and the politician or takes the respect due to the brave soldier and courageous prince as evidence that there is something wrong with all attempts to think about war in consistently moral terms. We have tried to bring into the open some at least of the philosophical and imaginative matter that underlies both of these oversimplifications.

In looking at Morgenthau we have argued that the division he attempts to make between morality and politics is indefensible and better understood as a conflict within morality. In considering Michael Walzer's instructive concept of dirty hands, we have tried to show that its likeliest lesson is that there are times when the moral law demands action which necessarily drives the good man into hatred of morality. From Bernard Williams we have derived the conclusion that the moral law readily generates situations in which a case can be made for defying morality: this case cannot be stated in moral terms, but its force must be felt by the good man. Although the analogies of Gauguin and Anna appeared to give some credence to Machiavelli's notion of the desirability of princes learning not to be so good, we argued that taken seriously the analogies condemn the Machiavel to remain nothing better than a mere gambler. In such contexts, we think, political realism can be seen to embody ethical truth confusedly stated rather than anti-ethical truth.

10. Relativism, subjectivism and the ethics of war

Throughout this book we have, of course, 'only been giving our opinion'. We have delivered a large number of moral judgments, and many people appear to think that moral judgments are problematic in a way that some other kinds of judgment – perhaps 'factual' or 'historical' or 'scientific' – are not. For, it is often said, moral judgments are or should be 'relative', are inescapably 'subjective'. A full treatment of such views would require a longer book than the present one to themselves; we can attempt no more than a brief epitome of some, perhaps the most important and influential, relevant arguments for and against.

Suppose, for convenience, we see the person who is making a moral judgment as claiming to be saying something that is true, and the sceptic as denying the moralist's claim to truth. The sceptic is not challenging the moralist with a counter-assertion: he is not countering the moralist's assertion that bombing is wrong with the counter-claim that it is sometimes right. Rather, he is trying in one way or another to undercut the debate that proceeds by assertion and counter-assertion, argument and counter-argument. The range of options open to the sceptic who is challenging the moralist but not denying all truth can be summed up under three heads:

(a) the sceptic may be claiming that there is no such thing as moral truth.

(b) the sceptic may be claiming that there is falsehood, or the possibility of falsehood, in the moralist's assertion which the moralist ought to acknowledge.

(c) the sceptic may be claiming that there is, or may be, moral truth in viewpoints which the moralist is rejecting.

The sceptic may be advancing more than one of these claims, of course, and may be denying *all* truth.

For present purposes, the challenge that there is no such thing as truth can be dismissed as absurd: if there is no such thing as truth, what does the sceptic think he is doing in saying so, still more in arguing so? Such scepticism is logically self-defeating.

The claim that there is no such thing at all as moral truth is readily countered by pointing out a rather minimal notion of 'truth' which the sceptic is likely to grant not too grudgingly, and probably somewhat scornfully. It is this. When one engages in moral discourse, there are certain things that count as a *false move* in the game of moral arguing. (The sceptic very likely thinks moral discourse is no more than a game.) An example is self-contradiction, another is maintaining some moral view which on one's own moral terms one should not be maintaining. Thus, if one is arguing from a pacifist viewpoint then one is contradicting oneself if one says that war is sometimes right, and coming out with an opinion that on one's own terms one should not if one says that black South Africa should rise up in armed rebellion. In short, there is a limited kind of rationality which is to be found in much moral discourse; and one can define a very unadventurous notion of moral truth in terms of it: a statement has moral truth if and only if it avoids things which, in terms of the moral position adopted by the person making the statement, would be a false move. This view could be refined at length, but we doubt whether many serious sceptics would doubt it.

It might be thought to represent a pyrrhic victory because if it represents all that can be said in defence of moral truth then it reduces the making of moral judgments to moves in a game. No doubt it is very galling to have one's opponent cry 'Checkmate', but defeat in a game matters only if one is playing that game. Must not any serious moralist want to show that his judgments must be accepted, or at least disputed, as having a force which holds regardless of what games a person chooses to play or not play?

Rather than embark on a general and necessarily highly abstract discussion of this fascinating question, we propose to consider it specifically by reference to the moral viewpoint adopted in this book. We have claimed that certain moral principles relating to war and all other activity having a military dimension (e.g. nuclear deterrence, arms races and the arms trade) are necessarily recognised as binding by anyone who has good wishes towards all men and who understands the good for man in terms of the need for each person to live his own moral life. That is, we have argued in some detail that for a man of good wishes, etc., any rejection or ignoring of these principles would be a false move. To that extent, acceptance and observance of the principles is, if our argument is correct, something that has truth on its side. Hence, if the sceptic wishes to circumvent our argument by saying that after all we are only playing a game then he can do so only by appealing to those – if any – who are prepared to play a game which involves not being a person with good wishes towards all men and/or not understanding the good for man in terms of the need for each to live his own moral life.[64]

And who wants to do that? This might seem a very naive question. Does one not know that there are very many bad people in the world, and that there is a portion of oneself that is relentlessly self-seeking and remorselessly misanthropic? This must be granted. But all that it points up is the very great difference between the law with which lawyers are concerned and the moral law. Speaking very roughly, legal law from Jim's viewpoint has sanctions attached to it because it is fundamentally addressed to those who are disposed to offend against fundamental decencies, or inescapable regulations of social conduct. The person, or part of oneself, to whom the legal law is most

[64] For an enlightening discussion of the slippery concepts of 'game' and 'play' see John Passmore *The Perfectibility of Man* Ch. 15.

importantly addressed characteristically asks – on being confronted with a rule – 'And what if I transgress? what is the penalty?' The penalty may be anything one likes, from boiling in oil to being shown up as a lawbreaker to people who have only a mild, passing interest and will do the transgressor no harm. The rather obvious point we are after is that the legal law is addressed to those who are disposed not to accept it for itself but only on account of some sanction.

The moral law is in this regard decisively different. It is addressed to people, and the part of the self, disposed to accept it 'for itself alone', and not on account of any sanction. The moral law is addressed to the better part of oneself, for its guidance in the struggle against the worse part of oneself – against the cruelty, selfishness, ignorance, idleness, indifference, etc., that lies within one. The moral law is addressed to the better part of a community, for its guidance in the struggle against the worse part.

This latter proposition might seem objectionably elitist, suggesting as it seems to do that there is a moral elite. This is far from being the case. Consider the moral law as it orders the relationships within a family, or among friends who are equals. It serves to guide each member of the family, each friend in his struggle against evil in himself and in others. Only if one believes, as we do not, that some segment of society enjoys a monopoly in the struggle against evil in others is there any reason for taking our assertion in an elitist way.

It might be thought that this sharp contrast between the moral law and the legal law ignores the well-entrenched view in Judaism, Christianity and Islam of God as the law-giver who punishes those who break his commands. No thorough treatment of this is possible, of course, but a brief comment may serve to show if not to justify our view of it. Some of Jesus' remarks claim that in serving the poor, the needy, and those other people on whose behalf the prophets spoke, a person would be serving Jesus, and that in failing these he would be failing Jesus. This, if it is believed, elucidates the meaning of being unjust or unkind. It is, in the context, a searing judgment by the man who is truly God. For it amounts to saying that persons who die having lived unjustly have betrayed Jesus as certainly as the disciples who slept while he suffered, or betrayed him. And worse: where those disciples were granted new life, there is no promise for the one who dies in injustice of any new life. What greater punishment or hell could there be than the thought that one has betrayed God and there is no new life in which to amend?

This question, like the earlier one about who would care to be a person without good wishes and/or without understanding of human good as something to be discovered in living, is not rhetorical. There are ways of playing games that rob it of its force. (Whether these games can be continued after death is a question not necessary to consider here.) Our point is that the religious 'sanction', leaving aside questions of what may happen after death, is quite unlike a legal sanction: it presupposes a spontaneous attachment on the part of the person addressed to Jesus; the absence of such deprives it of its force.

Because the moral law is addressed to the better part of humanity in oneself and in others, the possibility that the worse part of humanity will reject it by means of consistent argument is not a damaging possibility for the moralist. If the sceptic is to undermine his moral judgment, it must be on some other ground than by showing that the worse part of humanity may remain unconvinced by the best supported of moral judgments.

This stark argument will not please those who are impressed by the sceptical arguments listed above as (b) – that there is falsehood, or the possibility thereof, in the moralist's assertions which the moralist ought to acknowledge, and (c) – that there is, or may be, moral truth in viewpoints which the moralist is rejecting. Once again, we consider these propositions not in general terms but with reference to the moral judgments advanced in this book.

If the moralist, at the end of a long and complicated argument involving many complex premises and inferences, is reluctant to admit that he may be wrong then he is a fool. For he is merely under-estimating the great difficulty of rigorous argument and possibility of error. But this truism does not give the sceptic what he requires to substantiate (b). For evidence that one admits one may be wrong is to be found if the moralist goes out of his way to invite criticism and reply, patiently strives to see whether there is something he has overlooked or under-estimated, etc. In short, evidence that one regards oneself as fallible in the judgments one makes on matters one cares about is to be found in one's determination to stay at the level of assertion and counter-assertion, argument and counter-argument rather than any descent into scepticism which involves abandoning the search for truth.

The person who, on the contrary, delivers some moral judgment and then adds 'but of course this is only my opinion' is at least as likely to be rejecting the truth that he may be wrong as the foolish moralist who declines further argument. Suppose, for example, someone says 'Nuclear deterrence seems to me wrong, but of course that is only my opinion'. Depending on the context and tone of voice, he may merely be inviting a two- or many-sided discussion in which they are prepared to participate. But, and this is what is important, he may not be. He may be, often is assuming that the rider 'but of course that is only my opinion' reflects some sceptical truth (e.g. moral subjectivism) and renders him immune from criticism. The mixture of bad philosophy and timidity, self-mistrust, radical chic or whatever it is that makes subjectivism appear so desirable merely results in a dogmatism as uninteresting as that of the foolish moralist who will not argue. The truth that there is in (b) is that there is a need for argument, not that rational discourse is impossible.

Argument (c) is far more interesting. An extremely powerful form of it is to be found in Nietzsche's *On the Genealogy of Morals*. No brief summary can do justice to the rich suggestiveness of this masterpiece, but a sketch of a portion of it may serve to epitomise the kind of problem that is raised by (c), and the view we take of it.

11. *Nietzsche's* On the Genealogy of Morals

Nietzsche assumes that there is such a thing as objective truth about matters of fact. For example, he devotes a considerable amount of space to factual argument about the etymologies of certain words, and their implications for the history of morality. These arguments are not *ad hominem* but purport to prove something beyond reasonable doubt. However, Nietzsche attaches very great importance to the tendency which he thinks human beings always show to go far beyond the facts and to embrace speculative pictures of the world and their place in it which are frequently absurd and always far outrun the evidence for them. In particular, he argues, this is true of all the great philosophers. Kant is one of his leading examples: according to Nietzsche, Kant in developing his doctrine of the moral law is 'really' struggling for the optimal conditions in which he, the human being Kant, can live the life that is in him. Every philosopher is pleading in a special and deeply personal cause. Philosophy, Nietzsche thinks, can never be the same again after this has been pointed out.

Nietzsche attempts to show that there is a regular pattern in the self-seeking speculations about the world in which philosophers, the religious, and all men engage. The pattern that he 'uncovers' is closely related to his general assertion that every human being seeks those conditions in which it can live best. If this generalisation is true, the practice of *self-denial* is impossible: whatever a human being is doing when he 'engages in self-denial', he is assuredly not denying himself. What is he doing?

Nietzsche's answer to this leans heavily though not entirely on his etymological researches. He claims that there are two fundamental types of morality. In one, the fundamental word is 'good': those who practise this morality regard their own way of life, their own lives and the things that have a place in their way of life as 'good'; and things different from themselves as 'bad'. The word 'bad' is thus defined in terms of the word 'good'. Among themselves, the adherents of the morality of good/bad are mutually restrained by respect for one another's power. Each is brimming over with the life that is in him; so far from being our man of good wishes, he has little occasion to give others a thought except insofar as specific ties arise between him and them (e.g. he falls in love) or they are able to enforce his obedience to certain rules by means of sanctions. Law, but not the moral law as we have interpreted it, is important among these people. Nietzsche often invokes Homer's heroes and pre-Christian Rome as examples of the operation of the morality of good/bad.

What will happen when adherents of this morality come into contact with people who lack the power to restrain them by means of sanctions? Nietzsche goes a little further in answering this question than the logic of his argument strictly requires. In passages that have acquired notoriety through their perversion by Nazism, he suggests the view – recently again the subject of controversy – that individual human beings have a spontaneous desire to cause one another to suffer, or to fight and kill one another.[65] This dubious view is not necessary for his argument. All he needs to point out – as he does – is that there is nothing in the morality of good and bad to restrain men in their dealings with the powerless. If it should happen that the powerful, whether because of a spontaneous 'aggressiveness' or merely because of external circumstances, have occasion to treat the weak with cruelty then there is nothing in their values to stop them from doing so. It will only be a matter of time before some group of the powerful so oppress some group of the powerless that the latter are deprived of all opportunity for that search for optimal living conditions which, according to Nietzsche, is characteristic of all human beings.

What will happen then? According to Nietzsche, men would rather will nothing than not will.[66] To put it less epigramatically, the powerful will probably not have deprived the powerless of all opportunity for adaptation: there is one option that will probably remain open and which the powerful certainly cannot envisage in terms of their own ideas. It is possible for the powerless to turn inward. What this means is that everything that the powerful call 'good' the powerless call by a new name, that is their great contribution to world history – they call it 'evil'. They adapt to the

---

[65] Nietzsche II, 17 tr. Kaufmann and Hollingdale 86-7.
[66] *ibid.* III, 28 tr. Kaufmann and Hollingdale 163.

total repression under which they suffer by discovering for themselves a radically new self-understanding. Their suffering is rescued from being meaningless by their defining themselves as 'good' in terms of 'evil'. They, the powerless ones, are good in being utterly different from everything that they call 'evil' (i.e. everything that the powerful call 'good').

Here, for the first time, the paradox of 'self-denial' becomes resolvable. Those who engage in it are in one sense truly engaging in self-denial: for they have natural appetites that make them want the things that the powerful call 'good' and they systematically deny these things to themselves even when they can get them. But in a deeper sense they are not denying themselves but discovering, asserting themselves – for they solve the problem of adaptation by becoming persons who are 'good' in contrast to the 'evil' which the powerful, and their own natural appetites, call 'good'.

By a process which Nietzsche never fully explains, and for his purposes does not need to explain fully, the adherents of the morality of good/evil succeed in spreading their view of the world to other people. (Nietzsche suggests that it is very congenial to slaves and to those suffering from clinical depression.) Eventually, the adherents of the morality of good/bad capitulate and accept their former victims' view of the world. That is, they learn to see themselves as 'evil' rather than 'good'. By the cunning of history, the victims have triumphed as completely in this story as in the philosophies of Hegel and Marx.

A description of the capitulation is not strictly necessary for Nietzsche's argument but an imaginary example may serve to suggest the kind of process it might be. Suppose that the adherents of the morality of good and bad are Homeric heroes, whose life is one of fighting. The warrior class maintains itself in being by a mixture of, let us say, judicious restraint in battle and recruitment of members from outside itself, which cuts the newcomer off from his roots and insures against loss of group identity. Then, something happens which makes the warrior class beholden to people outside itself. Perhaps some innovation in the technology of war forces the warriors to appease skilled craftsmen and financiers whom they previously treated with unrestrained disdain. To preserve itself in being, let us suppose, the warrior class has to present its activity in terms that will commend it to the newly powerful. These newly powerful men happen to be adherents of the morality of good and evil. At this point, the old morality is doomed. It may linger on in a murky twilight, perhaps for centuries, but the operative understanding of the warrior's activity will necessarily be in terms of good and evil rather than good and bad. This schematic example could, of course, be altered in a variety of ways. For example, it might be tactical innovation, or population change, or an increase in that part of the population freed from subsistence agriculture, that caused the warrior class to need mass armies in conditions that necessitate appeasement and ultimate capitulation to the morality of good and evil. The defeated ones may not be warriors at all. The triumph of good and evil might have many different historical sources and not just one. And so on.

However this may be, Nietzsche's analysis does not stop with the triumph of good and evil. He regards this victory as catastrophic, for obvious and good reason. With the triumph, all men learn to hate themselves, to call 'evil' all their natural impulses. The initial point of this self-hatred – adaptation to total powerlessness, to slavery and physiological depression, to the tactical necessities of appeasing those who have a grip on supplies that the warriors need – has passed for society is radically altered with the triumph of good and evil. But people with natural impulses and little or nothing to gain from the morality of good and evil continue to be born. Nietzsche considered the nineteenth-century cult of nihilism to be a symptom of the plight of these strong ones, systematically prevented from understanding themselves or finding their optimal conditions for life. Nietzsche was at one with many writers of the time in being nauseated by man, the sheer boring, mediocre, average human being.

Like all human beings, he searched for his own optimal conditions for living and thought he found them. It was not for him to reverse single-handed the cunning of history and give back to those not born for good and evil their birth-right. For one thing, he knew that too much of himself was committed to seeing the world in ascetic terms, in terms of good and evil rather than good and bad. What he could do and tried to do was to proclaim, like a new John the Baptist, the coming of the new Messiah (Zarathustra) who would once more speak the clean, free language of good and bad rather than the now old, putrefying language of good and evil. He is emphatic that the new, free men cannot be called on to minister to the weak, the oppressed, and those others commended by the Hebrew prophets:

> Or is it their task, perhaps, to be nurses or physicians?
> But no worse misunderstanding and denial of *their* task can be imagined: the higher *ought* not to degrade itself to the status of an instrument of the lower, the pathos of distance *ought* to keep their tasks eternally separate! Their right to exist, the privilege of the full-toned bell over the false and cracked, is a thousand times greater: they alone are our *warranty* for the future, they alone are *liable* for the future of man. The sick can never have the ability or obligation to do what *they* can do, what *they* ought to do: but if they are to be able to do what *they* alone ought to do, how can they at the

same time be physicians, consolers, and 'saviours' of the sick?

And therefore let us ... keep clear of the madhouses and hospitals of culture ... So that we may, at least for a while yet, guard ourselves, my friends, against the two worst contagions that may be reserved just for us – against the *great nausea at man*! against *great pity for man*![67]

Nietzsche's argument gives formidable support to the view of the sceptic that there is, or may be, truth in viewpoints which the moralist is rejecting. Culminating perhaps in Kant, there is an extremely vigorous and still potent tradition in ethics of regarding the moral life as, in Kant's words, 'unconditionally good'. Nietzsche gives reason for rejecting this tradition.

But he does not, in rejecting it, opt for scepticism. He commends the revaluation of all values. A cosy interpretation of this sees it as calling upon us to rethink our values. But this is to reckon without the psychological and historical underpinning of Nietzsche's theory. The weak cannot revalue their values – their values suit them very well! Nietzsche's hope is that those who need, in the depths of their being, to revalue all values will do so. In his terms, there is no reason to believe that the process will be anything but a terrible one.

Nietzsche gives reasons for a mighty onslaught against Kantian morality. He certainly seeks to undercut much of the assertion and counter-assertion of moral discourse by showing what game the protagonists are playing (self-assertion, rules by good and evil). But it is equally true to say that what he is trying to do is to give a new twist to the moral life. This is plain in the passage just quoted which speaks repeatedly of what the new men 'ought' to do in terms irresistibly moral.

The question that is crucial for our argument is this: is the moral life that Nietzsche is commending at odds with that commended in this book? The case in favour of seeing Jim as one of Nietzsche's new free men, even if he is wearing the English botanist's clothes in which he first appeared in this book, is easily made.

Jim seeks to treat the humanity in himself and in others as an end and never merely as a means. We pointed out in our discussion of Bernard Williams' Gauguin that this could lead Jim into an impossible conflict, in which everything that needed saying to satisfy a decently informed moral intelligence could not be said from a moral point of view. There are necessarily the possibilities of conflicts in which the moral case against a certain action is overwhelming but in which the moral intelligence must grant that there is a strong counter-argument which cannot be framed in moral terms. This appears to us

[67] *ibid.* III, 15 tr. Kaufmann and Hollingdale 124-5.

to be Nietzsche's point. The conflicts in question arise because of a clash between what the moral law demands in the given case and what is demanded of someone immersed in one of those pursuits that give meaning and direction to human life, give significance to the Kantian concept of the human being as an 'end'. We have stated the point in terms of activities. Nietzsche states it in terms of that which the adherent of good and evil dubs 'evil'. Our interpretation is more specific, but there is a coincidence of view.

If this is correct, the very great difference between Nietzsche's style and our own requires explanation. It will not do to point out merely that of course Nietzsche is a great writer who can be expected to have a style incomparably more interesting, memorable, pungent, etc. Nietzsche writes of the adherents of the morality of good and evil with the relish of a great military commander for his most formidable enemy, cherished for the greatness of the battles between them. As a result of this magnanimous recognition of what he owes his enemy (namely, the glory of prowess in the fight) Nietzsche's writing about the priests whom he sees as the stinkingly revengeful cherishers of the morality of good and evil never disgusts. His writing is extremely violent, but always with the frame, the perspective of the great struggle between good and evil and good and bad – the struggle for that which shall save the moral law from collapse into vacuity and the final triumph of human self-hatred. Nietzsche, at least, always keeps his good taste (it is one of his best weapons).

12. The death of Nietzsche's enemy

The kind of hatred of morality that Nietzsche deploys is absent from this book (the hatred of morality for the monstrosities it requires, e.g. killing the innocent, is another matter, outside the range of Nietzsche's sharply drawn interests). The reason is historical and not merely personal. Although he detected the collapse of all consensus about values, Nietzsche was writing for an audience still committed, or believing themselves committed, to a Kantian moral understanding of the world. The old allegiances and pictures of the self were still vigorously alive.

Today, we think, the intellectual world – so far as one can generalise – has altered radically. Scepticism rules in thought, if not in action. We are not suggesting that people are worse or morally inferior to what they were – maybe they are better, e.g. more compassionate and caring. But the intellectual frame of reference within which the moral life is lived and not lived has altered. In place of a shadowy Kantian consensus there is scepticism. To view the world in a utilitarian, or an absolutist, or a religious way is to take a leap of faith. The more obvious kinds of compassion are unable to explain themselves and are suspicious of the suggestion that explanation might be needed. Scattered humanistic 'feelings' may be widely shared, but their form (the fact that they are feelings without arguments) as distinct from their admirable humane content attests a general scepticism about morality. Particular theories of morality proliferate, and there is no consensus on what they are theories about.

In this situation, Nietzsche's enemy has died. Where he threatens to rear his head again, paperback Nietzsche stands ready to cut him short. The necessary enemy now is not Kantian morality but the very many thoughts which collectively imply that any finer morality than that of mere pity is impossible. We have addressed ourselves to some of the relevant thoughts with, we hope, duly magnanimous recognition of the enemy's value for us.

Other prophets who have fuelled the scepticism about morality that derives from subjectivism and relativism could be discussed, but space is lacking. To conclude this brief critique of moral scepticism, we want to glance at two linked suspicions that our argument invites. First, an argument as long and complicated as ours might seem suspect – should not the truths of morality be able to speak for themselves? Second, an argument purporting to be as consistent and – in outline – as comprehensive as ours might be accused of ignoring the conflicts and tensions that are a necessary part of the human heart, and the imperfections that are incident on the human condition.

In general terms, we agree with the suspicion of the sheer length and complication of our argument. Anyone who has talked at such length has talked too long. But the 'truths' of morality cannot be left to speak for themselves in a time of collapsed consensus because the very meaning of 'truth' has become problematic. It was necessary to develop the viewpoint of our argument at considerable length in order to make plain the 'game' we were playing and thus demonstrate what in our terms would count as a false move, and therefore what could be accounted truth. It was also necessary to consider a large number of alternative views to see whether they provided a refuge for one disposed to reject our conclusions. Doubtless our argument contains mistakes, but these require counter-argument and correction rather than the dismissal of the whole as a hunt after bad reasons for believing things already known by instinct.

Is our argument too cool, analytic, and unemotional? We believe, and have argued, that the Kantian philosophy does insufficient justice to the emotions, dismissing them as the lower part of the self forever at war with reason. We have sought a partial reconstruction of Kant by replacing the good will with good wishes. We regard wishes with intense seriousness, and have sought to pay careful attention to the emotions incident upon war. Our argument is not unemotional but exhibits a sharp preference among the emotions for those that a person integrates into his personality, as the impulses by which he lives. Of course, one is also subject to emotions that rock and wreck one's stable, personal view of life. But we have thought it right to regard these – insofar as they cannot be thought through and seen as intelligent emotions – as a part of the enemy.

It is sometimes said that modern war has changed the world so much that what is needed is a new ethic. We do not share this view. We have relied on the intelligent emotions of men and women schooled in the Western tradition that begins with Homer's poem about a war crime. Our final appeal is to such emotions – is it not the case that the traditional principles of proportion, noncombatant immunity, and individual responsibility, together with the more unsettling notions of the pacifism of scruple, existential choice of the hopeless fight, and the passionate execration of morality itself elicit recognition and respect?

Conclusion

We undertook to try and show what ethics of war is like. We began with a contemporary problem – the bombing of cities practised by states against one another, practised by insurgents and counter-insurgents, threatened in nuclear deterrence. We pointed out that the bombing of cities has evolved in an almost complete moral vacuum. It is the work of men with a job to do, a job other than the elaboration, clarification, defence and application of morality. We suggested that the contemporary context in which bombing has developed and must be discussed is one of collapsed consensus: instead of political uniformity, each individual bound unequivocally to his own state, a fragmented world of divided loyalties in which the politically divided man is typical; instead of some over-arching moral and religious or philosophical uniformity such as that against which Nietzsche inveighed, an overwhelming scepticism in which all systematic moral principle is a leap of personal faith and very many are moved to retreat into their specialisms – the lawyer into legal positivism, the theologian into parochial ministry,[1] the soldier into the demanding business of defending his country or maintaining deterrence, the philosopher into subtle issues that trample on other specialisms not too much.

In this context, we examined and discarded a number of well-known ethical theories – utilitarianism, the moralities of absolute

[1] We do not mean to disparage theological positivism. Karl Barth's devastating critique of liberal theology retains too much force for any easy dismissal. (Cf. the late and gentle statement of his position in *The Humanity of God*.) But it should be remembered that what is here in question is not church dogmatics but ethics. On this, Barth's friend Dietrich Bonhoeffer comments:

> Barth ... called the God of Jesus Christ into the lists against religion ... That was and is his greatest service ... Through his later dogmatics he enabled the Church to effect this distinction in principle all along the line. It was not that he subsequently, as is often claimed, failed in ethics, for his ethical observations – so far as he has made any – are just as significant as his dogmatic ones; it was that he gave no concrete guidance, either in dogmatics or in ethics, on the non-religious interpretation of theological concepts. (8 June 1944 *Letters and Papers* 109)

principle, the Kantian worship of the moral law, the natural law tradition, situation ethics. Instead, we followed Hume into the analysis of personal merit. A consideration of a number of deliberately schematic examples suggested that the just war tradition and pacifism – often but wrongly regarded as rivals – could be restated in terms of a reinterpretation of Kant that gives weight to the dignity of human wishes of good towards all men. From the moral viewpoint adopted, the bombing of cities was seen to be highly problematic. Every measure, at every level of command, was seen as demanding justification, and carrying the battle to noncombatants was shown as specially objectionable. A number of alternative perspectives, which seemed to promise release from the guilt of indiscriminate killing were found wanting: the truth of them was insufficient to release the offenders from their crimes.

The Nuremberg trial, in which the Allies took a stand on the side of the victims of Nazi oppression and against the oppressors, was defended. Although the Allied bombing offensive was not an issue at the trial, Nuremberg provides a good precedent for speaking without apology of breaches of the moral law relating to war as *criminal*.

We did not infer from this that the men who made the bombing of cities could reasonably be regarded as criminals distinct from the rest of us. Doubtless, large sections of the population are without any share in the crime. But there are those with the capacity and opportunity for reflection on the larger issues involved in activity with a military dimension. Against these, who have done so very little to push into the political arena the moral issues relating to war that the collapse of consensus has done so much to obscure, we believe that we have established at least a prima facie case that they are criminals.

A comprehensive restatement of the just war tradition, although urgently needed, has not been attempted. On some issues, e.g. conscientious objection, we have made no comment. It seemed necessary to suggest something of the flavour and variety of ethics of war, the massive complication and paradoxical simplicity of the philosophical dialogue, as an invitation to others to join in carrying further this experiment in practical philosophy.

Bibliography

This bibliography details all works cited in the text and notes, makes a few suggestions for further reading, and comments on some material not discussed elsewhere in the book. Several important books which appeared too late for discussion in the text are marked*.

Acton, H.B. (ed.) *The Philosophy of Punishment* (London 1969). A useful selection of essays with bibliography. Should be read alongside the remarks on punishment in Nietzsche's *On the Genealogy of Morals*.

Allison, Graham, *Essence of Decision: Explaining the Cuban Missile Crisis* (Boston 1971).

Ambrose, S.E., *Rise to Globalism: American Foreign Policy 1938-70* (Harmondsworth 1971).

Anscombe, G.E.M., *Intention* (Oxford 1957).

Anscombe, G.E.M., 'Modern Moral Philosophy' *Philosophy* XXXIII (1958), 1-19.

Anscombe, G.E.M., 'War and Murder' in *Nuclear Weapons: a Catholic Response* (ed.) Walter Stein (London 1961); reprinted in *War and Morality* (ed.) Richard Wasserstrom.

Aquinas, Thomas, *Summa Theologiae* (London 1964- in progress), vol. 35 (ed.) T.R. Heath (1972).

Arendt, Hannah, *Eichmann in Jerusalem: a Report on the Banality of Evil* (London 1963).

Arendt, Hannah, *The Human Condition* (Chicago 1958).

Arendt, Hannah, *On Violence* (London 1970).

Aristotle, *The Ethics* (tr. J.A.K. Thomson, Harmondsworth 1953).

Aristotle, *The Politics* (tr. J.A. Sinclair, Harmondsworth 1962).

Aron, Raymond, *The Imperial Republic: the United States and the World* (London 1975).

Augustine, *The City of God* (tr. Henry Bettenson, Harmondsworth 1972).

Bailey, Sydney, *Prohibitions and Restraints in War* (London 1972).

Bainton, Roland, *Christian Attitudes toward War and Peace* (Nashville N.Y. 1960).

Baldwin, Hanson W., *Great Mistakes of the War* (New York 1949).

Barth, Karl, *The Humanity of God* (London 1961).

Batchelder, Robert C., *The Irreversible Decision 1939-1950* (New York 1961).

Bedau, Hugo (ed.) *Civil Disobedience: Theory and Practice* (New York 1968).

Bekker, Cajus, *The Luftwaffe War Diaries* (London 1966).

Bennett, Jonathan, 'Whatever the Consequences' *Analysis* vol. 26 no. 3 (1966), 83-102.

Bettelheim, Bruno, *The Informed Heart: the Human Condition in Mass Society* (London 1961). Still the most penetrating analysis of the meaning of the Nazi concentration camps.

Bienen, Henry, *Violence and Social Change: a Review of the Current Literature* (Chicago 1968). Makes some useful points but is needlessly heavy going.

Bodycount: Lieutenant Calley's story as told to John Sack (London 1971).

Bonhoeffer, Dietrich, *Letters and Papers from Prison* (London 1953).

Bosch, William J., *Judgment on Nuremberg: American Attitudes toward the Major German War-crime Trials* (Chapel Hill, N.C. 1970).

Bramson, Leon and Goethals, George (ed.) *War: Studies from Psychology, Sociology, Anthropology* (New York 1964). An old but handy reader.

Brierly, J.L., *The Law of Nations: an Introduction to the International Law of Peace* (6th ed. Oxford 1963).

Broad, C.D., *Five Types of Ethical Theory* (London 1930). A dated but admirably clear and open-minded study.

Brock, Peter, *Pacifism in Europe to 1914* (Princeton 1972).

Brock, Peter, *Pacifism in the United States from the Colonial Era to the First World War* (Princeton 1968).

Brock, Peter, *Twentieth Century Pacifism* (New York 1970).

Brodie, Bernard, *War and Politics* (New York 1973).

Brown, Peter, *Augustine of Hippo* (London 1967). An outstanding biography with much relevant background material but unfortunately very little on Augustine's attitude to war.

Butow, Robert J.C., *Japan's Decision to Surrender* (Stanford 1954).

Calvocoressi, Peter, *Nuremberg – the Facts, the Law, and the Consequences* (London 1947).

Calvocoressi, Peter and Wint, Guy, *Total War: Causes and Courses of the Second World War* (London 1972). An excellent general history.

Cargile, James, 'On Consequentialism' *Analysis* vol. 29 no. 3 (January 1969), 78-88.

Carr, E.H., *The Twenty Years' Crisis 1919-1939* (London 1939).

Carritt, E.F., *Morals and Politics* (Oxford 1936).

Chapman, George, *The Works of George Chapman: Homer's Iliad and Odyssey* (ed. R.H. Shepherd London 1875).

Chatfield, Charles, *For Peace and Justice: Pacifism in America 1914-41* (Knoxville 1971).

Chatfield, Charles (ed.) *Peace Movements in America* (New York 1973).

Clausewitz, Carl von, *On War* (tr. Michael Howard and Peter Paret, Princeton 1976).

Clor, Harry R., *Civil Disorder and Violence* (Chicago 1972).

Cohen, Marshall, Nagel, Thomas and Scanlon, Thomas (eds) *War and Moral Responsibility* (Princeton 1974).

Corti, Axel, *The Refusal*. A deeply moving and intelligent film about a conscientious objector beheaded under Hitler's regime. Cf. Zahn below.

Davidson, Eugene, *The Nuremberg Fallacy: Wars and War Crimes since World War II* (New York 1973).

Davidson, Eugene, *The Trial of the Germans: an Account of the Twenty-two Defendants before the International Military Tribunal at Nuremberg* (New York 1966).

Davidson, Mildred, *The Poetry is in the Pity* (London 1972). This short study of war poetry from Owen to Keith Douglas is a helpful supplement to the more substantial analyses by Johnson and Silkin.

Deane, Herbert A., *The Political and Social Ideas of St Augustine* (New York 1963).

Dixon, Norman, *On the Psychology of Military Incompetence* (London 1975).

'John Doe', *Report from Iron Mountain* (Harmondsworth 1968). A witty way of exploring the question of how 'total' the military dimension is in modern society.

Donelan, Michael (ed.) *The Reason of States: Essays in International Thought* (London 1978).

Douglass, James W., *The Nonviolent Cross: a Theology of Revolution and Peace* (New York 1969).

Douhet, Giulio, *The Command of the Air* (tr. Dino Ferrari, New York 1942).

Dunstan, Gordon, *The Artifice of Ethics* (London 1974).

Earle, Edward Mead (ed.) *Makers of Modern Strategy* (Princeton 1943).

Edwards, Peter and Leaman, Oliver, 'Justified Terrorism and Unjustified Apathy' (unpublished).

Falk, Richard A. et al. *Crimes of War* (New York 1971). Scrappy but useful.

Fanon, Frantz, *The Wretched of the Earth* (Harmondsworth 1967).

Feis, Herbert, *The Atomic Bomb and the End of World War II* (Princeton 1966).

Ferro, Marc, *The Great War 1914-1918* (London 1973).

Findlay, J.N., 'The Structure of the Kingdom of Ends' British Academy Henrietta Hertz lecture 1957; repr. *Values and Intentions* (London 1961) 419-35.

Finn, James (ed.) *A Conflict of Loyalties: the Case for Selective Conscientious Objection* (New York 1968). Somewhat broader and less occasional than its title suggests.

Fischer, Fritz, *Germany's Aims in the First World War* (London 1967).

Fletcher, Joseph, *Situation Ethics: the New Morality* (London 1966).

Ford, John C., 'The Morality of Obliteration Bombing' *Theological Studies* vol. 5 (1944), 261-309; part reprinted in *War and Morality* (ed.) Richard Wasserstrom, 15-41.

French, Peter A. (ed.) *Individual and Collective Responsibility: Massacre at My Lai* (Cambridge, Mass. 1972).

Fromm, Erich, *The Anatomy of Human Destructiveness* (New York 1973).

Fuller, J.F.C., *The Second World War: a Strategical and Tactical History* (London 1948).

Galbraith, J.K., *The Affluent Society* (Harmondsworth 1963).

*Gallie, W.B., *Philosophers of Peace and War* (Cambridge 1978). A trenchant discussion of the need to interrelate the writings on war of Kant, Clausewitz, Marx, Engels and Tolstoy.

Gendzier, Irene L., *Frantz Fanon: a Critical Study* (London 1973).

Gowing, Margaret, *Britain and Atomic Energy 1939-1945* (London 1965).

Gray, J. Glenn, *The Warriors: Reflections on Men in Battle* (New York 1970). Among the most enlightening of all books about war.

Gray, J. Glenn, *On Understanding Violence Philosophically* (New York 1970).

Green, Philip, *Deadly Logic* (Columbus Ohio 1966).

Greenspan, Morris, *The Modern Law of Land Warfare* (Berkeley 1959).

Greenwood, E.B., *Tolstoy: the Comprehensive Vision* (London 1975). Crammed with insights.

Hallé, Louis, *The Cold War as History* (New York 1967).

Hamilton, Bernice, *Political Thought in Sixteenth Century Spain: a Study of the Political Ideas of Vitoria, Suarez and Molina* (Oxford 1963).

Hanke, Lewis, *The Spanish Struggle for Justice in the Conquest of Latin America* (Philadelphia 1949).

Hare, R.M., *The Language of Morals* (Oxford 1952).

*Harrison, Tom, *Living through the Blitz* (London 1976).

Heisenberg, Walter, 'Research in Germany on the Technical Application of Atomic Energy' *Nature* vol. 160 no. 4059 (16 August 1947) 211-15.

Held, Virginia, Morgenbesser, Sidney and Nagel, Thomas (eds) *Philosophy, Morality and International Affairs* (New York 1974).

Higham, Robin, *Air Power: a Consise History* (London 1972).

Homer: see Chapman.

Hobbes, Thomas, *Leviathan* (many editions).

Horowitz, Irving, *War and Peace in Contemporary Social and Philosophical Theory* (2nd ed. London 1973).

Hume, David, *Enquiries Concerning the Human Understanding and Concerning the Principles of Morals* (ed. L.A. Selby-Bigge Oxford 1902).

Huntington, Samuel P., *The Soldier and the State: the Theory and Politics of Civil-Military Relations* (Cambridge, Mass. 1964).

*Hyde, H. Montgomery, *British Air Policy between the Wars 1918-1939* (London 1976).

Ilké, Fred, *The Social Impact of Bomb Destruction* (Norman, Oklahoma 1958).

'International Conference on Military Trials' Department of State Publication No. 3080 (Washington 1949).

International Institute for Strategic Studies. The journal *Survival* and the series of *Adelphi Papers* are a reliable and up-to-date guide to current strategic thinking (London 1959-in progress).

Irving, David, *The Destruction of Dresden* (London 1963).

Irving, David, *The Rise and Fall of the Luftwaffe: the Life of Luftwaffe Marshal Erhard Milch* (London 1973).

Johnson, James T., *Ideology, Reason, and the Limitation of War: Religious and Secular Concepts, 1200-1740* (Princeton 1975). A second volume is promised, carrying the story down to the present.

Johnston, John H., *English Poetry of the First World War: a Study in the Evolution of Lyric and Narrative Form* (Princeton 1964). Perhaps the most perceptive study yet published.

Jones, David, *In Parenthesis* (London 1963).

Jones, Neville, *The Origins of Strategic Bombing: a Study of the Development of British Air Strategic Thought and Practice up to 1918* (London 1973).

'Judgment of the International Military Tribunal for the Trial of German Major War Criminals (with the Dissenting Opinion of the Soviet Member)'. Cmd. 6964 (London 1946).

Kamenka, Eugene, *The Ethical Foundations of Marxism* (2nd ed. London 1972).

Kant, Immanuel, *Critique of Practical Reason* (tr. L.W. Beck, New York 1956).

Kant, Immanuel, *Critique of Pure Reason* (tr. Norman Kemp Smith, London 1929).

Kant, Immanuel, *The Moral Law: Kant's Groundwork of the Metaphysic of Morals* (translated and analysed by H.J. Paton, London 1948).

Kant, Immanuel, *Perpetual Peace* (tr. L.W. Beck, New York 1957).

Keen, Maurice H., *The Laws of War in the Late Middle Ages* (London 1965).

Kegley, C.W., and Bretall, R.W. (eds) *Reinhold Niebuhr: his Religious, Social and Political Thought* (New York 1961). Useful collection of critical essays.

Kennan, George, *Memoirs 1925-1950* (Boston 1967).

Khadduri, Majid, *The Law of War and Peace in Islam* (Baltimore 1969).

Kirk, G.S. and Raven, J.E., *The Presocratic Philosophers* (Cambridge 1957).

Lewy, Guenter, 'Superior Orders, Nuclear Warfare, and the Dictates of Conscience' *The American Political Science Review* vol. 55 (1961), 5-23; part reprinted in *War and Morality* (ed.) Richard Wasserstrom, 115-34.

Liddell Hart, Basil, *Paris or the Future of War* (London 1925).

Lifton, Robert Jay, *Home from the War* (London 1974).

Little, Franklin H., and Locke, Hubert G., (ed.) *The German Church Struggle and the Holocaust* (Detroit 1974) provides a useful guide to the copious literature on the relation between the German churches and Nazism. It also contains a piercing exchange on being a Jew after Auschwitz, see 'Some Perspectives on Religious Faith after Auschwitz' by Richard L. Rubinstein and 'Talking, Writing, and Keeping Silent' by Elie Wiesel.

Lorenz, Konrad, *On Aggression* (London 1966). Fromm gives a devastating critique.

Lyons, David, *The Forms and Limits of Utilitarianism* (London 1965).

McCarthy, Mary, *Medina* (London 1973).

MacGregor, G.H.C., *The New Testament Basis of Pacifism* (Fellowship of Reconciliation 1958).

MacGregor, G.H.C., *The Relevance of an Impossible Ideal* (Fellowship of Reconciliation 1960). A sympathetic, Christian pacifist critique of Niebuhr.

MacQuarrie, John, *The Concept of Peace* (London 1974).

Maddox, John, 'Prospects of Nuclear Proliferation' *Adelphi Paper no. 113* (London 1975).

Martin, David A., *Pacifism: an Historical and Sociological Study* (London 1965).

Martin, Laurence W., *Arms and Strategy* (New York 1973).

Mason, H.A., *To Homer through Pope: an Introduction to Homer's Iliad and Pope's Translation* (London 1972).

May, Ernest R., *'Lessons' of the Past: the Use and Misuse of History in American Foreign Policy* (New York 1973). It is not only US makers of foreign policy who abuse history in the ways May brings out so well.

Melville, Herman, *Billy Budd* (many editions). Classic expression of the tragic dilemma of military command.

Mendl, Wolf, *Deterrence and Persuasion* (London 1970).

Mendl, Wolf, *Prophets and Reconcilers: Reflections on the Quaker Peace Testimony* (London 1974).

Michel, Henri, *The Shadow War: Resistance in Europe 1939-45* (London 1972).

Middlebrook, Martin, *The Nuremberg Raid 30-31 March 1944* (London 1973).

Mill, John Stuart, *Autobiography* (many editions).

Mill, John Stuart, *Utilitarianism* (many editions).

Minear, Richard H., *Victor's Justice: the Tokio War Crimes Trial* (Princeton 1971).

Mitchell, William, *Winged Defense: the Development and Possibilities of Modern Air Power – Economic and Military* (New York 1925).

Moore, G.E., *Principia Ethica* (Cambridge 1903).

Morgenthau, Hans, *Politics Among Nations: the Struggle for Power and Peace* (5th ed. New York 1973).

Murphy, Jeffrie G., (ed.) *Civil Disobedience and Violence* (Belmont, Ca. 1971).

Narveson, Jan, 'Pacifism: a Philosophical Analysis' *Ethics* 75 (1965), 259-71; reprinted in *War and Morality* (ed.) Richard Wasserstrom, 63-77.

Nietzsche, Friedrich, *On the Genealogy of Morals* (tr. Walter Kaufmann and R.J. Hollingdale, New York 1969).

Nuttall, Geoffrey, *Christian Pacifism in History* (Berkeley 1971).

Owen, Wilfred, *The Collected Poems* (London 1967).

Paret, Peter, *Clausewitz and the State* (Princeton 1976).

Paskins, Barrie, 'Conscience in the Seventies' *Theology* LXXVII (July 1974) 365-75.

Paskins, Barrie, *On Wishing People Well* (Doctoral Dissertation Cambridge 1978). Generalised discussion of the modified Kantian position adopted in the present work.

Paskins, Barrie, 'Some Victims of Morality' *Proceedings of the Aristotelian Society* XCVII (1975-6), 89-108.

Paskins, Barrie, 'What's Wrong with Torture?' *British Journal of International Studies* vol. 2 no. 2. (July 1976), 138-48.

Passmore, John, *The Perfectibility of Man* (London 1970).

Pelton, Leroy H., *The Psychology of Nonviolence* (New York 1974). Probably the most readable book now available of the many on nonviolence.

Plato, *Apology* (tr. Hugh Tredennick, Harmondsworth 1954).

Plato, *Republic* (tr. F.M. Cornford, Oxford 1941).

*Powers, Barry D., *Strategy without Slide-Rule: British Air Strategy 1914-1939* (London 1976).

Quinton, Anthony, *Utilitarian Ethics* (London 1973).

Ramsey, Paul, *The Just War* (New York 1968).

Ramsey, Paul, *War and the Christian Conscience* (Durham N.C. 1961).

Reid, W.R., *Tongues of Conscience: War and the Scientist's Dilemma* (London 1969).

Reynolds, Charles, *Theory and Explanation in International Politics* (London 1973).

* Richards, Denis, *Portal of Hungerford: the Life of Marshal of the Royal Air Force Viscount Portal of Hungerford* (London 1977).

Richards, Denis and Saunders, Hilary St. John, *Royal Air Force 1939-1945* (London 1954, 3 volumes).

Ross, W.D., *The Right and the Good* (Oxford 1930).

Rothwell, V.H. *British War Aims and Peace Diplomacy* (Oxford 1971).

Russell, Bertrand, *Portraits from Memory* (New York 1969).

Russell, Frank, *Theories of International Relations* (London 1936).

Russell, Frederick H., *The Just War in the Middle Ages* (Cambridge 1975).

Sampson, R.V. *Tolstoy: the Discovery of Peace* (London 1973). Digs deep but a bit too respectfully.

Sartre, Jean-Paul, *Existentialism and Humanism* (tr. Philip Mairet, London 1948).

Silkin, Jon, *Out of Battle: the Poetry of the Great War* (London 1972).

Simmons, Clifford, (ed.) *The Objectors* (Isle of Man and London, no date).

Slessor, J.C., *Air Power and Armies* (London 1936).

Slessor, J.C., *The Central Blue* (London 1956).

Smart, J.J.C., and Williams, Bernard, *Utilitarianism For and Against* (Cambridge 1973).

Smith, Bradley F., *Reaching Judgment at Nuremberg* (London 1977).

Sorel, Georges, *Reflections on Violence* (London 1950).

Speer, Albert, *Inside the Third Reich* (London 1971).

Stanage, Sherman M., *Reason and Violence: Philosophical Investigations* (New York 1974).

Stone, Robert, *Dog Soldiers: a Novel* (Boston 1974).

Suarez, Francisco, *Selections from Three Works by ... Suarez* (Oxford 1944).

Taylor, A.J.P., *English History 1914-1945* (Oxford 1965).

Taylor, A.J.P., *Lloyd George: Twelve Essays* (London 1971).

Taylor, A.J.P., *The Origins of the Second World War* (Harmondsworth 1965).

Taylor, Telford, *Nuremberg and Vietnam* (New York 1971).

Tolstoy, Leo, *War and Peace* (tr. Rosemary Edmonds, Harmondsworth 1957, 2 vols). Tolstoy receives unsatisfactory treatment in most histories of pacifism: he emerges as excessively serene and simple, pompous and uncomic. For a brilliant corrective see Troyat.

Troyat, Andre, *Tolstoy* (tr. Nancy Amphoux, Harmondsworth 1970).

United States Strategic Bombing Survey (Washington 1945-1947 316 volumes).

Vitoria, Francisco de, *De Indis et de iure belli reflectiones* (Washington 1917). Contains an English translation.

Waltz, Kenneth R., *Man, the State, and War* (New York 1959).

Walzer, Michael, *Just and Unjust Wars: a Moral Argument with Historical Illustrations* (London 1978). Differs profoundly from the present book in method and theory. Walzer offers 'a book of practical morality'; ours is an essay in practical philosophy. Walzer rests much of his argument on an aggressor-defender theory rooted in the social contract perspective of his *Obligations*. The resulting disagreements are revealing about both Walzer's position and our own.

Walzer, Michael, 'Moral Judgment in Time of War' *Dissent* vol. 14 no 3 (1967), 284-92; reprinted in *War and Morality* (ed.) Richard Wasserstrom, 54-62.

Walzer, Michael, *Obligations: Essays on Disobedience, War and Citizenship* (Cambridge, Mass. 1970).

Walzer, Michael, 'Political Action: the Problem of Dirty Hands' in *War and Moral Responsibility* (ed.) Marshall Cohen et al. 62-82.

Walzer, Michael, *The Revolution of the Saints: a Study in the Origins of Radical Politics* (Cambridge, Mass. 1965).

Wasserstrom, Richard, 'The Laws of War' *Monist* 56 (1972).

Wasserstrom, Richard, (ed.) *War and Morality* (Belmont, Ca. 1970).

Watt, D.C., *Too Serious a Business: European Armed Forces and the Approach of the Second World War* (London 1975).

Webster, Charles and Frankland, Noble, *The Strategic Air Offensive Against Germany 1939-1945* (London 1961, 4 vols).

Wells, H.G., *War in the Air* (London 1908).

Wilkinson, Paul, *Political Terrorism* (London 1974).

Williams, Bernard, 'Moral Luck' *Aristotelian Society Supplementary Volume L* (1976), 115-35.

Williams, Bernard, *Morality: an Introduction to Ethics* (Harmondsworth 1973).

Williams, Bernard, *Problems of the Self* (Cambridge 1973).

Winch, Peter 'Ethical Reward and Punishment' *The Human World* vol. I (1970); repr. *Ethics and Action*.

Winch, Peter, 'The Universalizability of Moral Judgments' *Monist* 49 (1965); repr. *Ethics and Action*.

Winch, Peter, *Ethics and Action* (London 1972).

Wittgenstein, Ludwig, *Philosophical Investigations* (Oxford 1953).

Woetzel, Robert K. *The Nuremberg Trials in International Law* (London 1960). Reliable and not excessively technical.

Wood, Derek and Dempster, Derek, *The Narrow Margin: the Battle of Britain and the Rise of Air Power 1930-1940* (London 1963).

Wright, Quincy, *A Study of War* (2nd ed. Chicago 1965).

Yoder, John H., *Nevertheless: a Meditation on the Varieties and Shortcomings of Religious Pacifism* (Scottdale, Pa. 1971). Brief but profound by a Mennonite pacifist.

Zahn, Gordon, *In Solitary Witness: the Life and Death of Franz Jägerstätter* (London 1965).

Zellner, H.M., (ed.) *Assassination* (Cambridge, Mass. 1974).

Index